Marxism Missing, Missing Marxism

Studies in Critical Social Sciences Book Series

Haymarket Books is proud to be working with Brill Academic Publishers (www.brill.nl) to republish the *Studies in Critical Social Sciences* book series in paperback editions. This peer-reviewed book series offers insights into our current reality by exploring the content and consequences of power relationships under capitalism, and by considering the spaces of opposition and resistance to these changes that have been defining our new age. Our full catalog of *SCSS* volumes can be viewed at https://www.haymarketbooks.org/series_collections/4-studies-in-critical-social-sciences.

Series Editor
David Fasenfest (Wayne State University)

Editorial Board
Eduardo Bonilla-Silva (Duke University)
Chris Chase-Dunn (University of California–Riverside)
William Carroll (University of Victoria)
Raewyn Connell (University of Sydney)
Kimberlé W. Crenshaw (University of California–LA and Columbia University)
Heidi Gottfried (Wayne State University)
Karin Gottschall (University of Bremen)
Alfredo Saad Filho (King's College London)
Chizuko Ueno (University of Tokyo)
Sylvia Walby (Lancaster University)
Raju Das (York University)

Marxism Missing, Missing Marxism

From Marxism to Identity Politics and Beyond

Tom Brass

Haymarket Books
Chicago, IL

First published in 2021 by Brill Academic Publishers, The Netherlands
© 2021 Koninklijke Brill NV, Leiden, The Netherlands

Published in paperback in 2022 by
Haymarket Books
P.O. Box 180165
Chicago, IL 60618
773-583-7884
www.haymarketbooks.org

ISBN: 978-1-64259-770-7

Distributed to the trade in the US through Consortium Book Sales and Distribution (www.cbsd.com) and internationally through Ingram Publisher Services International (www.ingramcontent.com).

This book was published with the generous support of Lannan Foundation and Wallace Action Fund.

Special discounts are available for bulk purchases by organizations and institutions. Please call 773-583-7884 or email info@haymarketbooks.org for more information.

Cover design by Jamie Kerry and Ragina Johnson.

Printed in the United States.

10 9 8 7 6 5 4 3 2 1

Library of Congress Cataloging-in-Publication data is available.

*For Amanda,
Anna, Ned, and Miles;
and in memory of my parents*

Contents

Acknowledgements XI

Introduction
Marxism Missing – Presumed Dead? 1
How Marxism Went Missing 3
Why Marxism Went Missing 6
As Clear as Mud(de) 10
Essentializing Rurality? 14
Marxism Missing, but ... 18
Themes 23

PART 1
Marxism Missing

1 **Marxism(s) within/beyond the Nation** 29
   Introduction 29
   The External/Eternal 'Other' 31
   The Source of Social Miracles 36
   Because the Country Is Hungry 38
   Winning the Peasantry? 40
   A Huge Part of the People 42
   Class Solidarity and/or Cultural Autonomy 43
   Nationalism beyond the Nation 46
   Privileged Sections, Cheap Immigrants 48
   An Indispensable Attribute 50
   Conclusion 52

2 **From Marxism to the Cultural Turn (*via* Social History)** 55
   Introduction 55
   Marxism and Third World Development 57
   Populism, Social History, and Third World (Non-)Development 59
   Enemy of the (Capitalist) State? 64
   History, Methods, Politics 68
   Social History and/as the 'Cultural Turn' 72
   Ambiguity + Authenticity = Absent Marxism 75
   Conclusion 78

3 **From Marxism to Nationalism (*via* Imperialism)** 81
   Introduction 81
   The Authenticity of Populism 84
   The Inapplicability of Marxism 88
   Down the Drain (Once Again) 92
   India's Chief Curse 96
   Populism, Nationalism, Postmodernism 101
   What Did the Romans Ever Do for Us? 104
   Conclusion 107

4 **From Marxism to Agrarian Populism (*via* the Cultural Turn)** 109
   Introduction 109
   Peasants, Marxism, Populism 111
   The 'Cultural Turn' and/as the 'New' Populist Postmodernism 112
   Russia Then, India Now 115
   Old Believers? 118
   Farmers, Peasants, *Kulaks* 121
   Old/New Agrarian Populism? 124
   A Sense of Robust Realism? 129
   Conclusion 131

PART 2
Missing Marxism

5 **From Marxism to Late Antiquity (*via* Postmodernism)** 137
   Introduction 137
   The World beyond 141
   Citizens, State, and Economy 148
   Not Death but Resurrection 154
   Postmodernizing Premodernity 158
   Conclusion 165

6 **From Modern to Ancient Capitalism (*via* Bourgeois Economics)** 167
   Introduction 167
   Capitalism, Capitalism Everywhere 171
   Money Makes the World Go Round? 174
   Fear of Feudalism 177
   All Modes Lead to Rome 180
   Had Marx Lived … 185

Marginalism Is Not Marxism   187
Building Castles in the Air   189
Conclusion   195

7 **From Class Struggle to Identity Politics (*via* 'Otherness')**   197
Introduction   197
Film, Sameness, Otherness   201
To Keep Them Divided   204
Solidarity, Struggle, Socialism   208
Magical (Un-)Realism   212
Diasporic Discourse   215
On the Shoulders of Giants?   218
Placid Multiculturalism   220
Celebrating Otherness?   223
Conclusion   227

8 **Great Replacement, or Reaping the Capitalist Whirlwind (*via* Populism/Nationalism)**   230
Introduction: The Last Taboo   231
White Fright, White Fight   233
Demography, Culture, Civilization   236
Who/What Is Responsible?   239
Rival Ethnicities, Rival Populisms   242
Political Economy and/as Great Replacement   245
Migration and/as Surplus Labour   250
Marxism and the Industrial Reserve   252
Conclusion   255

Conclusion
Beyond Marxism, What?   258

Bibliography   271
Author Index   287
Subject Index   291

Acknowledgements

The title of this book – *Marxism Missing, Missing Marxism* – encompasses a number of distinct meanings. First, the palpable fact that nowadays Marxist theory is faced with the difficulty that many of those who espouse it tend either to discard components that are themselves crucial to Marxism or else to combine it with epistemologies that are incompatible with – or indeed antagonistic to – Marxist politics. This is the missing-as-absence aspect of the title. Second, and ironically, this void occurs just at the moment when the presence of Marxism – both as an explanatory approach and as a guide to future action – is most necessary. And third, the same term – missing Marxism – refers also to the fact that those who object to Marxism on economic or political grounds nevertheless fail to hit their target. Here the meaning invokes a failure-to-land-a-blow on Marxism. All these different meanings inform the content of this book.

This is not to say that what follows is the construction of Marxism as monolithic theoretical edifice; rather that, when stripped of any or all of its core epistemological components – such as class formation/consciousness/struggle, socialist transition as a desirable/feasible objective, and revolutionary agency – Marxist theory in effect ceases to be what historically Marxists have claimed it is. Such is the case especially when, having discarded both revolutionary agency and socialism, Marxism is said instead to be about recuperating a 'nicer' capitalism by means of multi-class alliances. The latter path is the outcome of a politics that, having substituted organic evolution for revolution, advocates empowerment not of class but of non-class identities, including zealous forms of nationalism hidden behind a thinly-clad disguise of anti-imperialism, and marginally less potent – but similarly problematic – versions merely orientalising the origins of capitalism.

Marxism – or more properly 'Marxism' – becomes as a result indistinguishable ontologically not just from non-Marxist theory but also from its anti-Marxist variants. It might be objected that all this is now of little or no consequence, as every form of Marxism has long since ceased to exercise any kind of theoretical – let alone political – influence it may once have had. The intellectual context, however, is not wholly unfavourable. These days public acknowledgements surface periodically to the effect that in some sense capitalism 'isn't working for everyone', and thus ought to be reformed. Into this political space ideas emanating from Marxist theory would in the past have been inserted and could do so still. Hence the importance of being clear, both about what Marxism is, and equally about what it isn't.

Special thanks are due to the following people. To Professor David Fasenfest, the Series Editor, for encouragement; to Debbie de Wit, Jennifer Obdam and Judy Pereira of Brill publishers, who guided the book through production; and to my daughter Anna Luisa Brass, who designed and drew the cover illustration. She not only drew the cover for five previous books – *New Farmers' Movements in India* (1995), *Labour Regime Change in the Twenty-First Century* (2011), *Class, Culture and the Agrarian Myth* (2014), *Labour Markets, Identities, Controversies* (2017), and *Revolution and Its Alternatives* (2019) – but also did the drawings which appear at the start of each section in the present volume. The cover and subsequent illustrations refer to the theoretical maze in which Marxism currently finds itself, and from which it is trying to exit whilst at the same time remaining epistemologically intact. Symbolized thereby is the endeavour by Marxist political economy to extricate itself from mistaken attempts to conflate it with the cultural turn, identity politics, bourgeois economics, or varieties of populism and nationalism, together with the danger of not doing so.

This volume draws on materials which appeared previously in *Critical Sociology, Science and Society, Critique of Anthropology, Capital and Class, The Journal of Peasant Studies*, and *The Journal of Contemporary Asia*. Others have not been published before and appear here in print for the first time. Like all my previous monographs, this one is dedicated to two sets of kin. To my family: Amanda, and Anna, Ned, and Miles. Also, to the memory of my parents: my father, Denis Brass (1913–2006), and my mother, Gloria Brass (1916–2012).

Introduction
Marxism Missing – Presumed Dead?

> Throughout the civilised world the teachings of Marx evoke the utmost hostility and hatred of all bourgeois science (both official and liberal), which regards Marxism as a kind of "pernicious sect". And no other attitude is to be expected, for there can be no "impartial" social science in a society based on class struggle.
>
> An observation made by LENIN more than a century ago, as relevant now as it was then.[1]

∴

As anyone who, as an undergraduate, was engaged in the study of the social sciences during the late 1960s, will attest, this was an era when a particular relay in statement circulated within the news media and, more generally, popular culture. Licensed thereby were a number of conflations: higher education was being undermined by calls for a different curriculum and more intellectual autonomy; critiques of the existing social order were blamed on those who were university students; moreover, this kind of political criticism aimed at capitalism was seen as emanating from university sociology departments; for its part, sociology as an academic discipline was regarded as wholly under the influence of Marxist theory; and all the latter characteristics were in turn perceived as combining to inform research conducted in the then-burgeoning area of development studies.

Symptomatic of this conflation – all students = discontents, all sociologists = Marxists, all development studies = Marxist theory – was the antagonism embodied in the many observations made at this conjuncture by, among others, conservative academics and writers.[2] Typical, perhaps, were the hostile views expressed by Kingsley Amis, who not only objected to having his books analysed by sociologists ('Sometimes I would meditate on how nice it

---

1 Lenin (1963: 23).
2 For an example of this kind of attack, along the lines of a spurious juxtaposition between what was presented as on the one hand an intellectually acceptable 'academic mode' and on the other an unacceptable 'Marxist mode', see Cox, Jacka, and Marks (1977).

would be if one's novels were read as novels instead of sociological tracts') but also dismissed the claim of the discipline to be considered as a serious form of intellectual activity.[3] About Marxism his views were unambiguous: 'I have had Marxism – in both senses of the words. I have experienced the ailment and so am immune. And I have also utterly rejected it'.[4]

One effect of such hostility was that many in the social sciences who considered themselves leftists, or were perceived by others as such, predictably regarded themselves as more radical than in fact they were. Accordingly, it is evident that from Worsley and Hobsbawm to Graeber and Breman, there has been – and is still – a tendency on the part of many academics to see themselves as victimized on account of their politics.[5] This despite the fact that holders of this view in equally many instances have not only ascended the academic hierarchy eventually to hold senior posts, but also have never been imprisoned or expelled from a research area (or a country) because of their political beliefs.[6] Ironically, therefore, the external attack on Marxism was compounded by an analogous but opposite internal process: many of those who regarded themselves (and were regarded by others) as Marxists turned out to be nothing of the sort.

---

3   See Amis (1970: 166), and also Amis and Conquest (n.d.: 70), whose definition of sociology goes as follows: '1) An academic, bourgeois, irrelevant (qq.v) study of society and its institutions now largely outmoded by 2) a polysyllabic briefing on the decadence of Western society and the means to overthrow it'.
4   This condemnation (Leader, 2000: 502–3) was a response in February 1957 by Amis to what was a favourable review published in the *Daily Worker* of a pamphlet by him. Significantly, a major reason for rejecting Marxism was that, although he accepted 'there is a class struggle … I think there are other struggles (racial, national, etc.) of equal political importance'. This is the same view as that held currently by exponents of the 'cultural turn'.
5   Worsley (2008) recounts how from the outset of his academic career the British security services regarded him as a 'person of interest'; Hobsbawm also saw himself as victim of sustained political interest by the security services (Evans, 2019), a view at odds with his absorption into the ranks of the British establishment (see Chapter 2 below). Analogous forms of self-perception as political victim in the case of Breman and Graeber are examined by me elsewhere (Brass, 2017: 68ff.; Brass, 2019: 116ff.).
6   This lack of obstacles placed in the path of institutional advancement is not just curious but also contrasts with the experience of early Marxists. In response to a letter from a fellow socialist who no longer had a job because of his politics, Engels (Marx and Engels, 2001a: 7) observed in 1887: 'The great problem is that we socialists are not only politically but also civilly proscribed, and for the entire bourgeoisie it is both a pleasure and a duty to see that we starve. This anathema falls principally upon educated and cultured men, whom they consider to be deserters from their own class that have passed over to the enemy camp. This problem presents itself everywhere; we [Marx and Engels] faced it ourselves in 1844 and 1849'.

That same conjuncture, one in which an expansion of higher education occurred, witnessed also the entry of Marxists into academic posts, thereby transferring Marxism from the street (where it served as a guide to political action, organization and policy) into the university (where it became largely a subject for study). Given its intellectual fashionability at this time, during the 1960s Marxism was unsurprisingly espoused by some in academia, only to be discarded once it ceased to be in vogue. Equally problematic was the fact that others who for similar reasons had declared themselves Marxists displayed a limited understanding of what this involved in terms of theory and practice. This contributed to a situation when in the 1980s Marxism could indeed be said to be missing, a dearth epitomized in dismissive approaches to debates about systemic transition generally, and that to socialism in particular, now regarded as pointless ivory-tower discussion.[7] Such discourse of pessimism in effect is complicit with the conservative view that beyond capitalism there lies – and cannot but lie – nothing that is politically achievable or desirable.

How Marxism Went Missing

Two conjunctures demonstrate how in metropolitan capitalist nations progressive opinion generally, and especially that in academia, moved away from Marxist theory based on class, and towards the perception of non-class identities as empowering. The first of these occurred during the 1950s and 1960s, when a misguided perception that Keynesian demand management had solved the problem of capitalist economic crisis licensed a search for forms of 'otherness' which did not entail the need for revolution and socialism. This became more pronounced during the second conjuncture, from the 1980s onwards, when the re-essentialization of traditional rural 'otherness' meant that economic development was itself increasingly dismissed as an inappropriate Eurocentric imposition on Third World peasant farmers.

Failing to realize the limits to post-war affluence, many socialists differed little from conservatives when it came to endorsing over-optimistic prognoses during the 1950s and 1960s. What all the latter missed, therefore, was that as capitalism became global the industrial reserve army would have to

---

7 A recent example is Wark (2019: 22–23), who maintains that '[t[here was once a language about transitions between modes of production. There's an elaborate argument about how feudalism became capitalism, about whether there might be multiple routes toward capitalism, about whether there could be more than one kind of socialism to come after. The debates about where capitalism comes from are fascinating but mostly of academic interest'.

be reintroduced.[8] That conservatives should misrecognize this is unsurprising, since they countenance no alternative to capitalism.[9] Rather more surprising, however, is the fact that the same kind of misrecognition informed the approach of those on the left, many of whom described themselves as socialists of one sort or another. Imagining that the welfare state, full employment, and better wages/conditions were here to stay, adherents of this approach wrongly concluded that economic conflict between capital and labour had either ceased or at least was no longer of political significance. Among them were Stuart Hall, Herbert Marcuse, and Regis Debray.

In part, this misrecognition derived from what was perceived by some on the New Left to be a causal link between 1950s affluence and political apathy. Thus the working class in Britain was regarded by Hall as having been co-opted politically by the welfare state, full employment, prosperity, and the consumer boom of the immediate post-war era.[10] In the following decade Marcuse argued similarly that, by economically seducing the working class ('The integrated man lives in a society without opposition'), capitalism had succeeded in avoiding struggle designed to transcend it as a system, and that consequently neither bourgeoisie nor proletariat were any longer historical agents of transformation.[11] Much the same kind of view was advanced at the end of the 1970s by Debray, who argued that, rather than being a challenge to the capitalist social order, the events of May 1968 in Paris gave it a new lease of life, and thus paved the way for its

---

8   Amidst the end-of-ideology triumphalism of the 1950s and 1960s, a few Marxists correctly recognized that full employment was a temporary phenomenon, which employers would seek to eradicate at the earliest opportunity. Among them was Dobb (1955: 215–255) who pointed out that, sooner or later, capitalist profitability would require the restoration of unemployment.

9   Noting that '[w]artime spending in the United States in the 1940s touched off a boom that has continued for more than thirty years [and] pumped money into every class level of the population without parallel in any country in history', an influential conservative pundit (Wolfe, 1976: 136) concluded that: 'In America [workers] make so much money … that the word "proletarian" can no longer be used in this country with a straight face'. Since in his opinion affluence had succeeded in banishing economic crisis and with it class struggle, Wolfe (1976: 167) felt able confidently to declare prognoses of capitalist demise – by, among others, Marx and Marxism – redundant: 'But once the dreary little bastards [= workers] started getting money in the 1940s, they did an astonishing thing – they took their money and ran! … The prophets are out of business!'

10 Hall (1960).

11 About the pessimism of Marcuse, Mattick (1967: 377) has commented that 'hope for a socialist working class revolution is given up in the expectation that social problems are solvable by way of reforms within the confines of capitalism. In this view, revolution has become not only highly improbable but entirely unnecessary'.

continuation.¹² This it did by eradicating institutional obstacles to further consumption on the part of French youth.

What leftists holding the view that capitalist crisis was now largely a thing of the past, and with it had dissipated the conditions giving rise to revolution leading to a socialist transition, should have seen coming, but didn't, was the subsequent emergence of a counter-revolutionary trend: originally ideological (the 'new' populist postmodernism), then economic (neoliberalism), and now political (the rise of the far right). In the case of journalism, here too the question is raised periodically as to why did no one foresee the emergence at the grassroots of populism, nationalism and 'nativism' (= 'these events came as a tremendous surprise')?¹³ The twofold answer, of course, is that a few, mainly Marxists, did in fact see this coming, while most of those who should have foreseen this process (but didn't) were themselves in thrall to the 'new' populist postmodernism.

It is perhaps only after having participated in such academic debates over a period of years that it is possible to identify what is a pervasive aspect of such exchanges. As has been noted previously, these discussions tend to be characterized by the transfer of interpretations from the margins to the core, a procedure accompanied by a process of political deradicalization.¹⁴ What is originally a problem the resolution of which, it is argued initially on the margins, can only resolved by a transition to socialism, in the course of this kind of transfer metamorphoses into its opposite: an issue that can be resolved within capitalism, and thus without a threat to the continued reproduction of accumulation. In this way, an interpretation premised on the desirability/feasibility of a socialist transition is stripped of the latter outcome, and when it reappears in the academic mainstream

---

12   Observing that 'May '68 was the cradle of a new bourgeois society', Debray (1979: 46, 48, 49) maintained that '[t]he sincerity of the actors of May was accompanied and overtaken, by a cunning of which they knew nothing [because capitalist] development strategy required the cultural revolution of May'.

13   'It is now a truism to say that we live in a world where the liberal, progressive and secular have ceded ground to the populist, nativist and nationalist [and] the secular has retreated before the religious. It is also a truism to say that these events came as a tremendous surprise'. See 'Imran Khan's rise is a metaphor for a changing world the west has failed to see', *The Observer* (London) 3 June 2018.

14   For more details about this, see Brass (2019). It is, unfortunately, not possible to address the margin/core transfer without contextualizing it in terms of the way academic institutions operate. Specifically, the contradiction between two rather obvious antinomies: the necessity, on the one hand, of incorporating cutting-edge theory (which is radical), yet on the other the inadvisability of antagonizing senior elements in the academic hierarchy (which tend to be conservative).

becomes instead a problem that capitalism is perfectly able (and willing) to address and resolve without danger to itself. Where an understanding of this dynamic – invariably unacknowledged, and thus largely hidden – is lacking, it is difficult to assess the both the continuities and discontinuities in the all the contributions to academic debate. Needless to say, political transfers of this sort on occasion entail silences and/or denials, particularly when the original interpretation on the margins has been the object of a critique prior to resurfacing in the core, and especially so when the critique and the subsequent endorsement is carried out by the same individual.

Why Marxism Went Missing

Possibly the most problematic instance of Marxism-missing-but-necessary combination, particularly as this affects theory about development, is the way in which two key debates have changed over the recent past: that about the capitalism/unfreedom link, and that about the 'new' populist postmodernism. Each issue is generally positioned by Marxism in terms of a problem to be solved only through a socialist transition. Now, however, there are attempts to recuperate them for capitalism, by claiming both unfreedom and populism are structural difficulties that can be resolved adequately within the confines of the accumulation process itself. The latter systemic form is thereby rescued, in the course of which all the dynamics – class consciousness, organization, and struggle – leading to a socialist transition are rendered unnecessary.

Accordingly, there are still those who maintain, in the face of substantial evidence to the contrary, that accumulation and unfree labour-power are incompatible. This was the orthodoxy during the 1960s, when politically distinct approaches ranging from the semi-feudal thesis to modernization theory all declared unfree production relations an obstacle to capitalist development in Third World nations. Since economic growth required the abolition of such 'pre-capitalist remnants', the presence or absence of capitalism was as a consequence determined by whether or not the unfree worker – categorized as subordinated by what is a feudal or pre-capitalist relation – has been replaced with free wage labour. When and where it had, capitalism was deemed to be present; when/where it hadn't, capitalism, it was said, was either absent, or insufficiently developed. For this reason, political alliances between workers and a national bourgeoisie were thought to be appropriate, in order to usher in a proper accumulation project. Those holding such a view, influential in the study of agrarian development in

INTRODUCTION: MARXISM MISSING – PRESUMED DEAD?

India and Latin America from the development decade onwards, included many on the left.[15]

From the 1980s onwards, however, the hitherto orthodox view that capitalist development required the eradication of unfree production relations was challenged by the Marxist deproletarianization framework.[16] The latter showed, much rather, the opposite to be the case: in many instances, producers were restructuring the labour process by replacing free workers with unfree equivalents. In a global economy where producers have to become increasingly cost-conscious so as to remain competitive, therefore, enterprises reproduce, introduce, or reintroduce unfree relations in preference to labour-power that is free, a process of workforce decomposition/recomposition. As such, deproletarianization is part of the way class struggle is waged 'from above'. Along with downsizing/outsourcing, this is a method whereby nowadays capital restructures its labour process, cutting costs so as to maintain/enhance profitability. An expanding industrial reserve army makes this kind of restructuring not just possible but also necessary, enabling multinational corporations, rich peasants, and commercial farmers to compete with rival enterprises. Whereas in the past the colonial state in India attempted to eliminate debt bondage and similar unfree working arrangements there, because they were thought to be obstacles to economic development, currently the neoliberal state (lip-service apart) is content to see them continue – and even flourish – as they contribute to profitability.

If unfree labour is not a pre-capitalist remnant but in many cases a relation of choice where capital is concerned, used as much by a national bourgeoisie as by a foreign one, then it is difficult to see how entering alliances with the employing/owning class within the nation to further the cause of capitalist development there is still on the political agenda of workers' organizations. This suggests that it is socialism, not a progressive form of capitalism, which should be the objective of any 'from below' political mobilization and programme. Furthermore, the use of these kinds of unfree production relation tends to hinder and/or undermine the formation of class consciousness among labour, particularly when they involve the recruitment of migrants (who are unfree and thus cheaper to employ) in order to displace unionized

---

15   On the subject of semi-feudalism, see Brass (1995; 2002). Among its many exponents at that conjuncture were Pradhan Prasad, Utsa Patnaik, Terry Byres, Jan Breman, Amartya Sen, Jairus Banaji and Amit Bhaduri. Some continued to hold this view, whilst others abandoned the semi-feudal thesis when it was subject to criticism.

16   On deproletarianization and its centrality to an understanding of the role of unfree production relations in the class struggle between capital and labour, see Brass (1999, 2011).

and politically militant workers (who are free and thus more costly to employ). Since employers benefit from unfreedom, and consequently the state permits its continuance, abolition of such oppressive/exploitative forms will be achieved only by a working class organized in pursuit of socialism.

Additional dangers – ones that crucially affect all Marxists in many different ways – are twofold. First, more recent contributors to this debate maintain – wrongly – that capitalism and its state can and will indeed eliminate unfree labour, thereby returning in part to the earlier claim that accumulation on a world scale can do without such oppressive/exploitative relational forms.[17] As problematic, therefore, is the absence of any mention about sudden and unexplained changes of mind, treated as unimportant, despite the fact that in particular instances such transformations entail an attempt to attach a non-Marxist political agenda to what was originally a Marxist one, an issue that is hardly of negligible importance.[18] And second,

17 Substantial and continuing evidence periodically confounds the oft-heard claim that, because capitalism is able to 'self-regulate', it will always and everywhere seek out and eliminate those (residual) production relations that are unfree. That the presence of the latter will not be 'solved' by capitalism, however, is underlined by the regularity with which 'scandals' – involving sweatshop conditions, low payment, and coercion – surface, are quickly said by employers to have been addressed, and then vanish from the headlines, only to resurface subsequently as 'scandals', often featuring the same enterprise. A case in point is the way the pandemic uncovered the fact of underpaid/overworked sewing machinists employed in 'fast fashion' clothing sweatshops, when the rising incidence of Covid-19 in one particular city was traced to the fact that such machinists were required to come in to work, regardless of whether or not they displayed pandemic symptoms. See 'Boohoo accused over Leicester's virus setback', *Financial Times* (London), 2 July 2020 'Leicester's dark factories show up a diseased system', *Financial Times* (London), 4–5 July 2020; 'Boohoo's Leicester suppliers face crackdown', *Financial Times* (London), 6 July 2020 'Boohoo shares tumble over concerns of illegal low pay at Leicester factory', *Financial Times* (London), 7 July 2020; 'Virus has shone a light on UK's dark factories – Britain needs better enforcement of existing protections for workers', *Financial Times* (London), 7 July 2020.

18 Among the many who currently maintain – implausibly – that capitalism and its state can and will eradicate unfree labour are Breman (on which see Brass, 2019: Chapter 5) and Fudge (2019). In what purports to be a review of Marxist contributions to the capitalism/unfreedom debate, a new account (Rioux, LeBaron, and Versovšek, 2020) displays a striking misunderstanding of this discussion and its political implications. It privileges recent interpretations – in particular those by a co-author of the piece in question – and misrepresents, downplays, or ignores earlier and more radical contributions to the debate (absent are key texts by Alex Lichtenstein and Yann Moulier Boutang). Not only are a number of participants wrongly identified as Marxists, therefore, but Rioux, LeBaron, and Versovšek also fail to point out that what they term 'a more faithful Marxist tradition' is nothing other than the class struggle argument based conceptually on theory about

that the longer a socialist transition is postponed, by not putting this objective on a leftist political agenda, together with that of migration – free and unfree – and the industrial reserve army, the more workers will in periods of crisis move towards reactionary populist solutions which seemingly offer to protect their jobs, culture, and livelihoods.[19] By shifting the emphasis from the economic role performed for capital by an expanding industrial reserve army of migrant labour to the attainment by the latter subject of citizenship in the receiving nation, this kind of reformism envisages only piecemeal changes to unfree labour and downgrades the importance of class struggle.[20]

---

deproletarianisation. Missing from the review is any reference to the crucial detail that some who have now joined 'a more faithful Marxist tradition' – rather late in the day – had earlier dismissed the very views they currently endorse. Frequent references to the publications of late adopters misleadingly conveys the impression that they have always and consistently supported this view. Furthermore, the review overlooks the additional fact that their claim about the longstanding neglect of unfree relations was an inaccurate accusation levelled by them at Marxist approaches. Not only do these late adopters receive a relatively privileged consideration in terms of weight given to their publications and arguments, therefore, but they all feature in the conclusion as representing the way forward in the capitalism/unfreedom debate. The Marxist who originally made the case about deproletarianization ('a more faithful Marxist tradition'), however, does not, despite having formulated many of the arguments subsequently taken up by the late adopters.

19   None these days makes a distinction between the supplementing and displacing function of migrant labour, and thus miss its implications for political economy. Seeking legislative interventions designed to achieve what is termed an 'appropriate balancing' between migrant and local worker, ends up regarding the State as benign, almost above the fray. This despite the fact that currently the State is not merely a capitalist but a neoliberal institution, the agency of which is to formulate/implement legislation favouring the accumulation process. For those holding this view, the assumption is that, even in such a *laissez-faire* environment, it is still possible to protect the rights of migrants and locals, whereas employers attempt to enhance competitiveness/profitability by playing one off against the other. Under a neoliberal capitalist labour regime, therefore, the State will not seek to disadvantage producers striving for economic growth by protecting the rights of their migrant and local workers, much rather the opposite: any rights labour has managed to gain over the years will be stripped away. Hence the fatuity of a search for 'appropriate balancing', an objective that amounts to no more than legislative tampering within a rampant market system.

20   Shorn of a role in the transition to socialism, such relational forms are henceforth to be situated somewhere along a continuum of capitalist occupations, their place determined by nothing more than subjective perceptions of how 'nice'/'nasty'/'very nasty' unfreedom is thought to be. Mapping the distinction between free and unfree labour onto the citizen/migrant binary also overlooks the fact that workers who are already citizens can become and remain unfree, no less than those deemed foreign.

As Clear as Mud(de)

Like those who locate solutions to the problem of unfree labour solely within the ambit of capitalism itself, so current views lamenting the rise of populism and the far right similarly insist that such politics can be contained by reinforcing bourgeois democracy. Neither approach realizes how accumulation in a global context generates – and indeed depends on – their respective object of analysis: production relations that are unfree in the one instance, and populist discourse in the other. In each case, therefore, the proposed redemption merely reproduces the systemic form that originally gave rise to what is still perceived by them as an anomaly in an otherwise benign economic structure.

Where populism is concerned, nowhere is this difficulty more apparent than in the attempt by Mudde both to explain its dynamic and to offer a political alternative. His object is 'to assess the key challenges that the far right poses to liberal democracies [and] to defend liberal democracies against these challenges'.[21] Defining populism in a restrictive way, as 'a (thin) ideology that considers society to be ultimately separated into two homogeneous and antagonistic groups [composed of] the pure people and the corrupt elite', he misses the full extent of its historical longevity, of its particular affinity with both the agrarian myth and foundation myths, of its overlap not just with the far-right but also with conservatism, and its being a long-standing target of Marxist theory.[22] These absences help explain the kinds of difficulties that permeate his attempts to explain populism, its causes, the reasons for its support, and its close historical and current link with immigration.

Coupling populism and immigration, the latter giving rise to the former, Mudde outlines how populist/far-right support that was originally 'white, predominantly male, and lower middle class', became over time working class.[23] As Marxism has long argued, such a change in social composition suggests that those in jobs were increasingly feeling the competitive impact of immigration. Although Mudde records the fact of this shift, he seems indifferent to the 'legitimate concerns' expressed by workers about such a development.[24] Instead, he points out that, due to 'the postindustrial revolution and immigration', the

---

[21] See Mudde (2019: 5, 178–79), who concludes in much the same vein: 'The ultimate goal of all responses to the far right should be the strengthening of liberal democracy … strengthening liberal democracy will, by definition, weaken the far right … we should be better at explaining why liberal democracy is the best political system we have'.
[22] For his most recent definition of populism, see Mudde (2019: 6–7, 36).
[23] Mudde (2019: 77).
[24] Mudde (2019: 100).

job prospects of 'lower educated, working class males' affected by this development are anyway on the decline in Western democracies.[25] The inference is that young workers in this category will no longer be around to provide support for populist/far-right movements. Overlooked, however, is a different – and Marxist – interpretation: that it is capitalism which generates this development; that immigration permits employers to restructure the labour process using members of the industrial reserve army; and that – although 'lower educated, working class males' are the victims of this restructuring, as members of the lumpenproletariat they nevertheless continue to provide the kind of support on which the populist/far-right thrives. Immigration control is regarded by Mudde simply as a 'key populist right' policy, whereas in the form of curbing the growth of the industrial reserve it also forms part of the Marxist case against capitalist exploitation/oppression.[26]

Keen to stress his long-term analytical engagement with the study of populism, Mudde perceives immigration as a matter not of political economy but rather of moral/humanitarian concern, regarding it as 'more a matter of personal judgment than objective condition'.[27] This generates in turn a doubly problematic teleology. On the one hand, populism is depicted in simplistic terms, as a discourse without an ensemble of complex internal elements (= 'thin ideology') or history, and thus lacking an adequate explanation as to why it gains the support it has and does. On the other, because immigration is seen by him mainly through the lens of moral concern, it is presented largely as an issue of refugee flight, and as such a phenomenon that can and should be accommodated – financially and in other ways – by European nations.[28]

---

25 'Populist radical right values', indicates Mudde (2019: 107–108), 'are disproportionately supported by specific subsets of the populations, particularly lower educated, working class males from the majority "ethnic" or "racial" group. However, because of the postindustrial revolution and immigration, these groups are becoming a smaller part of the population in most western democracies'.

26 Mudde (2019: 107).

27 See Mudde (2019: 4). As if to emphasize how far ahead of the game he has been, Mudde (2019: 2, 72, 98) makes constant reference to the length of time he has spent investigating the populism/far-right connection, along the lines of '[a] lot has changed since I started working on the far right in the late 1980s', how he saw the elder Le Pen speak 'in Paris in 1986', and '[t]he first time I came across this debate was more than thirty-five years ago [c. 1985]'. His criticisms of others (Mudde, 2019: 76, 97–98) notwithstanding, the scientific basis of methods he himself employs are not always clear ('over the years I have observed several far-right meetings myself, ranging from demonstrations and party meetings to more casual social meetings, like barbeques and concerts').

28 As suggested by references (Mudde, 2019: 39, 122) to the 'so-called "refugee crisis"', the latter is not viewed as constituting an economic crisis. Since for Mudde (2019: 4) immigration appears to be sociologically undifferentiated, composed simply of those seeking

However, contrary to the way Mudde perceives immigration, it is for political economy an issue not of 'financial resources' but rather of labour market competition, and the hostility it generates – in the form of populism – arises when capital is perceived by those who have (or aspire to) jobs as using migrant workers to further its own economic advantage.[29] Curiously, however, he upholds 'liberal democracy' against the challenge posed by populism, whereas for Marxism bourgeois democracy is not the solution but the problem. Ironically, therefore, Mudde is defending capitalism from a 'from below' reaction to a situation that capitalism itself has brought about for economic reasons, and indeed on which accumulation depends and from which it benefits. Part of the difficulty facing this view about the populism/far-right/immigration link is the confusion generated by many and frequent changes of mind.

When writing originally about populism in 2001, Mudde was adamant in making a number of claims about its nature. Like others, he dismissed the Marxist view linking agrarian populism with postmodernism, on the grounds that it was too abstract.[30] Equally insistent was his view that agrarian populism was 'progressive', and that consequently to regard it as reactionary – as do Marxists – overlooked this positive aspect.[31] Again like others, he asserted that populism 'plays a much more prominent role in contemporary Eastern European politics than in the West'.[32] Each of these claims turns out to be mistaken. To begin with, his contention that there is no empirical support for an agrarian-populism/postmodernism link is quite simply wrong, based as it is on a lack of familiarity with substantial evidence structuring the postmodern discourse of agrarian populist approaches such as the Subaltern Studies framework and

---

asylum/refuge, blame is consequently attached by him to the unpreparedness of the receiving context: 'The EU had the financial resources to deal with even these record numbers of asylum seekers, although for years it had neglected to build an infrastructure to properly take care of them'.

29 Because he sees 'liberal democracy', or what is perceived by him as a benign variant of capitalism, as a political alternative to populist/far-right mobilization, Mudde overlooks the extent to which such movements/organizations are financed/subsidised by large and powerful corporate interests (Koch, Coors), or precisely the dominant components of the very economic system – capitalism – which he does not question but wishes to recuperate.

30 In his opinion (Mudde, 2002: 231, n.4), therefore, Marxist analysis equating agrarian populism with postmodernism operated 'at such a high level of abstraction that it hardly still justifies the term "agrarian populism"'.

31 On the positive aspects of populism, see Mudde (2019: 215). Others who make the same erroneous claims are considered in Chapter 4 (this volume).

32 Mudde (2002: 231).

'everyday forms of resistance'.³³ As misplaced is the claim about the 'progressive' character of populism, which not only overlooks the persistence of reactionary components (among them nationalism and anti-semitism) that have informed this discourse throughout its long history, but – as he now seems to accept – there is little difference between populist ideology and that of the far right.³⁴ Similarly mistaken is the argument that populism is mainly an Eastern European phenomenon, a view that ignores its strong purchase in the West, again a claim that presumably he would now find necessary to disavow.

To the above list Mudde himself now adds a number of his own retractions. Not only did he dismiss the threat posed to 'liberal democracy' by the populist radical right as 'a relatively minor nuisance', therefore, but concluded – similarly mistakenly – just before the Brexit vote that 'Europe's troublemakers' from the same end of the political spectrum would have little or no influence on foreign policy.³⁵ The reasons for these errors, both unacknowledged and acknowledged, are in all cases the same: because he attributes the rise of populism simply to 'globalization', and nowhere mentions the crucial need of capitalism for an industrial reserve army, Mudde is unable epistemologically to connect increased levels of immigration and support for the populist far right either with the resulting process of labour market competition or with recent shifts in academic debate about identity politics, and how this in turn feeds into wider political discussion concerning the desirability or otherwise of pursuing a systemic transcendence of capitalism.³⁶ Beyond a call for reinforcing 'liberal democracy', therefore, and in response to the question as to how the

---

33   On the agrarian-populism/postmodernism connection, with particular reference to paradigms like Subaltern Studies and 'everyday forms of resistance', see Brass (2000).

34   Compare what Mudde said about the 'progressive' nature of populism in 2002 and what he says about it now (Mudde, 2019).

35   'In a 2012 lecture', accepts Mudde (2019: 113), 'I concluded that the populist radical right was a "relatively minor nuisance" to liberal democracy in Western Europe [and] I foresaw neither the extent of political mainstreaming of the populist radical right nor the transformation of some of this "political mainstream" into full-fledged radical right parties'. Similarly, '[a] think tank report on "the populist challenge to foreign policy", of which I was co-author', concedes Mudde (2019: 124), 'concluded only a few years ago that "Europe's troublemakers" had only modest influence on foreign policy and the international community … was published just a few months before a majority of Brits decided to leave the EU, undoubtedly one of the most important foreign policy decisions in Europe in the twenty-first century'.

36   On the way in which arguments supportive of the 'new' populist postmodernism transcended the boundaries of academia and moved outside the latter contexts to influence the broader political debate about the cultural desirability of open-door immigration, see Brass (2017: 377ff.).

far right can be defeated, he confesses that 'even after more than two decades, I still do not have the answer'.³⁷

Essentializing Rurality?

Although noting the dominance in Europe of 'identity politics', Mudde does not explore this further in terms of cause and effect. In keeping with his analysis of the populism/immigration/far-right connection, however, he maintains that identity politics amounted to 'a more or less explicit defence of white supremacy', thereby missing the crucial element of chronology.³⁸ Contrary to the way Mudde presents the issue, as a case involving the assertion simply of 'white supremacy', the latter was preceded by the postmodern invocation of identity politics, depicting national/ethnic 'otherness' in Third World countries as empowering and innate. This same discourse in turn informed debate about the desirability (or otherwise) of immigration into metropolitan capitalist nations, privileging the non-economic identity of the migrant over considerations of political economy. What postmodernism has done is to move into an ideological space occupied historically by populism: to the postmodern argument emphasizing the cultural identity of the migrant-as-'other'-nationality, the populist/far-right counterposes an argument similarly emphasizing cultural identity, only this time the nationality of the non-migrant worker (= British selfhood).

By transferring the concept of victimhood from class to non-class identities, therefore, postmodernism moved onto the ideological terrain occupied historically by conservatism. Empowerment was henceforth no longer about class, but now about national/ethnic/religious identity. As was pointed out long ago,

---

37   Mudde (2019: 129). He is not the only one to confess to bewilderment. Vehemently anti-communist conservatives – such as Applebaum (2020), who expresses surprise at the fact that many of those she knows personally have moved in a direction she abhors – like to present the rise of populism and the far-right as a political anomaly, an unexpected and inexplicable deviation from what they regard as the democratic norm, whereas it is much rather the wholly expected and thoroughly explicable outcome of bourgeois democracy, rooted as it is in capitalism as a system, and exhibiting all the contradictions thrown up by the latter.

38   According to Mudde (2019: 165), therefore, 'in the last two decades socio-economic issues have come to dominate the political agenda. In most European countries … the political debate is dominated by socio-cultural issues and so-called "identity politics", including a more or less explicit defence of white supremacy in the face of increasing politicization of ethnic and religious minorities'.

this has created a space for the populist anti-capitalism of the political right. Moreover, where/when postmodernism declares the Third World rural poor empowered, the inference – equally supportive of conservatism – is that no more change is necessary: the objective has been realized. Insofar as it privileges cultural identity as empowering, postmodern theory is also complicit with the kind of nationalist ideology in metropolitan contexts represented by UKIP. In the absence of socialist ideas/practice, and as capitalism spreads across the globe, this form of nationalist discourse can be deployed effectively by populists who claim it is the only way to safeguard/retain workers' jobs and living standards in situations where immigration results in acute forms of labour market competition.

Departing from attempts by those such as Mudde to counter the influence of populism through reinforcing 'liberal democracy', others by contrast have embraced populism, declaring it empowering and/or 'progressive'.[39] Current attempts to 'rescue' populism as a viable political theory, capable of being deployed in the present as a democratic 'from below' alternative both to neoliberalism and to Marxism, adhere to a familiar pattern. The concept is split, enabling the attachment of the word 'authoritarian' as a prefix to one form. Supporters can then concede that a 'nasty' (= reactionary) variant does indeed exist but maintain that the other ('nice') form is not it. In this way, the concept itself is salvaged, politically sanitized and declared positive theoretically. Accordingly, the difficulty facing views that exclude Marxist critiques of accumulation in favour of more optimistic populist endorsements, whereby traditional peasant economy/culture and citizenship inside the capitalist system are seen as politically desirable ends in themselves, is clear. By framing solutions that are compatible with continued accumulation, as these affect migration (resolved by extending citizenship), unfree labour (to be made 'nicer') and the peasantry (bolstering individual proprietorship), not only is a socialist transition ruled out but politically worrying *laissez-faire* trends are reinforced.

Given the extent of misunderstanding on the part of those who interpret populism as negative or positive as to how and why the identity politics of postmodern discourse empower *laissez-faire* capitalism, leading to the rise of populism and the far-right, it is important to trace – briefly – the recent history of what amounts to a political shift. Many aspects characterizing the 'new' populist postmodernism of the 1980s were already present in the United States some two decades earlier in what has been termed 'Radical Chic'. The

---

39 One cannot be entirely sure as to which of these two categories Mudde belongs, since earlier he insisted that populism was progressive, whereas now it is coupled by him with far-right political mobilization.

latter demonstrated just how quickly a national bourgeoisie ceases to be 'progressive', and consequently how rapidly a corresponding notion about the desirability of 'from below' empowerment dissolves. Significantly, the reason for this emerged clearly: it occurs when such 'progressives' are faced with the prospect of a challenge to their wealth, power, and property relations. In such circumstances 'progressives' reveal their true class interests, and swiftly distance themselves from those advocating an overthrow of capitalism and/or a revolutionary socialist transition. This is precisely what Marxists argued was the case in their earlier critique of *katheder*-socialism.[40]

That all the tropes characterizing the 'new' populist postmodernism – privileging non-class identities as empowering for 'those below'; combining rurality and 'otherness' in a discourse about 'noble savage'; wanting to 'do something' about socio-economic inequality without, however, relinquishing power and wealth; espousing an anti-capitalism bereft of socialism and revolution – also informed 'Radical Chic', is clear both from the overlapping discourse and also from exchanges between wealthy New York socialites and the Black Panthers in the context of a fund-raising meeting arranged for the latter by the celebrated musician Leonard Bernstein in 1970.[41] This was a conjuncture when an expansion in media, communications and culture made it necessary for those producing or benefitting from such economic developments – such as the political 'progressives' attending 'Lenny's party' – sought to legitimize their wealth in the form of *noblesse oblige*, thereby paying 'their dues to "the poor"'. Once the Black Panther movement made it clear that its form of political opposition to capitalism could not – and would never – involve a peaceful

---

40 On the discarding by *katheder*-socialism of the central tenets of Marxism – class formation/struggle, revolution and socialism – plus the attempt to recuperate peasant economy, and how such views resurfaced after the 1939–45 war, see Brass (2000, 2014).

41 Coined by Tom Wolfe (1970), the term 'Radical Chic' denotes the attempt by the rich and powerful to undertake a public show of concern for the plight of the poor, a display that in the end lacks sincerity, not least because of the class contradictions it reveals. Although a conservative, Wolfe accurately chronicled the antinomies when those he described as 'limousine liberals' engaged in 'elegant slumming': hence the anxiety on the part of wealthy socialites giving fund-raising parties for the urban poor at which a Black Panther was present, a situation which necessitated hiring servants of a different ethnicity (not black, but white) so as to avoid embarrassment. 'Just at this point', Wolfe (1970: 11, 12, 78–79) goes on to note appositely, 'some well-meaning soul is going to say, why not do without servants altogether if the matter creates such unbearable tension and one truly believes in equality?' The real function of such display is described thus (Wolfe, 1970: 26, original emphasis): 'And suddenly everyone feels, really *feels*, that there are two breeds of mankind in … Park Avenue, the blue-jowled rep-tied Brook Club Junker reactionaries in the surrounding buildings … and the few *attuned* souls here in Lenny's penthouse'.

transition, however, support for its objectives on the part of rich and powerful 'progressives' vanished.⁴²

The link between this earlier conjuncture, in the form of 1960s 'Radical Chic', and its later counterpart, the 'new' populist postmodernism of the 1980s, is clear. A turn away from political economy and towards culture at each conjuncture led, amongst other things, to an embrace of ethnic 'otherness' in what was thought by those who did this to be politically progressive. Much like the 'new' populist postmodernism, therefore, 'Radical Chic invariably favours radicals who seem primitive, exotic, and romantic … such as [those] who are not merely radical and "of the soil" but also Latin'; the same kind of favour, however, was not extended to 'the white working class'.⁴³ In terms similar to those deployed by the 'new' populist postmodernism some two decades later, 1960s Radical Chic displayed an uncritical approach to grassroots rurality (= *nostalgie de la boue*), which – when linked to plebeian cultural/ethnic identity politics ('primitive, exotic, and romantic') – was supported by the haut bourgeoisie of metropolitan capitalism simply because it was not perceived to be a class-based form of 'otherness'.⁴⁴ Finally, and most significantly, the shared characteristics include a political underpinning that is conservative. As in the case subsequently of the 'new' populist postmodernism, Radical Chic 'is only radical in style; in its heart it is part of Society and its traditions'.⁴⁵

---

42   A wealthy media personality – white and female – who was at that party (Wolfe, 1970: 72–74) told those present how she asked the wife of a Black Panther during a television interview whether their children 'will be able to grow up and live side by side in peace and harmony', to which the reply was 'not without the overthrow of the system'. Asked how she felt 'about the prospect of your child being in that kind of confrontation, a nation in flames', the Black Panther spouse replied, 'Let it burn!'. The interviewer persisted, noting 'what I'm talking about [is] the way you refer to capitalism … whether you see any chance at all for a peaceful solution to these problems, some way out without violence', adding 'I'm talking as a white woman who has a white husband, who is a capitalist, or is an agent of capitalists, and I am, too, and I want to know if you are to have your freedom, does that mean we have to go!'. Shortly thereafter, and unsurprisingly, Leonard Bernstein and other 'progressives' attending the party broke with and condemned the Black Panthers.

43   Wolfe (1970: 12, 42ff.).

44   As described by Wolfe (1970: 31ff.), therefore, '[w]ithin New York Society *nostalgie de la boue* was a great motif throughout the 1960s', it being a process whereby the rich 'can take on the trappings of aristocracy [and simultaneously] indulge in the gauche thrill of taking on certain styles of the lower orders. The two are by no means mutually exclusive; in fact, they are always used in combination'. Although not regarded by Wolfe as populist, Radical Chic nevertheless shares many of its characteristics.

45   Wolfe (1970: 91). It is hard to disagree with his dismissive tone (Wolfe, 1976: 149) with regard to what is termed 'the Me movements' of late 1960s and early 1970s America (the anti-capitalism of which took the form of avoidance, not struggle), particularly when observing '[i]t is entirely possible that in the long run historians will regard the entire New

Marxism Missing, but ...

One exception to the Marxism-missing-but-necessary combination is both interesting and surprising, given its genre (film) and locus (popular culture). This seeming anomaly emerges from a comparison of the different ways the agrarian myth is portrayed on film in the same context but at two specific conjunctures, six decades apart. On the one hand, the films *A Canterbury Tale* (1944), directed by Michael Powell and Emeric Pressburger, and *Tawny Pipit* (1944), directed by Bernard Miles, each set in war-time England; and on the other *Hot Fuzz* (2007) and *The World's End* (2013), both of which are directed by Edgar Wright, and set in a present or future England. The agrarian myth features in similar ways within these two conjunctures, but very differently between the conjunctures themselves.[46] This divergence might be represented in terms of the gap separating the earlier discourse, where the emphasis is mainly on 'what we are fighting for', from the later one, where there is a similar but opposite emphasis on 'what we are fighting against'.[47]

Left experience as not so much a political as a religious episode wrapped in semi-military gear and guerrilla talk'. To some degree, this view is echoed by Debray (1979: 63): 'And on the extreme left, which made people sit back to back in the New-World-campus manner, Jesus-freaks, rock and love arrived: Berkeley '68'.

46 For the definition of the agrarian myth, its overlap with populism and the foundation myth, together with the oppositions structuring its discourse – between categories (utopic/dystopic), between economic sectors (urban/rural), between class identities (aristocratic/plebeian), and between harmony/struggle (pastoral/Darwinian) – see in general Brass (2000). The way in which all these aspects of the agrarian myth can be applied to the analysis of film – ones that are not considered here – is outlined in Brass (2000: Chapter 7).

47 It must be emphasized that criticisms made here of these two 1940s films in terms of the way the agrarian myth is portrayed does not mean they are 'bad', quite the contrary. It is precisely because each constructs such an effective (not to say lyrical) image of national identity, highlighting its connection to nature, landscape, and character, that narrative sublimates the underlying political discourse. In short, it corresponds to a process of 'filmic seduction' well described by Truffaut (1968: 94) when interviewing Hitchcock about *The Lady Vanishes* (1938): 'They show it very often in Paris; sometimes I see it twice in one week. Since I know it by heart, I tell myself each time I'm going to ignore the plot, to examine the train and see if it's really moving, or to look at the transparencies, or to study the camera movements inside the compartments. But each time I become so absorbed by the characters and the story that I've yet to figure out the mechanics of that film'. The same capacity to 'draw in' the audience is also true of *A Canterbury Tale*, rightly perceived now as a cinematic masterpiece in what is anyway an impressive Powell/Pressburger *oeuvre*, responsible – jointly or individually – for films such as *The Thief of Bagdad* (1940), *The Life and Death of Colonel Blimp* (1943), *A Matter of Life and Death* (1946), *Black Narcissus* (1947) and *The Red Shoes* (1948). Among those influenced by and admirers of Powell/

In what is superficially a film illustrating a war-time episode of British eccentricity, the plot of *Tawny Pipit* recounts how villagers occupying different class positions join together to protect a rare species of bird nesting in the nearby countryside from egg-collectors interested only in the commercial value of their sought-after trophies. Mobilized to protect the birds and their eggs, the whole village is led by a local member of the ruling class who proclaims that 'love of animals and of nature are part of the British way of life' and for this reason it is necessary to provide the nesting birds with 'fair play' and a 'square deal'. This sporting theme is taken up by a local fighter pilot, a wounded hero recuperating in the village, who informs young cricketers from the village that 'we are playing the best side in the world [Germany] and playing for England'. Soldiers on manoeuvres in the local fields eventually detain the egg-stealers, announcing that this was done because the tawny pipit eggs 'belong to England'. Subsequently, the fighter pilot rejoins his squadron, to defend the nation against invasion, the last image being of him flying his plane over the village and its fields, on the way to join battle with the German airforce. The symbolism is clear: the protection of the bird nesting in the countryside – undertaken by all its inhabitants regardless of age or class – is a metaphor for the defence and also the continuity of nature, of the rural, and of the nation itself.[48]

Agrarian myth discourse also structures the film narrative of *A Canterbury Tale*, about four characters in war-time England (one of whom is an American, and all in the services), three of whom retrace the Chaucerian journey along the old pilgrim road, in the course of which they solve the mystery of the 'glue-man', a hitherto anonymous local inhabitant who attempts to frighten off women from visiting the area lest they form a distraction to soldiers encamped near the city. As in the case of *Tawny Pipit*, *A Canterbury Tale* presents an harmonious/pastoral image of the nation, epitomized in multiple visual depictions, not just of farmyard, horse and cart, and a blacksmith at work, but also of Canterbury and its cathedral seen across the fields (= 'a glorious prospect'). All the latter combine to project a discourse about nation-as-arcadia, an ancient

---

Pressburger films are directors such as Martin Scorsese, Francis Coppola, and Brian de Palma (on which see Christie, 1985).

48   Much the same kind of agrarian myth discourse, depicting England as a rural idyll seemingly devoid of an urban industrial economic sector, was reproduced during the 1914–18 war, with the difference that then it took the form largely of the written word: for example, the volume edited by Rhys (1917). This bears out the veracity of an observation by Baldwin (1976: 80), that '[t]he English can be said to exemplify the power of nostalgia to an uncanny degree'.

and – to the American soldier – an inexplicably quaint country. Significantly, the urban/rural tension at the heart of the agrarian myth is not avoided: of the three characters from the metropolis, two are won over by the pastoral ambience, while the third is compelled to defend his antagonistic views about 'the rural'.[49] Gradually it emerges that the local gentleman farmer and magistrate is in fact the 'glue-man', his principal motive being to protect the girl-friends of local men serving abroad.[50] However, the film ends with every character in receipt of 'blessings', much like those sought by and conferred on the original Canterbury pilgrims. One character learns that her fiancé, whom she thought dead, was still alive and awaiting her arrival; another is given rerouted letters from a girlfriend with whom he had lost contact; a third gets to play the cathedral organ, a long-held ambition of his; and the fourth, the erstwhile 'glue-man', is not reported to the police, and thus escapes prosecution and humiliation.

Displaying all the familiar tropes of routine detective fiction, *Hot Fuzz* has at its centre an efficient policeman sent from the metropolis to a small village in the provinces in order to investigate the occurrence there of a high incidence of unsolved fatalities.[51] Presented as suicides, all these deaths turn out to be homicides. Although the unfolding narrative hints that the spate of murders are due to plans for the capitalist modernization of the locality, such as the desire to replace a small shop with a large supermarket, this is deceptive, and a device to mislead the film audience. It transpires that the reason for the violent death of each victim is not economic, but an aesthetic/cultural one.[52] That of

---

49   Among the pro-rural sentiments uttered by those won over as a result of their time in the village near Canterbury are 'what wouldn't I give to grow old in a place like that', and 'why should people who love the country have to live in cities'.

50   Although the 'glue-man', the character in question is depicted in a sympathetic manner, as a benign individual who wants mainly to instil a love of the Kent countryside and its history into the British and American soldiers billeted in the locality.

51   The most familiar trope is that of the good policeman, a staple of film noir. In terms of characterization, it is epitomized by the lone private eye in the stories of Raymond Chandler, a principled individual who adheres to the chivalric code of the traditional aristocracy, and as an urban (and urbane) outsider upholds this same code when engaged in struggle against a rural hierarchy. Whereas in *Hot Fuzz* the policeman from the metropolis not only survives but settles in the village to which he was originally posted, in an earlier film covering the same ground – the *Wicker Man* (1973), directed by Robin Hardy – his equivalent is eventually murdered by those living in the rural location to which he was sent.

52   Lest this be though an unlikely narrative, or just an exaggeration, a recent story in the British press contains the following report: 'Prince Charles's designer town accused of putting aesthetics over safety: Poundbury village backtracks on plan to install yellow lines at spot where motorcyclist was killed ... putting the prettiness of the town above saving lives'. *The Guardian* (London), 24 October 2019.

a local newspaper journalist because he is unable to spell correctly, casting the village in an unfavourable light; that of a wealthy developer because his modern home offends against good taste; that of two actors because they make a mess of a Shakespeare play; that of the owner of a florist shop because she was about to take her flower-growing talent to a rival village; and that of a group of travellers because they spoiled the pristine appearance of the village itself. Every one of them was killed by the local Neighbourhood Watch Alliance, composed of bourgeois residents (police chief, supermarket owner, vicar): not because the victim opposed or blocked economic development, however, but much rather because s/he posed a threat to the locality winning the 'Village of the Year' award. Unusually, therefore, *Hot Fuzz* breaks with a longstanding filmic convention depicting impoverished/downtrodden farmers menaced by powerful outside capitalists in a struggle for economic resources – water in the case of *Chinatown* – and instead doubly relocates the conflict: both within 'the rural' itself, and involving nothing more than the preservation of a aesthetic/cultural identity that is traditional, pristine, and rustic. The latter corresponds to the Darwinian variant of the agrarian myth, the aesthetic/cultural values of which the bourgeois residents of the village are prepared to kill in order to defend.

Unlike each of the three previous films, *The World's End* is in many ways politically the most ambivalent.[53] Like *Hot Fuzz*, it begins by adhering to a familiar trope: a group of male friends reliving their youth by going on a pub crawl in the small town where they grew up. As this unfolds, however, it is increasingly evident that an alien invasion has replaced the whole local population with replicants, physically indistinguishable from their real selves. These androids become steadily more menacing, attacking the group and converting its members into replicants. On reaching the final pub, the two remaining members

---

53   This political ambivalence is reflected also in the way films by other directors seamlessly transited from a 1940s anti-fascist theme to the anti-communism of the 1950s and 1960s. A case in point is the work of Frank Launder and Sidney Gilliat, in which the enemy changed from the political right in films such as *The Lady Vanishes* (1938), directed by Alfred Hitchcock, and *Night Train to Munich* (1940), directed by Carol Reed (Launder and Gilliat providing the screenplay for both) to the political left in *State Secret* (1950), directed by Gilliat (and produced by Launder) and *Ring of Spies* (1963), directed by Robert Tronson (screenplay by Launder). Ironically, in other respects the narrative plus structure remained the same: both *Night Train to Munich* and *State Secret* – brilliant stories in filmic (but not political) terms – contained the same kind of chase scenario, involving an escape over the mountains (from Germany in the former, and from 'Vosnia' in the latter) into a safe and/or a neutral Switzerland. On Launder and Gilliat, see Brown (1977) and Babington (2002).

are transferred into an underground chamber, there to confront the Network, composed of technologically advanced aliens. In this exchange the still-human group leader asserts his right to individuality against the desire of the Network to establish a shared identity of uniformly happy/accepting beings. Patiently, the disembodied voice of the Network explains that it itself is responsible for all the technical advances found on earth and thus also for the betterment of humanity, to which the group leader Gary – played by Simon Pegg – replies aggressively that all he wants is 'to have a good time'.[54] The Network relents and agrees to pull out, leaving humanity to its own devices: all technological advance is erased, the town explodes, civilization collapses, and life on earth goes back to the dark ages.

Departing from the usual zombie apocalypse narrative, whereby the non-human replicant is depicted as an unambiguously negative force, *The World's End* portrays the Network in a more nuanced fashion, effecting a contrast between the inferred mindlessness of Gary – whose sole objective is 'to have a good time' – and the benign contributions (technology, betterment) on offer from the alien 'other', whose departure (unenforced) leads to the apocalypse, rather than the more usual film narrative in which it is a wholly malign force that generates the apocalypse. The Gary/Network difference is presented in terms of a struggle between individual and collective interests: the triumph of the former at the expense of the latter heralds a dystopic era bereft of economic development. In short, the conquest by 'the rural' of 'the urban', and the dominance of individuality over the collective, which – together with the end of development itself – are issues fundamental to an understanding of

---

54   Some of credit for the narrative is due to Simon Pegg, who not only starred in but also co-wrote *Hot Fuzz* and *The World's End*. The significance of this lies in the title of his undergraduate thesis, 'A Marxist Overview of Popular 1970s Cinema and Hegemonic Discourses', which suggests the narrative is not unintended. A clue to this can be found in his account (Pegg, 2011: 252–53) of engaging with film discourse whilst at university: 'It was at Bristol [Drama Department] that I discovered the joys of critical analysis which eventually inspired me to pick apart my beloved *Star Wars* as part of my final-year exams. Lectures and seminars on populist cinema were hugely interesting, since they enabled me to consider what I had previously assumed to be a disposable art form as a source of academic study. I was able to watch my favourite films again then address them as historical "texts", reflecting a host of psychoanalytical complexities … the process was fascinating and enlightening. At the beginning of our first film studies lecture [we were told that] we would never be able to view a film in the same way again. By developing and engaging our critical faculties we would effectively be given the ability to see through the artifice in three dimensions, able to detect meaning both intentional and unintentional [as well as] understand the intellectual mechanics at work in the narrative. …'

agrarian myth discourse.⁵⁵ In the two 1940s films, *Tawny Pipit* and *A Canterbury Tale*, the agrarian myth variant is the pastoral, whereby an harmonious rural setting comes under attack mainly from the outside, by a nationalist/fascist enemy located on the European mainland. In *Hot Fuzz* and *The World's End*, however, the enemies are internal and class-based, and the discourse is that of the Darwinian variant of the agrarian myth: the aristocratic version in *Hot Fuzz*, and the plebeian one in *The World's End*. This element of dissimilarity extends also to the physical aspect, which in the case of films at each conjuncture is equally marked: whereas in both the earlier ones the landscape is light, and open, as befits utopia, in each of the later films it tends to be dark and closed, in keeping with a dystopia.

Themes

The focus of Part 1 (Chapters 1–4) is on aspects of the debate, recent and current, within the domain of development studies, centrally about political and economic questions relating to Third World countries (socialism, colonialism, reparations). As applied to the issues covered, the argument made in this section is that Marxism is interpreted in a problematic manner (= Marxism missing): in short, what passes for Marxism, isn't. Though present, therefore, in this kind of approach Marxism is in reality absent. Part 2 (Chapters 5–8) deals with the same conceptual framework and issues, but now as these relate both to areas beyond the Third World and to a broader historical period. Accordingly, the contexts/conjunctures extend from debates concerning ancient society (systemic transition, decline of the Roman Empire, Late Antiquity) to ones about present-day metropolitan capitalist nations (the United States, Britain).

Since a Marxist approach is largely or wholly absent from the latter discussions, the case made in this section is that such a theoretical framework is analytically and politically necessary (= missing Marxism). That is, since there is no longer an attempt to deploy Marxist theory to account for the phenomena examined, it is an approach that is not merely lacking but essential. It must be stressed, however, that the distinction between Parts 1 and 2 is mainly one of emphasis. If certain themes and issues – not just the Marxism-missing-but-necessary combination but also the link between economic development and labour market competition, a process in its most acute form accompanied

---

55   See Brass (2000) for the different elements (aristocratic/plebeian, pastoral/Darwinian, Nature-on-the-attack/Nature-under-attack) composing agrarian myth discourse.

by the emergence or re-emergence of identity politics, a discourse privileging opposed variants of national/ethnic 'otherness' as evidenced currently in populism, postmodernism, and an assortment of nativist mobilizations – keep on surfacing throughout the volume, this is because they are all relevant to an understanding of the question being considered, which as a result can be explained in terms of an underlying theoretical and political unity.

The focus of Chapter 1 is on two debates, one between agrarian populism and Marxism about the way rural economy and society changes historically, and the other within Marxism itself concerning how the peasantry is transformed by capitalist development. Whereas family farmers cultivating smallholdings were essentialized by agrarian populism as independent proprietors, regardless of whether they sold the product of labour or labour-power, Marxism by contrast differentiated peasants along class lines, into a kulak, middle and poor stratum. Debate within Marxist theory involved Stalin, Trotsky, and Lenin, each of whom formulated strategy as to how different rural strata should be mobilized politically against capitalism and imperialism. Advocating anti-imperialist alliances with a 'progressive' national bourgeoisie, and supportive of cultural autonomy, Stalin maintained a 'strong' middle peasantry could be drawn into socialism; opposing this, Trotsky warned against kulak power, and was critical of peasant support for conservative and reactionary political movements. Recognizing the same danger, Lenin opposed national oppression, but also fought against nationalism.

Outlined in Chapter 2 is how aspects of these debates influenced 1960s development theory, especially the way identity politics informing 'new' populist postmodernism fused with social history, and the crucial role of Eric Hobsbawm in this epistemological merger. Endorsing an unheard voice-from-below as authentic and empowering, social history witnessed the rise of non-class selfhoods that licensed the championing of traditional culture as a bulwark against imperialism. Adopting a positive view of pre-industrial society and applying this to the Third World rural 'other', Hobsbawm not only equated Third World peasant movements with 'primitive rebels' of the Middle Ages, but also viewed such agency as 'progressive' because it was rooted in popular culture (= authentic). Significantly, and the self-image of Hobsbawm as political victim notwithstanding, a recent biography reveals the extent to which his deradicalization coincided with his absorption into the ranks of the British establishment, in the course of which his theory/politics became increasingly disconnected from Marxism.

In Chapter 3 a similar political contrast informs the way development case-studies (Africa, India) have been and are analysed. Because concepts like class, capitalism, and peasant differentiation are deemed by Worsley to be absent from the Third World countryside, Marxist theory is viewed by him as inapplicable to an understanding of economic development in such national contexts, while populism is viewed as an appropriate mobilizing discourse. In support of her call for reparations, Patnaik revives the colonial 'drain' theory and extends this to present-day exchange relations between ex-colonies and erstwhile colonizers. Initially absent from her analysis, the industrial reserve now surfaces, but in a way that breaks with Marxism. She maintains that two reserve armies exist, and that the one in the periphery is economically separate from its equivalent in metropolitan capitalism, overlooking or downgrading thereby the unity of capitalism as a system.

Chapter 4 examines the claim that agrarian populism can be – and is currently – progressive, a view evaluated in relation to recent pro-peasant/farmer-first accounts (Bernstein, Dhanagare) of rural mobilization in Russia at the start of the twentieth century and India at its end. Against this, it is argued that from the perspective of Marxist theory, agrarian populism cannot be regarded as progressive, for two reasons in particular. First, it overlooks or downplays the fact that capitalism requires of peasant households only their labour-power, as components of an increasingly global industrial reserve army. Opposed merely to certain forms of capitalism (foreign, large-scale) and not to accumulation *per se*, populists were and are unable to address this contradiction. And second, agrarian populism unleashes – or, once unleashed, endorses – discourses about the innateness of national/ethnic/religious difference associated historically and currently with the political right.

Considered in Chapter 5 is a somewhat unexpected departure from the pantheon of Marxist theory. In the case of recent historiography of ancient Rome, the central Marxist concept of systemic transition has been discarded. Instead of the longstanding account of Roman Imperial decline, characterized by increasing polarization of wealth/property ownership, impoverishment leading to social conflict, underconsumption and economic stagnation, decentralization, ruralisation, and political crises, this narrative has been replaced by the term Late Antiquity, a period which it is now claimed was exemplified by social harmony, enhanced religious belief, economic growth, and general prosperity. Of significance to the Marxism-missing-but-necessary combination is that Marxist (and other materialist) analyses subscribing to the decline thesis have been replaced by postmodern-influenced historians and historiography.

Where this kind of benign historiographical interpretation can end up is demonstrated by the economically benign argument that is criticized in Chapter 6. Not only does Banaji uphold the positive view about Late Antiquity, but he denies that the Roman Empire underwent a decline, and with it a process of change leading to systemic transition. Where the presence of capitalism in ancient society is concerned, Banaji favours the approach of Mommsen (who endorses its existence) over that of Marx (who denies this), this despite the fact that the description by the former of provincial economic organization does not quite accord with the notion of widespread economic dynamism. Many elements in the analysis of Banaji are drawn not from Marxism but from non-and anti-Marxist frameworks, and he signals his break with Marxism by eliminating the crucial distinction between merchant and industrial capital, and then claiming further that the latter category is merely a variant of the former. Capital is declared an ever-present systemic mode, as much a feature of Late Antiquity as of the twenty-first century global economy.

Chapter 7 compares two approaches to the debate about ethnic/national 'otherness', ones that are contextually, ideologically, and politically distinct. For intellectuals/activists such as Paul Robeson and C.L.R. James, not only did the importance of class solidarity and socialist objectives transcend ethnic/national boundaries, but 'from below' empowerment was to be realized within the home country itself (the United States, the Caribbean and African nations). Current post-colonial discourse, by contrast, equates nations with a specific ethnic identity and a concomitant role as either oppressor/exploiter or oppressed/exploited. The discourse of the post-colonial diaspora not only essentializes national/ethnic 'otherness' and celebrates wealth and accumulation, therefore, but also relocates the achievement of empowerment from the home country to metropolitan capitalist nations. In the latter context the objective is no longer systemic transcendence, but simply a better deal within the existing system.

Finally, Chapter 8 traces the different approaches that compose Great Replacement discourse, which attributes European cultural erosion and de-authentication to immigration, a mobilizing ideology fuelling the rise of populism and the far right. In this discourse blame for this process is attached to the left, deemed responsible for promoting identity politics that privilege any and all forms of 'otherness'. It is argued, however, that what Great Replacement discourse perceives as being on the left politically is more accurately interpreted as a rival form of populism: the 'new' populist postmodernism. Unlike Marxism, therefore, both the cultural turn and Great Replacement itself misrecognize the economic causes structuring their respective discourses.

PART 1

Marxism Missing

∴

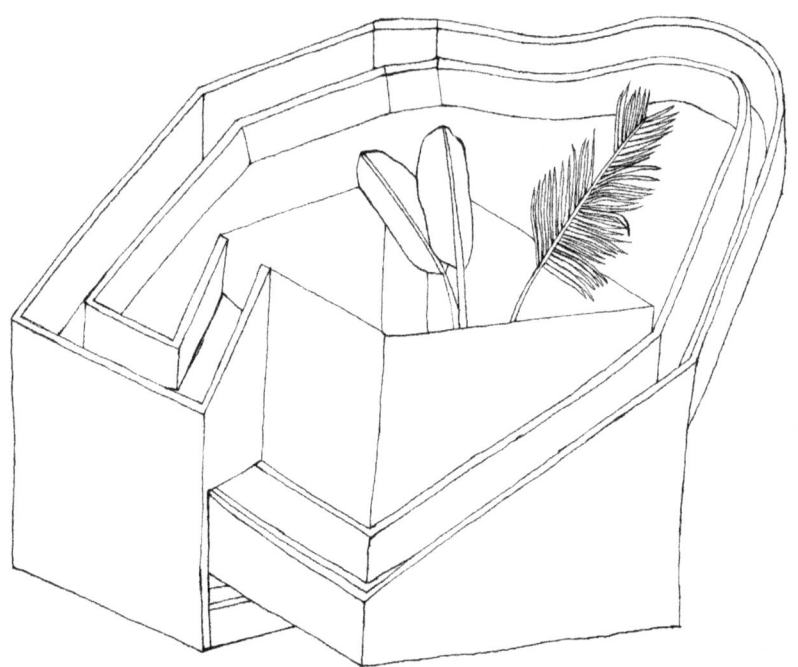

INSIDE THE MAZE © ANNA LUISA BRASS

CHAPTER 1

Marxism(s) within/beyond the Nation

> All's Whiggery now, / But we old men are massed against / the world.
> WILLIAM BUTLER YEATS.¹

∴

Introduction

Among the many reasons why Marxism can be regarded as missing are two in particular. First, as a result of what might be termed 'departures from within', by those who – whilst claiming to be Marxists – nevertheless discard (or fail to address) crucial aspects of its theoretical framework. And second, its absence can be attributed to an external displacement, most frequently by its political and economic 'other', agrarian populism, exponents of which make no secret of their hostility to Marxism. On occasion, and especially now, these two positions merge, with the result that what is presented as a Marxist argument can, on closer inspection, turn out to be an agrarian populist one.

All too often, these days behind an attack on imperialism lies an endorsement not of socialism but rather of nationalism. Lurking behind the latter, moreover, is a defence of bourgeois democracy, a 'progressive' national bourgeoisie, and ultimately a return to a 'nicer'/'kinder' form of capitalism. The origins of this purportedly-leftist strategy can be traced to the multi-class alliances Popular Front policy of the 1930s backed by Stalin; the same kind of approach is found currently among exponents of the semi-feudal thesis.²

---

1 Yeats (1933: 23).
2 A recent defence by Laibman (2015) of the stages framework – a variant of the semi-feudal thesis – maintains that the current public/private sector dualism be replaced with a trisectoral model, combining a dominant capitalism, a pre-capitalist remnant, and a postcapitalist harbinger. Along with servitude, feudal peonage and sweatshops, therefore, prison labour is in this model classified as a 'pre-capitalist remnant' on account of it (and them) having been 'important in the early history of capitalist accumulation'. A corollary is that, because 'pre-capitalist remnants' abound, capitalism proper is viewed as still rare: asking 'to what extent capitalist production relations are actually forming [in the Middle East, China and Latin America]', Laibman (2015: 175–76) replies that '[t]he answer [is], I believe: to a

Indeed, it is possible to construct a lineage from the 1930s Popular Front, via the Eurocommunism of Santiago Carrillo, privileging as it did not revolutionary class struggle waged against the bourgeoisie and its State but class alliances with the 'progressive' bourgeoisie, only resistance against the State, in furtherance not of socialism but rather of bourgeois democracy and nationalism, to the paradigms that influenced the development debate from the 1960s onwards.[3] The latter included not just the semi-feudal thesis, but also the 'new' populist postmodernism or the 'cultural turn'. As will be argued in the chapters which follow, therefore, academia has played an important role in the consolidation of this revisionist political trend, culminating in what is termed here the Marxism-missing-but-necessary combination. Over the last four decades the latter process has in effect hindered the formation within the ranks of the intelligentsia of a socialist alternative to the rise of populism and the far right.

That Marxism is deemed to be missing immediately raises the question of which Marxism, and why should one specific variant be privileged over any other. It could be argued that the choice of Trotsky as the absent Marxism is seemingly perverse, in that not only have such views been criticized strongly both from within and outside Marxism itself, but his interpretation of the dynamics generating systemic transformation no longer appear relevant to an understanding of the current epoch. About the economic, political, and ideological links between on the one hand the peasantry and on the other socialism, capitalism, nationalism, class, and much else besides, Trotsky was nothing if not consistent.

From the outset, therefore, he pointed out the danger of concessions made by communist parties in order to gain the support of an undifferentiated peasantry, in terms of the formation of an alliance with the 'progressive bourgeoisie' in defence of democracy and the nation.[4]

---

much lesser degree than we customarily assume'. Since what exists in such contexts are simply 'capitalist enclaves', we should 'support a national bourgeoisie' in its project to accumulate, thereby establishing capitalism proper, an objective 'I think we need to revive'. In short, this is the Popular Front logic informing the advocacy by the semi-feudal thesis of patience, as against those on the left – supporters of Trotsky's concept 'permanent revolution' – who in the opinion of Laibman are in 'a hurry' to bring about a socialist transition.

3   On Eurocommunism, see Carrillo (1977), whose reformist approach is explicitly aimed at the revolutionary Marxist theory of Lenin and Trotsky (Carrillo, 1977: 9–10, 118).

4   It is important to recall the lessons Marxism teaches about the political objective and outcome of Popular Frontism. In order to counter the rise of fascism, Stalin and Comintern instructed autonomous working-class parties and/or organizations throughout the world to ally themselves politically not just with the peasantry and the national bourgeoisie but also with conservatives in their respective national contexts. Popular Frontism in the mid-1930s accordingly entailed the replacement of working-class struggle and revolutionary internationalism with a nationalist and multi-class defence of democratic capitalism. Based on

Of the five sections in this chapter, the first outlines the way peasants feature both in Marxist theory and that of its 'other', agrarian populism. The second and third sections contrast the approach of Trotsky, for whom peasant commitment to traditional culture and political support for nationalist/conservative ideas threatened socialism, and Stalin, for whom the working class should ally itself with a 'strong' middle peasantry, thereby drawing the latter into socialism. Further contrasts are examined in sections four and five, involving two particular issues. First, the cultural autonomy favoured by Stalin in the struggle with imperialism, and how this breaks with the political approach of Lenin (fight national oppression, but also nationalism). And second, although critical of the 'privileged section' of the working class in metropolitan capitalist nations, and how this component was in the forefront of struggle against the presence of the industrial reserve army, Lenin nevertheless was equally critical both of divide-and-rule tactics used by employers to undermine working class unity, and of populists who dismissed the impact of surplus labour as 'an anomaly'.

I

The External/Eternal 'Other'

When addressing sources of external displacement, central to any understanding both of an absence of Marxism and of a necessity for its presence, are the claims advanced historically and currently by agrarian populism, epistemologically and politically the 'other' of Marxism. It could be argued that, as capitalism develops, over time the peasantry declines, and with it the potency of agrarian populism as a mobilizing ideology. Despite the separation of independent smallholders from their means of production, many of whom then join the industrial reserve, however, in many national contexts agrarian populist discourse continues to thrive. Even when separated from their means of labour, therefore, erstwhile petty commodity producers cling onto a peasant identity. The latter in turn can be invoked by conservative and/or reactionary political movements, which project traditional non-class forms of 'selfhood' (nationalism, ethnicity) as alternatives to any consciousness/agency of class.

---

peasant essentialism, this populist strategy has a long history, and Popular Frontism represented the culmination of revisionist views advocated some forty years earlier by Eduard Bernstein and Eduard David. Of equal length is the history of revolutionary socialist opposition to this kind of political strategy.

Agrarian populism has its roots in the antagonism towards Enlightenment discourse and the 1789 French Revolution expressed by Romanticism, a hostility which took the form of support for pre-revolutionary traditional forms/institutions and both the specificity and innateness of cultural/ethnic/national identity. At the centre of this discourse was an essentialist concept of an homogenous smallholding peasant, whose pristine and immutable cultural 'otherness' was said to embody both Nature and nationhood. The same identity structured not only Russian populist/neo-populist ideology at the end of the nineteenth century and the beginning of the twentieth, but also Italian fascism and German Nazism. In common with this prefigurative discourse, therefore, agrarian populism is supportive of small-scale economic activity (peasant family farming, individual proprietorship, artisanry) in the countryside, and also on rural cultural forms/institutions based on this activity: the family, village, regional, national, ethnic, and religious identities which are perceived as being derived from Nature.

This positive image of rural society is contrasted to a negative counterpart. Thus, agrarian populism opposes large-scale economic activity (collectivization, massification), particularly urban-based forms (finance capital, industrialization, planning). It is also hostile to their accompanying institutional, relational, and systemic effects (class formation/struggle, revolution, bureaucracy, the state), all of which are regarded as inauthentic/non-natural internationalisms imposed on rural populations by external (= 'foreign') agency/processes (socialism, capitalism). Unsurprisingly in view of its essentialist perception of rural identity, the historical subject of agrarian populism is an undifferentiated peasantry, the repository of traditional culture and thus emblematic of people/nation/Nature. In keeping with this is the view that a consequence of peasant de-essentialization – a result of separation from means of production (land) – is the erosion of cultural and national identity. Equally unsurprisingly is the fact that the main target of agrarian populist hostility is Marxism.

Peasants were – and are – central to Marxist theory about the dynamics informing the trajectory in pursuit of modernity and systemic transition: from feudalism to capitalism, and from the latter to socialism. Hence the process of accumulation is itself premised on an agrarian transition, whereby a marketed surplus is transferred to industry. This in turn requires the differentiation of the peasantry, and its fragmentation along class lines, thereby providing accumulation with both the employer and worker. A result of capitalist development in agriculture, therefore, was the emergence of rich, middle, and poor strata: the top component became part of a rural bourgeoisie, while the bottom stratum was converted into a proletariat. Middle peasants, or petty commodity producers, were depeasantized, and over time the majority of them also joined the ranks of landless labour. For Marxism, therefore, the historical agent of transformation is – and can only ever be – the proletariat.

However, because they perceived the labouring subject in rural areas as a 'natural' smallholder cultivating his/her land (leased or owned) – that is to say, an essentialist view of peasant economy – agrarian populists missed the fact that what poor peasants sold was not the product of labour but rather labour-power itself. From this error stemmed a failure to recognize both the presence and the role of those in the rural sector in providing capital with its much-needed industrial reserve army. The latter was – and is still – composed of those who, despite being perceived (and, indeed, seeing themselves) as independent peasant farmers, should more accurately be viewed as de facto workers. It is this contradiction – between an essentialist concept of peasant-as-cultivator-on-his/her-own-behalf and peasant-as-worker-for-other(s) – that informs much of the historical and contemporary debate about how politically to characterize rural mobilization and/or agrarian social movements.

For agrarian populism, there is no difficulty in this regard: the rural subject is nothing other than actually or potentially an independent peasant, and in terms of political and economic interests should always be seen as such. However, for Marxism this issue is more complex, since two conflicting sets of political and economic interest are at stake. On the one hand, therefore, it is possible to interpret as positive the fact that peasants who migrate to urban conurbations in search of better-paid work are acting as a potential or actual proletariat, and thus engaged in a process of class formation/consciousness. On the other, by contrast, it is equally possible to hold a negative view of this same process, in that these rural migrants can on occasion pose an actual/potential threat to those already in employment, especially where the former are prepared to undercut – and thereby replace – the latter. In these circumstances, the resulting contradiction takes the form of a split within the ranks of the working class: between its upper stratum defending its 'privileged' position in the urban workforce against an oppressed (and politically more worthy) lower stratum, composed for the most part of migrants from rural areas.

Not the least problematic aspect of populisms old and new which imagine that opposition to imperialism in general, and to neoliberalism in particular, is 'progressive' on account of its hostility to capital, is a failure to differentiate between two antithetical forms of anti-capitalism. As both Lenin and Trotsky made clear, one type of opposition emanates from the political left, and another has its origins in the discourse of the political right.[5] Whereas

---

5 The reactionary nature of certain forms of anti-capitalism was elaborated by Trotsky in his analyses of the connection between economic crisis and peasant support for fascism.

the former posits socialism as the transcendent 'other' of capitalism *as a system*, the latter is antagonistic only to certain kinds of capital (financial, foreign, large-scale, agribusiness). Hence the invocation by those on the political right of trajectories that avoid a socialist transition: instead, such paths involve either a return to a rural social order in which landlord and peasant (= 'the people') live in harmony, or the continuation of one in which petty commodity producers undertake smallscale accumulation.

Central to the anti-capitalist discourse of the political right, therefore, is the idea of cultural innateness rooted in nationhood, an eternal identity disturbed and undermined by an external (and alien) capitalism. From this stems the ideological potency of the agrarian myth, a discourse proclaiming the pristine nature of rural society, one that overlaps with both the foundation myth and agrarian populism.[6] In this kind of narrative the village community is regarded as being composed of an undifferentiated peasantry; neither the smallholder nor the rural context is perceived to be tainted by an external capitalism. Within such a discourse it becomes possible – historically and contemporaneously – for agrarian populism to depict peasants as embodying all the positive and culturally specific attributes of an 'authentic' national identity. Depeasantization effected by capitalism or socialism becomes an attack on the nation itself.

Arguing against the Popular Front of Stalin during the mid-1930s, therefore, he (Trotsky, 1979a: 38, emphasis added) made the following point: 'Naturally, the petty proprietor prefers order so long as business is going well and so long as he hopes that tomorrow it will go better. But when hope is lost, he is easily enraged and is ready to give himself over to the most extreme measures ... *The despairing petty bourgeois sees in fascism, above all, a fighting force against big capital*, and believes that – unlike the working class parties that deal only in words – fascism will use force to establish more "justice". The peasant and the artisan are in their manner realists. They understand that one cannot forego the use of force'.

6   As has been noted in Chapter 1 (and in many of my earlier publications), there is an ideological and political overlap between on the one hand the constituent elements of the agrarian myth, and on the other populism and historical/contemporary forms of conservative ideology. In broad terms, therefore, the agrarian myth endorses 'natural'/harmonious rural-based smallscale economic activity (peasant family farming, handicrafts) and culture (religious/ethnic/national/regional/village/family identities derived from Nature). By contrast, it expresses opposition to urban-based largescale economic activity (industrialization, finance capital, the city, manufacturing, collectivization, planning, massification) and hostility towards its accompanying institutional/relational/systemic effects (class formation/struggle, revolution, socialism, bureaucracy, the state). All the latter are perceived as non-indigenous/inauthentic/'alien' internationalisms imposed on an unwilling and mainly rural population by 'foreigners', and therefore as responsible for the erosion of hitherto authentic local culture, traditions and values.

In every respect, therefore, Marxism has been and remains the 'other' of agrarian populism. Although the Marxist critique of populism is rightly associated with the work of Lenin and Trotsky, their opposition to its discourse is prefigured in the work of Marx and Engels.[7] This kind of mid-nineteenth century populism was identified by Engels as one which sought 'to establish the rule of the aristocracy', composed of 'adherents of feudal and patriarchal society which has been or is still being daily destroyed by large-scale industry, world trade and the bourgeois society that they have both brought into existence. From the ills of present-day society this group draws on the conclusion that feudal or patriarchal society should be restored because it was free from these ills'.[8] His conclusion was that 'it always gives away its real intentions every time the proletariat becomes revolutionary and communist, when it immediately allies itself with the bourgeoisie against the proletarians'.

Such a pattern remains extant, with the difference that it is now a rural bourgeoisie that seeks to gain the support of plebeian elements by invoking a shared non-class identity when engaged in struggle against rival producers. As will be seen in a later chapter with regard to the new farmers' movements in India, unlike Marxism – which is antagonistic to capitalism tout court – agrarian populism is opposed only to particular variants of capital (financial, foreign), ones moreover that in the form of largescale agribusiness enterprises compete successfully with rich peasants and commercial farmers in the market for agricultural commodities. Obtaining the political collaboration of plebeian elements requires a non-class ideology which purports to advance the cause of 'those below': in short, a pro-peasant discourse that ignores or downgrades class distinctions transecting the peasantry. It is precisely this ideology – labelled by Marxist theory as 'false consciousness' – which is not only supplied by agrarian populism, but also endorsed by postmodern, post-colonial, and

---

7 For these critiques see Lenin (1964a) and Trotsky (1969). Marx and Engels (1976: 507ff.) had attacked agrarian populism half a century earlier, when in the *Communist Manifesto* they considered 'feudal socialism', defined thus: 'The aristocracy, in order to rally the people to them, waved the proletarian alms-bags in front for a banner ... so little do they conceal the reactionary character of their criticism that their chief accusation against the bourgeoisie amounts to this, that under the bourgeois regime a class is being developed, which is destined to cut up root and branch the old order of society'. In the sentence that follows, the underlying political fear of landowners who mobilize on the basis of agrarian populism is made clear: 'What they upbraid the bourgeoisie with is not so much that it creates a proletariat, as it creates a *revolutionary* proletariat' (original emphasis). In a letter to Vera Zasulich written in 1890, Engels (Marx and Engels, 2001c: 167) observed: 'That it is imperative to combat Narodnism, no matter where – whether German, French, English or Russian – I entirely agree'.
8 Engels (1976: 355).

post-development approaches, via arguments championing as 'progressive' and empowering cultural identities that transect class.[9]

II

The Source of Social Miracles

In his critique of populism Trotsky focused on its idealized perception of 'the rural' generally, and in particular on the way its discourse/agency was supportive of peasants – conceptualized by populists as undifferentiated – experiencing the impact of capitalist penetration of the countryside. Equally critical, therefore, were his observations about the role of intellectuals who in the main promoted and reproduced such views.[10] Noting the pervasive influence among intellectuals in Russia (and elsewhere in Europe) at the beginning of the twentieth century of a discourse about culture, Trotsky dismissed 'the cliquish self-importance of the intelligentsia' for indulging in what he termed 'self-congratulation, narcissism and pretension'.[11] This was because in his view many of the intelligentsia had shifted from upholding a political economy approach when addressing grassroots problems – and consequently regarding such issues as a form of disempowerment – to one featuring the same locus as a site much rather of cultural empowerment.

Not the least problematic aspect of this shift, argued Trotsky, was that culture – insofar as this refers to an already constituted ideological ensemble

---

9   As indicated elsewhere (Brass, 2017, 2019), those holding these kinds of view subscribe to paradigms such as global labour history or every-day-forms-of-resistance, and deploy concepts like 'multitudes', 'subalterns', 'classes of labour', 'food commodity chains', 'food security', 'food sovereignty', 'land sovereignty', and 'land grabbing'.

10 'The intelligentsia', noted Trotsky (1999: 91), 'has been substituting itself for the political parties, classes, and the people. The intelligentsia has experienced entire cultural epochs – on behalf of the people. The intelligentsia has chosen the paths of development – for the people. Where has all this titanic work being going on? Why, in the imagination of this same intelligentsia!'.

11 Hence the view Trotsky (1999: 84, 85) expressed in 1912 that 'all in one way or another cast off … their former passions, sympathies and hopes … Taking different paths and turnings – unbridled individualism, aristocratic scepticism, crude anarchism … and unprincipled satirical mockery – everyone aspired to "culture"'. He continues: 'It became clear just how unreliable were the intelligentsia's reserves of moral fibre. But such is the ironic nature of history: it was in this very period of near-universal self-denial and retreat from previously-held positions that the cliquish self-importance of the intelligentsia revealed its highest intensity … Never before had it indulged in such self-congratulation, narcissism and pretension … I am religion! I am culture! I am the past, present and future!'.

at the rural grassroots – reproduced and thus in an important sense perpetuated social and economic forms that were politically conservative.[12] Where the peasantry was concerned, therefore, rural culture reflected organizational dynamics and beliefs that were not just reactionary but also ones representing the political and economic interests of elements at the top of the class hierarchy (landlords, merchants, traders, rich peasants). For this reason, rural culture and peasant agency has on many occasions and in many different historical contexts privileged nationalist ideology and mobilization. In making the case that he did, moreover, Trotsky was in effect describing an earlier instance of the 'cultural turn' on the part of those intellectuals who pursued emancipation on the basis of protecting longstanding (national) agrarian institutions/traditions/customs/practices from erosion by (foreign) capitalism. That is, a future embodying nothing more than a return to the past: composed, in short, of those economic, political, and ideological structures reproduced historically at the rural grassroots, where populists maintain they have always existed.[13]

Despite – or perhaps because of – his theoretical contributions to Marxism, together with his considerable organizational achievements leading up to and in the course of the 1917 October Revolution, Trotsky (and his ideas) was the object of sustained political criticism from the 1920s onwards. As is well-known, this was a process culminating in his expulsion from the party in 1927, followed by his subsequent exile two years later, and finally his assassination in Mexico during 1940. Against this negative trajectory, with its implied rejection of everything that Trotsky represented politically, it will be argued here that over a whole range of issues – including class struggle, peasant differentiation, and the combined threat of populism and nationalism – his interpretation has not merely been vindicated but is now more relevant than ever.[14] As such, therefore, the approach of Trotsky corresponds to the kind of Marxism that is deemed to be missing.

---

12 On this point, the view of Trotsky (1999: 89) was unambiguous: 'Culture binds people together and imposes constraints; it is conservative, and the richer it is, the more conservative it is. In Europe, every new idea cutting its way through the solid body of the old culture was met by the deadening resistance of the old outworn ideology, and by a keen rebuff from entrenched interests'.

13 Hence the view (Trotsky, 1999: 88, 94) that '[t]he Narodniks wanted to make the country's economic primitiveness the source of social miracles ... We have had plenty of "original" social utopianism, and even today we have more than enough of it ... Narodnism [= populism] is nothing more than the ideological reaction of our barbarism to the capitalist progress that is corroding it'.

14 Since it has been covered by me elsewhere (Brass, 2019), among the concepts not considered here in any detail is permanent revolution.

Because the Country Is Hungry

During the civil war, although opposed to landlordism and capitalists, Russian peasants generally wavered between support for the Bolsheviks and the Whites, thereby demonstrating their political unreliability either by joining (or deserting to) the latter, or by not taking sides.[15] Such was the capacity of kulaks to undermine socialism that its defence, plus the avoidance of famine, required taking grain – by force, if necessary – from kulaks, who were described by Trotsky as 'beasts of prey, the exploiters of hunger and misfortune' on account of the fact that in wartime rich peasants refused to part with their surplus produce at prices offered by the state.[16] Kulaks, he noted further, were thus rightly perceived by socialists generally as 'the advance-guard of the counter-revolution', on which 'all the hopes of the bourgeoisie are founded'.[17] This was particularly so during wartime scarcity, when they held back grain and waited for prices to rise, the result being that workers and poor peasants starved, a situation culminating in a famine that would lead to the collapse of socialism. In order to prevent 'a war of town against country', therefore, what was needed in such circumstances was 'an alliance [involving the working class] with the rural poor … not a war between town and country but their joint struggle against the rural kulak class'.[18]

Less than ten years later, Trotsky and the Left Opposition noticed and were critical of the policy 'shift towards the upper strata in the village', a process of 'betting on the strong' that entailed promoting the leadership in agrarian cooperatives of middle peasants. This was accompanied by keeping hidden the presence and role in such units of rich peasant kulaks. Where poor peasants owed debts, policy decreed that they sell off their implements in order to meet these payments. All this, maintained the Left Opposition, amounted

---

15 In rural areas of Russia, Trotsky (1979b: 14, 15) noted, the Cossack cavalry was 'the most important arm wielded by Denikin and Wrangel', adding that more broadly '[t]he mood of the peasantry vacillated unceasingly'.

16 Because 'the country is hungry', argued Trotsky (1979b: 84), 'the towns are beginning to suffer from hunger, [consequently] the Red Army cannot resist the attackers owing to lack of food, and in these conditions all the hungry elements in the country must understand that there is grain to be had, that it is held by the kulaks, the beasts of prey, the exploiters of hunger and misfortune: that [the Bolsheviks] are offering to these kulaks a price determined by what the state's finances will bear, and that they are not giving us the grain at that price; and that, this being so, we are going to take the grain from them by force of arms; by using force against the kulaks we shall feed the workers, women and children! There is not now and there will not be any other road'.

17 Trotsky (1979b:99ff.).

18 Trotsky (1979b: 102).

to the empowerment of the well-to-do ('strong') middle peasant, described by Trotsky as being 'a junior edition of the kulak'. It went against the initial objective of the cooperatives, which was to 'bring the poor peasants out of their dead-end situation'. Instead, being 'extremely indulgent toward the kulak' could not but undermine the support among the rural poor that socialists had built up in the villages. As the Stalinist policy remained one of expanding the position, role, and influence in the cooperatives of a 'strong' middle peasantry, however, the outcome inevitably would be to subordinate the poor peasants to the middle peasants, and through the latter to the kulaks.[19]

Two decades later, in the midst of the New Economic Policy, Trotsky again pointed to continuing peasant differentiation – this time after collectivization – and once more warned of its implications for socialism. As long as individual holdings still persisted within larger agrarian units owned by the state (in the form of private plots), and with it the sub-letting of land inside and between such units, he insisted that the collectivization process could not be regarded as complete.[20] On the basis of the fact that 'the income of every one of these big collective farmers is ten to fifteen times more than the wage of the "average" worker and the lower-grade collectivized peasant', Trotsky concluded

---

19   Hence the following case made in 1926 by Trotsky (1980: 80, original emphasis) against Stalinist policy towards the countryside: 'In questions of agricultural policy, the danger of a shift toward the upper strata in the village has become more and more plainly delineated. Influential voices are already heard openly advocating the transfer of the actual leadership of the agricultural cooperatives into the hands of the "strong" middle peasant; they argue also that the kulaks' contribution can remain veiled in total secrecy; and that careless or inefficient debtors, i.e., poor peasants, should be made to sell the implements they need the most; and so on. The alliance with the middle peasant is more and more transformed into an orientation toward the "well-to-do" middle peasant, who more often than not proves to be a junior edition of the kulak. One of the primary tasks of the socialist state is, through the formation of cooperatives, to bring the poor peasants out of their dead-end situation. The inadequate resources of the socialist state itself deny it the possibility of carrying out any dramatic changes immediately. But this does not give [it] the right ... to be excessively indulgent toward the kulak. This kind of approach, which is met with more and more often in our party, threatens to dig a deep chasm between us and our main base of support in the village – the poor ... even at the upper levels of administration there is a noticeable desire to push back as much as possible the Communist or poor peasant layer of cadres in the agricultural cooperatives or to replace them with "strong" middle peasants ... under the pretext of an alliance of the poor with the middle peasants we everywhere observe the political subordination of the poor to the middle peasants and through them to the kulaks'.

20   See Trotsky (1967: 128ff., 132), who drew attention to 'the strength of bourgeois tendencies in this still extremely backward branch of the economy [where] market tendencies are inevitably strengthening the individualistic tendencies, and deepening the social differentiation of the village, in spite of the new structure of property relations'.

that even within the rural sector under the control of the state the 'exploitation of certain strata of the population by other strata has not disappeared, but has been disguised'.[21] What remained hidden, therefore, was that 'successful collectives often hire labour power from the poor ones, and the authorities shut their eyes to this', with the result that 'state power itself becomes less and less capable of socialist control'. Consequently, '[i]n agriculture as in industry, [the state] seeks support and friendship of the strong, successful "stakhanovists of the fields", of millionaire collectives'.[22]

III

Winning the Peasantry?

Contrasting the development of agriculture in the West and Russia, Stalin maintained that in the latter context it would entail 'organizing millions of small and middle peasants in cooperative societies', a process he described as 'socialist construction' which depended in turn on the provision by the state of credit.[23] His claim that peasants generally could be 'led into socialism' was linked to the view that the 'winning of the peasantry' followed more or less automatically from revolutionary agency conducted by the proletariat. Encouraged by the example of the October revolution, therefore, peasants in other countries, especially ones that were colonies, would see how in Russia their counterparts had 'received land from the proletariat, having defeated the landlords with the aid of [workers]'. As a consequence of overcoming landlordism and acquiring property, peasants would in the opinion of Stalin 'proceed under the banner of the proletariat, under its red banner', towards socialism.[24]

Although accepting that '[t]he peasantry is not socialistically inclined', therefore, Stalin nevertheless insists that petty commodity producers 'as a whole' will be drawn into socialism via cooperative organization. In response to the question as to '[w]hat will be the significance of the widespread cooperative

---

21 Also underscored by Trotsky (1967: 133) at this conjuncture was a reminder that earlier (in 1927: see above) the Left Opposition had already shown that in the Russian countryside kulak income was increasing more rapidly than that of workers.
22 Trotsky (1967: 134).
23 Stalin (1952: 68).
24 See Stalin (1940: 165–66), where he delineates the acceptability of socialism to peasants benefitting from the expropriation of the landlord class: 'If it was formerly difficult for a Socialist to come out openly among the non-proletarian middle strata of the oppressed or oppressor countries, today [1923] he can openly come forward and advocate socialist ideas among these strata and expect to be listened to'.

organization of the peasant masses under a system in which socialist industry rules', he answers: 'It means that petty-peasant farming will be withdrawn from the old capitalist road ... and will be transferred to a new path of development, to the road leading towards socialist construction'.[25] This, he went on to explain, 'is why the new opposition [= Trotsky] exaggerates the part played by capitalist elements in our economic life, and underestimates the part played by the motive forces of our socialist development'.

Most significantly, Stalin then adds that '[t]his is why the new opposition overstates the case as regards the differentiation which has taken place among the peasants, why it is so much alarmed about the kulaks (the rich peasants), minimises the role of the middle peasants, [and] tries to counteract the endeavours of the Party to enter into a firm alliance with the middle peasants'. During this stage, Stalin argued, class war in rural areas must be avoided, because it is a Trotskyist 'deviation' that consists of revisiting a system of villages run by poor peasant committees.[26] It was, in short, a policy not just of 'trying to destroy the kulaks root and branch', but also and thereby 'fanning the flames of class war [and] a proclamation of civil war within our country, and thus to the ruining of all our work of socialist reconstruction'. What Stalin argued for, therefore, was that peasants generally, and kulaks in particular, could and should be 'led into' socialism.

By contrast, Trotsky and the Left Opposition maintained that, once the rural population had been differentiated in terms of class, this would reveal that specific strata in the countryside – kulaks certainly, and probably better-off elements among the middle peasantry – would not only not be 'led into' socialism but actively oppose such an outcome. Rather than attempting to draw all peasants into socialism, as Stalin had intended, Trotsky more realistically understood that such an objective was problematic, faced as it was with a central obstacle: namely, that most actual/aspiring smallholders will always hold out for a redistribution of land in an individual form. As such, they become not just the main defenders of private property but also provide support for bourgeois political movements and nationalist (or counter-revolutionary) ideologies opposed to the eradication of individual ownership by advocating further redistribution and/or socialization of the means of production. Once they became individual proprietors, as a result either of land seizures or of an agrarian reform, peasants were regarded by Trotsky as the main obstacle to a

---

25   Stalin (1928: 69–70, original emphasis). As is shown in Chapter 4 below, this is position currently held by those such as Henry Bernstein who advocate similarly drawing middle peasants into a broad alliance with workers.
26   Stalin (1928: 412).

socialist transition. This was one of the reasons why he advocated an immediate transition to socialism (= permanent revolution).[27]

A Huge Part of the People

This problem notwithstanding, the political and theoretical views of Trotsky were increasingly replaced – not just in the Soviet Union – by an uncritical espousal and defence of Stalinism. Already criticizing the 'class political line of Comrade Trotsky' by the early 1920s, therefore, the Communist Party of Great Britain (CPGB) supported the policy of class collaboration, advocating what it termed 'a durable working alliance' between labour and the middle classes generally and farmers in particular.[28] This approach was consolidated during the 1930s, when the CPGB upheld the Stalinist concept of 'the democratic dictatorship of the proletariat and the peasantry': Trotsky was accused of ignoring 'the colossal revolutionary force of the peasant movement', and castigated for 'his utter contempt for the peasantry as a revolutionary force', since the latter would be in the vanguard of the 'colonial revolution [that] will be bourgeois-democratic in its content'.[29] The tenor of what passed for criticism emanating from the CPGB can be gauged by the vehemence of its discourse: 'Trotskyism is terrorism. Trotskyism is anti-working class. Trotskyism is a foul conspiracy against the interests of all who want to ensure the preservation of democracy, peace and Socialism'.[30]

Much the same is true of the United States at that conjuncture, where – as in the case of the CPGB – the Stalinist line was that workers should 'ally

---

27   The main (but not the only) target of his argument (Trotsky, 1969: 113) was populism, because it 'regarded all workers and peasants simply as "toilers" and "exploited ones" who were equally interested in socialism, while to Marxists a peasant was a petty-bourgeois, capable of becoming a socialist only to the extent that he either materially or spiritually ceased being a peasant ... [a]long that line was fought for two generations the principal battle between the revolutionary tendencies of Russia'.

28   'The class political line of Comrade Trotsky ... would mean and could mean nothing else but the minimising of the role of the middle classes and the farmers, the neglect of the colossal role of the colonial peasantry as reserves for exploitation by British imperialism', insisted the CPGB (1925: 27), since 'the task of the proletariat to feed the population of this country demands not an antagonizing of the remaining agricultural forces, but essentially a durable working alliance. ...'

29   See Andrews (1934: Chapter IV).

30   Pollitt and Palme Dutt (1937: 11). Similar kinds of vilification can be found in Pollitt (1937), and also in Soria (n.d., but c.1937) and Campbell (1937), who maintained implausibly that in Spain Trotskyism – in the shape of POUM – aided the nationalist coup of Franco.

themselves with great masses of the other exploited and oppressed groups and classes of the population, in the first place the exploited farmers [and] the lower middle classes of the cities'.³¹ This required the working class to unite with rural producers 'as a whole' – a category that in the United States at this period consisted of 'small and middle farmers [and] small traders' – so as to accomplish what was termed the 'bourgeois-democratic revolution'.³² The view of Trotsky was accordingly dismissed on the grounds that it 'implies that the sharecroppers of the South in the USA will turn against the workers the moment they begin, after the seizure of power, to take away the mines and the mills from the capitalists of, say, Alabama; that the tenant farmers of the Middle West will join the armies of Morgan and Ford to fight the taking over by the workers of the automobile plants, railroads and banks'.³³

IV

Class Solidarity and/or Cultural Autonomy

Among those who have delineated characteristics that constitute nationalism, Stalin occupies a problematic role, not least for having formulated yet also defended the conceptual validity and positive aspects of national 'belonging'. Although nationhood was based initially on shared economic activity, equally significant in his view was the consolidating role played by territory, language, race, and tribe in a 'psychological makeup' leading to the construction and stability of national identity, or what he termed 'a community of culture'.³⁴ From this emphasis stem the ideological, political and economic contradictions generated by this attempt to build a consistent Marxist theory about the historical

---

31 See Olgin (1935: 24).
32 'In the United States', observed Olgin (1935: 41, 45), 'there are tens of millions of small and middle farmers, small traders, petty-bourgeois intellectuals – a huge part of the people'. It was with all these elements, which it was accepted were not friendly towards socialism, that the proletariat had to ally itself in order to push for a 'bourgeois-democratic revolution'. The latter objective was made yet more complex politically by other factors. To begin with, the additional presence of ethnic difference which was used by employers to undermine any solidarity achieved within the rural population as a whole. As crucial was the unreliability of petty-bourgeois components in any alliance that workers managed to form. Both these issues are examined in more detail below, in Chapter 7 (this volume).
33 Olgin (1935: 48).
34 Hence the observation (Stalin, 1940: 7) that a 'nation is a historically evolved. Stable community of language, territory, economic life, and psychological makeup manifested in a community of culture'.

and current function of nationalism, and especially its relation to the (class or multi-class) struggle against imperialism.

National oppression was defined by Stalin as plunder of subject peoples combined with the forcible restriction of their sovereign rights, and differences in its severity were an effect of the presence or absence of democracy.[35] In contexts where the landlord class was dominant, therefore, national oppression was severe; where democracy and political freedom existed, however, it bore 'a less brutal character'. An additional cause of severity in the colonies was the presence there of imperialism and its allies, which included not just the landlord class but also 'the petty bourgeoisie, a section of the intelligentsia, and a section of the upper strata of the workers, who also enjoy the fruits of plunder'. Because of this, the target of any national struggle had to be imperialism.

Accepting that 'peoples' should have the right to secede (= regional autonomy), Stalin opposed 'the principle of national cultural autonomy', on the grounds that once it had developed, capitalism scattered whole populations, in the process severing them from their nations.[36] Subsequent attempts to reassemble these communities, he maintained, was to construct 'a nation artificially', which 'is to adopt the standpoint of nationalism'. The latter corresponded to 'cultural autonomy', since 'from numerous and valid questions which interest a nation it singles out the purely cultural group of questions'.[37] Stalin then added that: 'It is assumed that within a nation are, on the one hand, interests which tend to disintegrate the nation, for instance, economic interests, and on the other hand, interests which tend to weld it into a single whole, and that the cultural question is a question of the latter kind'.

The source of contradiction is not difficult to discern. On the one hand, therefore, Stalin recognized that claims to 'cultural autonomy' surfacing within a larger national context led inexorably to micro-level nationalisms composed (or recomposed) of a population long ago scattered by capitalism. Similarly, he was aware that any nationalist ideology advanced thereby constituted a threat to the reproduction of class solidarity in the same context. Also acknowledged was that such a discourse privileged a 'purely cultural group of questions', ones that promoted national unity ('tend to weld [the nation] into a single whole') at the expense of economic issues which, because they divided a nation along

---

35 Asking '[h]ow are we to explain the differences in attitude towards [subordinated] nationalities in different states?', Stalin (1940: 54–55) answered that it was due to 'differences in the degree of democracy prevailing in these states'.
36 For this and what follows, see Stalin (1940: 57).
37 'The basis for singling out these questions', noted Stalin, 'is the proposition that what unites a nation into a single whole is its culture'.

class lines, transcended national/ethnic identities. A comprehension of these issues suggests that Stalin was embarking on a critique of the kind of views currently applied to the rural Third World by 'new' populist postmodern analyses.

However, later Stalin adopted a different view, and promoted the cause of nationalism and multi-class alliances in pursuit of capitalism and bourgeois democracy, thereby laying the ground for the position eventually advanced by exponents of the 'cultural turn'. Hence the insistence by him that religious and educational practices specific to national minorities must in all cases be protected, a policy which in effect conceded the very 'cultural autonomy' he previously opposed.[38] This was contradicted yet again when rejecting – correctly – the proposal that 'workers should be organized according to nationality', since '[e]xperience has shown that the organization of the proletariat of a given state according to nationality only leads to the downfall of the idea of class solidarity'.[39] The reason for this, insisted Stalin, was that primacy must be allocated to the conflict against imperialism, an objective which downgraded the different class positions and interests of those engaged in this struggle.[40]

The necessity of countering national oppression of minorities was a position Lenin and Trotsky shared with Stalin; unlike the latter, each of the former opposed also the promotion of a separatist national/ethnic cultural 'otherness', both inside and outside Russia. Against the encouragement of such 'otherness', Lenin summed up the crucial distinction informing the Marxist position on nationalism in the following manner: 'Combat all national oppression? Yes, of course! Fight *for* any kind of national development, *for* "national culture" in general? – Of course not'.[41] In a similar vein, Trotsky pointed out that the Bolshevik Party 'did not by any means undertake an evangel of separation', and went on to observe that it 'insisted upon a rigid centralism, implacably warring against every taint of nationalism which might set the workers one against the other or disunite them'.[42] He took issue with the claim by Stalin that national oppression was an effect simply of the rule by a non-capitalist landlord class, and consequently was milder in countries governed by a bourgeois democratic

---

38   Stalin (1940: 57).
39   Stalin (1940; 58).
40   'We must support every movement directed against imperialism', argued Stalin (1940: 59), despite opposition from those belonging to the Left Opposition who pointed out that 'every national movement is a reactionary movement'.
41   See Lenin (1964b: 35, original emphasis) and also Trotsky (1934: 908ff.). Earlier, Marx himself had warned that a working class divided along national and/or ethnic lines undermined the solidarity necessary for a successful struggle against capital.
42   Trotsky (1934: 891).

regime, indicating much rather that 'national oppression developed unprecedentedly during the epoch of capitalism'.[43]

Nationalism beyond the Nation

One important consideration is the legacy of Stalin's 1930s Popular Front policy on the post-1960s debate about development, both in the Third World and in metropolitan capitalism. Designed initially to unite opposition to fascism, by promoting nationalist mobilization on the basis of multiclass coalition in defence of democracy, such objectives continued long after the defeat of fascism. This despite the fact that the period after World War II was a politically auspicious era for the left: not only has it had been in the forefront of the victorious struggle against fascism, but the desirability of modernity and economic development was now firmly on the global political agenda. Positioned, consequently, to play a major role in influencing the post-war settlement, and hence to advocate struggle by workers to bring about a socialist transition, many communist parties opted instead for political alliances with what they termed a "progressive" bourgeoisie, supporting bourgeois democracy by pursuing national objectives in a never-ending search for an as-yet unrealized "pure" capitalism.

In colonial and post-colonial Third World contexts, therefore, this reformist policy of Stalin involved cooperation between communist parties and the national bourgeoisie in an anti-imperialist popular front (peasantry + working class against imperialism).[44] The abolition of landlord capitalism (= the Prussian path) would lead to peasant capitalism (= the American path), a process whereby one form of capitalism (unbenign, landlord, undemocratic) is replaced not by socialism but by another 'pure' form of capitalism (benign, peasant, democratic). Based on the notion of an intervening bourgeois democratic stage, this would be characterized by 'progressive' capitalists striving for a 'pure' capitalism: that is, a stage in which peasant proprietorship reigned supreme. In this kind of transition, the two-fold duty of socialists was: first, to argue for the redistribution of land on an individual basis to smallholders (= 'repeasantization'); and second, to press not for socialism but rather to support elements of the 'progressive' national bourgeoisie.

---

43   Trotsky (1934: 905).
44   Stalin (1928: 124ff., 276ff.).

The deleterious impact and effects of this privileging by Stalin of nationalism, the consequent advocacy of political alliances with 'progressive' national bourgeoisie against imperialism, plus the downgrading of struggle by workers for socialism, and the pursuit of development policies favouring individual peasant proprietorship, are not difficult to discern. To begin with, and as Trotsky pointed out, such class collaboration led directly to the massacre of workers in China and Spain during the 1930s, when capitalism demonstrated to all concerned just how 'progressive' it was prepared to be.[45] Furthermore, and as will be seen in the chapters which follow, a long-term result of the popular front strategy promoted by Stalin – on the one hand supporting bourgeois democracy, accumulation, and nationalism, and on the other of demoting both the importance of struggle by workers to transcend capitalism and establish socialism – has been to create a space filled by those from the other end of the ideological spectrum. Namely, in periods of economic crisis, when workers desire radical political solutions to their predicament, it has become much easier for far-right populists to colonize the political space that leftism has ceased to occupy.[46]

Insofar as it privileges cultural identity as empowering, therefore, current populism feeds off *laissez-faire* accumulation where economic crisis – generating both an expanding industrial reserve army of migrant labour and also more intense competition, between capitalists themselves and between workers seeking employment – results in political crisis. In the absence of a radical leftist discourse advocating a break with capitalism and a socialist transition, therefore, workers are encouraged by populists to experience labour market competition as an effect of non-class identity. Currently and historically, evidence suggests that in these circumstances a radical politics remains on the agenda, but with the difference that working class support can be transferred instead to right-wing populist movements offering empowerment on the basis

---

45   Trotsky (1932, 1936, 1973).
46   In the light of a desire by Foucault and others (see below, Chapter 2) to incorporate the lumpenproletariat within the working class, it is important to recall the warning issued by Trotsky (1975: 125) during 1932 about the support these 'marginals' provide to fascism: 'At the moment that the "normal" police and military resources of the bourgeois dictatorship, together with their parliamentary screens, no longer suffice to hold society in a state of equilibrium the turn of the fascist régime arrives. Through fascist agency, capitalism sets in motion the masses of the crazed petty bourgeoisie, and bands of the declassed and demoralized lumpenproletariat; all the countless human beings whom finance capital itself has brought to desperation and frenzy. From fascism the bourgeoisie demands a thorough job ... And the fascist agency, by utilizing the petty bourgeoisie as a battering ram, by overwhelming all obstacles in its path, does a thorough job'.

of nationalism and/or ethnicity. This, it could be argued, is in part a legacy of the continuities in Stalin's 1930s popular front approach.

v

Privileged Sections, Cheap Immigrants

Imperialism was characterized by Lenin not merely as the highest stage of capitalism, but also as the dominance of capital rather than goods, the consolidation of monopolies, and the struggle by the latter to divide up the world between themselves.[47] British capital exports were designed to foster industrial development in the colonies, whereas those of France were designated by him as 'loan capital ... not invested in industrial undertakings'. For this reason, Lenin described French imperialism, unlike its British counterpart, as 'usury imperialism'.[48] Against Kautsky, who claimed that the principal characteristic of imperialism was a need by advanced countries to obtain possession of countries with agrarian economies, Lenin maintained that the division of the world pursued by capital was one in which monopolies sought to bring *all* nations under their control.[49]

Monopolies are specific to this particular stage of capitalist development, since they are the inevitable outcome of an imperialism which generates company debt that, in a period of crisis, leads to widespread restructuring. The latter procedure follows a familiar pattern, whereby large enterprises annex small equivalents, consolidating property and labour-power under their control.[50]

---

47   Lenin (1964c: 226) quotes with approval the definition of Hilferding ('capital controlled by banks and employed by industrialists').
48   Lenin (1964c: 243). This, it should be noted, is a different interpretation from that of Patnaik (see Chapter 3 below).
49   Hence the view (Lenin, 1964c: 268ff., original emphasis) that the 'characteristic feature of imperialism is precisely that it strives to annex *not only* agrarian territories, but even the most highly industrialized regions [since] the world is already partitioned [this] obliges those contemplating a *redivision* to reach out for *every kind* of territory ... an essential feature of imperialism is the rivalry between several great powers in striving for hegemony, i.e., for the conquest of territory, not so much directly for themselves as to weaken the adversary and undermine *his* hegemony'. Once again, this is different from the conceptualization of imperialism undertaken by Patnaik (see Chapter 3).
50   'During periods of industrial boom', notes Lenin (1964c: 234–5) profitability is substantial, 'but during periods of depression, small and unsound businesses go out of existence, and the big banks acquire "holdings" in them by buying them up for a mere song, or participate in profitable schemes for their "reconstruction" and "reorganization"'.

It is this procedure that generates an equally familiar reaction, one that – as Lenin notes – takes the form of 'small capital's old complaint about being oppressed by big capital'.[51] Unsurprisingly, such conflict involving small/big enterprises can – and does – feed into the populist/nationalist anti-capitalist discourse of the political right.

In the view of Lenin, monopoly profits enabled imperialism to buy off what he categorized as 'the upper strata of the proletariat', differentiated by him from the lower stratum, or 'the proletariat proper', which imperialism did not need to incorporate in a similar manner.[52] This he linked in turn to immigration from low-wage backward countries into imperialist ones, thereby creating 'privileged sections' in the latter contexts, and detaching them from the 'broad masses' of the proletariat.[53] The widening gap separating the upper and lower strata of the working class enhanced the capacity of populism and nationalism (= 'social-chauvinism') to undermine the solidarity necessary to any success of a working class movement in imperialist nations. Capitalists in the latter contexts were able to do this, emphasized Lenin, simply by driving a wedge between the existing workforce, composed of labourers in permanent and well-paid employment, and immigrant workers in casual and/or poorly-paid jobs, who are used by capital to undercut those in the former category.

On the face of it, therefore, Lenin belongs in the camp of those Marxists who criticize workers belonging to the upper stratum as 'privileged'. This despite the fact that historically such elements have been in the forefront of the 'from below' class struggle to obtain and then maintain wages/conditions, a struggle which may indeed pitch them against employers who attempt to roll back these gains by replacing these 'privileged' categories of labour with cheaper migrants recruited from low-wage countries. The difficulty with this argument is that, in economically advanced nations, precisely these kinds of struggle have been interpreted by most Marxists in positive terms, as a conflict against the use by capital of an industrial reserve army.

---

51   Lenin (1964c: 224).
52   Lenin (1964c: 281).
53   See Lenin (1964c: 282–83), who observes: 'One of the special features of imperialism ... is the decline in emigration from imperialist countries and the increase in immigration into these countries from the more backward countries where lower wages are paid ... Imperialism has the tendency to create privileged sections also among the workers, and to detach them from the broad masses of the proletariat'. On the need of capitalism for cheap immigrant labour, see also Lenin (1963).

An Indispensable Attribute

It is, however, incorrect to conclude that the presence/function of the industrial reserve army, particularly its role in undercutting those already in employment, was of no concern to Lenin.[54] On the necessity of class solidarity between workers of different nationalities or ethnicities, and how for Marxism the former identity always transcended the latter, therefore, Lenin was adamant.[55] Calling for unity, both linking Swiss workers to foreign equivalents, and among the German, French, and Italian migrant labourers employed by capitalist enterprises in Switzerland, he emphasized the importance of 'bringing them [all] together in the same unions'. Indeed, his view was that every attempt must be made 'to create an *internationalist* trend', with the object of avoiding fragmentation along the lines of national/ethnic differences culminating in 'social-patriotism'. This, Lenin argued, was because imperialism exploited foreign labour, and 'bases its hopes on estrangement between these two [local/foreign] categories of workers'. Needless to say, the emphasis placed by Lenin on working class unity in the face of the divide-and-rule tactic pursued by an imperialism that privileged the national/ethnic identity of the capitalist workforce, is wholly at odds with many current interpretations of grassroots mobilization, not least – and as will be seen in the following chapters – those advanced by exponents both of the 'cultural turn' and of formulations of imperialism-as-'drain'.

---

54 In the factory, argued Lenin (1960a: 70), 'the master sets no great store by the worker at all, because he can always easily find another one among the crowd of unemployed ready to hire themselves to anybody. Thus, the power of the employer over the worker increases, and the employer makes use of this power ...' That machinery performs for capital much the same role as does the industrial reserve is also clear (Lenin, 1960b: 102): 'Taking advantage of the fact that where machines are used far fewer workers are wanted, [the capitalist] throws them out of the factory in masses and then takes advantage of this unemployment to enslave the worker still further. ...'

55 On this, and what follows, see Lenin (1964d: 146–47), where he states 'it is necessary, first, consistently and unswervingly, to fight for organizational rapprochement between foreign and Swiss workers bringing them together in the same unions ... The specific feature of imperialism in Switzerland is precisely the increasing exploitation of disenfranchised foreign workers by the Swiss bourgeoisie, which bases its hopes on estrangement between these two categories of workers'. He continued: 'Second, every effort must be made to create a united, *internationalist* trend among the German, French and Italian workers of Switzerland, a trend that will make for genuine *unity* in all *practical* activity in the labour movement and will combat, with equal determination and on principle, French ... German and Italian social-patriotism'.

This concern about the presence and impact of the industrial reserve emerged in relation to his critique of populism (= romanticists), for whom the growth of a reserve army was somehow an anomalous dimension of the accumulation process, whereas for Lenin it was much rather the *sine qua non* of capitalism, 'which could neither exist nor develop without it'.[56] The focus of his critique aimed at populists, therefore, was that – contrary to their view (surplus labour = 'a mistake') – the industrial reserve was (and remains) central to the capitalist dynamic.[57] To make this point, he began by taking issue with Malthus, who regarded surplus population as an effect of 'natural' causes and not of an 'historically determined system of social economy'.[58] Lenin then criticized Sismondi for making the same error: that is, avoiding the contradiction between accumulation and the seemingly 'anomalous' presence of surplus labour. Sismondi, therefore, 'makes no attempt even to analyse the relation between the surplus population and the requirements of capitalist production, neither do our Narodniks [= populists] ever set themselves such a problem'.[59]

For Lenin, therefore, the reason for the overlap between the Narodniks and Sismondi, and the inability of the latter to comprehend the crucial economic role discharged by industrial reserve in the accumulation process, was due to a corresponding incapacity to 'understand the connection between small production (which he idealises) and big capital (which he attacks)', and consequently 'that his beloved small producer, the peasant, is in reality becoming a

---

56   See the description by Lenin (1960c: 180–81, original emphasis) of those in the industrial reserve army as 'the workers needed by capitalism for the *potential* expansion of enterprises, but who can never be regularly employed', adding that 'on this problem ... theory arrived at a conclusion diametrically opposed to that of the romanticists. For the latter, the surplus population signifies that capitalism is impossible, or a "mistake". Actually, the opposite is the case: the surplus population, being a necessary concomitant of surplus production, is an indispensable attribute of the capitalist economy, which could neither exist nor develop without it'.

57   'While noting the formation of a surplus population in post-Reform Russia', observed Lenin (1960c: 181, 182), 'the Narodniks have never raised the issue of capitalism's need for a reserve army of workers'. Consequently, 'on the subject of surplus population, the Narodniks adhere entirely to the viewpoint of romanticism ... Capitalism gives no employment to displaced workers, they say. This means that capitalism is impossible, a "mistake", etc. But it does not "mean" that at all. ...'

58   Lenin (1960c: 178).

59   See Lenin (1960c: 179, original emphasis), who continues: 'The scientific analysis of this contradiction revealed the absolute falsity of this method [whereas the Marxist] analysis showed that surplus population, being undoubtedly a contradiction [and] an inevitable result of capitalist accumulation, is at the same time an indispensable component part of the capitalist machine'.

petty bourgeois'.[60] As will be seen in later chapters, this is a discourse Sismondi and Narodnism share with current variants of the same discourse: that is, a failure to realize that there is an anti-capitalism of the political right, opposed only to large-scale capital (foreign, finance) and not to small-scale accumulation.

Conclusion

Many of the theoretical and political disagreements about present-day economic development, together with their concomitant disputes as to the desirability or otherwise of systemic transition, can be traced back to late nineteenth and early twentieth century debates between Marxism and agrarian populism about changes to rural society. Historically, populists have regarded peasants as either actually – or anyway potentially – independent proprietors, thereby ignoring the distinction between smallholders who sell the product of labour and those who sell their labour-power. Because it does not view peasants as a uniform category possessing the same economic and political interests, Marxism by contrast has differentiated the peasantry in terms of class. Unlike either rural capitalists belonging to the rich stratum, or the middle stratum composed of family farmers, poor peasants are considered de facto workers. For this reason, poor peasants are viewed as more accurately forming part of the rural working class or – when they migrate to the urban – as joining the industrial reserve army. That those in the latter category may continue to see themselves (and be seen by others) as actual/potential smallholders, despite the economic reality of their situation, not only sustains populist discourse but – as such – is at the root of much intellectual discord among those who continue to study economic development.

Within Marxist theory itself, this disagreement is embodied in the different approaches of Trotsky and Stalin. Unlike the Marxism of Trotsky, which was critical both of nationalism and of an undifferentiated peasantry as the subject of the historical process, that of Stalin privileged not just nationalism but also insisted that – initially at least – the kulak could be drawn towards socialism. By ousting of Trotsky and the Left Opposition, Stalin replaced class struggle, revolution and socialism with class alliances, democracy and nationalism as the objectives Marxists should pursue. When the different Marxist approaches of Trotsky and Stalin are extended beyond Russia, a significant distinction emerges. Whereas for Trotsky, a United Front represented political alliances

---

60   Lenin (1960c: 221).

confined to workers' parties in Europe, by contrast Stalin endorsed a Popular Front approach in which parties of the left combined with bourgeois equivalents. The latter corresponded in effect to class collaboration, whereas the former embodied class unity.

Trotsky opposed Popular Frontism on a number of grounds. First, he objected to the peasant essentialism advocated by the Popular Front: because an undifferentiated category 'peasants' included in its ranks small agrarian capitalists whose interests were not merely distinct from but actually opposed to those of workers, he emphasized the importance of recognizing agricultural workers as part of the proletariat and not as an incipient peasantry. Second, he maintained that the target of working-class mobilization should be capitalism and not feudalism, since fascism was a reaction not by the feudal *ancien regime* but by the bourgeoisie. Third, he warned against the dangers of categorizing the national bourgeoisie in less developed countries as 'progressive', and thus also of the risks to a proletariat of entering supra-class (= Popular Front, 'national-popular') alliances with a colonial or semi-colonial bourgeoisie in order to carry out the tasks of 'democratic' capitalism. And fourth, Trotsky argued that confidence in the existence of a 'progressive national bourgeoisie' itself was misplaced, since it, too, would turn to fascism were its own interests to be threatened by working class mobilization. In short, the middle classes were not interested in anti-fascist struggle if this in turn opened up the prospect of socialist revolution, as happened in both China during the late 1920s and 1930s Spain.

Some of these same contradictions also inform Marxist debates about imperialism, particularly when this involves labour market competition that is acute, between workers located in the metropolis and those on the periphery. The deleterious function of the present-day industrial reserve in metropolitan capitalism suggests a change (positive → negative) is needed in the way Marxism interprets migration. Originally, therefore, the journey from countryside to town was seen as positive, a way in which rural populations were 'civilized' in the course of migration, in the sense that they left behind them the ideological backwardness of agrarian society and were drawn into politically empowering – and thus more progressive – discourses circulating among workers employed in urban areas. Lenin saw this as essential to the formation of a specific consciousness of class on the part of an already constituted proletariat, which in the late nineteenth and early twentieth century it certainly was. In the twenty-first, however, the same migratory pattern can be seen as a very different kind of process.

Together with the more general recuperation of the Popular Front approach, this endorsement by academia of the 'cultural turn' in a large part helps explain the current existence of the Marxism-missing-but-necessary combination. Of interest to Marxists, therefore, are the following questions. Why did political economy not feature in that debate, and why did it focus principally on the issue of culture? And why did those on the left subscribe to this in the unleftist way they did? In the past, even non-Marxists linked race and class, showing how the former acted as a proxy for the latter. These days, by contrast, postmodern anti-Marxists have dispensed with class as a concept, dismissing this as Eurocentric and 'foundational', and instead essentialize non-class identities as innate. The sort of problems that result are explored in the following chapters.

Whereas Marxists who grew up in the first half of the twentieth century did so in the shadow of fascism, at a time when the political right was flexing it muscles, those who grew up during the second half, by contrast, did so in a period when, following the defeat of fascism, the political right was dormant. For this reason, the discourse of the political right, with which most early twentieth century Marxists were familiar and against which a constant guard was mounted, was ignored by many of those to came to Marxism during the latter half of the century. This led in turn to a lack of vigilance and a corresponding false sense of security, with the result that when this same nationalist politics re-emerged in the period after 1968 and rose to prominence once again from the 1980s onwards, many of those who perceived themselves as being on the left were caught unawares, and consequently wrongly identified elements of its discourse as progressive. In short, because socialists have forgotten who their enemy is, too often they have mistaken the latter for a friend.

CHAPTER 2

From Marxism to the Cultural Turn (*via* Social History)

> *Influence, n.* In politics, a visionary *quo* given in exchange for a substantial *quid*.
> A definition by AMBROSE BIERCE.[1]

∴

> Pride has always been one of my favourite virtues. I have never regarded it, except in certain cases, as a major sin.
> An observation by EDITH SITWELL.[2]

∴

Introduction

As will be seen in this chapter and the ones which follow, the earlier interpretations the populists, as well as those of Trotsky, Stalin, and Lenin, all resurface in later debates about the Third World peasantry during and after the 1960s development decade. This some do in ways that, whilst purporting to be Marxist, were not just non-Marxist but anti-Marxist. That the latter tended to be presented unchallenged compounded the difficulty, since crucial aspects of Marxist theory were diluted, misrepresented, or simply missing from many of the interpretations – or, more accurately, reinterpretations and misinterpretations – which informed discussions about Third World development that took place in the course of this later period.

These kinds difficulty became evident in the rise to academic prominence and fashionability of a variety of frameworks, either claiming to be Marxist, or sharing its commitment to 'from below' emancipation – but only or largely in

---

[1] Bierce (1967: 156).
[2] Sitwell (1962: 15).

terms of non-class identities. Among these were two in particular: on the one hand the semi-feudal thesis, possessing epistemological and political affinities with the views of Stalin; and on the other, the 'new' populist postmodernism (= the 'cultural turn'), which sought to replace Marxist theory in general, and political economy in particular, especially with regard to development studies. Given his political and intellectual influence, not just on the left, the focus here is on Eric Hobsbawm (1917–2012), with particular reference to social history and Marxist historiography. A recent biography makes this possible, not least because of the in-depth coverage of his life as well as his work.

In order to establish whether in his case Marxism is indeed missing, and why, three sections in this chapter trace debates in which Hobsbawm not only participated but in an important sense formulated and influenced. A first section considers the way in which agrarian transformation is conceptualized by Marxism, the semi-feudal thesis, and populism, and how theory about desirable forms of rural empowerment shifted from class to non-class identity. The focus of the second is on the political contradictions arising from the life and work of Hobsbawm, while his views about the connection between Marxism, social history, and the 'cultural turn' are examined in the third section.

I

The continuing influence of Stalin, combined occasionally with criticisms of Trotsky, is evident in the arguments of many who contributed to debates about economic growth in the Third World during and after the 1960s development decade.[3] This was particularly true of the way certain Marxist and populist interpretations of what happens to the peasantry in a developing economy, and why. In keeping with Stalinism, therefore, the semi-feudal approach to the rural Third World at this conjuncture allowed capitalism off the hook, postponed socialism *sine die*, and permitted the myth of a 'progressive' national bourgeoisie to flourish. By the 1980s, all forms of Marxism were being expelled from the development agenda by the 'new' populist postmodernism, which sought instead to recast peasants as economically undifferentiated and culturally 'other'.

---

3 Post-1960s criticisms of Trotsky include those by Hodgson (1975) and Mavrakis (1976). For his part, Hobsbawm (1973: 64, 90) oscillated between damning Trotskyism with faint praise, and dismissing it outright as a 'Marxist deviation', the adherents of which sought unsuccessfully to 'impose specific ideas and perspectives on the masses and in doing so isolated themselves'. Evans (2019: 58, 99, 148–9, 229), too, confirms the antagonism expressed by Hobsbawm towards Trotsky, along the lines of 'revolution-mongers of the Trotsky gang who find nothing better to do than provoke risings and riots among strikers'.

Marxism and Third World Development

It is clear that the concerns expressed by Trotsky about the potential threat to socialized agriculture in mid-1930s Russia were equally relevant to the agrarian reforms of the 1960s and 1970s in Latin America, where the same kinds of problems emerged, not least the presence and effect of private holdings within cooperatives, an issue the State was unwilling and/or unable to address. When applied to Third World countries at subsequent conjunctures, therefore, the emphasis Stalin placed on the necessity of proceeding not to socialism but to a benign form of capitalism – effected by an equally benign progressive national bourgeoisie committed to upholding democracy – resulted in backing for development strategies promoting accumulation by, among others, rich peasants located inside agrarian reform units of the Third World.

Notwithstanding the eventual call by Stalin for the 'liquidation' of the *kulaks* within the Soviet Union, his foreign policy ensured, ironically, that the same kind of rural capitalist in colonial and/or less developed nations would henceforth receive political support from communist parties in such contexts. This was because landlordism was equated by him with feudalism, making the next task in the agrarian sector of these countries one of establishing what was deemed to be a hitherto absent capitalism. Under the auspices of a 'progressive national bourgeoisie', accumulation was an economic objective that would be accompanied by a political transition to bourgeois democracy.

Adhering closely to the views of Stalin, exponents of the semi-feudal thesis maintained from the 1960s onwards that because capitalism was yet to develop in Third World countries, the political economy agenda consisted of two objectives. Henceforth working-class mobilization and struggle, aimed at the realization of socialism and against capitalism and the bourgeoisie, had to be subordinated to the pursuit of nationalist alliances between labour and capital so as to establish bourgeois democracy, enabling among other things accumulation by better-off peasants. Intellectually, such claims informed the mode of production debate in India, and in terms of approach guided many of the reformist policies formulated by the political left throughout Latin America.[4]

If socialism in developing nations was postponed by the semi-feudal thesis, then it was banished altogether by the 'new' populist postmodernism that

---

4 The best accounts of the mode of production debate in India at this conjuncture are to be found in the volume edited by Ashok Rudra (1978) and a series of articles by Alice Thorner (1982): the same debate as applied to Latin America is summarized in Goodman and Redclift (1981). On the reformist approach of leftist parties in Latin America, see Debray (1970) and Petras (1978; 1981).

emerged and consolidated from the 1980s onwards. Major intellectuals who formulated, promoted, or embraced postmodernism – both then and earlier – include Derrida, Foucault, Lyotard, and Baudrillard: a political characteristic shared by them all was, to a greater or less extent, hostility towards Marxism and Marxist theory.[5] In the case of development studies, the impact of postmodernism has been negative, in that the 'cultural turn' set out to deprivilege socialism, materialism and class as illegitimate Enlightenment/Eurocentric forms of 'foundationalism' inapplicable to the Third World. Quotidian resistance by (undifferentiated) peasant subalterns in defence of indigenous culture and tradition is instead seen as a legitimate part of the struggle against capitalism, a result being that rural struggle is no longer about class but identity politics. This recuperation by postmodernism of an essentialist peasant culture/economy leaves intact the existing class structure and reproduces the populist mobilizing discourse of the political right. It is, in short, a conservative form of anti-capitalism.

In the analytical framework of the 'new' populist postmodernism, the meaning and object of rural mobilization – historical and contemporary alike – was reconfigured. Instead of movements based on class, which attempt to realize the economic fruits and benefits of economic development by capturing and exercising political control over the state apparatus (as Marxists argued), the action/identity invoked by (undifferentiated) peasants and (undifferentiated) workers in many Third World contexts were – and are – unconnected with socialism.[6] Rather, they adhere to non-class identities and pursue a different

---

5 Thus, for example, Foucault (1996: 128) insists 'we have to talk about a certain powerlessness of traditional Marxist discourse to account for fascism. Let's say that Marxism has given an historical account of the phenomenon of Nazism in a determinist fashion, while completely leaving aside what the specific ideology of Nazism was'. Similarly, he (Foucault, 1996: 131) maintains '[i]t's a trait of many Marxists nowadays – ignorance of history. All these people, who spend their time talking about the misrepresentation of history, are only capable of producing commentaries on texts'. Neither of these assertions is correct. The twofold claim, about a supposed inability on the part of Marxism to account for fascism, plus an unawareness of its ideological specificity, ignores the fact that each of these 'absences' was filled by Trotsky (1975) in his analyses of 1930s Germany. Equally mistaken is the contention that Marxists are ignorant of history, and consequently focus on textual commentary. Much rather the opposite is the case: the majority of Marxist theory is not only based on empirical research, and its conclusions suffused with historical examples, but the accusation concerning a tendency to exegesis is more accurately levelled at postmodern theoretical practice. In other words, conducted by those who have an intellectual affinity with Foucault himself.
6 A case in point is the defence by Foucault (1996: 90–91) and colleagues of the lumpenproletariat (= undifferentiated worker) because it is composed of 'marginals' who – since they are not producers – are of no interest to Marxism. Lamenting that 'the lumpenproletariat, in Marxist theory, is a sort of residue [which the authorities] do their best to "stigmatize"',

kind of agency, each of which is categorized as empowering by the 'new' populist postmodernism. Peasants and workers struggle on an everyday basis, as subalterns engaged in resistance, and generally only at a local level, merely so as to retain their existing culture and traditions.[7] It is the latter process, and not class or development, which defines and exalts the rural 'other', insists postmodern theory.

Populism, Social History, and Third World (Non-)Development

Over the past four decades, many of those writing about the undesirability of further economic development in rural areas have done so from a 'new' populist postmodern theoretical framework.[8] In support of this view, exponents of such an approach dehistoricize and essentialize culture, declaring it innate and the basis for the construction – or reconstruction – of village society outside and against capitalism and its state. From the 1980s onwards, therefore, the

---

a colleague of Foucault states that 'we are discovering ... there is a possibility of bringing the real marginal into social and political action which would be that of all workers'. To this Foucault replies that 'there is a split between the proletariat on the one hand and extra-proletarian, non-proletarianized plebeian on the other ... We should not say: there is the proletariat and then there are these marginals. We should say: there is in the overall mass of plebeians a split between the proletariat and the non-proletarianized plebeian'. Another discussant then adds that 'the Marxist perspective must be broken with, which is centred solely on the producer'.

7   On quotidian resistance, see Scott (1976; 2012). On subaltern agency, see among many others Bhagavani and Feldhaus (2008), Andolina, Laurie, and Radcliffe (2009), Mahajan (2011), and Zene (2013). On 'from below' struggle as local level agency, see Wankankar (2011) and Mignolo (2012).

8   Put bluntly, postmodernism enabled many in academia to adopt a seemingly radical stance, a theory that did not require a practice, an approach which of course Marxism criticizes. Although it is fashionable to affix the rise of identity politics to US academia, its intellectual origins can be traced to a revisionist historiography in India, where the subaltern studies project recuperated a nationalist discourse based on two things: on the one hand the rejection of Enlightenment discourse as an inauthentic Eurocentric colonial imposition, and on the other the recovery of an 'authentic' grassroots voice. The latter, it was argued, was mainly rural, an unheard or silenced narrative of the peasant subaltern, unnoticed but heroically engaged in resisting colonialism in the name of India. It was this interpretation – aided intellectually by, amongst others, the critique of 'orientalism' by Said – which took American scholarly discourse by storm, for three reasons: its privileging of an anti-colonial theme (which the US has in common with India), its privileging of nationalism, and its deprivileging of internationalism, materialism class and – in particular – class struggle. The latter identities and agency – all central to Marxist theory – could accordingly be expelled from the analytical canon.

'now' populist postmodernism deployed the very same arguments opposing further economic development in the Third World countryside as had reformists and conservatives earlier in the case of Europe. Together with other non-class identities, the quotidian resistance by (undifferentiated) peasants against capitalism became the focus of the increasingly fashionable social history that rose to academic prominence alongside the 'new' populist postmodernism.

During this same period, therefore, social history as a form of academic study, regarded by Marxism as recognizing – and, where possible, giving voice to – the political interests of workers ignored by mainstream historiography – has fragmented into a never-ending plethora of competing microhistories: among the latter are religious history, gender history, oral history, ethnically-specific history, the history of sexuality, and the history of the body.[9] A focus on the presence and ideological structure of 'other' identities is, from a Marxist view, itself unproblematic, in that it helps explain why and how a variety of non-class 'selfhoods' on occasion pose obstacles to the consciousness and/or struggle of class.

The problem arises when some of these same kinds of non-class 'otherness' are deemed politically empowering and autonomous, to the extent of overriding and analytically displacing class as a category, in terms of its multiple effects (formation, consciousness, struggle). It is precisely this imperceptible epistemological shift, from non-class identity as one among a number of political issues that require addressing by Marxists, to the single dominant component subordinating those outside itself to its own will; an exclusionary

---

9   Some of these non-class identities are covered in a survey of social history (Burke, 1998). Many of the same themes feature in an earlier volume (Samuel and Stedman Jones, 1982), celebrating the ideas and contributions of Hobsbawm to social history. Among the issues it covers are 'everyday life – the personal and the political', religion, gender, and environmentalism. As noted in another volume (Zunz, 1985: 4), 'social historians actively participated in the new pluralist vision of the 1960s. At stake was more than a simple enlargement of history's vision. By devising methods which allowed them to build judgments from thousands of observations of ordinary people, they could investigate groups heretofore ignored or at best misunderstood. For the first time, historians could divide the social structure into an infinite number of segments and explain the positive role of diverse communities within the society at large. They could, for example, envision the "proletariat" as a group of heterogeneous and often conflicting human beings, not simply as the idealization projected by the international labour movement'. In a wood-for-the-trees methodology, a downwards focus on proliferating minutiae – a quest that ended at the level of the individual him/herself – has meant that the way the wider systemic dynamic functions (together with the reasons for this) is lost. What this involved, analytically and politically, was not merely the fragmentation but the replacement of class by numerous forms of non-class 'otherness', a harbinger of the identity politics to come.

approach, moreover, that is usually announced by an accompanying coronation of the identity in question as one that is progressive in political terms. Just such a process of intellectual and ideological upgrading in effect transforms social history into the concerns and discourse of the 'new' populist postmodernism.

Part of the difficulty stems also from the way in which an undifferentiated Third World 'other' tends to be regarded simply as victim of cultural imperialism. Objecting to the ideological onslaught on Third World populations by electronic media owned/controlled in Western nations licenses a slide into support for the culture of the 'other' subjected to this sort of attack.[10] In the absence of a critical political approach to what, precisely, the culture of the 'other' itself advocates, this epistemological shift can involve a defence of pre-modern traditions/institutions/practices, all of which are consequently sanctified as empowering.[11] Dismissed in the process is not just a concept of modernity as a broadly desirable objective – in effect, castigating every form of development – but also all theories espousing ideas of systemic change as positive. Excluded thereby is, of course, Marxism; installed thereby is its rival approach, populism, for which any form of economic development – promoted

---

10 Although Tomlinson (1991) is aware of this difficulty facing those who oppose cultural imperialism, he has problems avoiding the trap that awaits: support for pre-existing cultural 'otherness'.

11 Prakash (1995) is just such an example of this sort of epistemological shift, from opposition to imperialism and colonialism into a vindication of pre-capitalist ideological and economic forms. Expressing approval of the views of Gandhi as 'the realignment of the colonial record [which is] a severe indictment of modern civilization', Prakash (1995: 6–7) accepts that 'Gandhi turns to India's ancient "village communities" as an alternative model', but immediately adds – inaccurately, but symptomatically – 'he does not do so as a nativist'. Blame for the latter is – again symptomatically – then affixed to the external 'other', in this instance Henry Maine, a representative of British conservatism. This attempts thereby – but does not succeed – to effect a double 'realignment': on the one hand an indigenous populist discourse, emblematic of nationalism, is recast as positive (= sanitized ideologically); on the other, any negative associations this discourse may carry (= nativism) is at the same time attributed to the colonial 'other'. To be absolutely sure, the double 'alignment' requires a further stage: the conversion of what is palpably a recuperation of pre-modern agrarian populist forms of 'otherness' into what it is claimed to be nothing more than an 'alternative modernity'. Indeed, this is precisely the step taken by Prakash (1999), who proceeds to recast 'otherness' as modern and scientific; again, one encounters claims such as '[t]he passionate belief in the existence of an indigenous tradition of science was no mere fantasy', insisting (Prakash, 1999: 228) that '[t]his was not nativism, but a carefully formulated proposition, arguing that the concept of science was culturally located'.

by imperialism and socialism alike – is seen as a threat to the culture of Third World peasants.[12]

Symptomatically, for the 'new' populist postmodernism the central epistemological problem is to construct a model that subsumes all kinds/forms of narrative, a framework that accounts merely for the fact of narrative, not its purpose. No significance is attached to the link between language and the material conditions that give rise to or sustain a particular narrative.[13] Indeed, it is a link the very existence – let alone the efficacy – of which postmodern theory denies. This means that there is no longer a necessary relation between ideological practice and infrastructure, a non-determinate view that the 'new' populist postmodernism inherited from structuralism.[14] Nor is there any form of consciousness that – from the point of view of a particular class – can be categorized as false.[15] Ignoring both the fact and effect of the presence of class

---

12 As will be seen in the Chapters which follow, arguments challenging or recasting modernity that in effect install (or re-install) pre-modern social forms championed by the 'new' populist postmodernism, are common and bring with them specific effects. Such a view is not just held by Hobsbawm (see below, this Chapter), but also informs the attempt to transform Late Antiquity into a triumphal kind of 'alternative' capitalism (Chapter 6). It also lies behind the reinterpretation of unfree production relations as merely a benign form of traditional cultural 'otherness'. And, finally, recasting modernity in this fashion plays directly into the hands of those who uphold Great Replacement discourse (Chapter 8), perhaps the most worrying outcome politically speaking.

13 The political and theoretical path away from Marxist materialism and towards what became the 'cultural turn' was clearly mapped in France in the influential review *Tel Quel* (ffrench and Lack, 1998). It moved from a sympathetic attitude towards communism during the 1960s to a critical stance on Marxism in the 1970s, for its focus on economic issues. The resulting transformation was signalled by a stratospheric climb into discourse theory, whereby a dematerialized language-in/for-itself announced the rule of aporia, a nihililism where the only reality seemed to be 'nothingness'. In the course of this change, the review espoused psychoanalysis, together with the innateness of violence/'evil'; what was termed the crisis of rationalism led in turn to a positive view of theology, the importance allocated to politically non-specific forms of 'dissidence', and the assertion that the subjectivity of the writer overrode any ideological considerations.

14 For evidence of this connection, see the contributions to the volume edited by Attridge, Bennington and Young (1987).

15 A central form of postmodern aporia involves the claim that, as the subaltern is unknowable, he/she cannot be represented, in effect not only abolishing the intellectual accessibility of peasants and labourers but converting them into the mysterious 'other' of conservative discourse. Those such as Spivak, Kristeva, and Prakash link the 'unrepresentability' of subaltern culture to the 'unknowability' of the subaltern him/herself: a subject thus defined cannot be represented by someone 'other' (= intellectuals) than him/herself, a view that verges on the solipsistic. A consequence of pristine subaltern 'otherness' being both unknowable and intellectually inaccessible, moreover, is that it is unalterable. Just such an epistemology is invoked not by Marxists but rather by conservatives who claim

within the ranks of those opposed to colonialism, therefore, this framework overlooked also the degree to which anti-imperialist/anti-colonial discourse/mobilization was that of small capitalist producers and rich peasants as much as that of poor peasants and agricultural workers.

Having shifted the concept of empowerment from class to ethnicity/gender/nationality, the 'new' populist postmodernism has also made it difficult for Marxists to pose questions about the industrial reserve army of labour without risking accusations of racism/sexism/xenophobia. Grass-roots resistance as envisioned by the 'new' populist postmodernism is deemed to be simply about cultural empowerment, with little or no reference to political economy. Viewed in latter terms, an expanding industrial reserve army is disempowering, and as such can be blamed by workers on capital; the struggle accordingly becomes one of class.

Viewed through postmodern lens, however, the same process alters in meaning and agency. Struggle becomes about non-class identity, workers seeing the impact on them of the industrial reserve army of labour as the fault not of capital but of migrants belonging to a different ethnicity, gender or nationality. What is of particular interest in this epistemological change – Marxism increasingly missing, as a result of its distortion by the semi-feudal thesis or displacement by the 'new' populist postmodernism – is the contributory role of perhaps the most influential social historian in the past half century: Eric Hobsbawm.

II

Hobsbawm was one of the very few public intellectuals widely acknowledged as having represented the voice of the political Left throughout the second half of the twentieth century, not just in Britain but globally.[16] For this reason alone he merits a biography, examining both his rise to and transcendence of academic prominence, and accounting for this burgeoning influence. The

---

that, as the subaltern likes the way he/she is and feels empowered by his/her culture (of which the economic is merely a part), consequently no one – and especially not intellectuals on the left – should presume to advise him/her otherwise. This of course leaves power and control in the hands of the bourgeoisie, since according to this kind of argument it is impermissible for an intellectual even to put to a subaltern a non-subaltern idea: because the subaltern is unknowable, the nature of the subaltern and therefore of its 'other' cannot even be posed. Even if it could, intellectuals are disbarred from this, because to do so is to privilege a non-subaltern discourse.

16   The view (Samuel and Stedman Jones, 1982: 332) that Hobsbawm 'must be known internationally to a greater extent than almost any other post-war British intellectual' is one commonly held by historians and social scientists.

book itself belongs to what is now emerging as a recognizable genre: the 'celebrity biography', whereby an eminent British academic chronicles the life (and times) of an equally distinguished predecessor, outlining the many and lasting contributions made by the latter to the relevant discipline.[17] Since the recipients of this kind of accolade are generally what might be termed mainstream intellectuals, or in the case of historians those who are regarded by their peer group as politically uncontroversial, the biography of Hobsbawm by Richard Evans appears on the face of it to be something of an anomaly. Whether or not this is actually so will be the focus of this chapter.

What is beyond dispute is that the biography of Hobsbawm is in a fundamental sense comprehensive: it is a vast tome, consisting of almost 800 pages and some 2,200 endnotes, and Evans probably knows more about him than anyone else does or ever has, including in all likelihood Hobsbawm himself. Nothing escapes the attention of his biographer, and the detail is at times overwhelming. Along with conversations Hobsbawm had and books he read and wrote, therefore, every institution or location through which he passed, almost every person he encountered, and certainly every political and/or historiographical debate in which he participated, is given its own mini-history and/or recorded in minute detail.

Enemy of the (Capitalist) State?

The advantage of such an all-embracing approach is that its thoroughness enables the reader to form an opinion not necessarily shared by Evans.[18] Its disadvantages are equally clear. Since much of the information in the biography is drawn from what Hobsbawm recorded in letters he wrote/received or diaries he kept, it is at times difficult to separate out whose voice one is hearing: that of the subject of the biography, or of the biographer himself? At some points, therefore, Evans appears to be rather too much in awe of Hobsbawm,

---

17   Recent examples of this genre include biographies of G.M. Trevelyan (Cannadine, 1992), of A.J.P Taylor (Sisman, 1994), of Isaiah Berlin (Ignatieff, 1998), of E.H. Carr (Haslam, 1999), and of Hugh Trevor-Roper (Sisman, 2010). Among the historians whose influence has yet to be chronicled in a similar manner are Peter Gay and Geoffrey Elton.
18   It should be noted that in the course of an amicable exchange of views with Richard Evans about the biography, although I questioned a number of points he made, both of us accepted two things. First, that 'our disagreements are matters of emphasis and degree' (RJE to TB, 21 July 2019). And second, that the biography had indeed succeeded in being as much about the wider historical context as it was about Hobsbawm's own place in it (TB to RJE, 21 July 2019). Acknowledging the latter underlined, in my view, the importance of the biography.

and thus on these occasions gives him the benefit of the doubt in assessing both the claims advanced by his subject and criticisms made of them by others. However, Evans is an astute and insightful historian, and at other points does indeed question – albeit gently – the claims and self-image advanced by Hobsbawm on his own behalf.[19]

Not the least of the many contradictions informing the academic career of Hobsbawm was the contrast between his self-perception as victim on account of his political views, and the steady institutional advance, in terms of employment, promotion, travel, and publication. This journey coincided with his ascent into the ranks of the British Establishment, a process marked by recognition and honours.[20] In what is at first sight an anomaly, he was lionized and feted by Establishment academics – among them Noel Annan and Isaiah Berlin – not noted for showing a sympathetic political attitude towards Marxism and socialists.[21] Significantly, perhaps, it was a journey marked by the fact that, increasingly, his most damning political criticisms tended more often than not to be directed at those belonging to the far left (Tony Benn, the Labour politician, and Arthur Scargill, leader of the 1984–5 miners' strike).[22]

Claims made by Hobsbawm to victimhood notwithstanding, time after time attempts to block his advance came to naught.[23] Thus the security services

---

19 Although Evans is broadly critical of Marxist theory, his is nevertheless an even-handed approach to the biography and its subject, not least because of the extent and detailed nature of the coverage. Not only is Evans knowledgeable about the period involved – having produced important analyses of German history – but he has also defended the practice of historiography from postmodern (and other) attempts to undermine it (Evans, 2002, 2014).

20 About this process Evans (2019: 487–88) comments 'his gravitation towards the Establishment did not please everybody on the left', and recounts one observer as saying that 'at the party [after a public lecture] someone came up [to Hobsbawm] and attacked him quite violently for having sold out to the Establishment. He was quite disconcerted ... and sheepishly murmured the rather lame excuse that it was best to join something to change it. It made me smile, for in the settings of the [British] Academy and the Atheneum [club], where I saw most of him, so far as I am aware he made not the slightest move to change anything'.

21 Evans (2019: 121, 254, 397, 447–49, 454–55, 480). Annan and Berlin – who facilitated Hobsbawm's travels, publication, and institutional recognition/advancement – were responsible for blocking the academic careers of, respectively, E.H. Carr and Isaac Deutscher. Berlin approved of Hobsbawm because the latter agreed with his own critique of communism.

22 See Evans (2019: 517ff.), who comments that '[b]y now, Eric had launched a full-scale assault on what he called "the retreat into extremism' in parts of the labour movement'.

23 For this self-perception by Hobsbawm as political victim, see Evans (2019: 302). One early claim by Hobsbawm of victimhood is dismissed by Evans (195–6, 689–90 n.12 Chapter 1)

were unable to prevent him either from broadcasting on the BBC, from travelling abroad, or from obtaining travel grants.[24] Unlike Paul Robeson, whose passport was confiscated by the US authorities, Hobsbawm travelled extensively from the 1950s onwards, without encountering obstacles, either financial or political. Despite the occasional setback, his institutional progress in terms of academic posts and promotions followed a conventional trajectory, to the extent of being able eventually to turn down offers of senior appointments. Nor did negative appraisals of manuscripts he submitted prevent their eventual publication; indeed, Hobsbawm appears to have had a privileged input to the world of publishing, exercising a lot of influence at Weidenfeld and Nicolson, from whom he received substantial book advances and for whom he recruited other authors.[25]

From the 1980s onwards, Establishment honours and/or recognition multiplied apace: Hobsbawm was elected to membership of the Athenaeum Club, and Fellowships at King's College, Cambridge, and the British Academy (FBA).[26] Significantly, he himself accepted this as 'natural', admitting that 'the Establishment is increasingly clasping me to its international bosom – and frankly, I am vain enough to like this kind of initial-collecting [FBA, CH] ... there are considerable compensations'.[27] Unsurprisingly, the culmination of his ascent into the ranks of the British Establishment was the offer of a knighthood and then a Companion of Honour (CH, an Establishment bauble) from Tony Blair for 'laying the intellectual foundations for New Labour'.[28] Not the

---

on the grounds that other historians who were known members of the Communist Party obtained appointments 'without difficulty'.

24   About these issues, see Evans (2019: 262, 404–5, 407, 237, 384–5, 387, 445–6, 447–8), who records that MI5 regarded Hobsbawm as unthreatening (Evans, 2019: 220).

25   Evans (2019: 381, 467). Where book publication is concerned, Hobsbawm (2002: 310) acknowledges the assistance of George Soros, an ardent defender of the capitalist system and an equally doughty opponent of socialism.

26   Evans (2019: 479ff.).

27   Evans (2019: 482). This pursuit of Establishment recognition on the part of Hobsbawm was also the subject of criticism by his colleagues, one of whom observed (Evans, 2019: 480) that he 'had a strong sense of what was or wasn't the establishment and in his way a bit of a tuft-hunter, certainly an intellectual snob', whilst another commented 'Eric the Marxist, who opposed established society, had at the same time a profound respect for the traditions of this British society that had welcomed him into its arms'.

28   See Evans (2019: 560–61), who describes this ascent into the ranks of the establishment thus: 'Blair clearly felt he owed a debt to Eric for the role he played in laying the intellectual foundations for New Labour ... Keith Thomas, President of the British Academy from 1993 to 1997, was one of a number of senior figures to recommend Eric for a knighthood ... Tony Blair, as Prime Minister, also held out to him the alternative of appointment as Companion of Honour (CH) ... Eric accepted the CH because, he said, his mother would

least of the many ironies is that Hobsbawm was one of those who in 1998 contributed to the final issue of *Marxism Today,* announcing that he – and they – had been critics of New Labour all along, on account of its refusal to break with the *laissez-faire* project of Thatcherism.[29] Only those who are unfamiliar with academic practices should be surprised at this *volte face*, since keeping in step with prevailing orthodoxy or fashion invariably requires a seamless and unacknowledged change of this kind.

At first glance, the receipt by a Marxist historian of such recognition and appreciation from capitalist institutions seems to be an anomaly. As has already been noted, there can be no doubt as to the influential role exercised by Hobsbawm during the 1960s and 1970s in what is described by Evans as 'a revolution in British historiography ... the coming of social history'.[30] Evidence suggests, however, that much of this had in Hobsbawm's case little or nothing to do with Marxism. This, perhaps, helps explain both the acceptability of his views to academics hostile to socialist theory, and the ease with which he was absorbed into the ranks of the establishment. It comes as no surprise, therefore, that increasingly his publications elicited criticisms along the lines of 'there was nothing particularly Marxist about them', 'the absence of any viable Marxist analysis', 'an elegy for mid-Victorian, middle-class liberalism', and

---

have wanted him to ... Many noted the symbolism of the fact that at the formal ceremony of investiture at Buckingham Palace, as Eric knelt on the footstool provided for the Queen to put the ribbon with the medal of the Companion of Honour round his neck, a piece of plaster fell from the ceiling onto the floor'.

29 Also among the contributors denouncing New Labour were Stuart Hall, Martin Jacques, and Geoff Mulgan, all of whom had earlier championed either the market or postmodernism, and frequently both. The final contribution, by David Edgar, contained a somewhat muted *mea culpa*: 'It was a bit of a cheek, some people said, for a resurrected *Marxism Today* to organize a critique of the Blair project. Was this the same Marxism Today which declared the forward march of Labour halted? Which argued, so loudly and so long, that Old Labour had lost its working class millions? Which insisted that the era of socialism had been overtaken by New Times? Were not these people in effect the harbingers of Blairism, at the very least playing John the Baptist to its Jesus Christ? And having the immortal gall to do so in the name of a political giant [Karl Marx] whose project they had set out to consign to the dustbin of history?' See David Edgar, 'Marx with Sparks', *Marxism Today*, November/December 1998, page 64. The same irony was not lost on journalists, a number of whom also drew attention to the complicity of most contributors with the very project they now rejected as having failed. See 'The Marxists return to pronounce on the fruit of their ideas: Blairism', *The Guardian* (London), 9 September 1998; 'These aged teenagers at Marxism Today, guiltily shuffling their feet', *The Guardian* (London), 23 October 1998.

30 Evans (2019: 444–45).

'he does not use the category "class" in his depiction of the twentieth century'.³¹ Neither is it a surprise that the sorts of political mobilization and agency promoted by Hobsbawm were tactical alliances and electoral pacts between workers and the middle classes, an approach described by Evans as 'his trademark note of paradoxical compromise'.³²

Hence the kind of theory and politics advocated by Hobsbawm possessed only a tenuous connection to Marxism. When asked to define the latter, he replied that 'it suggests that … human society is capable of change', a definition which, as Evans records, was derided as either meaningless or tautological.³³ In keeping with this, Hobsbawm also maintained that '[c]ommunism first and foremost represents a demand for human rights', a view that is quite simply wrong.³⁴ What Marxist theory upholds is not human rights, a very general and non-class-specific political objective that can be invoked and realized by all class elements defensively within capitalism, but rather control of the State in order to establish socialism. Neither does it advocate an equally unspecific notion of 'change' – a term used thus is one associated with Whig history and not Marxism – but rather formation of and struggle by opposing classes, a process which generates systemic transformation.

This uncertainty as to what Marxists believe and advocate in turn raises two other questions: might not the rewards/honours received by Hobsbawm have been, after all, just for his being a pathbreaking historian; and if not Marxism, then with what sort of theoretical approach was his social history consistent?

History, Methods, Politics

These problems with theory stem in part from methodological causes: often, therefore, Hobsbawm simply took at face value accounts he heard, either

---

31 The books against which these criticisms were directed are Hobsbawm (1987, 1989, 2000). A not dissimilar view about the earlier books by Hobsbawm is taken by Genovese (1984: 19), who observes that there is 'a paradox in his big books on industrial capitalist society [since] there is much less in them than some might demand about working-class culture and related matters'.
32 Evans (2019: 254, 510–11, 516ff., 578). Tactical alliances and electoral pacts with the bourgeoisie – in short, the Popular Front strategy of Stalin – was an approach Hobsbawm applied from the outset. In France during 1936, therefore, he maintained that with the far right growing in strength, 'this situation [was one in which] the Communists needed the petty-bourgeoisie' to avoid a fascist coup (Evans, 2019: 99), a position that ignores the many historical instances of support given by the petty-bourgeoisie to the far right (as emphasized by Trotsky).
33 Evans (2019: 610).
34 Hobsbawm in Bethell (2016: 195).

from fellow academics or from peasants met briefly in the course of his travels.³⁵ Evans notes in passing how, after attending meetings of the Communist Party Historians' Group in the early 1950s, Hobsbawm used to gather up ideas that had been discussed in note form and then write them as articles.³⁶ This suggests that at least some of the arguments contained in his publications during that decade were those put forward by other attendees, and therefore did not originate with him. Similarly, the arguments informing *Primitive Rebels* – described by Evans as having 'introduced novel concepts into the historiographical debate' – emerged mainly from conversations with others at that conjuncture.³⁷ Much the same is true of his knowledge about rural Latin America.³⁸ When in the following decade Hobsbawm agreed to collaborate with George Rudé on *Captain Swing*, he gave as a reason that his understanding of the issues came from having supervised a doctorate on the subject: in this instance, too, neither the idea nor the research appears to have been that of Hobsbawm himself.³⁹

In keeping with this pattern, E.P. Thompson hinted that Hobsbawm was somewhat cavalier with regard to his influences, being reluctant to credit others who made the same case and/or used the same sources.⁴⁰ Notwithstanding claims about the originality of his approach to historiography – made not just by Hobsbawm himself but also by his biographer and others on his behalf – there are grounds for questioning such assessments.⁴¹ Hence the argument by Evans that he 'pioneered an entirely new approach to British labour history' is not correct.⁴² There is a long – very long – lineage where this kind of

---

35   Evans (2019: 380).
36   Evans (2019: 318).
37   Evans (2019: 379, 383).
38   On this point, see Bethell (2016: 19).
39   According to Evans (2019: 439), 'most of the detailed research was carried out by Rudé'.
40   Evans (2019: 336–37). The observation by Thompson raises the same difficulty noted earlier by Engels (Marx and Engels, 2001b: 477–78, original emphasis) in a 1890 letter to Conrad Schmidt: 'I know the said Loria; he was over here and he also corresponded with Marx. He speaks German and writes it as in his article – that is to say, badly – and he is the most consummate careerist I have ever met. At one time he believed that world redemption lay in smallscale peasant landownership, but whether he still does, I cannot say. He writes one book after another and plagiarises with an effrontery that would not be possible outside Italy – even in Germany. For instance, a few years ago he wrote a little book in which he proclaimed Marx's materialist conception of history as *his* most recent discovery, and sent the thing to *me*! When Marx died, he wrote and sent me an article in which he maintained that ... Marx had based his theory of value on a sophism which he himself had recognized as such. ...'
41   For these claims, see Evans (2019: 335–36, 532–33).
42   Evans (2019: 432). The same kind of question can be raised with regard to *The Invention of Tradition*, a concept popularized in 1983 by Hobsbawm and Terence Ranger (Evans,

analysis is concerned, extending from Government Commissions and Reports, via accounts by, among others, William Cobbett, William Howitt, Richard Heath and William Dodd in the nineteenth century, to similar approaches in monographs written by W. Hasbach, F.E. Green, Wal Hannington, Reg Groves, and Page Arnot in the early twentieth. In fact, labour, its international context, characteristics, and political direction/organization was central to most political economy discussion (Cobden, Bagehot, Sidgwick, Kay-Shuttleworth, Fawcett) throughout the Victorian era, thereby anticipating Hobsbawm by at least a century.[43]

Methodological issues such as these notwithstanding, diaries and letters reveal that Hobsbawm had a high opinion of his own abilities, a perception reinforced and shared by many of those he encountered, inside and outside academia: the biography records numerous examples of fulsome praise – 'academic brilliance', 'exceptionally brilliant', 'I am intelligent, very intelligent … I already see myself at Oxford', 'the most brilliant historian of our generation at Cambridge', 'precociously brilliant', 'very brilliant', and so on and so forth.[44] Such encomia sit awkwardly with the reality of his intellectual practice, however, involving as it did serious political misjudgements and historiographical misinterpretations leading to or necessitating subsequent changes of mind.

Not only did Hobsbawm accept what was claimed to be the case against the accused at the Moscow trials, therefore, and thought the Molotov-Ribbentrop Pact would prevent war, but he also dismissed the likelihood of a military coup in Chile just before its occurrence and was similarly overoptimistic about the impact of Gorbachev on the Soviet Union.[45] Equally misplaced was his view

---

    2019: 530, 732 n.30 Chapter 2). It, too, was anticipated some three decades previously by C.P. Snow (1951: 383) who noted then that '[n]ine English traditions out of ten … date from the latter half of the nineteenth century'.

43   Many of the components and issues attributed subsequently to studies by Hobsbawm – among them labour conditions, trade depressions, foreign competition, and capital accumulation – were covered earlier in publications by Thomas Brassey (1872, 1879). That historians should be aware of what social theory says about their subjects of study was also addressed previously, in contributions to the volume edited by Hughes (1954).

44   These praises, and many others besides, are recounted by Evans (2019: 46, 51, 80, 91, 116, 123, 171, 319).

45   On these mistaken views, see Evans (2019: 148–9, 174–5, 408, 545–46). It is incorrect to maintain, as does Evans (2019: 552), that events following the breakup of the USSR vindicated the importance Hobsbawm attached to 'identity politics'. As will be seen below, he recognized the politically reactionary underpinnings of the 'cultural turn' only rather late in the day, long after others had done so. Accordingly, the ones whom the events of the 1990s proved right were those who from the start accurately recognized the political trajectory which erstwhile Soviet bloc nation-states would follow – a far-right ethnic/national populism.

that Yugoslavia would not fragment along national/ethnic lines.[46] As problematic was underestimating the impact of nationalism in nineteenth century European revolutions, and idealizing rural banditry as a way of redistributing wealth away from the rich towards the poor. Also missed was the fact that Peasant Leagues in Brazil were organized by the Communist Party, and that unfree production relations on *latifundia* in Peru were not obstacles to economic growth and would therefore not vanish once landlords were expropriated.[47]

Given its centrality to his reputation as a leading social historian, perhaps the main error Hobsbawm made concerned the labour aristocracy in nineteenth century Britain.[48] Initially – at the start of the 1950s – he subscribed to the view that British workers were less revolutionary inclined than their European counterparts as a result of benefitting from imperialism, and consequently having been bought off by capitalism. In versions of this same argument published later, Hobsbawm conceded that in the British context it was incorrect to say that unskilled workers were more revolutionary than their more skilled equivalents. Nevertheless, his stance on this debate is defended by Evans, who contends that Hobsbawm sparked a fruitful historical controversy, a hallmark of his career to come. About this misinterpretation and its justification, a number of observations are in order.

To begin with, it was not until the 1980s that Hobsbawm recognized his error where misinterpretation of the labour aristocracy thesis is concerned.[49] By then, it was all too clear that capitalism was changing for the worse, as the

---

46   For this view, see Hobsbawm (1973: 71).
47   That Hobsbawm overlooks the connection between Peasant Leagues in Brazil and the Communist Party is pointed out by Evans (2019: 405). The failure of Hobsbawm to understand the connection between unfree labour and economic growth in rural Peru is outlined in Brass (2019: Chapter 9).
48   Evans (2019: 249). Of interest in this regard is a revealing aside (Evans, 2019: 250), detailing the way in which Hobsbawm dealt with potential/actual criticism of his ideas: 'Determined that the article [about itinerant skilled artisans] would not be shot down by his seniors, who would, almost inevitably, be asked to review it for publication … Eric sent it for informal, preliminary comment to two of the men who up to this point had proved the major obstacles to his academic career: R.H.Tawney and T.S.Ashton … [Hobsbawm] tactfully noted his appreciation of Tawney's advice … Through this tactic, Eric ensured that the piece would glide smoothly into the pages of the *Economic History Review*, as indeed it did … in 1951'. Here, surely, is an aspect of the explanation for the academic rise of Hobsbawm. That is, not his 'brilliance' or breadth of knowledge, nor his sparking of fruitful historiographical controversy, but rather cultivating the approval of his seniors for what he had written – including from an opponent of Marxism such as Ashton. In short, the not uncommon practice of not antagonizing senior (and conservative) academics in the same discipline, a tactic that surprises when followed by Marxists.
49   Evans (2019: 696–97 n.35).

neoliberal project took hold in metropolitan contexts – once again, rather late in the day for someone to have to rectify a mistake. More generally, and including also all his other misinterpretations, there is an issue here that the biography does not address. Put bluntly, how can being incorrect, repeatedly so, be taken as a sign of intellectual and/or academic distinction, and in what way is Hobsbawm's case different in this regard from all the other historians and social scientists who over the years have similarly advanced views that turn out to be wrong? As such, it highlights the contradiction between on the one hand the inexorable paeans to the analyses undertaken and/or positions held by Hobsbawm, and on the other a consistent pattern of being wrong-footed in many of his political and historiographical judgments. In short, the question posed once again is: why Hobsbawm?

III

Institutional and methodological issues covered thus far – a closeness to the British Establishment, an uncertainty as to what constitutes Marxism, and a misrecognition of crucial issues in debates – pose difficulties for any view of Hobsbawm as a radical and innovative historian. It is therefore necessary to turn to what is possibly the most problematic aspects of his approach: the connection between Marxism, social history, and the 'cultural turn'.

Social History and/as the 'Cultural Turn'

Accordingly, it is necessary both to agree and yet to disagree with Evans when he observes that for Hobsbawm '[b]ecoming a Communist meant embracing poverty as a positive virtue ... This was surely a key psychological impulse behind his growing self-identification as a Communist'.[50] Whilst it is true that this was probably a motivating factor where Hobsbawm was concerned, turning poverty into a virtue in this manner is not really a Marxist view, more of religious one (= 'Blessed are the poor'). Much rather socialists regard poverty as a blight to be eradicated, a disempowering systemic effect of capitalism. This distinction is important, since Hobsbawm's perception of poverty as empowering helps explain his understanding of social history and the 'cultural turn', each of which also claim to endorse 'those below' simply because they are 'below' and an 'unheard voice'.

---

50   Evans (2019: 35).

Epistemological clues to this difficulty, and his resulting take on social history, lie in his espousal of non-Marxist form of pro-rural/anti-urban Romanticism: as set out in the biography he was 'more [of] a Romantic rebel' who 'developed a strong love of the English countryside ... Nature was important to Eric [who experienced] an almost ecstatic feeling of communing with nature'.[51] This can be linked in turn to the way Hobsbawm approached many of the issues he investigated, not least his idealization of bandits as the epitome of peasant activism, an authentic voice-from-below.[52] As he himself observed, 'I have the bad habit of always sympathizing with the weaker side', and indeed it could be argued that his negative interpretation regarding the social impact of the industrial revolution may have led in turn to a positive view of pre-industrial rural society in Europe and Latin America, an idealization that is the hallmark not of Marxism but of agrarian populism.[53]

The search by Hobsbawm for 'authenticity' and 'otherness' in the domain of popular culture – a quest informing his love of Jazz – opens up a space not just for the celebration of pristine culture as an unheard voice from below, a position that was to generate advocacy of the 'cultural turn' and – where rural society was concerned – the 'new' populist postmodernism, but also rural

---

51 Evans (2019: 37, 61, 62). In keeping with this, a profile of Hobsbawm at Cambridge in 1939 (Keuneman, 1982: 366) recounts that 'Eric had a large and vulgar patriotism for England, which he considered in weak moments as his spiritual home'. According to Evans (2019: 41, 60–61, original emphasis), at that same conjuncture Hobsbawm 'only half wanted to talk about Hitler [he] wanted to talk, expansively and sentimentally, about lakes and boats': indeed, he dreamed of 'a Magnum Opus, and that's a Marxist analysis of culture [adding] "I want to know as little as possible of the big city and big city culture"'.

52 On the idealization by Hobsbawm of social banditry, see Evans (2019: 382–3, 405–6) and also Blok (1988: 99–100). Significantly, perhaps, a similar idealization of bandits as 'redistributors of wealth' is encountered in Foucault (1996: 193). As in the case of his championing of the lumpenproletariat simply because its components were regarded as 'marginal', Foucault maintains that thieves and bandits were 'popular heroes' by virtue also of being 'marginals' ('the same is true of the bandits of Corsica and Sicily and the thieves of Naples').

53 Evans (2019: 193, 335–6). As has been noted earlier in this volume (and also elsewhere), whereas Marxism differentiates peasants in terms of opposed class positions and interests (rich, middle, and poor strata), agrarian populists by contrast regard petty commodity producers as an homogeneous category. A consequence of not differentiating the peasantry is seen in Third World agrarian movements, when better-off elements (rich peasants and capitalist farmers combining trading and money-lending with large-scale cultivation) claim they are basically no different from the mass of smallholders (poor peasants with just a few acres); hence the frequent occurrence of the populist mobilizing slogan 'we are all peasants'.

agency as a form of reasserting such traditional cultural 'otherness'.[54] It is true that eventually Hobsbawm became a critic of postmodern theory, but this was only after those who remained Marxists had done so earlier.[55] Rather late in the day, he finally recognized the tainted impact of the 'cultural turn' on the study of politics and history, ironically after he himself had spent many years contributing to its epistemological foundations.[56]

This failure by Hobsbawm to spot the anti-Marxist epistemology of the 'new' populist postmodernism until long after it had become an established component of academia is not difficult to discern, since its trajectory possesses origins in the earlier Marxist debate about nationalism, and whether or not it discharged a progressive role historically in the accumulation process. Part of the difficulty he faced, therefore, stems from his initially supportive perception of nationalism, a view Hobsbawm inherited from Stalin, which prevented recognition of its political dangers once exponents of the 'cultural turn' took over and deployed key elements of this discourse when championing the Third World rural 'other'. Having espoused the semi-feudal thesis, in which nationalism was seen by him (and others) as a positive contribution to the struggle for political democracy and economic development, an objective to be realized by multi-class alliances between workers, peasants and the national bourgeoisie against international capital (as advocated by the 1930s Popular Front), Hobsbawm was in effect committed from the very outset to a defence of this political identity.

Among other things, the espousal by Hobsbawm of the semi-feudal thesis helps explain his appeal to Third World scholars, for whom a positive image of nationalism was linked ideologically to political action aimed at its realization. The argument that British economic development was due mainly to empire fed directly into the nationalist discourse about exploitation being a nation-to-nation

---

54 On the importance to Hobsbawm of Jazz, see Evans (2019: 367ff.). From the start, Hobsbawm privileged culture analytically (Evans, 2019: 139, 201–202, 242, 334); he was in the opinion of his biographer 'not an economic historian [since] he came to history via literature'. Elsewhere Hobsbawm (1998) describes himself as 'a historian of the twentieth century who has tried to reflect on the relations between the arts and society'.

55 For these later criticisms by Hobsbawm of postmodernism, see Evans (2019: 529–30, 550ff., 595).

56 Evans (2019: 529–30) records that, although Hobsbawm retired from the board of the *Past & Present* in 1987, he nevertheless continued informally to make contributions to editorial activity 'well into the 2000s'. It was at the latter conjuncture – somewhat late in the day, as noted, that 'where he smelled a whiff of postmodernism he was … dismissive' of submissions to the journal.

(not class) relationship.⁵⁷ Such a view licenses a shift in the cause of continuing underdevelopment, from class relations found within a nation, and onto the external 'other', whether capitalist or imperialism – both of them 'foreign'. This is the position Hobsbawm adopted with regard to Latin America in the transition debate, making capitalism not socialism the next stage in the political agenda of the left.⁵⁸

Furthermore, this positive vision of nationalism (and its kindred conceptual apparatus) was bolstered in his case by an earlier adherence not just to romanticism, but also his backing for the 'popular culture' as the 'unheard voice', his perception of the 'cultural turn' as empowering, and an essentialist view of peasant economy. Unsurprisingly, it then proved difficult for Hobsbawm to pull back and recast these same kinds of identity as politically conservative – not to say reactionary – when they resurfaced in the discourse of the 'new' populist postmodernism. The latter is fundamentally opposed to the central political case that Marx made: namely, the ultimate objective of his materialist analysis was class agency (by workers and poor peasants) and systemic transition (from capitalism to socialism). It is precisely the possibility of thinking/doing these kinds of things that postmodern discourse has banished politically.

Ambiguity + Authenticity = Absent Marxism

Even in the late 1980s, Hobsbawm was still ambivalent about this issue, warning against nationalism yet at the same time admitting that he sympathized with 'national feelings' since 'there is something I find pleasant about small nations and their attempt to build or maintain a separate culture'.⁵⁹ The latter

---

57 It was this approach which, having informed both *The Age of Revolution* (Hobsbawm, 1962) and *Industry and Empire* (Hobsbawm, 1968), was one that he then applied to rural Latin America, arguing that capitalism there was either absent or foreign (on which see Brass, 2019: Ch.9).

58 As will be seen below in Chapter 3, an identical nationalist discourse was deployed in the case of India by other exponents of the semi-feudal thesis. There it labels workers in metropolitan capitalism as complicit in the imperialist project. Because exploitation and underdevelopment are regarded as externally caused, they are consequently decoupled from an internal capitalist class.

59 Historians, warned Hobsbawm in 1988 (Evans, 2019: 551, original emphasis), ' "must resist the formation of national, ethnic and other myths, as they are being formed", adding that: "I remain in the curious position of disliking, distrusting, disapproving and fearing nationalism *wherever* it exists [but it] must be harnessed for progress if possible ... I also happen to like some peoples and sympathize with their national feelings, but that's a

contradicted what Marxists such as Lenin, Trotsky, and Rosa Luxemburg (but, significantly, not Stalin) cautioned about embracing nationalism; it also overlooked the difference between the historical role of nationalism as capitalism develops, and how the same discourse is deployed now by neoliberalism and its political representatives in order to divide-and-rule workers opposing the extension of the market in general and the industrial reserve army in particular.

Hence the errors he made about Latin American feudalism stem largely from such misinterpretation: that peasant activism was rooted in the ideology of the Middle Ages, and the belief by Hobsbawm that the model to analyse this was the subaltern of Gramsci.[60] That an essentialist view of the peasantry (= undifferentiated, subsistence-oriented) underwrote his intellectual approach to rural contexts, both in Europe and the Third World, is clear from his observation that 'the destruction or at least the weakening of the self-sufficiency of the peasants [pointed to similarities] between European history and that of backward colonial countries'.[61] Unsurprisingly, Hobsbawm endorsed a pre-modern 'way forward', whereby peasant agency = Middle Ages discourse = grassroots 'authenticity'.[62] Not only is this inconsistent with Marxist theory, but it is also precisely what 'new' populist postmodernists argue.[63] In other words, *this* is the trajectory away from a socialist transition that Hobsbawm followed.

---

matter of personal taste: there is something I find pleasant about small nations and their attempt to build or maintain a separate culture"'.

60   Evans (2019: 380, 498–99). When asked in the course of a 1980s interview (MARHO, 1983a: 37–38) whether the work of Gramsci had 'led to fruitful advances in Marxist history', Hobsbawm replied: 'I don't know that the Gramscian influence on Marxist history is particularly new. I don't think myself that Gramsci has much of a specific approach to history other than Marx's own approach … [Gramsci has] got an enormous amount of very beautiful things to say about the history of the subaltern classes, as he calls it, that I've certainly benefited greatly from'.

61   Evans (2019: 166). It is noteworthy that the championing by Hobsbawm of the 'authenticity' of an undifferentiated peasantry is not so different from the similar endorsement by Foucault (see above) of the 'marginality' of the lumpenproletariat as an undifferentiated worker.

62   Evans (2019: 382).

63   As in the case of the 'new' populist postmodernism, therefore, Hobsbawm moved from a critique of modernity in aesthetic terms, in which a failure of modernity in aesthetic terms slides imperceptibly into an endorsement not just of a contrary view (that the pre-modern is a form of empowerment) but also of bourgeois democracy and its mass market. This much is clear from his (Hobsbawm, 1998: 30) observation that 'it is impossible to deny that the real revolution in the twentieth-century arts was achieved not by the avant-gardes of modernism, but outside the range of the area formally recognized as "art". It was achieved by the combined logic of technology and the mass market, that is to say the democratization of aesthetic consumption'. Hobsbawm's view about a pre-modern

This is clear from his claim that during 'the periods in which intellectuals have attached themselves to the people, they have performed their finest tasks. In the periods in which the intellectuals have retreated into their "ivory tower" they have produced nothing of value due to their disassociation from the people'.[64] Such a view could in part explain a number of things. To begin with, Hobsbawm subscribed to an over-optimistic perception of the way Marxist intellectuals might fare in academic institutions.[65] For this reason, he regarded the entry of leftists into university posts during the 1960s expansion of higher education as positive, a development that in his opinion would lead politically to a more 'progressive' institutional outlook.[66] Much rather the opposite happened, in that the admission of such intellectuals into university jobs turned out to be conditional. It resulted in one of two outcomes: either inclusion based on discarding of socialist beliefs and Marxist theoretical approaches; or exclusion of those who refused to recant politically in this manner.[67]

More importantly, the idealization of intellectuals 'going to the people' also helps explain his initial uncritical espousal of the 'new' populist postmodern approach to the agrarian sector of Third World nations. Hence the seeming realization of this very link between intellectuals and 'the people' (*not* the class) in the form of first uncovering and then championing what was presented as an homogeneous category of rural 'others' (= the 'unheard voice' of those below), suppressed by imperialism and colonialism. In the light of this it comes as no surprise that Hobsbawm reacted with enthusiasm for the kind of social history reflected in the 'cultural turn'. It was deemed progressive in

---

'way forward' mimics that of Escobar (1995), whose postmodern approach rejects development as an inappropriate foundational/Eurocentric model imposed by Marxists on rural populations in Third World nations.

64 Evans (2019: 302).
65 'What was new was the unexpected scale of the conversion of intellectuals to Marxism', noted Hobsbawm (2011: 365), 'largely because of the dramatic expansion of institutions of higher education and their students all over the world in the 1960s, an expansion for which there was no historic precedent'.
66 In his own words (Hobsbawm, 2011: 364), 'Marxist elements came to permeate the language of public discourse of students, and as men and women emerging from student radicalism [in the 1960s] became teachers and communicators. And indeed – not only in the emerging countries – decision-makers in politics, state service and the media, areas in which recruitment was increasingly from among university students of the radical generations. Marxism acquired a firmer lodgement than before in the institutions concerned with education and communication. This stabilized its influence. The young products of the 1960s embarked on what would ... be for many of them long careers'. But not as Marxists, one might add somewhat cynically.
67 For details about such academic inclusion/exclusion, see Brass (2017: Chapter 18).

political terms, by him and others, on the grounds that grassroots reassertion of traditional culture was simply an expression of 'from below' opposition to colonialism.

Because Hobsbawm omitted to ask about the extent to which peasants were differentiated along class lines, and what kind of smallholders were involved in grassroots rural agency, therefore, he failed to spot the effectiveness of traditional/'authentic' ideology in the pursuit of capitalist economic and political objectives. This shortcoming – not differentiating rural producers, their activism and objectives – led in turn to a tendency on his part to over-optimism when evaluating the 'potential for a genuine social revolution'. Overlooked by him, consequently, was that in Peru and India it was usually the better-off peasants who mobilized, not just against the landlord class but also (and later) against sub-tenants and agricultural workers. More often than not, peasants generally are to be found in the ranks of the counter-revolution, activism that has nothing to do with a socialist transition, to which property-owning smallholders are frequently opposed.

Conclusion

Whether or not Marxism can be said to be missing from post-1945 debates about Third World development, and if so why, is an issue posed here with regard to the respective fates of two dominant paradigms: the semi-feudal thesis, which claimed a theoretical affinity with Marxism, and the 'new' populist postmodernism, which was antagonistic to it. Because large property was categorized as feudal, and capitalism deemed absent from the countryside, exponents of the semi-feudal thesis advocated political alliances between workers and 'progressive' capitalists in furtherance not of socialism but rather of nationalism, bourgeois democracy, and economic growth. As applied to the agrarian sector of Third World nations during the 1960s 'development decade', this was an approach that favoured better-off peasants who were actual or aspiring capitalist producers. It was, in short, a framework – necessitating a 'bourgeois democratic' stage, with nothing beyond – from which a revolutionary socialist form of Marxism was indeed missing.

If the roots of the semi-feudal thesis were found in Stalinism, then the source of the 1980s 'cultural turn' was late nineteenth and early twentieth century agrarian populism, supportive of smallscale rural production and opposed to 'the curse of bigness' (capitalist and socialist alike). Buying into this prefiguring narrative, the 'new' populist postmodernism contested all forms of Marxism as inappropriate Eurocentric impositions on the Third World rural 'other'. Recuperated thereby was not just an essentialist image of an undifferentiated peasant, but also a number of non-class identities – national, gender, ethnic, local, religious – all of which were subsumed under the rubric of a silenced/unheard traditional subaltern voice. The latter mobilized outside and against the state, an emblem of the 'foreign' modernity which the subaltern resisted. Academically, 'new' populist postmodern discourse merged with – or, rather, colonized – the research interests and broad approach of social history, which as a result became less recognizably a practice compatible with Marxism. Given his contribution to social history, plus his political and intellectual eminence, not just on the left, the focus here has been on the theoretical and political approach of Eric Hobsbawm.

Any answer to the question asked here – why Hobsbawm, or what was it about him that merits the attention his analyses or views have attracted – has to start with an unavoidable contradiction. Hobsbawm regarded himself, and was regarded by others, as victimized for his leftist political views, a commitment that affected his academic employment prospects and publishing output. Yet in terms of posts held, promotions conferred, conferences attended, and books/articles published, his academic career does not seem to have been unduly affected in negative terms, nor did he suffer hugely simply on account of his leftist politics, much rather the opposite. Early opposition to his views came not from agents of the State as from fellow historians, and concerned not his politics so much as his competence. Consequently, it is possible to tell a different story about the story of Hobsbawm's political difference.

Not only was he never imprisoned for his political views – unlike many socialists whose opinions are considered 'dangerous' in countries where they live or which they visit – but the security services proved singularly ineffective in blocking his institutional advance, publications, broadcasting, or travel. Much rather, Hobsbawm was friends with and cherished by members of the British Establishment not known for their sympathetic attitude towards holders of socialist views. After reading the biography, therefore, the impression that remains is one of an unresolved contradiction: between on the one hand Hobsbawm's own self-image of victimhood on account of his politics, and on the other the seemingly limitless recognition and honours accorded him by Establishment institutions and persons, plus the relative ease of his access to publishing outlets and the extensive nature of his publication record. When added to the fact of his mistaken historical and political judgments, the element of contradiction looms yet larger, and requires explanation.

The argument of those regarded as most critical of Hobsbawm is that he gradually moved rightwards politically as he grew older, making his peace with capitalism as a system in his later years. Advanced here is a somewhat different contention: it is that he was never that radical politically, and further that this was evident from the very first. It was precisely because of this that the British Establishment grasped him to its bosom, and he was able to do all the things – travel, publish, broadcast, ascend the academic hierarchy – that those on the left usually find difficult to do because of institutional and other obstacles placed in their path. This acceptability to the powers that be can also be linked to the fact that Hobsbawm was a precursor of the 'cultural turn'; all the views he formulated or expressed with regard to social history and rural society in the Third World subsequently emerged in the form of the 'new' populist postmodernism which not only became academically fashionable but opposed and undermined Marxist theory from the 1980s onwards.

Historically, the ruling class everywhere has always endeavoured to pursue a well-tried tactic: pick out the least threatening and dangerous individual from amongst its political opponents, and lionize him/her. The object is to depict as politically harmful those views which in reality pose the least risk, thereby defusing/displacing ideological hostility to its own political survival, a particularly effective manoeuvre where intellectuals are concerned.

Not the least important roles discharged by academics who have a privileged access to public platforms are three in particular. First, to question continuously the possibility/desirability/feasibility of revolutionary socialism. Second, to endorse, seemingly from a leftist position, an 'alternative' politics that does not threaten the power/wealth of those who own/control the means of production/distribution/exchange. And third, to convey or reinforce the image of a benign capitalism that does not suppress criticism from its political opponents. All these roles, it could be argued, were ones that Hobsbawm fulfilled to perfection.

CHAPTER 3

From Marxism to Nationalism (*via* Imperialism)

> As to the working class of the oppressed nation, national oppression restrains it in the class struggle, not only by restricting its liberty of organization ... but also by arousing in it a feeling of solidarity with its national bourgeoisie. Tied hand and foot, corrupted politically by nationalism, the proletariat of the oppressed nation turns into a defenceless object of exploitation and at the same time into a dangerous competitor (wage-cutters, strikebreakers) to the workers of the oppressing nation.
> ROSA LUXEMBURG writing about the national question in 1916.[1]

⋯

> PATRIOTISM – too often the hatred of other countries disguised as the love of our own; a fanaticism injurious to the character, and fatal to the repose of mankind.
> An early nineteenth century definition of nationalism by HORACE SMITH that clearly has no relevance whatsoever to the present.[2]

⋯

Introduction

As has been noted elsewhere, the 1960s 'development decade' signalled an important break in the interpretation of village society in Third World countries.[3] It marked a shift in the conceptualization of 'the rural', and in particular the role of peasant economy: from a pre-war image of perpetual stasis, embedded in never-changing subsistence cultivation, to the possibility/desirability of modernity and economic growth. Third World agrarian structures became

---

1 Luxemburg (1976: 303–4).
2 Smith (1890: 270).
3 See Brass (2014: Ch.3).

the focus of development theory, policies, and planning, generating important debates – involving Marxists and non-Marxists alike – between social scientists (economists, sociologists, anthropologists) and historians. These discussions covered a wide range of questions, including the mode of production, labour regimes, the state, decolonization, and capitalist development in both metropolis and the periphery. The political and epistemological dilemmas this raised surface all too clearly in Marxist approaches to development issues, not just that of Hobsbawm (see previous Chapter) but also by Peter Worsley and Utsa Patnaik, whose analyses of Third World political economy had their roots in that era, and consequently were – and are – informed by unavoidable antinomies.

It could be argued that, as someone who started out as an anthropologist and then metamorphosed into a sociologist, Worsley accurately embodies the very epistemological contradictions emerging at that conjuncture.[4] Anthropological research has tended to emphasize the a-historical character of micro-level village/tribal units composing rural society, plus the enduring nature of custom and tradition within these small-scale environments. By contrast, the focus of sociology has been on the dynamics structuring the wider context, an approach necessitating the deployment of macro-level analysis informed by the broad theory (or theories) emanating from political economy. An additional contradiction involves theory: despite being aware, generally, of the epistemological difficulties informing postmodernism, and in particular the antagonism between the latter and Marxism, he nevertheless approaches Third World development with an analytical framework that in many respects turns out to be no different from that of the 'cultural turn'.[5]

---

4 Discussing the distinct methodological approaches of these two social scientific disciplines, Worsley (2008: 198) concludes: 'Both kinds of study – the wide-scale sociological survey, and the fine-grained anthropological kind – were needed, for there had been more theories than research on the ground'. About his own methods, Worsley (1984: xii-xiii) observes: 'My framework is not one of events, but one of meta-theory: of theory set against and lodged in history ... I did not do "research" in the usual, fieldwork sense of that word ... What I did was to visit as much of [the Third World] as possible, keeping my eyes and ears open, talking to people, and reading the specialized studies others had spent years producing'. His approach was, in short, not so different from that of Hobsbawm, who similarly based his analyses of the rural Third World on short visits and 'talking to people'.

5 As early as the 1980s, Worsley (1989: 11, original emphasis) noted that '[i]n the West, Marxism, feeble between the Wars and under strong repression during the Cold War, has experienced a veritable renaissance in the last two decades [the 1960s and 1970s]. But although a great deal of fine research has been done by Marxists, the dominant characteristic of those who specialize in *theory* – as distinct from using Marxist theory to investigate the world – has been not just its scholasticism, but also a very rapid turnover of fashions in Marxism, including regular attempts to compensate for obvious inadequacies by borrowing from non-Marxist

Moreover, in the view of Worsley himself the antinomies did not stop there: where the study of the Third World was concerned, therefore, 'I was myself one of these contradictions: a communist officer in the colonial forces, who, like so many, later came to reject Stalinism, though not socialism ...'[6] Notwithstanding this self-identification as a socialist, his having written a monograph on Marxism, and his clear sympathies with the oppressed/downtrodden in Third World societies, the espousal of Marxism by Worsley can be said to have been problematic from the outset. Much the same is true of Patnaik. In the case of Worsley, reasons for this include not just a perception by him of nationalism and populism as 'natural' identities in Third World countries, the pre-independence absence in the latter contexts of class, but also a disparaging view about Marxism as having little or nothing to say about both the history and future of these social formations. Such an assessment emerges from a comparison of the principal texts by him about Third World development, published two decades apart: one in 1964, the other in 1984.[7]

In what is also presented as a Marxist analysis of Third World development, specifically of the historical and current impact of the 'drain' of wealth from periphery to the metropolis, and the role in this of the industrial reserve army, Patnaik extends the characteristics of colonialism to imperialism, the latter becoming in effect a variant of the former. She thereby perpetuates beyond decolonization and the end of formal political rule the process of economic appropriation by Britain from India. In other words, the 'drain' continues not merely past independence itself but also into the present: according to this model, it is the nation, not capitalism, which is both oppressor and victim. Whereas Lenin pitched his theory of imperialism mainly at the level of relations between countries, Patnaik manages to turn the equivalent analysis into a form of pro-peasant discourse. In effect, she parts company with Leninism on the subject of capitalist development, based in his case on peasant differentiation along class lines.

This chapter consists of three sections, the first of which outlines the interpretation by Worsley of colonial and post-colonial political change in Third World countries. The second examines the way in which Patnaik interprets economic development in such contexts, with particular reference to how the 'drain' persisted after the end of colonization, and why in her view it continues

---

("bourgeois") thinkers, notably Freud'. His critical assessment of this epistemological development was accurate: 'Most of these hybrids have not been very impressive'.
6 Worsley (1984: xi).
7 According to Worsley (1984: xiii), his 1964 book was mainly about Africa, whereas the focus of his 1984 volume was on Latin America. Neither volume, he accepted, contained enough about India.

to be a part of imperialism. Difficulties faced by each of these approaches to development theory, Marxist and otherwise, are considered in the third section.

I

Contributing to the formation of what became the New Left during the early 1960s, Worsley was critical of the 'Big Corporations' that undertook what he termed 'paternal exploitation' that characterized the penetration of Third World nations by the new imperialism.[8] For him, this – and only this – was capitalism: foreign, large-scale, and indeed visible to any observer as such. Apart from agribusiness plantations, therefore, a similar kind of economic activity was not to be seen among peasants in the countryside. According to this view, accumulation in the newly-independent nations of the Third World was – and by inference was destined to remain – an externally-driven process and foreign owned.[9]

The Authenticity of Populism

Traditional African societies were depicted by what Worsley called 'racial mystics, political militants, poets, and African historians' as embodying the values lost by the industrial West.[10] This endorsement by them of 'communitarian values [in] African village society' necessitated in turn their denying that class differentiation was present in decolonized nations, which were consequently 'held to be *classless*, indeed conflictless'.[11] Where conflict was present, they

---

8   See Worsley (1960: 124–5, 129), where he notes: 'The explanation of colonial poverty, and of continued impoverishment even after independence, begins to take shape in the light of ... foreign investment and profit'.
9   Even sizeable enterprises like these were regarded by Worsley (1984: 164) as not necessarily fulfilling the conditions required by an accumulation process ('The efficiency of large-scale agriculture ... cannot be judged simply by using capitalist criteria of profitability').
10 According to him (Worsley, 1964: 126), 'racial mystics, political militants, poets, and African historians, could agree that traditional African society enshrined important human values which, they believed, the West had lost because of their proud but also sad ... history as the pioneers of modernized industrial society'.
11 Hence (Worsley, 1964: 127, original emphasis) 'the reassertion of the vitality and importance of a continuing African culture, could ... be summarized as an assertion of the "communitarian" nature of African society ... [a] stress on communitarian values, of the living *Gemeinschaft* nature of African village society ... the thinking of the new populists ... asserts that traditional society was particularly homogeneous ... The decolonized society, especially, is held to be *classless*, indeed conflictless'.

argued, it would 'be eliminated during the process of modernization' or blamed on colonialism.[12] As well as Africa, maintained Worsley, theorists in Asia also deployed the same populist approach, insisting on 'the homogeneity of their societies'; a unity, it was claimed, that derived from 'colonial pauperization'.[13] At this point, however, he poses two crucial questions that seemingly prefigure disagreement. First: 'To what extent does this ideological emphasis upon the "unity" of the nation and the homogeneity of society reflect a real absence of social differentiation in the new societies'; and second, 'to what extent is it merely another instance of the familiar rhetoric of all nationalists who ... have always appealed to an often-spurious solidarity, embracing all classes and conditions of the nation'?[14]

Ironically, having questioned, rightly, the claims made by populism as applied to Third World countries, Worsley then proceeds to uphold their veracity.

Although in the early 1960s Worsley dismissed as populist those terms projecting cultural 'otherness' in the Third World as innately empowering identities (negritude, the African personality), therefore, he nevertheless also endorsed them as authentic.[15] Pointing out that what the new élites wanted was 'larger representation in the legislature, and a greater share in Government employ', Worsley contended that populism was an acceptable way in which a national bourgeoisie might espouse and support the broader political objective of an all-encompassing 'progressive' move to oust the

---

12   Blaming colonialism for any/all ills that survive independence is, of course, also an argument made by Patnaik (see below).
13   On this point, see Worsley (1964: 128–30), who notes both that 'colonial pauperization of the people' was attributed to 'foreign' (= European) forms of imperialism which 'in India, pauperized an entire nation', and that 'Asian theorists have developed "populist" theories which emphasize the homogeneity of their societies'. Consequently, '[t]he societies of Asia and Africa are commonly seen by theorists in those countries not so much in terms of the class-divisions that the Westerner almost instinctively begins to look for, but in terms of the common life-situation of the whole population which derives from their past and present tradition of village-level democracy, and from the unifying experience of common political oppression and economic impoverishment at the hands of foreign imperialism'.
14   Worsley (1964: 130).
15   Hence the view (Worsley, 1964: 164ff., original emphasis): 'We embarked upon an examination of class structure in the new Africa largely because of assertions by the ideologists of the new states that their societies were "homogenous", that they lacked the antagonistic class divisions of the Euro-American world, and that they were, in consequence, peculiarly solidary'. Rejecting the Marxist critique of nationalism as a species of false consciousness, he continues: 'We now have to agree that the evidence shows them to be largely correct ... in very many of these countries, classlessness *is* a reality'.

landlord class in such Third World contexts.[16] Because of this, he asserted that ethnicity was a correspondingly more appropriate mobilizing discourse, replacing as it did class with non-class ideology, an identity which enabled the successful formation of a mass party capable of pursuing modernity and development.[17]

According to Worsley, therefore, populist discourse is an accurate depiction of the reality on the ground: in other words, during the early 1960s there was no class, no class differentiation, and no capitalism. In effect, at this conjuncture Worsley asserts the veracity of something akin to a Chayanovian model of African peasantry.[18] As lacking in surprise is the corollary: he then insists – like Fanon, and others at that same conjuncture – that throughout the Third World (not just Africa) it is peasants, not workers, who are the real 'revolutionary force'. Two decades later, these views had not changed fundamentally, except in one specific way.[19] Now he championed the rural cooperative as a production unit within which peasant economy would be able to reproduce itself and thrive, but accepted that such an arrangement entailed the continuation of private property.[20] What remained unaddressed was the way in which cooperative agriculture would (and, indeed, did) fuel the twin processes of peasant

---

16   See Worsley (1964: 143, 146), where he observes that 'the "business elite" is able to subscribe to "populist" values [because by doing so it] displays the classic "progressive" attributes that Marx described for the bourgeoisies of Western Europe, which also had to fight their way into the sun against the entrenched power of the landed nobility'.

17   'Ethnicity, then, in the present phase of development in the new African countries at least', declared Worsley (1964: 162–64), 'is a much more important bond between men than class; it is the ready-made basis for the mass party … ethnicity is still crucial'. This is because '[c]olour is the index of [a] common inferiority which unites Africans and Asians not only across class-lines, within their own states, but also across international, cultural, and geographical boundaries'.

18   'Africa is its peasantry', argues Worsley (1964: 162), 'subsistence-producers or cash-crop producers, but independent peasants. This is the basic fact about the social structure of the new African states – and of many new states elsewhere'.

19   Hence the later assertion (Worsley, 1984: 93) aimed at Marx, to the effect that his 'view of peasant inability to take class action is, of course, misguided'. This is doubly incorrect, in that for Marxism peasants do not constitute a class, and the economic and political objectives that rural movements embody are usually those of the better-off components – that is, the class interests of rich peasants.

20   Supportive of the rural cooperative as a way forward in Third World agriculture, Worsley (1984: 147ff.) nevertheless accepted that 'the basic unit was still the private farm, and it still had to compete on the capitalist world-market. The very success of the cooperative, paradoxically, strengthened the private farm and private farming'. On the role of cooperatives in the development process, see also Worsley (1971).

differentiation and the consolidation inside these very units of a rich peasant stratum.[21]

Explicitly backing what is termed by him a 'strong' Chayanovian approach to peasant economy, in which endogenous production/consumption patterns are based on kinship/household, Worsley cast doubt on the relevance to the rural Third World of peasant differentiation, preferring instead Chayanov's household/demographic cycle.[22] Similarly consistent with his earlier view that it is the (undifferentiated) peasant, not the worker, who is the true 'revolutionary subject, Worsley endorses the middle peasant thesis of Alavi, arguing that there was no consolidation of 'a permanent class status' due to the family demographic cycle, and further that 'the most radical of them were likely to be those that had a marginal stake as middle peasants'.[23] On the issue of 'from below' rural agency, he concludes emphatically: 'It was they [= middle peasants], not the poorest peasants, who [in Russia] became the most radicalised, just as it was to be in Asia half a century later'.[24]

At the same 1960s conjuncture, moreover, Worsley warned that – were they not to be accepted as such – these Third World forms of cultural 'otherness' would develop into 'Europe-hating exclusiveness'.[25] The irony with this seemingly prescient observation on his part about what became the 'cultural turn' is that, notwithstanding the widespread support for this discourse (that is, a recognition as authentic), identity politics nevertheless went on to become precisely what he thought acceptance would avoid: a form of 'Europe-hating exclusiveness'. Contrary to what he imagined would occur, that the recognition of 'otherness' would be necessary so as to preclude antagonism, therefore, not

---

21 An example of this process can be found in the agrarian cooperatives located in the eastern lowlands of Peru, in the Province of La Convención, during the mid-1970s (Brass, 2000: Chapter 2).

22 For positive references to Chayanov, see Worsley (1984: 72, 80, 82, 115, 130, 355 n.35 Chapter 2), who notes that populism opposed Lenin on the grounds that 'it was not class but the family that constituted the relevant framework for analysing peasant relationships'.. In keeping with this, he (Worsley, 1984: 119ff., 125, 355 n.23 Chapter 2) also endorses both the account by John Berger of the French peasantry, and the social banditry argument of Eric Hobsbawm.

23 Worsley (1984: 116, 354 n.56 Chapter 1).

24 Hence the view (Worsley, 1984: 158) that '[i]n the Third World, there is always the spectre of peasant revolution, more salient, hitherto, than that of proletarian revolution'.

25 '[W]e shall have to learn to appreciate the dynamism and pride lying behind the philosophies of "negritude" and "the African personality"', maintained Worsley (1960: 140), 'lest they decay into a Europe-hating exclusiveness. If we do all this, we shall not lose an old world but gain a new'.

merely did this not prevent hatred of Europe (= Eurocentric discourse) from arising but much rather enhanced it.

The Inapplicability of Marxism

During the 1960s, in a context where Third World nations were emerging from colonialism, Worsley was an early and insightful commentator on the nature and perils of populism. Describing the latter as 'a mystical top dressing of quasi-religious appeal to the unity of the people, land, and society', he argued that populism 'has been quite inadequately recognized as the very important genus of political philosophies it is'.[26] Subsequently, however, he seemed to retract this initial endorsement, arguing that 'this label [= populism] doesn't tell us very much because all parties, Left and Right, try to build mass support', adding that ' "Populism"... tends to be simply a residual category in between naked conservatism at one end of the spectrum and egalitarian, redistributive ideologies such as socialism or communism on the other'.[27]

Not only did the term now appear qualified by inverted commas, but populist movements are said by Worsley 'not to fit into the traditional European models of class society'.[28] In keeping with his idealized depiction of populism as an 'authentic' discourse appropriate for Third World countries, Worsley claimed that in these same contexts 1960s nationalism was not just different from its counterpart in Western Europe but also benign.[29] Neither claim has endured: a non-benign combination of nationalism + populism in Third World

---

26 On the characteristics of populism, see Worsley (1964: 165, 167; 1969: Chapter 10; 1984: 112–13).

27 Worsley (2008: 185).

28 Worsley (2008: 139). That populist movements do not contain within their ranks elements with specific class interests, and thus break conceptually with the process of class mobilization, is not correct. Historically, agrarian populism has been a means whereby rich peasants have been able to draw upon support from middle and poor counterparts, by means of invoking non-class identity, ideology (nationalism, ethnicity, sectoral distinctiveness) and discourse. During the pre-war era, this was a characteristic of agrarian mobilization in Eastern Europe, where such populist movements laid the ground politically and ideologically for – and merged with – what became fascism. This is misrecognized by Worsley (1984: 143), who maintains incorrectly that '[t]hese movements were wiped out by fascism'. They were not 'wiped out' by fascism, much rather amalgamating with the latter.

29 Hence the following optimistic view (Worsley, 1960: 138): 'Nor is the nationalism of the emerging countries patterned on the model of the older nationalism of Western Europe either in form or in spirit'.

countries is nowadays matched by a similar and equally non-benign combination in metropolitan capitalist nations.

Unmentioned by Worsley at the earlier conjuncture is that the importance of populism had long been recognized by Marxists, but its arguments and political conclusions were strongly disputed, again by Marxists. Hence the theory of Lenin and Trotsky was forged in the course of numerous political exchanges with Russian populists and populism; despite being critical of such views, the fact that neither of them regarded populism as unworthy of theoretical engagement underlines the political influence and ideological tenacity each attributed to this form of discourse. Like Marxism, therefore, Worsley characterized populism as a discourse that on the one hand is anti-urban, anti-class, and anti-largescale (whether capitalism or socialism), while on the other it is just as strongly pro-rural, pro-peasant, pro-smallscale, and supportive of non-class ('natural') identities.[30]

Despite claiming to espouse Marxism, therefore, Worsley is nevertheless at best ambivalent (and at worst dismissive) about its political and economic relevance to the study of development. In the 1970s he was already arguing that the intellectual value of Marxist theoretical approaches to the social sciences had not merely declined in importance but was now largely defunct; where sociology generally – and that applied to the Third World in particular – was concerned, therefore, Marxism in his opinion no longer possessed explanatory validity.[31] By the mid-1980s, his work had become anti-Marxist in orientation, maintaining that 'because of [its] inadequacy [when] theorizing about [ethnicity, nationalism, and class] Marxist materialism ... has had such dire consequences'.[32] This is particularly the case with regard to Marxist

---

30 'The populist commonly holds that the indigenous society is a "natural" *Gemeinschaft*', states Worsley (1964: 165), which 'implies an agrarian economy, based on the peasant or small farmer, as distinct from an industry-dominated economy. City-based capitalism, its banks, its factories, the whole array of urban existence, is believed to be unnatural and based on false values ... Big business thus comes in far strong criticism; a complementary stress upon small rural handicrafts and manufactures is not unusual'. Later, however, Worsley (1984: 75) attempts to distance his own view about the rural social structure by insisting '[t]his is not to romanticize the village [which] was no idyllic *Gemeinschaft*. ...'

31 See Worsley (2008: 174–5, 214, 233–35).

32 Outlining the reasons for updating the earlier volume about Third World development, in the Preface to his later book, Worsley (1984: xii-xiii) declared: 'My main hope [for writing the book] is that I may have thrown some theoretical light on ethnicity and nationalism and their relationship to class, because of the inadequacy of theorizing about these important forms of social life, particularly in Marxist materialism, which has had such dire consequences'.

interpretations about the peasantry, and especially those concerning the issue of socio-economic differentiation in the countryside.

Hence the criticisms directed by Worsley not only at Marx himself, accused generally of economic reductionism, but also and specifically at Lenin and Kautsky, on account of their argument that capitalist development necessarily involved – and, indeed, grew out of – a process of peasant differentiation.[33] This in turn was linked by Worsley to the contention that, in Russia and Third World contexts alike, rich peasants were not capitalists, and that capitalism itself was largely absent from the countryside: where accumulation occurred, it was the result of foreign investment in largescale agribusiness enterprises, such as plantations. Insisting that in Russia there existed neither a proletariat nor capitalist exploitation, as Marxists claimed, Worsley opts instead to follow the populist arguments of Shanin concerning on the one hand the absence both of peasant differentiation and of *kulak* as a sociological category, and on the other the corresponding economic viability of petty commodity production.[34]

Although rightly objecting to 'the mythical picture of the cultureless past of the colonial peoples, who had no history until the whites came along', Worsley nevertheless is unable to avoid falling into a now-familiar trap.[35] Whilst it is true that colonized populations did not have a 'cultureless past', it is but a short step

---

33   See Worsley (1984: 80, 114–15, 123, 129–30), who maintains that '[t]he predictions made by the leading Marxist authorities on agriculture, from Kautsky to Lenin, had therefore been falsified'. Ironically, later in the same text Worsley (1984: 160) draws attention to the fact that '[t]he historic poles of large-scale estates and small-scale peasant holdings which, together with those who had no land at all, provided the labour for those estates, have existed throughout history, and persist today', which is precisely what Kautsky argued was the reason why capitalist producers did not always expropriate neighbouring smallholders.

34   See Worsley (1984: 130, 355 n.35 Chapter 2). 'By the standards of developed capitalist agriculture, even a rich peasant was miserably poor', he asserts, noting that that: 'Nor was there [in Russia] any significant strengthening of the richer peasantry. The much discussed kulaks ... were more competent and entrepreneurial peasants, rather than capitalist farmers proper'. The same kind of claim, but applied to rural producers in pre- and post-1917 Russia, and to the new farmers' movements in India, are made by, respectively, Bernstein and Dhanagare (see Chapter 4, this volume).

35   Worsley (1960: 131), whose critique anticipates the following view expressed subsequently by the historian Trevor-Roper (1965: 9): 'It is fashionable to speak today as if European history were devalued: as if historians, in the past, have paid too much attention to it; and as if, nowadays, we should pay less. Undergraduates, seduced, as always, by the changing breath of journalistic fashion, demand that they should be taught the history of black Africa. Perhaps, in the future, there will be some African history to teach. But at present there is none, or very little; there is only the history of Europeans in Africa. The rest is largely darkness, like the history of pre-European, pre-Columbian America. And darkness is not a subject for history'.

from rejecting this argument to one that, because they do indeed have a culture, this is the specific form their empowerment is going to take.[36] In the end this is as mistaken a view – and a patronizing one at that – as the initial claim that they have no culture ('a cultureless past'). Equally problematic is the corollary: namely, that the 'obverse of all this [colonial populations lack a culture] was the uniqueness of Western civilization'.[37] Again, this cannot but anticipate the postmodern trope that emerged some two decades later: where the defence of an 'other' culture merges with an attack on 'Western civilization', therefore, not only does this surreptitiously licence a slide into an analogous defence of pre-capitalist systemic forms/institutions/organization that gave rise to this 'other' culture, but it also and simultaneously negates any progressive elements to be found subsumed under the general term 'Western civilization'.

II

The concept of the 'drain' informing the model of imperialism used by Patnaik is, as she herself makes clear, based largely on an original analysis undertaken by Dadabhai Naoroji (1825–1917).[38] Not the least curious aspect of her enthusiasm for his theoretical model is a political one: Naoroji was a member of Parliament for the Liberal Party in Britain, and a founding member of the Indian National Congress. Conceptualized by Patnaik as a fiscal mechanism whereby the wealth of India was transferred to Britain, the 'drain' entailed as a result a process of income deflation and impoverishment wreaked by means of colonial taxation, a burden that fell mainly on peasants (= petty producers) in India.[39] This was because industrialization in the metropolis depended on food crops grown in the tropical periphery, commodities the non-tropical area

---

36   Subsequent observations by Worsley (1984: xi; 1997: 147), both that 'I will surely be accused of the sin of "culturalism" ', and that '[i]n concentrating on culture in this book ... I am not preaching "culturalism" ', suggest that the epistemological shortcomings associated with a culture-as-empowerment approach was something he recognized later.

37   Worsley (1960: 132).

38   In the words of Patnaik (2017: 278): 'We cannot do better than to go to the classical pioneers, Dadabhai Naoroji and R.C. Dutt, who wrote over a century ago. Far from being outdated, their works show a deep qualitative insight into the economic processes underlying the drain, which is missing from much of present-day writing'.

39   Echoing the demands made by the new farmers' movements in 1980s India, she (Patnaik & Patnaik, 2017: xxvi, 29–30) maintains that peasants require subsidies and remunerative prices, which in turn have to be provided by the state. The latter, however, was prevented from doing this in the colonial era, when tax revenue was siphoned off from colonies to the metropolis, a transfer with which 'landlords and local feudal elements' were complicit.

could not itself produce.[40] Her political conclusion, one unconnected with Marxism, is a call for reparations.[41]

Down the Drain (Once Again)

According to Patnaik, among the negative outcomes of the 'drain' was that the allocation of land/resources in rural India to the cultivation of export crops necessarily diminished the amount of subsistence produced by cultivators, an impact which she claims 'is invariably ignored in development theory'.[42] The latter claim is quite simply incorrect, since the 'food availability decline' framework is currently a highly fashionable paradigm and central to the anti-development approach of agrarian populism, as exemplified by concepts such as 'food sovereignty' and 'food security', which – like Patnaik – proclaim not just the viability of peasant economy but also its moral right to survive as such.[43] This view about the peasantry is not one shared by the majority of Marxists. Nor, for similar reasons, is her inference that, had there been neither colonialism nor post-independence imperialism, peasant economy would have as a result been able to reproduce itself.

However, whilst in the earlier version as formulated by Naoroji, the 'drain' operated as an untoward (and almost regrettable) aspect of colonialism, the later one of Patnaik extends the same process beyond independence and into the present day. Her argument is that, through price adjustments effected in the post-war era, ex-colonial nations attempted to claw back the advantages of rising commodity prices that favoured peasant farmers in newly independent nations, thereby ensuring that the 'drain' mechanism continued much the

---

40 Patnaik (2017: 284) describes as 'asymmetric production capacities' the fact that the cold temperate regions of Europe were not merely incapable of producing tropical products (indigo, jute, cotton) but also themselves manufactured nothing that producers of such items wanted in return. Such an argument has more in common with the 'unequal exchange' thesis of Emmanuel (1972) than it has with Marxism.
41 'It is practicable', insists Patnaik (2017: 311–12), 'for the industrial nations as a whole to repay the transfers which they took, or from which they benefitted, in the past.
42 The export policy informing the 'drain' effected by British colonialism (Patnaik & Patnaik, 2017: xxvii) 'was always marked by a decline in the production and availability of food grains for local populations owing to the diversion of land and other resources to export crops. This inverse relation between the growth of export crops and the availability of food for the local populations, is invariably ignored in development theory'.
43 On the interconnection between these concepts, development theory, and agrarian populism, see Brass (2015).

same as before.⁴⁴ Unlike Naoroji, therefore, Patnaik decouples the 'drain' thesis from colonialism, and attaches it instead to imperialism. Like him, however, she continues to locate the main contradiction not between classes but rather between nations; in her case, an antimony involving on the one hand 'rich' metropolitan countries that are capitalist, and on the other 'poor' Third World nations. In short, her version is – like his – about nationalism, not class; and again like him, she overlooks the interests/agency of those within the nation.

Moreover, unlike not just Naoroji but also Marxism, the contemporary victims of this transfer are mainly (undifferentiated) peasants, not workers. From the outset, Patnaik makes it clear that in her view capitalism proper ('genuinely capitalist production') is still absent from the periphery, and that the presence there of an accumulation process is an external not an endogenous phenomenon.⁴⁵ Equally clear is what she opposes: the target of her analysis is the Marxist argument that the distinctions between the capitalist metropolis, composed of economically advanced nations (Europe, the United States), and the periphery, on which are located economically less developed countries (ex-colonies in the Third World) are less marked today than they used to be.⁴⁶

---

44   The crux of her argument, made early on (Patnaik & Patnaik, 2017: xxvi), is as follows: 'The main economic mechanism for ensuring an uninterrupted supply of these products to the advanced North at non-increasing prices has been an "income deflation" imposed on the working populations of the South, which restricts their demand for their own products. This has indeed proved to be a highly effective tool and continues to be used even in the absence of direct political control being exercised over Southern populations ...' The resulting claim made by her is equally unambiguous: 'In the process of asking and answering these questions, we found that we had formulated a theory of imperialism that has relevance not only for the past, but also in the present era'. References to the impact of the 'drain' on Third World nations pervade all the recent publications by her (Patnaik, 2007; Patnaik, 2017; Patnaik and Patnaik, 2017).

45   This absence is signalled by her use of the term 'genuinely capitalist production' (Patnaik, 1999: 290, 296), whilst the accumulation that does occur is labelled an 'encroachment' from outside India (Patnaik & Patnaik, 2017: 48, 51).

46   Patnaik & Patnaik (2017: 1–3, 6), where it is stated that '[t]he purpose of the present book is to argue a position contrary to the one outlined above [namely] that big capital *of the third world itself* is complicit in this process of undermining and squeezing the traditional petty producers, viz., the peasants, craftsmen, fishermen, artisans, and so on is not germane to the argument, just as the fact that metropolitan capitalism also squeezes its own residual petty producers, not to mention the workers directly employed by it, is not germane to the argument. What is important is the fact of this compression of income and livelihoods exercised by metropolitan capitalism upon the traditional petty producers of the third world, especially of the tropics '. What she objects to strongly, consequently, is the argument that, because capital is mobile, 'the implication is that workers in metropolitan countries are now competing against low-wage workers of the third world. They are no longer insulated from the low wages prevailing in the third world'.

In short, a degree of convergence has taken place, erasing many of the hitherto significant differences separating metropolis and periphery as regards the operation of and practices by capital, together with the kinds of production relations it uses. The result has been a corresponding similarity in both 'from above' class struggle waged by capital, and 'from below' class struggle waged by labour.

Unlike that of Patnaik, the critique by Naoroji of British economic policy in India included the recognition that, to some degree and in some areas, India had gained a number of advantages from colonial rule.[47] Among these were a variety of public works, including railway construction, canals, and irrigation projects. Furthermore, not all the negative elements affecting the Indian economy were attributed by him to colonialism. Thus, for example, he maintained that a decline in food production was on occasion due to the operation of the market, whereby public works attracted labour away from agriculture, leading to a decline in output.[48] Similarly, high prices for some agricultural commodities were of short-term duration, due in the case of cotton to the American Civil War.[49] Again unlike Patnaik, Naoroji both recognized and paid tribute to the efforts of British colonial authorities to alleviate famines in India.[50] This approach was itself reciprocated by the colonial authorities, who in the early 1880s noted that his criticisms were aimed directly at them, to the effect that 'the people of the country being so largely excluded from the higher walks of administrative work and responsibility', nevertheless commended his analysis

---

47 As Gupta (1911: 316) acknowledges, this was true of Romesh Chunder Dutt as well. Naoroji (1901: 52) also acknowledged that historically a 'drain' of wealth had affected Britain itself, as well as other European nations ('all Europe was tributary to the Pope'). It was a process that was not confined either to India or to colonized nations.

48 Railway construction in particular drew workers away from agricultural production (Naorji, 1901: 69), the outcome being that 'to a great extent agricultural labour is diminished in the neighbourhood, the want of good communication preventing other parts from supplying the demand. The result is that less food is produced and more mouths to feed, and, with the labourers well paid, a temporary and local rise in prices is the inevitable result ... it will be easily seen that, in every Presidency in good seasons, the localities of high prices have been those only where there have been large public works going on'.

49 'Thus, then, it is the old story', states Naoroji (1901: 75, 77), since 'prices kept going down under the British rule till, with the aid of railway loans, cotton windfall, etc., they have laboured up again, with a tendency to relapse'. Given his espousal of free trade, he understood that price fluctuations were sometimes an effect of economic cycles and not necessarily the fault of adverse policies enforced by a malign colonialism.

50 'No doubt', he (Naoroji, 1901: 212) accepted, 'the exertions of individual Europeans at the time of famines may be worthy of admiration; the efforts of Government and the aid of the contributions of the British people to save life, deserve every gratitude'. Dutt expressed a similar view (Gupta, 1911: 339–340).

('This essay is well worthy of close examination by any thoughtful politician into whose hands these papers may fall').[51]

In one sense it is strange that Patnaik – a self-proclaimed Marxist – champions the 'drain' theory of Naoroji, not least because he believed in free trade and – while castigating British colonialism for its economic appropriations from India as a whole – had little or nothing to say about surplus extraction within India itself, by Indian producers from non-property-owning Indians.[52] Unsurprisingly, therefore, who or what produced income – that is, the surplus extracted by the British from India – was an issue that he did not attempt to address.[53] What he wanted to see happen was not independence, just a better deal from British colonialism for the Indian bourgeoisie. As a late nineteenth century Liberal, he endorsed the free market and his approach was informed by the view that, rather than continuing to extract surplus from its colony, the British ought to permit India to enter the market and trade there on its own account. In another sense, however, her support for his ideas is theoretically consistent, in that – as a founder member of the Indian National Congress – he was, like Patnaik herself, an ardent nationalist.

As regards economic policy, Naoroji advocated free trade between the Britain and India, and lamented the absence of what today would be called 'a level playing field'.[54] To this end, he argued that India should be restored 'to her *natural* economical conditions', enabling the subcontinent not only to pay the

---

51   Naoroji (1901: 145).
52   For her self-description as a Marxist, see Patnaik (1999: ix-x). An identical case to that made by Patnaik, one that if anything is even more critical of British colonial policies, is found in Wilson (1909). Similarly endorsing the analysis of Naoroji, Wilson (1909: 12, 57–58, 60) observes that debt 'merely aggravates the virulence of cancer in the body economic [as] when the Simla Government of India decided arbitrarily to fix the exchange value of the rupee against gold', noting subsequently that 'these deficits are, by adding to the debt, steadily and surely plunging the people of India into deep and ever deeper misery'. Of particular interest is the political direction from which this critique is made: accordingly, Wilson (1909: 164–65) acknowledges that he is a 'Free Trader by conviction ... A Free Trader I am, and must remain'.
53   For him the element of appropriation occurred between nations, not within nations and between classes. Hence the following (Naroji, 1901: 188): 'As to the question, how and by whom, directly or indirectly, the income is actually produced, and how and by whom, and through what channels, this income is distributed among the whole people, that is an entirely different matter, and ... is quite separate from the first and fundamental question of the whole total of the means and wants of India'.
54   For example, see the observation by Naoroji (1901: 136, original emphasis) that '[u]nder the present unnatural policy England takes from India's scanty; under a natural and just policy, it will gain from India's *plenty*, and Manchester may have its free trade to its heart's utmost content'.

revenue demanded by its colonial rulers but also to form a market for British manufactures. In short, to 'become England's best and largest customer, instead of the wretched one she is at present'.[55] The object was not so much to gain independence as to secure a better economic deal for India within the existing colonial structure. In his words, '[t]he obvious remedy is to allow India to keep what it produces, and to help it as much as it lies in the power of the British nation to reduce her burden of the interest on the public debt', adding – loyally – 'with a reasonable provision for the means absolutely necessary for the maintenance of British rule'.[56] Throughout his critique based on the 'drain' theory, Naoroji was at pains to emphasize that the solution he envisaged involved not decolonization *per se* but rather a larger share accorded by the colonial government to India of the economic wealth generated by the latter.[57]

India's Chief Curse

Central to her theory about imperialism is the claim by Patnaik that both the fact and the scale of transfers from the periphery to the metropolis have been ignored by most western literature on Third World development, despite findings about the 'drain of wealth' having been set out in great detail by Naoroji (and confirmed subsequently by other Indian scholars).[58] Unlike him, however, she broadens the concept of victimhood, and links this through the nation to its peasantry. Patnaik explains this difference by noting that Naoroji omitted to describe the impact of the 'drain' on peasants because at the time he was writing they had yet to be affected by such transfers.[59] There is, however, an

---

55   Naoroji (1901: 201). 'Let natural and economic laws have their full and fair play', he maintained (Naoroji, 1901: 216), 'and India will become another England, with manifold greater benefit to England herself than at present'. For an identical view held by Dutt, see Gupta (1911: 336).
56   See Naoroji (1901: 136).
57   In essence the case made by Naoroji (1901: 206, 208) constituted a moral appeal to the British nation to 'do the right thing'. If this was not heeded, he (Naoroji, 1901: 206–7) warned, there was gathering a political challenge that colonialism might then have to face: 'Those Englishmen who sleep such foolish sleep of security know very little of what is going on. The kind of education that is being received by thousands of all classes and creeds is throwing them all in a similar mould; a sympathy of sentiment, ideas, and aspirations is growing amongst them; and, more particularly, a political union and sympathy is the first fruit of the new awakening, as all feel alike their deprivation and the degradation and destruction of their country'.
58   See Patnaik (2017: 277).
59   'The only matter Naoroji and Dutt did not write about, because it took place mainly after their time', notes Patnaik (2017: 279, original emphasis), 'was that the Indian peasantry and

alternative reason for this absence: namely, Naoroji saw the 'drain' for what it was – an appropriation not from peasants but from bourgeois and petty bourgeois elements (= small/medium capitalists), which constituted the kind of victims of colonialism that really concerned him.

An equally important feature of the 'drain', therefore, was the complaint by Naoroji that educationally qualified Indian nationals were as a consequence deprived of access well-paying employment in the professions, and thus unable to ascend the relevant career hierarchies (government, civil service, medical, teaching).[60] The real victim of foreign rule, for Naoroji, was the Indian bourgeoisie, who were denied thereby an ability to prosper: generally absent from his catalogue of the oppressed were poor peasants and workers.[61] Those most affected by the 'drain' were not the rural and urban plebeians but rather the middle classes – 'Natives of ability and high character' – who might otherwise expect both to fill the positions currently occupied by the colonizers and enjoy the remuneration (salaries, pensions) the latter received.[62] Exemplified in terms of 'a direct deprivation of the natural provision for similar classes of the people of the country', Naoroji underlines the extent to which his concern

---

workers produced the *second largest merchandise export surplus in the world* for at least four decades from the 1890s'. In terms of chronology, this claim is problematic: Naoroji published his findings about the 'drain' in 1901, when according to Patnaik colonialism had been extracting surplus from Indian peasants for a whole decade. This underlines the point being made here, that when formulating the 'drain' thesis, Naoroji perceived an altogether different category of victimhood. Nor is it true that Dutt ignored the impact of the 'drain', much rather the opposite: throughout his writings (Gupta, 1911: Chapter XXII, 'Agrarian and Economic Views') he made constant references to the plight of the 'agriculturalist'/'cultivator'.

60   'The educated find themselves simply so many dummies, ornamented with the tinsel of school education, and then their whole end and aim of life is ended', he (Naoroji, 1901: 205, 211) observed: 'We are made B.A.'s and M.A.'s and M.D.'s, etc., with the strange result that we are not yet considered fit to teach our countrymen'.
61   Although Naoroji (1901: 186, 188) lamented the poverty of the agricultural labourer, his main concern was clearly the impact of the 'drain' on the bourgeoisie. Dutt, by contrast, made extensive reference (Gupta, 1911: 376) to the fact that peasants had no say in the way they were ruled by colonialism ('There is no department of work in which an Indian member can make himself more valuable to the voiceless millions of cultivators and artisans').
62   See Naoroji (1901: 103–4, 183–84), who notes: 'It is these salaries and pensions [received by government officials and the non-official British] and all other expenditure incident to the excessive European agency, both in England and India, which is India's chief curse, in the shape of its causing the exhausting drain which is destroying India. In the ordinary and normal circumstances of a country, when all the salaries, pensions, etc., are earned by the people themselves, and remain in the country itself to fructify the people's own pockets ...'.

was principally the loss of job opportunities for the Indian bourgeoisie: that is, a specifically nationalist discourse.[63]

The contrast between on the one hand what Naoroji really objected to in the functioning of the 'drain', and its operation in India during the colonial era, and on the other the attempt by Patnaik to depict his concern as 'progressive' in a Marxist sense, could not be clearer. In her view, he worried that surpluses extracted by the British had 'a strongly deflationary impact on mass purchasing power', and it was this which informed the 'drain' thesis.[64] What concerned Naoroji, however, was not the mass purchasing power of peasants, but comparatively speaking a much narrower set of economic interests: that of the Indian middle classes, as a result of their not having access to the kinds of well-paying jobs that were held by the British as a result of having colonized India.[65] For this reason, the assertion by Patnaik concerning the reason why peasants were not a feature of the 'drain' theory as formulated by Naoroji is incorrect.

This aspect of the discourse about 'drain' – job competition between those of different nationalities/ethnicities – can itself be linked to a contemporary version. Categorizing 'England [as] the worst foreign invader [India] has had the misfortune to have', Naoroji frames the employment rivalry generated as a result of colonial rule in terms not of political economy but of national 'otherness': that is, an earlier variant of the now familiar identity politics.[66] Supportive of the proposal to set up an Agricultural Department, therefore, he observes both that 'India cannot afford to have more blood sucked out of her for more Europeans', concluding that 'Native agency ... would be the most natural and proper agency for the purpose'.[67] Indeed, his way of presenting this

---

63 Hence the following view (Naoroji, 1901: 184): 'All salaries and pensions, etc., paid to Europeans in England and India, beyond the absolute necessity of the maintenance or supervision of British rule, are actually, first, a direct deprivation of the natural provision for similar classes of the people of the country, and, second, a drain from the property and capacity of the country at large'.

64 As to the identity of those affected negatively by the 'drain', Patnaik (2017: 294, original emphasis) is clear: 'Both Naoroji and Dutt were acutely conscious of the fact that when monies raised from producers in India were not spent in their entirety within the country under normal budgetary heads, it meant a severe squeeze on the producers' incomes ... in effect, *surplus budgets* to an unimaginably large extent were being operated with a strongly *deflationary impact* on mass purchasing power'.

65 Like Naoroji, Dutt also subscribed to this view (Gupta, 1911: 377): 'We want Englishmen in all these departments, we welcome them to help us, but we do not wish them to monopolise all the higher services to the virtual exclusion of the children of the soil'. Unlike Naoroji, however, it was less central to his interpretation of the 'drain'.

66 See Naoroji (1901: 224–25).

67 Naoroji (1901: 227).

issue – along the lines of 'India does not get a moment to breathe or revive. "More Europeans," "More Europeans," is the eternal cry' – comes close to the way in which immigration is depicted negatively by much populist ideology – driven by nationalism – throughout Europe and America today.[68]

The transformation undergone in the theoretical approach of Patnaik is perhaps nowhere so evident as in the role played in her analysis by the industrial reserve army. The latter featured centrally in a debate between us conducted a quarter of a century ago over the link between capitalism and unfreedom.[69] With two notable exceptions, therefore, Patnaik has not deviated from case made then, which has remained within the parameters of the semi-feudal thesis. The two exceptions are, first, an extension of the 'drain' argument into the present day, so that where surplus extraction from India is concerned, there is no longer any break separating colonial and post-colonial epochs; and second, the emergence of the industrial reserve as a major aspect of the economic relationship between colonizer and colonized.

Earlier, therefore, Patnaik denied strongly that a 'pauperised Indian peasantry' constituted an industrial reserve army of labour. She was emphatically opposed to attempts by others to see a connection between the sale of labour-power by peasants in India and the formation/reproduction of an industrial reserve army. This was a view Patnaik sustained in the face of two critiques: in the course of exchanges, initially with Paresh Chattopadhyay during the 1970s mode of production debate itself, and subsequently with me in the mid-1990s. On each occasion she was adamant that no link existed – or could exist – between a 'pauperised Indian peasantry' and the industrial reserve army of labour. In her reply to Chattopadhyay, therefore, Patnaik complained that '[o]ne really fails to see what [he] is driving at here or how the "industrial reserve army" is at all relevant to my argument', adding: 'How is Marx's concept of the "industrial reserve army" within a capitalist mode of production at all relevant to my argument about a pauperised Indian peasantry forced to subsist on the land as wage-workers?'.[70] Her conclusion then was that any attempt to conceptualize a 'pauperised Indian peasantry' in terms of the industrial reserve army was an argument which 'we would reject ... emphatically'. Similarly, and subsequently, Patnaik was just as opposed to my argument that

---

68 See Naoroji (1901: 225).
69 The sequence of the four contributions that composed this exchange was as follows: Brass (1994), Patnaik (1995), Brass (1995), and finally Patnaik (1997). The last contribution can be discounted, since it was not only short but also largely an expression of indignation at the fact that her arguments had been criticized.
70 Patnaik (1978: 214).

unfree labour-power formed part of the industrial reserve army drawn on by capital when restructuring its labour process.[71]

Now, all of a sudden, the very same connection – an industrial reserve army composed of a 'pauperised Indian peasantry' – is made by Patnaik equally strongly, and looms large in her latest analysis.[72] She begins by distancing herself from Marxist interpretations of the industrial reserve for two reasons in particular: because its role is limited to suppressing real wages, not money wages; and because it disregards the fact that produce grown in the periphery is consumed in the metropolis.[73] Patnaik distances herself from Marxism yet further, accepting that the real/money wage 'distinction did not matter for Marx [as] he was talking about a commodity-money world [in which] real and money wages moved together [and] there was no separate discussion of the role of the reserve army for maintaining the value of money'.[74]

The full extent of this break is revealed when she proceeds to argue that Marxism ignores the presence of an additional reserve army of labour in the periphery, where its function is to keep a check on the cost of goods cultivated by peasants ('pre-capitalist petty producers') who hire labour to grow export crops for the metropolis.[75] Of these two industrial reserves, furthermore, it is the one in the periphery – not the metropolis – that is the more important, again a fact 'not recognized in traditional Marxist literature'.[76] This importance

---

71 As pointed out at the time (Brass, 1995: 100ff.), her problem with conceptualizing the industrial reserve army stemmed from a twofold difficulty. First, because Patnaik regarded unfree labour as evidence for a pre-capitalist/semi-feudal agriculture, consequently for her such production relations were incompatible with an accumulation process; and second, she perceived the labouring subject as essentially a 'pauperized' peasant rather than as a worker.

72 Hence the current emphasis (Patnaik and Patnaik, 2017: 58) on the fact that '[t]he maintenance of these labour reserves is essential for the systemic economic stability of capitalism'. Although the drain', plus the work of Naoroji and of Dutt, all feature in earlier publications by her (Patnaik, 1999; Patnaik, 2007), one looks in vain for a similar analysis there of the industrial reserve army.

73 Patnaik & Patnaik (2017: 48–49, 50).

74 Patnaik & Patnaik (2017: 49–50).

75 According to her (Patnaik & Patnaik, 2017: 50) the additional industrial reserve army in the periphery is composed of 'precapitalist petty producers, who supplement their own labour with that of hired workers in particular seasons [in order to] keep down the money wage rate/money incomes within the periphery and hence prevents any possibility of an autonomous cost-push in the case of such commodities'.

76 Hence the view (Patnaik & Patnaik, 2017: 50–51): 'Capitalism in short has always used two reserve armies of labour and not one: one of these located within the metropolis ... the other one located within the periphery ... The latter, not recognized in traditional Marxist literature, is far more important in a sense that the former, since it can be relied upon even to provide a source of recruitment for the capitalist sector's direct employment whenever the need arises'.

stems in her opinion from a qualitative difference: whereas that in the metropolis corresponds to a reserve army, in the periphery by contrast there exists only 'a massive labour reserve'. The capacity of the latter to discipline workers employed by capital in the metropolis is limited, according to Patnaik an effect both of its unskilled character and also distance.[77] Linked to this is her astonishing view that 'income deflation upon the workers in the metropolis itself is unlikely ever to be imposed, if it is imposed at all'.[78]

III

Apart from the gulf separating the analyses by Worsley and Patnaik from Marxist theory about Third World development, their approaches to the latter subject are faced with other but related kinds of difficulty. These extend from the perception of non-class identities as empowering and progressive, a tendency to categorize accumulation as external, to an inability to interpret capitalism as a system uniting the interests and agency of producers across national boundaries, and thus also of their geographically separate workforces.

Populism, Nationalism, Postmodernism

To some degree, the benign interpretation Worsley advanced during the 1960s about the homogenous, empowering and 'authentic' character of Third World populism and nationalism, was itself prefigured in an earlier analysis by him of Melanesian Cargo Cults.[79] Mobilizing on the basis of traditional culture, such millenarian movements in both the pre- and post-war era drew on rural support, and in his view 'have had a radical, anti-White and even communistic flavour'.[80] For

---

77 Asking 'why ... should capital need an internal reserve army in addition to the one located in the periphery', she (Patnaik & Patnaik, 2017: 51, original emphasis) answers that 'there is a qualitative difference between the two reserve armies. The one located within the metropolis can strictly be called a reserve army while the one located in the periphery is not so much a reserve *army* as simply a massive labour reserve whose disciplining role for the workers directly employed by capital in the metropolis can at best be an imperfect one. This is because such labour reserves are devoid of the skills that even the "unskilled" workers in the metropolis possess'.
78 Patnaik & Patnaik (2017: 46).
79 See Worsley (1957).
80 Accepting that 'ancient cultural ties may become factors of revived importance', especially in the case of Melanesian nationalism, Worsley (1957: 254–56) goes on to note that where Cargo cults flourished, now cooperative units operate along with the village council 'as forms of political and economic expression of indigenous aspirations'.

Worsley, therefore, there already existed at this conjuncture a link between this kind of 'from below' mobilization asserting traditional cultural forms of empowerment, and his positive view about Third World nationalism as an unheard indigenous voice. This interpretation was what the 'new' populist postmodernism went on to make its own a couple of decades later.

These claims made by Worsley, not just about the 'authentic'/'progressive' nature of populism and nationalism in Third World countries when faced by imperialism, but also about the reasons for the positive reception accorded to his ideas in such contexts, are faced with a number of difficulties. To begin with, labelling as 'progressive' the endorsement by a national bourgeoisie of populism in order to be able to join with workers and poor peasants in a common struggle against a landlord class overlooks the fact that, following the defeat and expropriation of large rural proprietors, bourgeois elements quickly turned against plebeian components which sought either to extend the redistribution process to rich peasant capitalists themselves or, indeed, to transcend capitalism.[81] Promoting ethnicity and not class as a means of establishing a common bond in such conflict also ignores both the exclusionary impact of such a discourse and also its capacity to reproduce false consciousness which constitutes an obstacle to further 'progressive' – let alone socialist – objectives. Put bluntly, how 'progressive' can the latter be, insofar as it renders impossible unity with those urban workers in metropolitan capitalism who are, more often than not, indicted as being complicit with imperialist exploitation, from which they are accused of benefitting.[82]

Equally problematic is Worsley's view that, although rightly noting both that 'the populist asserts that … class-divisions [are] dismissed as *external* ("imperialist") intrusions', and that '[t]he populist … is usually some kind of radical, hostile to Big-ness in general', s/he can be led 'either Left or Right'.[83]

---

81 Although he acknowledges the fact of class struggle, Worsley (1984: 87) sees its operationalization only under feudalism, where it takes the form of conflict between tenant and landlord.

82 Again, this is a view held by Patnaik.

83 Worsley (1964: 165, original emphasis). In keeping with this, elsewhere he (Worsley, 2008: 148–49) appears to argue that the populist denial of class was an effect simply of imperialist coercion of post-independence governments, rather than a pre-independence mobilizing ideology: 'The Western powers wasted no time in bringing the new, would-be independent African and Asian governments to heel … The sad, neigh-universal response to these pressures was to convert the nationalist claim forged during the struggle for independence that there were no class or cultural differences at all in the new states into the assertion that if there were there shouldn't be'. In other words, a non-too-subtle ideological shift, along the lines of 'we did this because it was forced on us after independence, not because we subscribed to aspects of this discourse prior to independence'.

Maintaining the existence of a leftist version of populism – as will be seen in other chapters in this volume, currently a claim made also by a number of those who insist that it is a 'progressive' ideology – he overlooked the politically reactionary historical role of mobilization linked to this discourse. Populism is opposed not just to some forms of capitalism but also to socialism. It is precisely this twofold form of hostility that drives the antagonism expressed by populism to the state *per se*, seen by it as an institution legislating/enforcing the rule on behalf of either capitalism or socialism.[84]

This in turn highlights an additional problem: namely, who backs populism, and why. Although he accepts that populism found support among new elites, this does not appear to include rural elements, since both class and capitalism were excluded by him from the pre-colonial rural Third World. Consequently, because it was opposed to landlordism, Worsley perceived rural cultural 'otherness' as progressive and empowering (pro-modernity and development). However, much agrarian populist mobilization in the Third World that invokes ethnic/national 'otherness' as empowering is antagonistic to modernity and development. It is, in short, a discourse that is anti-progressive, and hostile not to 'feudal' landlords but rather to the encroachment of 'foreign' capital. Neglecting both the internal class divisions of agrarian populist agency, and also its effects in terms of backwards-looking discourse generated as a result, poses fundamental difficulties for any theoretical framework applied to Third World development.

As presented by Worsley, therefore, such mobilizations in rural areas are sustained largely by peasant family farmers defending their economic identity as subsistence producers from expropriation by 'foreign' capitalists. This overlooks instances in the Third World where such movements have been led by rich peasants interested not in subsistence but in accumulation. Making a common cause with middle (and perhaps even poor) peasants necessarily requires a mobilizing ideology that does not draw attention to class distinctions within the ranks of the peasantry: hence the prevalence within populist movements of discourse emphasizing national/ethnic identity. Externalizing capitalism and class in this manner not only helps explain why populism is the ideology of choice where small capitalists are concerned, but also brings into question claims regarding the absence of capitalism in Africa during the pre-colonial era. Prior to the advent of colonialism in the late nineteenth century, therefore, evidence suggests that there did indeed exist black farmers,

---

84   Elsewhere Worsley (1969: 222) purports to discern a break between the attitude to the state of Russian populism, and that of its American counterpart.

merchants, and other kinds of producers, who employed workers, invested capital, and owned enterprises that generated profits.[85]

A related difficulty concerns the reason given by Worsley for the acceptability of his views about the Third World to those in the latter context.[86] Despite thinking that it was the occurrence of the 1962 Cuban Revolution that generated an interest in his ideas, and contributed to the commercial success of his 1964 book throughout Central and Latin America, the attention it received there was more probably due to his endorsement of populism and nationalism as 'natural' and 'authentic' political discourses in Third World contexts. The latter interpretation fits closely with the pro-peasant *indigenista* views that have had a long history and intellectual purchase south of the Rio Grande, not just in Mexico and Central America but also in Andean nations (Peru, Bolivia).[87]

What Did the Romans Ever Do for Us?

Over a whole range of issues, Patnaik parts company with Marxism, endorsing arguments that are not just nationalist but also supportive of neoliberalism (free trade, anti-taxation). Her call for reparations ignores the fact that economic restitution could be applied retrospectively by virtually every conquered – let alone colonized – nation on earth. This much was recognized by Naoroji, who noted that the colonial power had itself experienced a 'drain' historically; on the basis of this kind of infinite regression, therefore, Britain might conceivably invoke reparations from other European countries as a result of having been invaded first by Rome during the first century BC, and then by the Normans in the eleventh century.[88] It is an argument that in essence functions

---

85 On this point, see among others, the studies by Iliffe (1983) and Sender and Smith (1986).
86 Hence the view (Worsley, 2008: 179): 'My publisher told me that my book, *The Third World*, was a very "passionate" book, and that it would take me around the world. I thought this was a wild and surprising idea, but he proved to be right. Chicago quickly published it, where it became their number one academic best-seller … But it was the Spanish-language edition which had the greatest success, not in the [Iberian] Peninsula but in Mexico, where Siglo XXI sold five editions across the continent in a decade'.
87 *Indigenista* discourse permeates not only the work of anthropologists such as Robert Redfield, Ángel Palerm, and Arturo Warman on rural Mexico, but also much political theory, social science, and literature (José Carlos Mariátegui, Castro Pozo, Fausto Reinaga, Ciro Alegría) about Peru and Bolivia. For details, see Brass (2014: Chapter 1).
88 Advocacy of the 'drain' as a perpetual and unproblematically one-sided relationship brings to mind the justly celebrated scene in the film *Monty Python's Life of Brian* (1979), directed by Terry Jones, in which a discussion by members of the People's Front of Judea about the injustices of Roman rule ('They've bled us white [and] taken everything we had,

as an avoidance mechanism: a substitute for addressing surplus extraction by internal capitalist producers. For holders of this view, the exploiter is always abroad – little or no mention is made of the presence of an indigenous bourgeoisie and its role in the accumulation process. Reparations in this instance would be made to a country that has already entered the space race, possesses atomic weapons, and has a vibrant telecoms/media industry.

That Patnaik departs from Marxist theory, and in some instances fundamentally so, is also evident from her dismissal of the argument concerning the emergence of a double convergence, between capital in both metropolis and periphery, and labour in each of these contexts. Despite accepting that such a development undermines much of the theoretical veracity informing her conceptualization of the links between imperialism, the 'drain', and the industrial reserve army, Patnaik nevertheless insists that such considerations are somehow irrelevant ('not germane'). What really matters, for her, is the continuing ability of metropolitan capital to 'compress the income and livelihoods' of traditional peasants in the Third World. This is the 'logic' of her argument that colonialism never ended, and neither did the identity of its victims – undifferentiated peasants.

Recognizing – finally – both the presence and importance of the industrial reserve, Patnaik then attempts to insert it into her nationalist interpretation of a continuing 'drain' from ex-colony to erstwhile colonizer. To this end, she insists there is not one industrial reserve (as Marx argued) but two: one in the metropolis and a second in the periphery, the latter being the more important. According to her, therefore, the object of the industrial reserve is not to lower the cost of labour-power employed by capital in the metropolis, as it is for Marxism, but rather to keep down the cost in the periphery of export crops produced there by peasant cultivators. As such, she regards the operation of the reserve army as evidence for continuing income deflation – but only in India: that is to say, the persistence there of the 'drain' ('the essence of imperialism') long after the end of colonialism.

Equally problematic is the attempt by Patnaik to split the industrial reserve on the grounds of geography, and then to identify a difference between its separate components in terms of socio-economic impact and effect on metropolis and periphery. Because he regarded capitalism as a system, Marx did not divide it into different components each with a logic separate from the other

---

not just from us, from our fathers, and from our fathers' fathers') moves via the central questions ('what have the Romans ever done for us? And what have they ever given us in return?') to a list of improvements effected by the colonizers (aqueducts, sanitation, roads, irrigation, medicine, education, wine, public baths).

parts. Accepting that it is a distinction not found in Marxism does not prevent her from locating a twofold divergence: a national logic, operating in the Third World periphery; and a peasant economy logic in the same geographical context. However, where accumulation is concerned, Marxism does not allocate a 'separate' economic dynamic to Third World nations, especially not now. Much the same problem confronts her claim that the distinctiveness of each components of the industrial reserve is due to the inability of labour in the periphery to migrate as far as the metropolis so as to exercise downward pressure of wages/conditions – to discipline, in other words – of those employed there.

As the recent history of migration from the periphery – not just from the Middle East, but also from Africa – to the European metropolis attests, claims that physical distance nowadays constitutes a barrier to the movement of labour simply do not hold.[89] Neither do claims about a comparative absence of the requisite skills being an obstacle to the employment by capital of workers from the periphery as members of the industrial reserve in the metropolis. Elsewhere it has been shown that the element of skill is of decreasing significance, for two reasons: first, because many of those in the periphery now have the necessary skills; and second, the growing importance of deskilling.[90] The latter means that skill is not as central to the reproduction of the capitalist labour process in metropolitan contexts as it once was. When deskilling is combined with the fact current migration patterns indicate that distance is no object, it underscores the accuracy of the original interpretation by Marx, who argued for the existence of one – not two – industrial reserve army serving the needs of employers in a single capitalist system.

Similarly difficult is the assertion by her that income deflation will never be imposed on the metropolis, a view that is quite simply wrong, as the experience of workers in many parts of Europe and the UK from the 1980s onwards – in the shape of austerity, cut-backs in public spending, privatisation, restructuring, outsourcing, class struggle – underlines. The thinly-disguised nationalist discourse informing the case made by Patnaik amounts – again – to the refrain that 'we are more victimized than you', whereas the Marxist (as opposed to nationalist) argument would be 'we are *all* victims of capital, Indian and European worker alike'. Downplaying the oppressive impact of accumulation on those employed in the metropolis derives from the age-old trope, a staple of nationalist ideology, that all – as distinct from some – workers there were complicit with capitalist objectives because they, too, benefitted from them.

---

89 On this point, see Chapter 8 in this volume.
90 For details, see Brass (2011: Chapter 1).

Conclusion

In his 1960s analysis of Third World development, Worsley is clear about certain absences and presences: missing from the rural sector in such contexts are the categories of class, indigenous accumulation, and peasant differentiation; instead, what exists there is 'foreign' capital, and peasants as the main revolutionary force opposed to colonialism, their ideology/agency taking the form of populism. For these reasons, populism is regarded by him as the appropriate mobilizing discourse (= 'authentic' voice) of Third World nationalism. By contrast, Marxism is perceived as a theoretical framework that is inappropriate to an understanding of the rural Third World. Moreover, much like Patnaik, Worsley attributes poverty to appropriations effected by an external capital on a pauperized Third World peasantry.

Caught epistemologically and methodologically between sociology (with its emphasis on modernity) and anthropology (with its focus on tradition), Worsley rather neatly embodies some of the contradictions informing the 1960s development decade. Although he understood the theoretical difficulties with populist interpretations that had been dominant in the pre-war era, yet he simultaneously endorsed such views when applied to 'emerging' (= politically independent) nations in Africa. Hence the claim by him that the populist view of rural society as homogeneous and class-less was essentially correct. Consequently, populism as a mobilizing discourse was associated by him principally with an emerging nationalism in the Third World, an interpretation which cannot account for its current resurgence amidst metropolitan capitalism. Both the latter and the former, however, can be explained in terms of populism as a reaction to enhanced market competition, by employers and workers alike.

For her part, Patnaik not only constructs her model of imperialism on the basis of the earlier 'drain' theory of Naoroji, whereby British colonialism appropriated surpluses from India, but also extends this same process into the present day. That Naoroji, a Liberal champion of free trade, considered members of the Indian middle class blocked from access to jobs filled by the British as the principal victims of colonialism, does not prevent her from endorsing his bourgeois nationalist views as 'progressive' and of current relevance politically. In support of this model, Patnaik invokes the presence/role in India of the industrial reserve army of labour, a category initially absent from her argument. Unlike Marxism, however, which conceptualized the industrial reserve in the metropolis as a method of disciplining and/or lowering the cost of workers, she not only splits both the reserve itself plus its functions in terms of metropolis/periphery, but also dismisses its impact in the metropolis whilst privileging its role in the periphery.

Much like Worsley, therefore, one of the main issues Patnaik avoids confronting from the 1960s onwards is that blaming accumulation and its negative effects solely or largely on 'foreigners', in the process justifying this by invoking the agency of imperialism, cannot but divert attention from the presence of class within 'poor' Third World nations. Historically, this explanation has been a staple of nationalist discourse, particularly the 'drain' theory in the case of India, where the indigenous bourgeoisie have claimed that problems arising from poverty would be solved merely by ending colonialism. It is also supportive of the 'middle peasant' thesis, which itself has linkages with dependency theory and nationalist ideology. This begs the question of what, precisely, in such economic contexts a mobilization of peasant farmers would – and could – demand that is still 'progressive'; smallholders may indeed be a 'revolutionary force', but on the side of reaction. In short, the anti-capitalism of the right, mobilized as such by populist discourse.

CHAPTER 4

From Marxism to Agrarian Populism (*via* the Cultural Turn)

> My principles, sir, in these things are to take as much as I can get, and to pay no more than I can help. These are every man's principles, whether they be the right principles or no. There, sir, is political economy in a nutshell.
>
> > Words spoken by a conservative and anti-progressive clergyman in an 1831 satire by Thomas Love Peacock, expressing a view not so different from the twin policy objectives (remunerative prices + lower input costs) pursued by the new farmers' movements in 1980s India.[1]

∴

Introduction

The usual argument heard today, as so often in the past, is that Marxist theory is fundamentally wrong because it has always misunderstood the peasantry – and thus underestimated the enduring nature of their cultural and economic 'otherness' – in every form of society. Here this argument is reversed: it is because Marxism was right about peasants that it has posed awkward questions for those in academia who continue to study and write about agrarian change. Over the whole range of economic, ideological, and political issues, a clear-cut difference has always separated Marxist theory from agrarian populism, its main political rival where interpretations of the peasantry are concerned. This was a distinction embodied in their respective combinations of a discourse-for (what each of them endorses) and discourse-against (what each opposes). Whereas agrarian populism approved (and approves) of the kind of things and/or processes objected to by Marxism, the latter in turn disagreed (and disagrees still) with what is backed by the former.

The significance of this distinction lies in the fact that over the latter half of the twentieth century agrarian populism has resurfaced in the discourse

---

1 Peacock (1895: 152).

of the 'cultural turn'. Rejecting the previous modernity/development project as part of an inappropriate Eurocentric colonial imposition on the rural sector of Third World countries, the 'new' populist postmodernism analytically re-essentialized the identity politics associated historically with 'peasantness'. A major claim made by exponents of the 'cultural turn', however, is that – unlike its earlier counter-part – the current form of populism and the grassroots movements subscribing to this ideology are politically progressive, and thus models to be followed in the future. This re-emergence and consolidation of populism, both globally and academically, is itself reflected in the attempt to recuperate specifically populist interpretations of agrarian history.

Current analyses following this line justify their approach to peasant/farmer agency by claiming that a break exists between what they accept as old/reactionary forms of agrarian populism and what they argue are modern/progressive (= 'nice') variants. This is done by insisting that issues previously encountered at the rural grassroots – such as class divisions or backwards-looking rural nostalgia and tradition – are all identities/discourses belonging to the past, and as a result are now largely absent. Instead, these historical forms are said to have been replaced currently by a forwards-looking project in the countryside that is not only different but also based on modern/realist politics and ideology; the latter reflect the changed economic demands neither seen nor rooted in the past. The impression conveyed is that 'bad' populism is somehow an anomaly, not just unconnected with but a deviation from the contemporary norm of a 'nice' populism.[2]

For its part, Marxist theory is condemned for not recognizing this transformation, and thus for continuing to apply preconceived/outmoded critiques to present-day agrarian populism. This insistence on the progressive character of modern agrarian populism is also linked to the view that Marxist critiques have yet to establish its reactionary nature, or such objections as have been made are in some sense faulty. However, it will be argued here that these claims, advanced in defence of agrarian populism, are themselves problematic, both

---

2   As well as the two main case studies examined below, a recent example of this approach is Borras (2019), who attempts unsuccessfully to make a distinction between right-wing (= 'nasty') populism and what he terms 'progressive agrarian populism', a 'nice' contemporary variant. The latter, he maintains, consists of 'people of the land' who in his opinion have a natural political inclination towards socialism, defined by him as nothing more than 'a deeply democratic and egalitarian organization of power'. Missing from this pointlessly vague definition – which could just as well apply to some forms of accumulation – is any consideration of issues such as the ownership/control of the means of production, distribution, and exchange, property relations generally, collectivization, income redistribution, and central planning, not to say class struggle aimed at seizure/control of the state.

methodologically and in terms of theory. Furthermore, it will also be argued that the Marxist critiques deemed by agrarian populism to be absent or faulty are neither.

In the presentation which follows there are three main sections. The first contrasts agrarian populist interpretations with Marxist positions on the peasantry, together with the way each approach is endorsed or undermined by the 'cultural turn'. Recent claims about peasant movements made in case-studies of the Russian and Indian countryside are considered in the second, while the third appraises critically the view contained in these same case-studies regarding the existence of a modern/progressive (= 'nice') variant of agrarian populism.

I

Peasants, Marxism, Populism

In the two decades following the defeat of fascism, agrarian populism was supplanted both by bourgeois modernization theory and by Marxist approaches to Third World development. Each challenged static depictions of peasant smallholders long associated with pre-1939 analyses of rural societies in underdeveloped nations which tended to portray them as unchanging and unchangeable. Notwithstanding a shared commitment to 'progress', Marxism and bourgeois modernization theory subscribed to very different interpretations as to its systemic direction and outcome. From the 1950s to the 1970s, therefore, the object of agrarian reform policies advocated by bourgeois modernization was to generate a twofold process: by extending landownership, peasant proprietors would create a mass consumer market for commodities produced by domestic capital. For its part, Marxism viewed mobilizations by poor peasants and agricultural labourers throughout Asia and Latin America as heralding the possibility of a socialist transition.

The 1980s, however, were characterized by the academic decline of development theory itself, and in particular those approaches – such as modernization and Marxism – which adhered to notions of 'progress'. This was accompanied by the simultaneous rise of neoliberalism and postmodernism, both of which had a profound impact on the peasantry: one on its economic prospects, the other on its interpretation. Critiques of capitalism underwent a corresponding shift, away from political economy and towards culture/aesthetics, and increasingly took the form of opposition to the impact of accumulation on grassroots rural farming/tradition/culture/ethnicity. In keeping with this, class as an analytical concept was downgraded and/or replaced by non-class identity; modernity, revolution, and socialism as desirable objectives gave way to tradition, resistance, and a return to a benign (= 'nicer') capitalism.

The 'Cultural Turn' and/as the 'New' Populist Postmodernism

In order to understand the current relevance and significance of Marxist theory as the 'other' of the 'cultural turn', it is necessary to situate both approaches in the context of the development debate taking place over the last half century (and, indeed, earlier). Epistemologically, the 'cultural turn' (= 'new' populist postmodernism) encompasses a variety of frameworks, including those presented under the label of subaltern studies, ecofeminism, new social movements, everyday-forms-of resistance, post-colonialism, post-Marxism, post-development, and post-capitalism.[3] Of crucial importance, therefore, is how the 'cultural turn' represents an epistemological and political fusion of postmodernism (= identity choice) and neoliberalism (= economic choice), enabling its academic exponents to reassert the analytical validity of agrarian populism. This in turn has not just negated but reversed the political agenda informing much discussion in academia generally – and the social sciences in particular – whereby socialism was perceived as a desirable outcome of economic development.

At the root of the 'cultural turn' is the privileging by postmodern theory of language, and a corresponding deprivileging of socialism, materialism and class as illegitimate Enlightenment/Eurocentric forms of 'foundationalism' inapplicable to the rural Third World. No significance is attached to the link between language and the material conditions that give rise to or sustain a particular narrative. Indeed, it is a link the very existence – let alone the efficacy – of which postmodern theory denies. An important reason that poverty has vanished from the development agenda is, quite simply, that it has been redefined. Rather than being categorized as a problem, which is what Marxism and much modernization theory did in the 1960s and 1970s, rural poverty has been redefined by postmodernism as part of culture, and thus empowering for its grassroots subjects. Postmodernism has been able to do this for two reasons.

First, because many of those who regard themselves either as sympathetic towards socialism, or indeed as Marxists, have forgotten (or in some

---

3   Marxist critiques of the 'new' populist postmodernism as a result of long-standing theoretical and political engagement with the latter framework are outlined in Brass (2000, 2014), where further details about the case made in this section can be found.

cases never learned) what Marxist theory actually teaches.[4] They have as a result espoused postmodern theoretical positions (peasant essentialism, the innateness of nationalism, the desirability of grassroots ethnic empowerment, rural tradition as mobilizing discourse) that are epistemologically no different from the identity politics advocated by the political right. Postmodernists compare the nationalist discourse featuring subaltern identity to that developed in the first decade of the twentieth century, suggesting this is the way forward politically. In their view it is the model that the left should incorporate into its theory and practice because, in the present stage of capitalism, national difference and not class antagonism is the main contradiction.

And second, because the reproduction of capitalism no longer depends on the consuming power of peasants in the so-called Third World. What an increasingly international capitalism wants, however, is only their capacity as workers, for two reasons. On the one hand, to produce agricultural commodities that can be exported and consumed elsewhere, an old argument made by Kautsky a century ago, and still relevant today. On the other, as migrants to form part of a globally-expanding industrial reserve army, the object of which is to force down yet further wages and conditions throughout the world in what is now an international capitalist labour process.

This failure to understand the centrality of the industrial reserve army to the global accumulation project exposed the inadequacy of 'new' populist postmodern claims about the capacity of the rural economy and society effectively to resist systemic change. Namely, the truism long proclaimed by Marxism that hollowed-out petty commodity production is in the long run incompatible with the reproduction of independent smallholding proprietorship as envisaged by agrarian populism. Unlike the 1960s, when peasants were seen by varieties of modernization theory as contributing to economic development in two ways – as consumers and producers of commodities – now all that accumulation requires of them is their labour-power. However, because it does not advocate the transcendence of capitalism as a system, and perceives empowerment simply in terms of re-establishing/protecting rural culture, agrarian populism is unable to address this problem.

---

4   It is noticeable when comparing the extent and range of sources cited, that measured against earlier analyses of rural transformation many texts currently attempting to situate peasant economy in terms both of a global presence and of a *longue durée* are what might be called 'research lite'. The resulting absence of depth and breadth manifests itself in numerous ways, not least in misrecognizing – and thus conflating – theoretical approaches that are politically and epistemologically incompatible.

Just as the recent past has seen attempts to divide capitalism along 'nice'/ 'nasty' lines, so now we are presented with an analogous distinction between 'nice'/'nasty' populisms. In each case the object is the same: to present a tainted economic system and/or political opposition to it as essentially benign. Such attempts insist a better populism or capitalism is possible, despite being claims that have been strongly criticized historically and currently by Marxists, who argue that a better populism or capitalism is not possible. Neoliberalism is the logical outcome of capitalist development, to which agrarian capitalism is an equally predictable form of far-right political reaction. What advocates of a 'progressive'/'nicer' populism forget, therefore, is that in subordinating ever larger portions of the globe to the market, capitalism has triggered not a class but a non-class response. The dilemma faced by the 'new' populist postmodernism underlines what by now ought to be obvious: unless the very existence of accumulation is itself questioned, capital will always succeed in using agriculture for its own purposes, notwithstanding attempts to protect/re-establish a culturally 'other' form of peasant farming.

That a concept of an undifferentiated peasantry engaged in resisting modernity/progress is central to a postmodern approach to development theory is in fact conceded by one of its main devotees. Wrongly castigating Marxism (and bourgeois economics) for failing to notice that peasants have not disappeared, therefore, Escobar objects to development *per se*, on the grounds that it is an inappropriate foundational/Eurocentric imposition on Third World nations.[5] Maintaining inaccurately that 'one never finds in these [developmentalist] accounts ... how the peasants' world may contain a different way of seeing problems and life', he proceeds to endorse what is an unambiguously populist view of the peasantry – labelled by him 'post-development' – as an alternative to capitalism.[6] Development is in his view nothing more than a

---

5 Escobar (1995: 106). Needless to say, such an objection ignores the view of Kautsky (1984) who pointed out that peasant survival is an effect neither of its supposed economic efficiency nor of the desire of smallholders themselves, but rather of the need on the part of agribusiness enterprises and/or rich peasant farmers to have continuing access to the labour-power on the peasant family farm.
6 Escobar (1995: 111). For the claims which follow, see Escobar (1995: 205, 215, 219, 221, 225). Contrary to what he thinks – that development theory in general and its Marxist variant in particular has somehow overlooked the fact that peasants have 'a different way of seeing problems and life' – no theory of development ignores the presence, the content and the distinctiveness of rural opinion. The problem is that the latter is not uniform, and consequently economic and political interests diverge, for the simple reason that different class elements at the rural grassroots (rich peasants, poor peasants, agricultural labourers) hold opposed views about crucial issues such as the role of the state, land reform, property redistribution, wage levels, etc.

failed attempt to apply Enlightenment values to Asia, Africa, and Latin America, since '[i]n the Third World, modernity is not "an unfinished project of the Enlightenment"'. Much rather, instead of development linked to the Enlightenment, Escobar invokes 'grassroots movements, local knowledge and popular power', citing as an example the capacity of smallholders in Peru to 'reinvent ... elements of longstanding peasant culture'. The resulting 'culture-specific productive strategy' is categorized by him as alternative to capitalism grounded in 'the sheer fact of cultural difference'.

II

Russia Then, India Now

The two case studies examined here, by Henry Bernstein about rural Russia at the beginning of the twentieth century and by D.N. Dhanagare about rural India at the end of the same century, make the same kind of claims and exhibit similar contradictions. Both rely heavily on views expressed by and/or interpretations contained in populist and/or anti-Marxist sources: Shanin (cited no less than fifty times) and Figes (cited some thirty times) in the case of Bernstein, and Laclau and Mouffe in the case of Dhanagare.[7] Each ignores alternative explanations advanced either by earlier analyses of Russian peasants in the case of Bernstein, or in the case of Dhanagare by his own previous writings on Indian farmers' movements.

Replicating positions taken historically in debates about the role of agricultural production in the development process, Bernstein and Dhanagare subscribe to what might be termed broadly a 'farmer first' view. The latter has its epistemological origins in and is supportive of agrarian populist discourse/agency; it is also antagonistic towards Marxist theory which questions not just the political efficacy of a 'farmer first' approach to the study of economic development, but also claims that the current structure and political objectives of agrarian populism are progressive. Although accepting that his analysis is 'highly selective' in that it not only relies on a 'limited number of works' but also omits to address Bolshevik positions and debates about the agrarian question in Russia, Bernstein nevertheless fails to mention the outcome of

---

7 Notwithstanding his many endorsing references to the populist approaches of Shanin and Chayanov, Bernstein fails to mention, let alone to address, important critiques of them by Littlejohn (1973a, 1973b, 1977). Despite the fact that the *Journal of Peasant Studies* special issue in which the article by Bernstein appears is supposed to be about Marxism, it seems to be much rather a celebration of agrarian populism.

such an approach: the reification of an agrarian populist narrative.[8] Unsurprisingly, this has epistemological and political implications for the object of his analysis, which is to place 'the Russian experience' in the context of 'today's global capitalism'.

About the socio-economic characteristics and mobilizing discourse of the 1980s new farmers' movement, Dhanagare is nothing if not adamant. To begin with, his central point is that farmers are not peasants, and as such both the movement itself and the demands it makes are considered as being without precedent.[9] 'For the first time in the history of protest movements in postcolonial India', he declares, 'the new farmers' movements were not only advancing new agendas but also presenting new ideas in theoretical and ideological discourses'.[10] Hence the insistence by Dhanagare that the object of the movement was simply the realization of 'cost-based agricultural prices so that farmers (*not peasants* of the Chayanovian imagery) could compete in domestic and international markets'.[11] This emphasis on remunerative prices, moreover, was in his opinion proof both of a modern outlook and (consequently) of an absence of grassroots support for 'any strong nostalgia for "tradition"' based on backwards-looking ideological forms like nationalism, ethnicity, and caste.[12] According to Dhanagare, therefore, the sectoral divide informing the ideas of the farmers' leader in Maharashtra, Sharad Joshi – Bharat (= 'the farm sector') v. India (= industry) – refers to nothing more than an imbalance in terms of trade between 'the rural' and 'the urban', and is thus devoid of any backwards-looking ideological taint.[13]

---

8   See Bernstein (2018; 1128). Not addressing Bolshevik interpretations does not, however, prevent him (Bernstein, 2018: 1133, 1140) from dismissing Lenin in particular (see below) and, more generally, Bolshevism, both for 'ignorance of the realities of village life' because of a 'longstanding deficit in rural political work', and for not having a detailed agrarian programme. These claims about Bolshevik ignorance/absence, however, are not supported by other studies that are not Marxist – for example, Seregny (1989).

9   By the mid-1970s, therefore, (Dhanagare, 2017: 8, original emphasis), 'the Indian *peasant* had become a market-oriented *farmer*, although an overwhelming majority of them continued to be subsistence farmers, but now, less dependent on the landlord, but more dependent on the market'.

10 Dhanagare (2017: 62). The section continues: 'The ideology of the farmers' movements was a blend of economism and populism [a] calculation of the cost of farm production and the hiatus between the low support prices being offered to farmers and the rising costs of farm inputs. Such rational arguments were unheard of in the pre-independence peasant movements'.

11 Dhanagare (2017: 30, original emphasis).

12 Dhanagare (2017: 27).

13 Dhanagare (2017: 81–82, 84). Both at the outset and subsequently Dhanagare (2017: xiii, 36–38) acknowledges the influence not just of farmer leaders/activists, but also of Sharad

Agrarian populist ideology as a mobilising discourse is seen by Dhanagare as wholly positive: he insists that 'in the post-modern context, populist forms of protest politics cannot be discredited', adding – like Bernstein – that it is 'important to examine the emancipatory potential of populism as an ideology and of populist mobilisation'.[14] For this reason, Dhanagare approves of the positive interpretations of populism by Laclau, Mouffe, and Piccone, and – again, like Bernstein – is strongly critical of Marxists who question its progressive credentials.[15] Hence the antagonism expressed by Dhanagare – just as with Bernstein – towards Marxist analyses which seek to explain the social composition and mobilising ideology of the new farmers' movements in terms of class interests and class struggle.[16] Given this optimism where populist mobilising discourse is concerned, the decline of the new farmers' movement is regarded by Dhanagare as an unanticipated – almost inexplicable – political and ideological nadir.

Joshi himself, described effusively by Dhanagare (2017: 80) as a 'towering leader'. A result of interviewing Joshi seems to be that Dhanagare (2017: 92 n.17, 231, n. 16 and n.18) has become increasingly drawn to his views. Many of the arguments made by Dhanagare are prefigured in Varshney (1995: 118–19, 137) who not only demonstrates a similar enthusiasm for the leadership of Sharad Joshi, but denies both that the latter represents the 'old agrarians' (= backwards-looking pre-1947 populist discourse) and that the new farmers' movements are 'class-driven'.

14 Dhanagare (2017: 32, 34–5).

15 See Dhanagare (2017: 25, 27) who overlooks the fact that because they endorse populism, both Mouffe (2018) and Piccone also regard as positive the ideas of Carl Schmitt (2004; 2005), the right-wing Catholic political theorist responsible for legally justifying the Nazi seizure of power in Germany on the grounds that it restored stability/order in the name of 'the people' and thus in the interests of the nation. It is perhaps significant that this endorsement by those who still regard themselves as politically leftist has attracted scorn not just from Marxists but also from those belonging to the political right. Hence the view expressed by one of the latter (Lévy, 2008: 87) who observes that 'a whole part of the Left, deprived of Marx, is now embracing Schmitt – seeking in the latter the reasons for thinking and acting that they can no longer find in the former. A whole segment of the European ... intelligentsia is marching as a single man behind the strange and ... hallucinatory idea that we need a Nazi thinker to help the Left out of its gridlock'.

16 Dismissive views about explanations which focus on class identity/interests/ struggle surface periodically throughout his analysis. Thus, for example, the view (Dhanagare, 2017: 16) that 'the success of the farmers' movement ... cannot possibly be understood ... in terms of its being the 'old' *kulak*-rich peasant movement, that is, a class-based movement', and that 'it would be naïve to brand the farmers' movement as the rich farmers' or *kulak* movement'. Much the same point is made subsequently when Dhanagare (2017: 65) claims that 'the straightjacket theoretical and conceptual categories of Marxist class analysis [are] over-simplistic'. Following Laclau, therefore, Dhanagare (2017: 27, 66) maintains 'there is a need to go beyond stereotyped but meaningless formulas such as class struggle', describing the latter as 'a fetish of 'revolutionary praxis [and] infantile adventurism'.

Old Believers?

Where Marxism is concerned, the antipathy expressed by Dhanagare and Bernstein is difficult to miss. Nearly four decades ago, Dhanagare published what was then, and what is still, an important analysis of peasant movements in India in the period immediately before and after Independence.[17] Nevertheless, over time his political views have undergone a twofold change: to an increasingly benign view of populism and the new farmers' movements, and a correspondingly hostile perception of any Marxist critiques aimed at them. Based on what he argues is a framework informed by Gramscian hegemony, such positive/negative judgments pervade his recent analysis.

As he makes abundantly clear, the analysis of the new farmers' movements to which Dhanagare objects so strongly is a Marxist one. In what is a lengthy catalogue of shortcomings, Marxist interpretation is accused, variously, of 'failing to acknowledge the ability of populist ideological discourse to help the class-ridden agrarian hierarchy to transcend their class situations and interests'; of overlooking how rich farmers establish hegemony over middle and poor farmers 'through a populist ideological interpellation'; and, finally, of unjustifiably 'clubbing together' the Bharat v. India ideology of the new farmers' movements with 'postmodern articulations', thereby conflating subaltern historiography, eco-feminism, and new social movements with the conservatism, reaction, nationalism and populism of the BJP – all of which, claims Dhanagare, is 'far from convincing'.[18] Because of a 'theoretical and ideological commitment to orthodox Marxism', this framework is also charged by him with having too negative a view of populism: since 'populist movements have become a part of everyday life, especially in India today', contends Dhanagare, consequently 'this phenomenon cannot be written off as a potential area of sociological enquiry'.[19] Moreover, since Marxism applies 'the nineteenth century model

---

17 Dhanagare (1983).
18 See Dhanagare (2017: 29–32), who objects to what he terms the Marxist categorization of populism, the subaltern studies approach, the new farmers' movements, ecofeminism, and new social movements as all subscribing to postmodern theory, whereas the Marxist argument is actually somewhat different. Namely, that what subaltern studies, new farmers' movements, new social movements, ecofeminism, and postmodernism actually have in common is their *populism* – not quite the same epistemological linkage as that made by Dhanagare. Others who have subsequently made a similar connection between all these variants of populism include Roy and Borowiak (2003), Nanda (2004), and Cochrane (2007).
19 'Quite contrary to [the Marxist] negative depiction and delegitimization of populism', observes Dhanagare (2017: 32), 'Piccone [has] stressed the need to rethink the phenomena

of European peasantry to the post-Green Revolution, market-oriented Indian farmer', which he regards as 'completely misplaced and erroneous', it misses the fact that Sharad Joshi, 'always appealed to reason and rational thinking and not to arouse emotions'.

In the case of Bernstein, negative assessments of Marxism entail a dual approach, coupling outright condemnation of some analyses with the contention that others were sympathetic to the aims of agrarian populism. Accordingly, he cites the work of Trotsky, but manages to convey the misleading impression that he, too, shared the pro-peasant ideology of populism, whereas strong opposition to the latter view was a constant theme in all that Trotsky wrote about the agrarian question in pre- and post-1917 Russia.[20] Similarly, the case made by Lenin about class formation/struggle generally, and class differentiation of the Russian peasantry in particular, is dismissed by Bernstein, who follows Shanin in asserting that Lenin's analysis was not just methodologically flawed but its focus was also more on the urban worker and insufficiently on its rural counterpart.[21] Not only is no attempt to present – let alone engage with – the methodological approach of Lenin, but this assertion overlooks the fact that historically even those strongly opposed to Marxist theory have found value in his approach. Thus, for example, writing about the Russian factory system in the late nineteenth century, Tugan-Baranovsky not only upheld Lenin's calculations and findings but also endorsed his criticisms of populist methodology and data.[22]

The decoupling by Bernstein of peasant economic activity from Marxist theory about class differentiation and capitalist accumulation takes a number of forms, extending from on the one hand the assertion that exploitation/inequality had more to do with patriarchy than capitalism, to on the other the rejection of the view that *kulaks* were numerically/economically/politically significant, and the denial that they were producers (as distinct from moneylenders) and were anything more than middle peasants. Expanding on the view of Figes that exploitation within the peasantry is mainly patriarchal, Bernstein adds: 'that is, within "traditional" structures of inequality in

---

of populist ideology and movements as alternative discourse that its critics dismiss prematurely'.

20 See Bernstein (2018: 1127, 1133). The mistaken view that Trotsky subscribed to pro-peasant ideology is also found in one (Brenton, 2016) of the many centenary volumes purporting to assess – but the guiding theme appears simply to express hostility towards – the 1917 Russian Revolution.

21 Bernstein (2018: 1131, 1133).

22 Tugan-Baranovsky (1970: 302, 438–9, n.16).

the *mir* rather than manifesting capitalist accumulation'.[23] Where inequality and exploitation are found, therefore, this is merely an effect not of capital accumulation but rather of longstanding village organizational norms. Surplus appropriation is a consequence of family relations inside the peasant household (= 'patriarchal forms') and not capitalist differentiation and accumulation *per se*. This view exculpates capitalism and its rich peasant by transferring blame for exploitation/inequality onto 'traditional structures', thereby avoiding fixing this to rural capital and perhaps even denying the presence in the countryside of the accumulation process itself. Exploitation is decoupled, in part or in whole, from agrarian capitalism.

On the issue of peasant differentiation, Bernstein again follows Shanin in arguing that the rise of the *kulaks* was exaggerated, that such better-off peasants were 'never a serious political force', and that anyway 'it was difficult to distinguish *kulaks* from middle peasants'.[24] The inference is clear: by claiming that what were termed '*kulaks*' were actually no more than middle peasants, Bernstein is attempting to play down – if not deny – the existence of peasant differentiation and its negative role (both political and economic) in the pre- and post-1917 agrarian sector of Russia.[25] Not only are *kulaks* not numerous, therefore, but they are marginal to production. Contrary to what Marxists argued, Bernstein regards the presence and efficacy of *kulaks* at the rural grassroots in Russia at this conjuncture as negligible. Downplaying the presence/role of agrarian capitalism, peasant differentiation, and *kulaks*, creates a space in turn for the claim that current variants of agrarian populism are not just different but even more 'progressive' than earlier counterparts, and for this reason should be supported politically by Marxism. Among the characteristics which are said to be specific to current variants are 'ecological farming' and 'less emphasis on property rights'.[26]

That such antagonism extends to include additionally current Marxist analyses is evident from the denial by Bernstein that 'all agrarian populism [is] necessarily and equally "wrong" and "reactionary" '.[27] What is still lacking,

---

23 Bernstein (2018: 1130, n. 9).
24 Bernstein (2018: 1130–31). Significantly, perhaps, the same claim – that no difference existed between *kulak*s and middle peasants – was made by the Social revolutionaries, the agrarian populist party representing the interests of peasant proprietors (Radkey, 1963: 145, 249).
25 In his words (Bernstein, 2018: 1142), therefore, 'If the problem was above all that of the predominant middle peasantry, this casts a different light on … differentiation'.
26 Bernstein (2018: 1145–46).
27 Bernstein (2018: 1146). For an analogous complaint see Borras (2019: 6), who objects to the fact that what he perceives as 'broadly left-wing agrarian social movements … are often lumped together, perjoratively [by Marxism] as populist and dismissed as such'.

therefore, is 'a critical engagement' by Marxism with 'today's agrarian populism and the diverse rural struggles it embraces', which in his opinion elicits support because it 'appears a more vital ideological and political force [that] challenges ... any Marxist agrarian politics'. Not only is the claim that 'critical engagement' is lacking incorrect, but the 'wrong'/'reactionary' label clearly refers to what Marxist criticism says about the 'new' populist postmodernism.[28] Accordingly, negative appraisals are the result not of an *a priori* Marxist approach but rather of having examined agrarian populism in terms of its economics, politics, and ideology. It is precisely because of an engagement with the claims made historically and currently by populists and populism that Marxism has time after time declared agrarian populism to be politically wrong and ideologically reactionary.

Farmers, Peasants, *Kulaks*

The supposedly theoretical shortcomings/failings/absences on the part of Marxism identified by Dhanagare and Bernstein are extremely problematic. These are anyway surprising claims to make, not least because in the case of Dhanagare evidence to the contrary is found in two places, with both of which he is familiar: not only in the earlier collected volume to which Dhanagare himself contributed, but also in his monograph. Elsewhere, therefore, he accepts what initially he denied: namely, that 'the role of gender, nature or nation/ethnicity can and, in fact, does enter into the neo-populist discourse of the new farmers' movement', a view attributed to Marxism.[29] Equally contradictory, Dhanagare also cites approvingly the Marxist argument concerning the central role played by non-class identities – 'those that can be shared by them' uniting rich, middle, and poor peasants – in the populist discourse of the new farmers' movement.[30] So much for the supposed failure of Marxism to indicate

---

28   The call to back a movement or belief simply because it is 'a more vital ideological and political force' could have been advanced as a reason for shifting one's support behind the rise of fascism during the 1920s and 1930s.
29   Dhanagare (2017: 121–22 n.30).
30   Dhanagare (2017: 118). Lest there be any doubt as to what he agrees is the case, the citation in full goes as follows: 'It is precisely this development of a superior unity that helped a populist movement to deflect roles – of middle and poor peasants – that suggests ... "the possibility of identities/interests not only unconnected with class but also those that can be shared by them (disadvantaged otherwise in economic terms) with rich peasants (we-are-all-the-same by virtue of being rural-not-urban, peasants-not-workers, Hindus-not-Muslims, Maharashtrians-not-Gujaratis, Indians-not-foreigners) that populism discharges for an emerging/aspiring agrarian bourgeoisie"'.

how populist discourse is deployed in order to gain the support of those petty commodity producers who are not rich peasants.

Contrary to the assertion Dhanagare that '[a] simple class analysis of the farmers' movement in the traditional Marxist perspective would not, in our view, unfold either the secret of its mass mobilisation nor would it reveal the manner in which rich farmers succeeded in their hegemonic influence over the class alliance within the farmers' movement', therefore, class struggle requires that rich peasants – otherwise engaged in conflict with poor peasants who sell their labour-power – resort to populist discourse about sectoral and these other non-class identities specifically in order to divert attention from this class divide and its effects.[31] That is, precisely 'the ability of populist ideological discourse to help the class-ridden agrarian hierarchy to transcend their class situations and interests' which he earlier claimed was missing from Marxist analysis of populism. As misplaced is the inference that Marxism advocates writing off populism 'as a potential area of sociological enquiry': much rather the opposite is the case, in that Marxism has long argued the rightwards political trajectory of much academic writing about populism makes such enquiry crucial. That Marxism is critical of populism does not mean that it ought not to be analysed, far from it. Unfortunately, however, Dhanagare mistakenly conflates being critical of populism with a desire to avoid studying it.

With one notable difference, most of the arguments made by Dhanagare are prefigured in the agrarian populist framework of Charan Singh.[32] Regarded as 'the champion of India's peasants', he – much like Dhanagare – dismissed 'Marxist thinking' as 'a pathetic but unexplained faith', arguing that 'in agriculture there are many improvements which are not sufficiently remunerative'; not only did he advocate policies such as agricultural price supports and input cost reduction, but he also opposed land ceilings, wage increases for hired labour and was antagonistic to what he termed the 'socialistic'/'collectivist' agrarian programme of Nehru.[33] The main difference in approach

---

31 Dhanagare (2017: 16).
32 Proclaiming that data vindicates his view about the systemic viability of peasant economy, Singh (1964: 105) concludes in Chayanovian terms that 'these figures are an unmistakable tribute to the inherent internal strength of the system of peasant farming, its adaptability to changing circumstances, its capacity to bear the stresses of modernisation, and above all its power to endure'.
33 For these views, based largely on the peasantry in 1950s Uttar Pradesh, see Singh (1964: 25, 92, 96, 102, 336ff., 448–49). In keeping with the economic logic of the development decade, he observed (Singh, 1964: 102): 'It is high productivity per acre which is the crux of the matter. Once this is achieved, as it can be on small independent farms, the peasants will have more to consume and also more to sell'.

is simply put: cultivators described by Singh as peasants are labelled farmers by Dhanagare. It is perhaps no more than a measure of this ambivalence that Dhanagare not only uses the words 'peasant' and 'farmer' interchangeably, but also applies to farmers the same tripartite division – rich, middle, poor – as used by Lenin to differentiate the peasantry in terms of class.[34]

Nowhere is this more evident than in how what he wrote nearly a quarter of a century ago has metamorphosed in his most recent analysis. Then his view was that 'the peaceful assertion of *peasant* power through mass mobilization ... defines its class character', an interpretation which he accepted was 'not wholly untenable empirically'.[35] Exactly the same argument is reproduced now, but with one crucial difference: 'peasant power' has now been changed to 'farmer power'.[36] Further on he does indeed accept both that capitalist production in rural Maharashtra is reflected in 'the well-entrenched position of rich *peasants* in local power structures', and that 'the sugar lobby overlaps with the *kulak* lobby [which] consists of *peasant* producers who turn increasingly to cash-crop farming for market and profit'.[37] In short, his perception earlier was (and to some degree is still) unambiguous: that the farmers' movement was indeed no different from a peasant mobilisation, that in some sense it had a class dimension, and that empirically these characteristics accorded with reality obtaining on the ground. As presented currently, however, his view now appears to be exactly the opposite: it is a movement composed solely of farmers, all of whom are united by this identity and the economic demands to which such 'hegemony' gives rise. Indeed, Dhanagare seems at times to regard all rural producers uniformly as a species of 'economic man', striving relentlessly to enter and perform effectively in the capitalist market.

The claim by Dhanagare – like that of Bernstein – that the demand for remunerative prices is a modern phenomenon, and thus a characteristic not of peasant agency but only of farmer movements, is incorrect: he perceives a break where in reality there was none, there being significant continuities between peasant agency/organizations before and during the 1950s and the post-1980s farmers' movements. In a general sense, therefore, every agrarian producer engaged in market transactions can be said to have always been in favour of lower input costs and higher output prices. Historically, sharecroppers and tenants – no less than peasant proprietors – have pursued (and where possible organized in furtherance of) policies such as rent reduction,

---

34 Dhanagare (2017: 8, 39 n.6).
35 Dhanagare (1995: 73, emphasis added).
36 Dhanagare (2017: 98).
37 Dhanagare (2017: 108, 109–10, emphases added).

debt write-offs, and low-or-no-interest credit. Among the demands made by rich and middle peasant mobilizations in 1950s Andhra Pradesh, for example, was that for better provision by the state both of agricultural inputs (irrigation, electricity) and remunerative prices for their agricultural produce. In short, the economic objectives sought by the new farmers' movements during the 1980s are not as novel as Dhanagare appears to think.

Even in late nineteenth century Russia, rich peasants combined farming with trading and industrial economic activity, seeking to concentrate in their hands land, crop areas, livestock and implements. Characteristics attributed by Lenin to *kulaks* – such as usury, the production of marketable grain, all of which increased as capitalism developed – are no different from those attributed by Dhanagare to Indian farmers.[38] It is a view, moreover, with which Dhanagare appears to concur, in that elsewhere he himself uses the term 'rich farmers/ *kulaks*'.[39] Before the 1939–45 war, many peasant parties in Europe were members of the Green International, the forerunner of the present-day *Vía Campesina* (the umbrella organization to which are affiliated many of the farmers' movements in India), espousing a similar agrarian populist ideology and advocating much the same kind of political and economic policies.[40] Among the latter was the demand for high output prices and low input costs, or exactly the same policy objectives – sought by peasants – as made by the new farmers' movements in 1980s India.

III

Old/New Agrarian Populism?

The attempt to decouple peasant economic activity from capitalism, class differentiation, and exploitation ignores a number of things. To begin with,

---

38 References by Lenin to these characteristics as being those of rich peasants are found throughout his collected works. In a context of capitalist agriculture, objections by a better-off tenant to *corvée* or rental payments in kind or cash, or by a sharecropper to the percentage of the product taken by the landowner, are in effect demands for lower input costs. Similarly, rural agency to end the legal capacity of a landlord to appropriate a proportion from cultivators wishing to dispose of land itself carries with it the perception of what is (and what is not) a remunerative price for this commodity.

39 Dhanagare (2014: 52).

40 Peasant parties affiliated to the Green International were nationalist and supportive of religion, but against both collectivization and the State, blamed by them for low output prices and high input costs. See Vlado Matchek, 'The International Peasant Union', *The Tablet*, 19 March 1949, pp. 180–181.

early twentieth century sources emphasize both the fact and extent of *kulak* economic activity, together with rich peasant self-perception as 'benefactors'.[41] The various claims made by Bernstein, along the lines that exploitation was an effect not of accumulation but of kinship/family, that the presence of *kulaks* was exaggerated, that they were only money-lenders, essentially no different from middle peasants, and anyway posed no threat to socialist planning, is contradicted by the very sources he failed to consult: namely, early twentieth century accounts by a variety of politically different analyses. Far from being indistinguishable from middle peasants, therefore, *kulaks* were regarded as 'other', and perceived as being 'the bitterest enemies' of those at the rural grassroots: in short, opposition to *kulaks* was seen in terms of a struggle about class and was expressed in this kind of language.[42]

On the question of the link between patriarchy and capitalism, what must be understood is the extent to which it is capitalist production relations that transect the peasant household, and consequently kinship and/or fictive kinship (= 'traditional structures') present in the labour process correspond also to links between an owner of the means of production (a household head possessing land) and non-owning kinsfolk (sons, daughters not having

---

41 Stepniak (1905: 67, 69) notes both the reach and impact of exploitation by *kulak*s, which is 'imposed every year on millions of peasants in every region of the [Russian] empire ... Far from considering it as something to be ashamed of, the money-lenders always pose as the peasants' "benefactors" '. He concludes that it is a 'new economical regime which has struck root in Russia [and] is not only extending but acquiring permanent force ... There is no province, no district, in which the system does not extensively obtain'. In a similar vein, Mackenzie Wallace (1877: 105) reports: 'Not a few industrial villages have ... fallen under the power of the *Kulaki* ... By advancing money the Kulák may succeed in acquiring over a group of villages a power almost as unlimited as that of the proprietor in the time of serfage'.

42 Hence the following comment (Stepniak, 1905: 312–13): 'At the present day the bitterest enemies to the people are singled out from among their own ranks. They form a detached and numerous class, which has its adherents, and agents, and supporters. The hatred they inspire in millions of peasants is as legitimate as that inspired by the slave-owning nobility in times of yore. Modern hatred assumes the character of class-hatred, and extends to the whole social system, of which the rural plutocracy is the necessary outcome'. Much the same point was made by Walling (1908: 256–7), who observed that 'there is in every village a small class of peasants who have always been, and may for some time remain, loyal to the Czar. These are the privileged – the village usurers, the peasant landlords, the small merchants ... Between these and the majority of peasants there is arising the most brutal and terrible war ... From pillaging the landlords it is a short step to pillaging the rich peasants. The latter reply where they can with a forced confiscation of the weaker peasants' goods'.

property rights).[43] Furthermore, although he accepts the presence of *kulaks*, Bernstein maintains that their main economic activity is money-lending, and thus unconnected with production (= 'not to richer, more "progressive" peasant farmers, even those who might employ workers').[44] What he fails to note, however, is the link between money-lending and production: that rich peasants used loans to secure and maintain control over the labour-power of poor peasants, who because of debts owed to *kulaks* were compelled to work on land owned/leased by the latter.

Contrary to the argument that *kulak* economic activity was largely confined to usury, therefore, money lending was a method whereby capitalist peasants secured both land and labour-power (= means of production). Referred to by other peasants as '*mir*-eaters', *kulaks* use money-lending for productive ends: to lower costs and increase profitability across all their economic operations in the village commune.[45] Combining 'extensive land culture' with shopkeeping and trading, therefore, *kulaks* possess not only extensive property of their own, but lease-in additional land within the *mir*.[46] The object of money-lending

---

43   The way in which capitalist relations not only transected but overrode considerations of kinship in rural Russia is outlined by Stepniak (1905: 325ff.).
44   Bernstein (2018: 1130).
45   'On the whole', notes Stepniak (1905: 84), 'the *kulaks* and *mir*-eaters, as all observers agree, obtain by the bondage system tolerably good work. Working for a *kulak* exhausts the peasant's strength ... [e]mploying a much greater proportion of bondage work relatively to their capital than the regular landlords ... the *kulaks* and *mir*-eaters grow in numbers, riches, and power with startling rapidity'.
46   According to Stepniak (1905: 74, 75–76) some 25–33% of Cossack land – 'inalienable by law' – was in the hands of *kulaks*: 'Letting [of land] to *koulaks*, or peasant capitalists, is ... quite common and much in vogue ... At the present time, the new peasant *bourgeoisie*, the *koulaks*, legally have got into their hands vast quantities of inalienable communal land under the form of long leases'. Although only 5.4% of the population, such rich peasants have 54+ acres per household, and many possess between 270 and 810 acres 'of the richest black soil per household'. Other sources – not noticeably sympathetic to Marxism – confirm not just the increasing power and wealth of *kulaks*, but also how money-lending was used in order to get access to land. Hence the observation by Mavor (1914: 356): 'The prosperity of the *kulaki*, or well-to-do peasants, is one of the significant features of the period. The growth of this class was facilitated by the Peasants' Bank and its presence as an important fraction of the village population is noticed in all the reports from the districts ...' Similarly, Drage (1904: 120) notes that 'legal restrictions on sale of land and communal ownership, which hinder the richer peasants from extending their farms in a legal manner by the purchase of more land, force them into the position of moneylenders, in order to obtain the use of neighbouring fields ... Peasants who have been successful as farmers and invested much labour and money in their land are naturally opposed to the system of periodical redistribution, and where the number of prosperous farmers is large they are often able to prevent them'.

is also to obtain/control/cheapen the requisite labour-power for production on these rural holdings at a point in the agricultural cycle when competition for this commodity is at its height.[47] All this underlines the central dilemma the *kulaks* posed for Bolshevism. Unless their increasing economic power was reined in, therefore, any attempt by the October Revolution to transform the agrarian sector of Russia would be undermined.[48]

When considering old/new agrarian populist variants, it is not the case that what is termed the 'progressive' populism of today is in certain important respects that different from its historical counterparts. This challenges the view of Bernstein that current agrarian populist mobilizations and farmers' movements, in the form of the *Via Campesina*, are 'very different' from the rural agency of early twentieth century Russia: present-day agrarian populism is for him 'very different from anything that existed a century ago'.[49] Continuing in the same vein, he argues that 'the substance and styles of "peasant politics" have changed radically from the "heroic" period of peasant wars and their

---

47 'Credit is mostly given on the security of the peasants' work, their hands being their most valuable possession', observes Stepniak (1905: 60–61, original emphasis), adding: 'It assumes the form of payment in anticipation for work to be done in the next season ... A very important proviso [is that the] agreement never omits to mention that it retains its binding power for an indefinite number of years. Thus, if the [lender] should not require his debtor to work in the immediately following summer ... he is free to call on him to liquidate his debt in the following year, or even the year after, thus securing for himself cheap labour at a time when wages are likely to be at their *maximum*'. Many examples of wage differences between free workers hired in summer and unfree labour bonded during the winter months are provided by the same source (Stepniak, 1905: 63ff.), which notes that 'it is no uncommon thing ... to see labourers of each class working side by side, the one for ten the other for three and a half roubles per *dessiatine*'. For a similar account, see Walling (1908: 246ff.).

48 On this point see, among many others (again, not necessarily sympathetic to Bolshevism), Rosenberg (1934: 197ff., 220ff.) and Sukhanov (1955: 308). During the 1920s the Left Opposition (Serge and Sedova Trotsky, 2015: 142) warned that '[i]ndustry was still too weak to supply all the needs of the countryside, and large stocks of grain and of other primary products were accumulating in the hands of the *kulaks* ... private traders, more ingenious and flexible and also less scrupulous than the public sector, speculated in the products of socialized industry and resold them at extortionate profits; middlemen grew rich and the new capitalists were able to invest their surpluses in small businesses or to deposit them in the State Bank at a reasonably attractive rate of interest. These "NEP-men", profiteers created by the New Economic Policy, were a parasitic and demoralizing social phenomenon. Unless firm and prudent counter-measures were taken, the Opposition foresaw a multitude of evils: a conflict with the *kulaks*; industrial stagnation; food shortages in the cities and in the army; the growth of a counter-revolutionary bourgeoisie made up of *kulaks* and "NEP-men" ... and the final surrender of all the Revolution had stood for'.

49 Bernstein (2018: 1145).

contributions to the making of modern history'.[50] These claims in effect clear the ground for the main populist argument: namely, that insofar as contemporary forms of agrarian populism are different from their historical precursors, they can – and should – be regarded as 'progressive', politically speaking. Contrary to such assertions, however, the distinctions said by him to separate the old/new populisms are mostly non-existent. What remains a constant are on the one hand the political discourses and policy objectives, and on the other robust opposition to the state and anything resembling socialism.

Hence the 'ecological' dimension invoked by current peasant and/or farmer movements is merely a continuation of the longstanding agrarian populist discourse about Nature, and how petty commodity producers have always represented this (peasant = Nature = nation), so this ideological dimension is not in fact new. Similarly, property rights are still central to the discourse and political objectives of agrarian populism today, a presence registered by slogans such as 'peasant autonomy' and 'land sovereignty' (= the moral right of peasants to individual smallholdings) and 'land grabbing' (= struggle against depeasantization). Even the demand for higher agricultural prices – an objective currently affixed specifically to new farmers' movements – was made by peasants affiliated to the Green International, which emerged during the 1920s and was the precursor of the present-day *Via Campesina*. There *is* a difference, but not with regard to discourse/ideology. Whereas the latter has remained constant (= the agrarian myth), therefore, it is the *practice* that has changed. Nowadays academic populism is for the most part anchored in unthreatening agency (demonstrations, petitions, etc.), whilst the practice of earlier populists – the Russian intelligentsia who went to the people was not just physically and politically a more-risky kind of commitment, but also one that depended on a more sustained engagement with the rural grassroots.

The political object finally emerges: Marxists and Marxism, insists Bernstein, must accept the necessity, as he sees it, of change, by including agrarian populist claims and subjects in a broadly 'progressive' anti-capitalist mobilization. To this end he advocates a 'capacity ... to change positions, that goes far beyond the comfort zone of class purism and other illusions', by, among other things, 'accepting the need for some rapprochement with the middle peasant'.[51] If, as he argues, there is no difference between *kulak*s and middle peasants – that is, *kulak* ≠ rich peasant; instead, *kulak* = middle peasant – then what is advocated is clear: the inclusion within the ranks of a 'progressive'

---

50   Bernstein (2018: 1144).
51   Bernstein (2018: 1146).

mobilization of capitalist producers, on the grounds that the peasantry is, after all, undifferentiated in terms of class.

Instead of being differentiated by class, as Marxists argued, peasants have been re-essentialized by current agrarian populism as undifferentiated smallholders – or farmers – who are authentic bearers of national/regional/local culture. In this way, homogeneous petty commodity producers have resurfaced as the eternal 'other' of capitalist development. This is the discourse informing many 'new' populist postmodern analyses currently informed by concepts such as new social movements, the subaltern, ecofeminism, post-colonialism, post-marxism, and post-capitalism. Conceptually, the 'new' populist postmodernism replaced the disempowerment of class relations – the focus of Marxist political economy – with its opposite: the notion that, much rather, petty commodity producers in rural areas were empowered by the 'otherness' of their cultural identity. Contrary to the case made by Dhanagare, this applies also to the 'new' farmers' movements in India.

A Sense of Robust Realism?

If the economic distinction between the objectives pursued by peasant agency and farmer movements is less marked than Dhanagare imagines, then neither is the discourse used in furtherance of these ends. What he objects to is not just the application of a Chayanovian economic model to the new farmers' movements, but also to the view that such mobilization might in any way involve endorsement of a traditionalist (= backwards-looking) political ideology.[52] However, this objection is similarly contradicted by Dhanagare himself, where he states of 'the dominant class interests in rural India' that their 'political expressions and manifestations may be mediated through *caste, kinship and other similar ethnic or primordial identities*', and further that 'the sugar lobby ...

---

52 See Dhanagare (2017: 79–80), who notes that 'while the earlier peasant movements always involved one class or class interests against the other in rural society, the new farmers' movements have not tended to divide agrarian communities on economic (class), ethnic, caste, religious or political lines. The new farmers' movements have succeeded to a reasonable measure in bringing together the entire rural agricultural population and interests ... the earlier peasant movements had streaks of restorative consciousness; they at least tacitly glorified the pastoral agrarian *gemeinschaft* feeling of solidarity, with nostalgia, idealism and romanticism of the tradition (*à la* the Chayanovian peasant in Russia had). In contrast, the new farmers' movements faced the challenges posed by processes of industrialisation and modernisation with a sense of robust realism'.

is ridden with factional conflicts and competing interests, often mediated by *caste, sub-caste, clan or other similar primordial identities*'.[53]

In short, he himself underlines the presence of the very identities which in an earlier analysis he denies as having any relevance to or purchase on the discourse of the new farmers' movements, in the process castigating those who maintained the opposite was the case. Having championed Joshi's 'modern'/'rational' populism, therefore, a long way into his own analysis Dhanagare is suddenly confronted with what he terms 'obvious illusory and mystifying elements' in the discourse of the new farmers' movements hitherto regarded by him as progressive and 'emancipatory'.[54] It is a discovery so at odds with his own approach that, clearly, he remains baffled by it. Ironically, the main claim – concerning the unalloyed modernity of populist discourse – is also undermined by additional evidence, provided both by its author and by others.

During the mid-1990s, therefore, Joshi not only founded the BSP (*Swatantra Bharat Paksha*), so as to participate in electoral politics, but entered into alliances with Hindu chauvinist organizations such as the BJP (*Bharatiya Janata Party*), linked to the far-right RSS (*Rashtriya Swayamsevak Sangh*), and *Shiv Sena*, a Maharashtra-based rightist political grouping. Both the latter subscribe to a *Hindutva* discourse invoking ancient cultural traditions, practices, language, and religious beliefs, a backwards-looking ideology which proclaims Indian national identity as innate and ethnically-specific. Observing that Joshi's *Sanghatana* was beginning to admire the BJP, and further that the BSP was launched by him 'in an attempt to bring together all ideologically like-minded right-wing forces', Dhanagare notes further that 'impressed by Joshi's ideological articulations' *Shiv Sena* supported his bid to become an MP (2004–2010). Joshi in turn provided support for BJP-*Shiv Sena* candidates in Maharashtra.[55]

Dhanagare perceives this development as an anomaly, a regrettable and unnecessary deviation from the otherwise promising norm of a 'modern'/'rational' populist ideology, hitherto deployed successfully by Joshi so as to maintain new farmers' movement 'hegemony', rather than what it was: the culmination of an entirely predictable rightwards political trajectory. Part of the difficulty is that Dhanagare mistakenly equates Guha's 'subaltern category' simply with subsistence cultivation, and thus incompatible with those producers (= farmers) who grow cash-crops for the market.[56] However, as Guha himself makes clear, his definition of subaltern includes components of an agrarian bourgeoisie – or

---

53 Dhanagare (2017: 107, 109 emphasis added).
54 Dhanagare (2017: 88).
55 Dhanagare (2017: 217, 221–22, 226, 227).
56 Dhanagare (2017: 8).

precisely those elements which produce for the market.[57] Consequently, for Dhanagare the category 'subaltern' cannot be seen as linked epistemologically to the way in which rich peasants benefit from deploying a populist discourse.

In order to deflect from class divisions within the ranks of supporters divided by class, therefore, populism as a mobilising discourse has of necessity to invoke other, non-class identities, or the kinds of religious/nationalist/communal issues that historically feature most effectively in the ideology of conservatives and the far right. Misunderstanding this ideological role, due in part to his rejection of Marxist theory about false consciousness and class struggle, Dhanagare attributes the decline of the farmers' movement simply to the political ambition of Joshi ('despite its initial spectacular successes, started showing symptoms of decline rather too early [because] he was obviously harbouring political ambitions [and had a] hunger for power').[58]

Quite why Joshi's complicity with the existing political system may have undermined the farmers' movement is anyway open to a different interpretation. As leader of the Shetkari Sanghatana, he benefited directly from the religious discourse about Bali Raj, a mythological kingdom the presence of which is a pervasive component of rural grassroots ideology in Maharashtra.[59] Contrary to the claim made by Dhanagare, this confirms the important role in the farmers' movement of traditional ideology. Moreover, insofar as his person was identified by the members of the Shetkari Sanghatana with the deity Bali (the demon king) at the centre of this discourse, therefore, Sharad Joshi was associated with the restoration of a golden age era under King Bali. Once he joined the formal institutional structure of politics, however, Joshi in effect severed the link at the centre of this myth, and thus betrayed its object: the restoration of a golden age that would be not just different from but better than the present.

Conclusion

Any modern defence of Marxism necessarily entails engaging with what is now a globally resurgent populism. Accordingly, the question posed currently

---

57 According to Guha (1982: 8), therefore, among the social components of 'the subaltern' are 'the lesser rural gentry, impoverished landlords, rich peasants and upper middle peasants', which underlines the extent to which it is an agrarian populist category. This is one of the reasons why it is regarded by me as possessing ideological affinities with other, similar kinds of populism.
58 Dhanagare (2017: 244).
59 On the perception of Sharad Joshi as King Bali, see Youngblood (2016).

by Marxist theory about peasants is aimed directly at its political 'other', and concerns whether populism in its historical or present-day manifestation (the 'cultural turn', the 'new' populist postmodernism) is – or, indeed, can ever be – progressive (= 'nice') in a political sense. This is an issue that has been thrown into sharp political focus by the contemporary rise of populism in Europe, Asia, and the Americas. However, the deep roots of this question, both in historical terms and in long-standing debates about the role of the agrarian structure in socio-economic transformation (and systemic transition), are not always recognized, let alone addressed. The significance of these considerations is simply put: from the late nineteenth century onwards, agrarian populism has featured centrally in important grassroots movements and mobilizations, together with the debates and disputes such agency generated.

Regarding the main question posed by Marxism of whether or not agrarian populism is currently as progressive as its academic supporters claim, evidence suggests otherwise. Over a whole range of issues – among them the desirability/feasibility of the rural, nationalism, ethnicity, individual private property; the undesirability/infeasibility of the urban, Marxist theory, socialism, collective agriculture, state regulation – little or no difference separates new variants of agrarian populism from their older counterparts. Like its historical precursors, therefore, current agrarian populism is opposed not to accumulation per se but only to particular forms of capitalism (finance, 'foreign', largescale agribusiness). The wish of present-day agrarian populism to preserve/restore peasant economy, by resisting capitalist penetration of the countryside – but without advocating the systemic transcendence of the accumulation process itself, fails to confront the irony at the heart of this process: what capital wants from peasant economy is not its produce but its role as a source of cheap labourpower. This contradiction generates in turn the anti-capitalism of the political right, in that smallholders threatened with dispossession of necessity invoke non-class identity – nationalism, ethnicity, traditional culture – as their main (or only) political defence. In their struggle to compete or survive, therefore, peasant proprietors have shifted the debate with the neoliberal State from one simply about economic (which they feel they are bound to lose) to one about 'the social' (where they perceive their winning chances are better).

Of these supporters, Bernstein makes much the same case as Dhanagare: both maintain that current populist movements are not the same as earlier ones, the object being – where peasants are concerned – to recuperate and thus to exonerate the validity of populism generally as a mobilizing ideology, at the expense of Marxist theory about such agrarian movements. Each insists that, in contrast to the past, present-day farmer/peasant agency is neither reactionary in political terms nor does it advocate a backwards-looking/traditional ideology. Their reasons for thinking that contemporary populism is progressive are the same: because current peasant agency informed by agrarian populist ideology is aimed at neoliberal capitalism, consequently it cannot be regarded as backwards-looking and reactionary. Both undertake a double renaming: for Bernstein, therefore, no difference exists between *kulak*s and middle peasants, whereas for Dhanagare all peasants are simply farmers.

Crucial issues such as peasant differentiation, the class position and interests of rich peasant capitalists, plus the way these structure and inform grassroots agency in the countryside, are thereby downplayed or avoided. Where the interpretation of early twentieth century rural Russia is concerned, therefore, the fact that current agrarian populist approach insists – contrary to past and present Marxist views – no substantial economic and political difference separated *kulak*s from middle peasants, throws into doubt both the presence of class divisions at the rural grassroots, and thus the extent to which capitalism had penetrated the countryside. However, the shape and intensity of conflict at the level of the *mir* not only contradicts this assertion that no difference existed between the rich peasant *kulak* and the middle peasant but also suggests further that it was a *class* distinction fully recognized and opposed by all villagers involved in grassroots struggles.

That the struggle conducted by the new farmers' movements not only included better-off producers as well as those who were poorer but was also couched in terms of non-class identity does not mean that class is an inappropriate Marxist category to apply to an analysis of the new farmers' movements in India. The argument that categories such as 'peasant' and 'class' are relevant to an understanding only of pre-1947 rural agency, not to that of the new farmers' movements of the 1980s, is contradicted by evidence found in many different sources. This suggests that the difference between 'peasant' and 'farmer' in terms of characteristics and economic demands are not as stark as claimed. Furthermore, the transformation that has occurred over this period is much rather the consolidation of an agrarian capitalist stratum, an economic identity recognized by Lenin and other Marxists not just as an outcome of the accumulation process but also as compatible epistemologically with the concept 'peasant'.

Where Gramscian 'hegemony' is concerned, any view which follows uncritically the interpretation of Mouffe ends up subscribing to the notion of populism as an emancipator/progressive ideology simply as it is already constituted, rather than as a discourse possessing many reactionary components. Gramsci himself was clear that 'hegemony' entailed cultural struggle, precisely due to the fact that so much grassroots ideology was permeated by – and thus required opposition to – already existing 'common sense' discourse and concepts. In the battle over culture so as to establish 'hegemony', therefore,

Gramsci – like Lenin and other Marxists (then and now) – argued that much of the ideology circulating at the rural grassroots (customs, traditions) had to be challenged and transformed, not least because it was penetrated by landlord and/or bourgeois discourse hostile to fundamental change.

Since the connection between a backwards-looking ideology (= the *sine qua non* of populist mobilization) and the forwards-looking *economic* objectives of rich peasant capitalists is misunderstood, also missed is the significance of class interests/struggle. In their pursuit of lower input costs and higher output prices, therefore, rich peasants realize that, rather than agitating for such objectives on their own, it is better to obtain the support of middle and poor peasants for these same interests, which explains the crucial role that Bharat/India played as an 'us'/'them' mobilizing discourse. Hence the Bharat/India dichotomy informing the movement enables actual/aspiring rich peasants to make a number of interrelated claims: that all agrarian strata – large, medium, and small landed proprietors, sharecroppers, tenants, sub-tenants, and peasant families generally – are united by virtue of being rural producers: that such an identity ranges them all against the urban; and, consequently, that oppression/exploitation occurs/originates *outside* the ranks of the movement itself.

Again contrary to what is argued, there is nothing inherently 'mystifying' about the fact that the new farmers' movements subscribe to conservative and even reactionary politics, as is evident from the kind of political alliances (BJP, Shiv Sena) into which Sharad Joshi entered. Ironically, the similarity between the non-class identities deployed specifically as a populist mobilizing ideology in order to establish and reproduce 'hegemony', thereby avoiding political discord within the ranks of the new farmers' movements in India, and the populist discourse used by the far right have made it easier for the latter group to garner support from the former. It is precisely this process of ideological 'capture', together with the reasons for it, that a positive view of populism as an 'emancipatory' mobilizing discourse prevents one from understanding.

Against what its supporters claim, therefore, agrarian populist movements are neither inherently progressive nor currently so different from earlier variants. Historically and currently, populist mobilizing ideology – nowadays informing 'cultural turn' discourse – downgrades or ignores class consciousness/struggle while privileging those non- or anti-class identities (nationalism, ethnicity) which play directly into the hands of conservatism and the far right. This is precisely what Marxist critiques have always maintained was – and is still – the case.

PART 2

Missing Marxism

OUTSIDE THE MAZE © ANNA LUISA BRASS

CHAPTER 5

From Marxism to Late Antiquity (*via* Postmodernism)

> Claims of priority are common propaganda in all sorts of movements: we have had some remarkable examples in our own day.
> An observation by MOSES FINLEY about the role of religion in society.[1]

⋯

> It is the fate of great historians that their dicta are generally taken for granted in space-saving silence and are mentioned only on those rare occasions when their followers dare to differ.
> A reference by TENNEY FRANK to the work of Mommsen and Meyer, fellow historians of ancient society.[2]

⋯

Introduction

A central attack on the Marxist concept 'transition', involving as it does the general notion of an historical shift from one kind of economic system to another and different one, has occurred in what at first sight is perhaps one of the unlikeliest historical debates: namely, that about the decline of ancient Rome. This has led to replacing the question to be asked from 'When did the Roman Empire fall' to 'Did the Roman Empire actually fall?'. Notwithstanding their differences, claim and counter-claim in this discussion raise the same question: if the Roman Empire fell, or did not fall, then in each case why was this? Many of those who oppose the concept of decline now espouse the concept 'Late Antiquity', a period which it is argued by them was one of enhanced religious belief, economic growth, and general prosperity. However, this view

---

[1] Finley (1968: 177).
[2] Frank (1914: ix).

is faced by certain methodological and theoretical issues confronting the academic rise and epistemological consolidation of the term 'Late Antiquity'.

In the past, investigations of the later Roman Empire of the third, fourth and fifth centuries were scarce, because sources were deemed inadequate. Now that has changed, and the same kind of sources are mined for the information they provide. The problem is that the focus of the majority of these sources has been on Christian religion, which themselves contain little material on politics and the economy but plenty about culture. It is on the latter area, therefore, that research has focussed, and its study has become academically fashionable, a process that has in turn enabled the epistemological construction not just of 'Late Antiquity' but also a postmodern shift away from the equation of ancient Rome with a civilization and towards an emphasis stressing the empowerment of Barbarian 'otherness'.[3]

One aspect of more recent approaches to the historiography of ancient Rome is not merely setting aside but reversing the meaning of earlier arguments that have as a consequence all but vanished from the intellectual agenda. In the process, important details that – when brought together – provide a different picture or arrive at a divergent conclusion, have been lost. This, in some measure, helps to explain a noticeable tendency on the part of some current historiography about ancient society to celebration, an approach coupled with an equally pronounced tendency to dismiss previous analyses – not just Marxist ones – simply on the grounds of age (old = bad, new = good). Along the way, these revisionist approaches in many instances simply avoid engaging with prefiguring arguments contained in former analyses of the same processes and/or phenomena. Hence the recently expressed view that 'thinly disguised nativist tracts on how immigration … brought down the empire' by past historians who remain anonymous, since '[t]o name names would be invidious'.[4]

---

3 See Scott (2017: 219ff.) for a symptomatically postmodern instance of just such a shift. At a personal level, it is difficult to reconcile this conceptual downgrading with the visual impact of the Italian capital when visiting my daughter Anna during the year 2018/19, when she was based in the British School at Rome. The complex around the Imperial Forum, especially the multi-level building that is Trajan's Markets – an administrative centre – itself defies the removal of the term 'civilization' from what is seen there. Just as exponents of Late Antiquity turn to what architecture depicts in order to validate claims they make, so it is possible to invoke the architecture in Rome itself as evidence supportive of its designation as a 'civilization'.

4 Kulikowski (2019: 320). Although the latter declines to 'name names' of earlier approaches responsible for 'thinly disguised nativist tracts', it is probable that Kulikowski – like Beard and others (see below) – had in mind the work of Tenney Frank.

In view of this epistemological break, one can but turn to a magisterial account by de Ste Croix, which covers the reasons for the general absence of Marxist contributions to the historiography of ancient society, and also links this dearth to the prevailing silences, avoidance, and suspicion of Marxist theory on the part of many in academia.[5] In this chapter the object is somewhat different. Given the twofold purpose of this volume – both to trace why Marxist theory is missing from analyses of specific epochs, contexts, and issues, and to make the case for its return to a consideration of these topics – the requirement to place not just Marxism but its concept of systemic transition as embodied in the decline thesis firmly in relation to the way the rise of postmodern (= the 'cultural turn') has influenced analyses of Late Antiquity. A defence of Marxist concepts applied to ancient society necessarily extends to those analyses which, though not Marxist – and sometimes anti-Marxist – nevertheless share crucial elements (impoverishment, struggle, crisis, decline, transition, etc.) of a materialist framework. It is the latter, in its negative totality, to which those who subscribe to the Late Antiquity approach are opposed.[6]

The presentation which follows is divided into four sections. Specifically materialist approaches endorsing the decline thesis – including not just Marxists but also opponents of Marxism – are considered in the first section, the focus of which is on the negative aspects of religion and of the economy. A more positive interpretation of religion by exponents of Late Antiquity is examined in the second, whilst both opposition to and a championing of 'cultural otherness' at Rome, are examined in the third section.

---

5 See de Ste Croix (1981: 19ff.). The main influence on the historiography of ancient society of postmodern theory occurred in the decades following the publication of that pathbreaking Marxist analysis.
6 A rough pattern of the epistemological divide between on the one hand those who subscribe to the decline thesis, together with some or most of its accompanying conceptual framework, and on the other those who support an altogether more positive interpretation that structures the Late Antiquity approach, is set out in the following Table:

Later Roman Empire	Late Antiquity
Decline thesis	Flourishing thesis
Crisis	Stability
Transition	Continuity
Negative interpretation	Positive interpretation
Materialism	Postmodernism
Adherents include: Marx and Engels, Kautsky, Luxemburg, Frank, Rostovtzeff, Oertel, Walbank, Jones, de Ste Croix	*Advocates include:* Brown, Millar, Veyne, Fowler, Beard, Banaji

I

Accepting that the emergence and consolidation within the Roman Empire of early Christianity gave voice to the poor and oppressed, drawing a parallel in this regard with the nineteenth century pursuit of socialism by the working class movement, Marx and Engels nevertheless emphasized the huge difference between a struggle for social transformation within the existing socioeconomic system and the quest by Christianity for salvation that was merely spiritual, leaving the sources of temporal power intact.[7] As regards social composition, the Christian community – or 'congregation' as Kautsky termed its supporters – the heterogeneity of which meant that '[t]here was absolutely no common road to emancipation for all these elements'.[8] For them, as for the Roman Empire itself, a material form of transcendence was not possible.[9]

---

7   The duality informing this early Marxist view about religion was summed up in 1894–95 by Engels (Marx and Engels, 1957: 313) thus: 'The history of early Christianity has notable points of resemblance with the modern working class movement. Like the latter, Christianity was originally a movement of oppressed people: it first appeared as the religion of slaves and emancipated slaves, of poor people deprived of all rights, of peoples subjugated or dispersed by Rome. Both Christianity and the workers' socialism preach forthcoming salvation from bondage and misery; Christianity places this salvation in a life beyond, after death, in heaven; socialism places it in this world, in a transformation of society. Both are persecuted and baited, their adherents are despised and made the objects of exclusive laws, the former as enemies of the human race, the latter as enemies of the state, enemies of religion, the family, social order ... Three hundred years after its appearance Christianity was the recognized state religion in the Roman World Empire'.
8   'What kind of people were the first Christians recruited from?', asked Marx and Engels (1957: 330–31), and answered: 'Mainly from the "labouring and burdened," the members of the lowest strata of the people, as becomes a revolutionary element. And what did they consist of? In the towns of impoverished free men, all sorts of people, like the "mean whites" of the southern slave states and the European beachcombers and adventurers in colonial and Chinese seaports, then of emancipated slaves and, above all, actual slaves; on the large estates in Italy, Sicily, and Africa of slaves, and in the rural districts of the provinces of small peasants who had fallen more and more into bondage through debt. There was absolutely no common road to emancipation for all these elements. For all of them paradise lay lost behind them; for the ruined free men it was the former *polis*, the town and the state at the same time, of which their forefathers had been free citizens; for the war-captive slaves the time of freedom before their subjugation and captivity; for the small peasants the abolished gentile social system and communal landownership. All that had been smitten down by the levelling fist of conquering Rome'.
9   In answer to the question as to '[w]here was the way out, salvation, for the enslaved, oppressed and impoverished, a way out common to all these groups of people whose interests were mutually alien or opposed?', Marx and Engels (1957: 332) replied: 'This way out was found. But not in this world. In the state in which things were it could only be

Accordingly, early variants of Christian dogma were differentiated from later ones: the former contained progressive aspects that were erased from subsequent versions, once these became 'official' as a result of having been purged of any radical teachings.[10] Underlining the necessity of plebeian opposition having to 'wear the mask of religion', behind which there was 'a very tangible worldly interest', all forms of faith-based discourse were for Marx and Engels in the end ways of avoiding having to address the presence, the structure, and the impact on their respective congregations of secular power.[11]

The World beyond

The combined themes structuring the analysis by Marx and Engels of the reasons for the rise of Christianity were echoed by Kautsky. Not just the break separating its earlier radicalism from later conservatism, therefore, but also the fact of religion subsequently being recast as an ideological form of non-material transcendence.[12] It was, in short, the only 'way out' from the poverty

---

      a religious way out. Then a new world was disclosed. The continued life of the soul after the death of the body had gradually become a recognized article of faith throughout the Roman world. A kind of recompense or punishment of the deceased souls for their actions while on earth also received more and more recognition ... [with] Christianity ... a way out was found which would lead the labouring and burdened from this vale of woe to eternal paradise ... only with the prospect of a reward in the world beyond could ... renunciation of the world ... be exalted to the basic moral principle of a new universal religion which would inspire the oppressed masses with enthusiasm'.

10   'We therefore see that the Christianity of that time', observed Marx and Engels (1957: 326), 'which was still unaware of itself, was as different as heaven from earth from the later dogmatically fixed religion of the Nicene Council; one cannot be recognized in the other. Here we have neither the dogma nor the morals of later Christianity but instead a feeling that one is struggling against the whole world and that the struggle will be a victorious one; an eagerness for the struggle and a certainty of victory which are totally lacking in Christians of today. ...'

11   Marx and Engels (1957: 314–15), who note that although popular uprisings in the case of Islam were also rooted in economic causes, 'even when they are victorious, they allow the old economic conditions to persist untouched'.

12   'We have seen', concluded Kautsky (1925: 461, original emphases), 'that Christianity did not attain victory until it had been transformed into the precise opposite of its original character; that the victory of Christianity was not the victory of the proletariat, but of the clergy which was exploiting and dominating the proletariat; that Christianity was not victorious as a subversive force, but as a conservative force, as a prop of suppression and exploitation; that it not only did not eliminate the imperial power, slavery, the poverty of the masses, and the concentration of wealth in a few hands, but perpetuated these

and oppression experienced by plebeian elements in the Roman Empire.[13] Like Marx and Engels, Kautsky linked this systemic *impasse* to the heterogeneity of the workforce. Among the latter were found slaves, peddlers, and shopkeepers, as well as members of the lumpenproletariat, all of whom were united only by poverty and consumption linked to this, not by their position in the production process.[14] In this kind of pre-modern economy, the main object was to produce so as to consume: when describing the nature of the labour regime used in the Roman Empire, Kautsky is at pains to emphasize how different it was at the time he was writing when compared to that of early Christianity. The latter was largely urban, subsumed under a variety of relational forms, including labourers which Marxism interprets as unfree, and those working from their own homes.[15]

In contrast to the current pattern of accumulation, whereby deskilled labour that is unfree can be employed in conjunction with already established advanced productive forces, where the latter are historically absent the presence of bonded labour discourages the development of labour-displacing technique.[16] During the later Roman Empire, therefore, the labour-power of slaves and other unfree workers – for example, those who were bonded by debt – was according to Kautsky an obstacle to enhanced levels of productivity, and thus to economic growth premised on improved technique.[17] This was because, by virtue of their being unfree, and thus cheap, the presence of such workers – as

conditions. The Christian *organization*, the Church, attained victory by *surrendering* its original aims and defending their opposite'.

13 'For the slaves', explains Kautsky (1925: 412), 'the hope in the coming Messiah, the prospect of a kingdom of general bliss, necessarily was most attractive, much more so than practical communism, which could be realized only in forms that had little meaning for them so long as they were slaves'.

14 See Kautsky (410–411, original emphasis), who observes: 'Large establishments with free workers, resembling the large peasant family, were hardly known, slaves, domestic workers, burden-bearers, also peddlers, small shopkeepers, the *Lumpenproletariat*, these were the lower classes of the urban population of these times among whom communistic tendencies might arise. But these classes present no element that might have expanded the common possession of commodities into a common faculty of production. The common element remained a community of consumption only'.

15 Christianity in the first three centuries AD, Kautsky (1925: 464) notes, 'was exclusively an urban movement [of which] the free urban proletarians, workers and idlers did not feel that society was living on them; they all strove to live on society without giving any return. Work played no part in their vision of the future state'.

16 For more on this distinction, see Brass (2011: 32ff.).

17 Hence the view (Kautsky, 1925: 76) that 'the slaveholding economy technically involved not an advance but a retrogression … [it] lowered the productivity of the productive workers and retarded the advances in practical technique'.

long as supplies of them were abundant – provided employers with no incentive either to invent or to invest in technology, and thus held back the process of economic development.[18]

A combination of the plentiful supply of unfree labour that was cheap, plus a subsequent decline in its availability, was central to the process of transition affecting the later Roman Empire as envisaged by Rosa Luxemburg.[19] During the first century AD, a dearth in the amount of war captives – the main source of slaves on which much economic production depended – resulted from an extended time of peace. Since peasant agriculture had been weakened as large estates consolidated and expanded operations, the remaining stock of slave labour became more valuable economically.[20] It was this reduction in the availability of labour-power, argued Luxemburg, which – together with the need to enhance grain cultivation within Italy – necessitated what she terms 'a return to small peasant farming'. In order to obtain labour-power, therefore, large properties leased out plots of land in return for rental payments either in work (directly for the landlord) or in kind (indirectly cultivating crops for the owner of the estate). Her conclusion is that '[i]n Rome this was called [land worked] by the *colonus*', a form of tenancy that was the precursor of feudal tenure ('From this we can derive the first beginnings of the corvée economy of the Middle Ages').[21]

---

18 See Kautsky (1925: 63): 'In antiquity, this subjection took the form of a greater cheapness of labour power at the disposal of the possessors of great resources of money in the shape of an immense slave supply ... All of which are factors which decreased the productivity of labour instead of raising it. The necessary conditions were lacking in antiquity for a development and utilization of machinery ... the necessary incentive to thinkers and investigators to invent machines was also lacking'.

19 Composed at the start of the twentieth century, the analysis by Luxemburg (2013) of the Roman Empire was part of the *Introduction to Political Economy*, described by the editor of the complete works (Luxemburg, 2013: viii) as one of 'her most important books [containing] material not found in her other works, critiques of such theorists as Karl Bücher, Werner Sombart and Max Weber [plus] analyses of pre-capitalist societies, such as those in sub-Saharan Africa and pre-Columbian America [and] a detailed discussion of the role of wage labour in contemporary capitalism'.

20 'In the first century AD and thereafter a much milder form of slavery began', writes Luxemburg (2013: 324), adding: 'It is constantly maintained that Christianity brought this about. But it is exclusively the consequence of the fact that this labour power now had to be valued more highly, because there was no longer any surplus of it to be had'. Needless to say, the latter view is not one shared by the exponents of Late Antiquity (see below), whose positive interpretation of Christianity stands in absolute contrast to that of Luxemberg (and, indeed, other Marxists).

21 Her views about the emergence of feudalism are contained in Luxemburg (2013: 339ff.).

Important aspects of this same argument fed into the debate about whether or not the Roman Empire declined, deployed subsequently not just by Marxism but also – as will be seen below – by its opponents. Linking economic retardation and stagnation not merely to the rise of Christianity but to the wider process of imperial decline, Walbank extended the earlier case made by Kautsky.[22] Simply put, the trajectory identified by Walbank was as follows. Since landowners 'peopled the countryside' of Italy and Sicily with slave gangs, the effect of such unfree labour was that wages for work generally remained low, leading to a widespread pattern of underconsumption on the part of those employed, which meant that a demand for products was lacking.[23] As long as such labour-power was cheap, little or no incentive existed to replace it with productivity-enhancing technique. This in turn generated a trend towards economic decentralization, a retreat both to subsistence production in the countryside, and consequently to *re*peasantisation.[24]

This centrifugal process contributed to the growing economic self-sufficiency of large estates, 'the late Roman precursor of the feudal baron ...

---

22 Nowadays largely ignored by historians of the *Imperium Romanum*, and consequently unmentioned in most analyses of the Principate – but see de Ste Croix (1981: 550, 578, 643) – Walbank (1946) formulated his theory connecting the decline of empire directly to the economic stagnation arising from the employment of slave labour, an approach commended by Vogt (1993: 4).

23 This interrelated dynamic (Walbank, 1946: 26–27) took the following form: 'It was [the] landed class which peopled the countryside of Italy and Sicily with slave gangs ... Thus the atmosphere was wholly unfavourable to technical progress [and consequently] the classical world perpetuated that technical retardation which had been one of the most paradoxical features of the civilizations of the Nile and Euphrates – paradoxical because it was thanks to a unique crop of technical inventions – the plough, the wheeled cart, the sailing boat, the solar calendar, the smelting of copper ores, the use of the power of oxen and the harnessing of the winds with sails – that these civilizations had come into being. In both instances the cause of the retardation was the same – the bisection of society into classes with contrary interests'. He continues: 'Economically, the vast masses of empire never tasted the fruits of their labour; and this meant a permanently restricted internal market. Because wealth was concentrated at the top, the body of society suffered from chronic underconsumption. Accordingly industry had to seek its market either in the limited circle of the middle and upper class, together with the army (which therefore had considerable economic significance), or else outside the Empire, where of course there were even fewer markets for mass-produced goods. Consequently, the economic basis for industrialization was not to hand'.

24 According to Walbank (1946: 34), 'the large rural estate had always been the scene of a certain amount of industry', consisting of tanning, weaving, wagon-making, fulling, carpentry, blacksmithing, undertaken by craftsmen and specially trained slaves. As will be seen in Chapter 6, this volume, the process of repeasantizarion is the opposite of what Banaji claims occurred.

foreshadowing clearly the mediaeval monastery'.[25] As the source of slaves declined, large rural properties leased holdings to *coloni*, tenants and/or sharecroppers – 'forerunners of the later serfs' – whose rental payments to landowners took the form of labour. Furthermore, an effect of decentralization was that both consumers and producers were withdrawn from economic activity in urban areas, thereby putting in place a number of characteristics which Marxist theory – exemplified not just by Marx and Engels, but also by Kautsky and Luxemburg – associates with the rise of feudalism.

In keeping with the preceding interpretation of religion by historical materialism, Walbank also emphasized the dissonance between its being a 'from-below voice' and its disempowering economic impact. Hence the role of a Messiah as saviour was consistent with near eastern belief systems in which this discourse expressed the antagonism of 'those below' towards grassroots oppressions such as moneylending. As this messianic discourse spread, however, the more radical elements were discarded. Composed by the early fathers, the economic doctrine of Christianity, Walbank noted, 'corresponds exactly with the needs of the stagnating economy of the third-century Empire', which – in addition to locating salvation in the after-life – stressed both a 'modest income' and the need for 'prayer, holy conversation and good works'.[26] With the conversion of Constantine in AD 312, therefore, 'Christianity had come to terms with the Empire'.

A further indicator of disempowerment was the contrast between the rising incidence of religious belief and the decline in scientific advance, the latter being a condition of increased economic productivity (= the 'other' of systemic decline). The vacuum left by technical progress in Ionia, Athens and Alexandria during the fifth and sixth centuries BC was filled by religious cults that originated in the eastern Mediterranean, among them Mithraism and Christianity. Why the latter emerged as the dominant form is attributed by Walbank to a number of causes: the usefulness of its political and ideological discourse to the ruling classes, not just counselling acceptance by 'those below' of secular

---

25 See Walbank (1946: 35ff.), who notes: 'Each estate, in proportion as it became self-sufficing, meant so many more individuals subtracted from the classical economic system, so many less consumers for those commodities which still circulated on the old markets. So the large domain played its part in restricting trade and speeding up the general process of decentralisation'.

26 Walbank (1946: 60–61). Christian instruction about the desirability both of 'modest income' and more time spent on religious contemplation did not prevent the Church from becoming a wealthy institution. As Hardy (1931: 46) notes, in the fifth and sixth century Byzantine Egypt monasteries were among the most important ecclesiastical proprietors.

power, but also enhancing and legitimating this temporal authority in the form of Emperor-worship.[27]

Many of these themes inform a more recent and influential Marxist analysis, by de Ste Croix, of the issues and processes leading to the decline of the Roman Empire. His approach, however, marks a subtle change in emphasis where Marxist interpretation of ancient society is concerned: it is informed by an epistemological shift in attributing the main cause of decline not so much to the forces of production as to the relations of production. Whereas the focus of Kautsky and Walbank is on how the availability and cheapness of unfree labour (principally of slaves) prevented a technological breakthrough that would significantly augment productivity, that of de Ste Croix ascribes the same process of decline to class struggle. Over the period AD 138–235, therefore, the legal rights of the poor were 'gradually whittled away', a diminishing amount of surplus generated by slaves making it necessary for property owners to transfer the same economic burden onto the 'free poor'.[28]

To the prominence given by earlier Marxist interpretations to the ideologically disempowering impact on 'those below' of Christian religion, therefore, de Ste Croix adds an economic dimension: a requirement on the part of the Roman State to support the now-official but nevertheless materially unproductive clergy.[29] Coupled with a corresponding increase in the size of the army

---

27   'The increasing role played by religion in contrast to scientific thought', observes Walbank (1946: 59, 60), was linked to 'the services which religion could render to political stability [a role] recognized two hundred years later by Polybius, who expressed his admiration for the skill with which the Roman State kept its lower classes in subjection by a judicious compound of terrors and pageantry ... The political function of religion was reckoned high among the devices adopted by Hellenistic statecraft. The peoples of Greece, Asia Minor, Syria or Egypt were encouraged to satisfy their longings for a "Saviour", a "Benefactor" and a "Liberator" by deifying their various kings under these titles ... The practice had old-established roots in the monarchies of Babylonia and Egypt ... When Augustus made himself supreme head of the Roman State in 30 BC, he soon discovered the efficacy of deification. Julius Caesar, the hard-headed politician and general, now dead, was dubbed the 'Divine Julius'; subsequently it became usual to deify all Emperors'.

28   See de Ste Croix (1981: 454, 462–63). Taking issue with historiography that follows Gibbon in characterizing the Antonine era (AD 96–180) as a 'Golden Age', de Ste Croix (1981: 465–66, 469–70) outlines 'how the propertied class of the Graeco-Roman world as a whole were able during roughly the first two and a half centuries of the Principate ... to tighten their grip on those below them and place themselves in an even more commanding position than they had previously been, by reducing the political and constitutional rights of those members of the lower classes who were Roman citizens'.

29   On this see de Ste Croix (1981: 495), who observes: 'From the second decade of the fourth century onwards a new economic burden suddenly appeared, of a kind no one could previously have expected. With the adoption of Christianity as the official religion of the Graeco-Roman world, by Constantine and his successors, the economy had to support an increasingly large

and the civil service, this resulted in a situation whereby 'taxation became much heavier in the fourth century onwards'.[30] Because of this downward pressure, evidence for sustained 'from below' opposition on the part of peasants and urban labour to 'barbarian' invasions is lacking.[31] This, de Ste Croix suggests, is the reason for the decline of the Roman Empire: over time, the 'merciless exploitation of the peasants made many of them receive, if not with enthusiasm, at least with indifference, the barbarian invaders'.[32] In short, a form of class struggle undertaken by 'those below' against the increasing surplus extracted from them by the propertied classes.

II

Although hostile to Marxism, other historians of ancient society writing in the first half of the twentieth century – among them Rostovtzeff, Frank, and Oertel – nevertheless retain many aspects that are consistent with materialism, including the fact of economic decline, together with the centrality to an understanding of this process of the labour regime. Reading the decline narrative through the lens of the 1917 Russian revolution, whereby a Roman aristocracy and bourgeoisie were vanquished by armies composed of peasants and workers, Rostovtzeff nevertheless upheld the concept of economic decline caused – in an echo of de Ste Croix – by the 'hatred and envy' of plebeians subjected to increasing levels of oppression and exaction at the hands of the aristocracy.[33] Equally in line with materialism was his negative view about the role of Christianity in this process of systemic decline.[34]

---

body of clerics, monks and nuns, the vast majority of whom were not engaged in any economically productive activity and therefore – whatever their spiritual value to the community – must be counted, from the economic point of view, as so many "idle mouths"'.

30 On the increasing level of taxation, see de Ste Croix (1981: 498). The rising numerical strength of the Roman army and the civil service (de Ste Croix, 1981: 490ff., original emphasis) 'represented a tremendous drain upon the resources of the Graeco-Roman world', since many were '*withdrawn from the productive process*, and had to be maintained by those who remained within the process, above all of course the peasants and the slaves'.

31 de Ste Croix (1981: 485).

32 de Ste Croix (1981: 502–3).

33 Hence the conclusion (Rostovtzeff, 1927: 366) that 'the social and political catastrophe of the third century, in which the state, relying upon the army or, in other words, upon the lower classes, defeated the upper classes ... a fatal blow to the aristocratic and urban civilization of the ancient world. From this blow the ancient world never recovered'.

34 In keeping with the later view of Walbank, Rostovtzeff (1927: 364) maintained that '[t]hose who refused to surrender [to the effects of economic decline] took refuge in religion [and] sought deliverance from the pettiness of real life in the contemplation of God and in communion with the unseen world'.

Citizens, State, and Economy

With the anti-Marxist framework of Oertel, the narrative about the causes of economic decline alters somewhat. While the ire of Rostovtzeff was occasioned by a perception that the outcome of the 1917 Bolshevik revolution was prefigured in the plebeian struggle which ended Roman civilization, that of Oertel was aimed at the role of the state in suppressing what he deemed to be a functioning and prosperous *laissez-faire* economic system.[35] Although both objected to what each perceived as threats similar to those posed by the Soviet system, Rostovtzeff insisted the dangers came from below (in the form of peasant agency) while Oertel maintained they came from above (in the form of state intervention).[36] For Oertel, therefore, the operation of a *laissez-faire* economy was undermined by what he termed 'state-socialism', or tendencies 'that were opposed to the individualistic principle of economic theory'.[37]

According to Oertel, a combination of private enterprise and liberal economic policy during the first century generated a process of 'organic growth on the lines of *"laissez faire"*, *"laissez aller"*', the only limit to development being the obstacle to technological development posed by the agrarian sector.[38] In what is a veritable panegyric to the economic virtues of the Augustan Principate, Oertel chronicles an era of commercial prosperity which he labels 'capitalism'.[39] In no small measure he attributes this to the fact that a feature of

---

35 Speaking of the expanding *Imperium Romanum*, Oertel (1934: 384) asserts that '[a] worldwide economic system ... cannot develop when it is constantly disturbed through ... interference by the State in production and in the give-and-take of trade'.

36 Oertel (1939: 255–56) traces the chronology of decline to Vespasian (AD 69–79), when Italy ceased to lead the Empire, becoming as a result 'politically insignificant' at the time of Caracalla (AD 211–217). This was because army recruits came increasingly from the 'lower classes ... especially the peasant type', with the result that 'the centre of gravity shifts to these classes more and more'. It is important not to overemphasize the difference in approach between Oertel and Rostovtzeff, given that both feared Bolshevism and socialism, together with the implications for the bourgeoisie, property relations, and accumulation generally in their own time of what had occurred in Roman society under the Principate.

37 Of all the causes of decline, for Oertel (1939: 254) 'perhaps the most important of all was the promotion of State-socialist tendencies that were opposed to the individualistic principle of economic theory. ...'

38 Because Augustus eschewed the development of 'State-socialism', argued Oertel (1934: 386), consequently the 'old economic principle of *laissez faire*, *laissez aller* was left unchanged ... Free competition was to prevail throughout the Empire, and free trade ... Beside the principle of *laissez faire* there was a belief in the old doctrine of private enterprise'.

39 See Oertel (1934: 384–85): 'A fundamental change took place after Augustus had given the world the *pax Romana* and the *quies Italiae*, and had thus created an economic area

the period was the absence of agrarian reform legislation, plus the fact that it witnessed 'interference' neither with property relations nor with the 'old social order'.[40] Following the civil wars that characterized the last years of the Republic, the picture drawn by Oertel of the early Principate is an undeniably Panglossian one: industry, commerce, and a 'bourgeoisie' composed of citizen-farmers and freedmen all flourished economically, both within Italy itself, and in other parts of the Empire. This remained the case until the advent of 'State-socialism'.

What Oertel categorizes as 'State-socialism' – a threat as he saw it to to 'the economic system based on a private economy tending to individualism and [market] freedom' – emerged at this conjuncture, as urban production was decentralized or relocated to the provinces, and quantities of cheap slave labour declined.[41] This was accompanied by a shift of power from the individual to the state, the latter institution becoming more centralized ('State egotism') and interventionist – characterized by 'regimentation, standardization, and a dictatorial attitude' – from the second century onwards.[42] It was a change which, in the opinion of Oertel, amounted to a total transformation, 'of one economic system by the other', putting in place 'the substitution of a new civilization'; possessing roots at the start of the second century, it took one hundred and fifty years to accomplish, and was completed by the third century.

A different emphasis about the cause of decline, based nonetheless on the deleterious impact of religion, was advanced at the start of the twentieth century by Frank. His argument – now seen as controversial – was that in no small

---

characterized by an extent and peacefulness such as mankind had not previously seen [which] constituted a guarantee of peace and order'.

40   'Once the Empire was consolidated', writes Oertel (1934: 385) in a scarcely-disguised celebratory mode, 'there was, with few exceptions, no interference in the ownership of property. The time of *leges agrariae* was past. The distinctions marked out by the old social order were retained'.

41   For this and what follows, see Oertel (1939: 232ff, 238–39).

42   What Oertel (1939: 256) opposes is the kind of political development which Augustus had resisted: 'State egotism rather than altruism, by regimentation, standardization, and a dictatorial attitude rather than by control and paternal beneficence'. Although Oertel adhered to the economic concepts/issues consistent with historical materialism – decentralization, underconsumption, retardation – his attribution of decline to 'State-socialist tendencies' was criticized by Walbank (1946: 70ff.). The latter described Oertel as 'a liberal idealist' who – because he was a supporter of the market – disliked state intervention in the Roman Empire, believing that decline was due to government stifling the 'creative energy' of the market. For this reason he also defended 'the resistance of the bourgeoisie to the central bureaucracy'. This, Walbank concludes, 'merely proves that it is Oertel's own background in German liberalism which evokes his sympathetic attitude towards ancient "capitalism" '.

way the decline of Rome was due to 'orientalising', a process he equated with the decline of 'native stock' (= Italian population) and its replacement with 'oriental stock' from Asia Minor or Syria.[43] Unlike other and similar concepts that circulate in the present, however, in the case of ancient Rome this change occurred as a result of internal dynamics: locals were not displaced by immigration, since in economic terms immigrants were not attracted to Rome.[44] Instead, slaves acquired as a result of conquest or purchase eventually became freedmen, and – as citizens – increased in numbers.[45] To some degree, this approach was shared by A.H.M. Jones, when observing that 'a decline in public spirit in the later Roman Empire' was due to a corresponding decay of 'civic patriotism [whereby the] idea of public service waned'.[46]

This transformation, maintained Frank, underwrote the trend licensing political absolutism based on Emperor-worship and deification. The latter accompanied the process whereby the Italian population, which represented liberty and law, was increasingly replaced by those from the East who 'had never known self-government'. That is to say, inhabitants who had helped put in place the politics and ideology of the Republic, based as these were on a democratic ideal, gave way over time to non-Italians who did not subscribe to the same processes/ideals, and consequently lacked a similar commitment to their continuation, preferring much rather – or at least not objecting to – the anti-democratic rule of an Emperor.[47] An important aspect of this transformation was the change in religious belief, towards what Frank termed the 'emotional and mystical religions of the East' which privileged 'faith' and 'intuition'.[48]

---

43 In many respects, the case about decline made by Frank anticipates what is now termed the Great Replacement. As will be seen in Chapter 8, although Camus (2018: 163) maintains that, conceptually, the current Great Replacement thesis 'is of my own creation', therefore, much the same kind of approach was applied by the Frank at the start of the twentieth century to the study of ancient Rome.

44 The difficulties with this and later variants of the 'white fright' Grand Replacement discourse are not difficult to discern, involving as they do a focus simply on the ethnic or national identity of the migrant.

45 The rise in non-Italian population was attributed by Frank (1920: 156–7) to a liberal manumission policy that conferred freedom and citizenship, whereby those who started out as slaves were able 'to merge into the citizen body of Rome'.

46 See Jones (1966: 369).

47 For the influence of Eastern practices on Emperor-worship in Rome, see Garzetti (1974: 100).

48 Frank (1920: 164) sums up this position in the following manner: 'Did Rome's capacity to govern fail because the people of iron will, indefatigable purpose, and prudent vision that had built the state bequeathed its government to men of softer fibre'.

Although it is easy to dismiss this argument as racist, it is important to note that, economically speaking, Frank did not denigrate the foreign 'other' involved in the change he describes. Much rather the opposite is the case, in that he regarded such 'others' – Greek/Graeco-Syrian ex-slaves and their sons who originally came from the East – as extremely competent economic agents who deserved the success they achieved in the late republican era.[49] This admiration is evident from the way Frank described them, as '[t]hese clever Easterners', '[t]here was nothing they could not do', adding that '[t]hrift, cleverness, and fidelity were the qualities which gained them their liberty, and these were the same qualities which soon turned them into successful merchants and shipowners'.[50] Indeed, his criticism was directed not at these foreign 'others' but rather at the native Italians who – following the Punic wars – preferred to invest money in land instead of commerce and trade.[51] For this reason, concluded Frank, citizens of foreign extraction 'had little difficulty in outstripping

---

49 According to Frank (1914: 284–85) it was only under the Emperor Claudius that 'one [can] speak of state encouragement of commerce at Rome'. During the republic, those involved in commerce were not Romans but foreigners, who 'before the end of the second century [seemed] to predominate, and though they are called "Romans" by the Greeks ... a close examination of their names reveals that a very small percentage of them were Romans. The greater number of those whose birthplace is indicated on inscriptions came from ... Greek cities allied to Rome. The Italian names that occur are very largely such as found, not at or near Rome, but in inscriptions of Campania and Southern Italy. In other words, the merchants and shippers, the bankers and money-lenders, who followed the Roman flag eastward, were men who came from the old mercantile cities of Southern Italy, cities which, when allied to Rome, were able to extend their field of operation under the protecting power of this all-dominating ally'.
50 For these views, see Frank (1914: Chapter XIV).
51 The lack of interest in external trade/commerce on the part of Romans with money to invest is attributed by Frank (1914: 286–87) to an alternative source for investment, found within Italy itself: land. In an argument that anticipates the same argument by Wiener (1981) about how investment in land generated the industrial decline of Victorian England, that of Frank argues similarly that it was land inside Italy, not commerce outside it, which attracted Roman money. After the defeat of Hannibal, therefore, 'it was necessary to plant citizen-colonies [in] the north [where lands] were far richer than those in the south, and they could not easily be held unless colonized. We cannot doubt that for thirty years [203–173 BC] all the available capita;l and colonists were sent northward'. This could be seen as an alternative explanation to that of Walbank regarding the cause of systemic retardation. As has been noted above, Walbank argued that it was the availability of cheap/unfree labour (= slaves) which hindered the further development of the productive forces. By contrast, and with regard to a much earlier period, Frank contends that what lay behind a lack of investment in commerce and industry during the republican era *circa* 200–160 BC was the attraction of land for those with money to invest. In this framework, however, the non-interest of Rome in external commerce/trade is linked to a different case being made. Namely, that Romans were uninterested in foreign trade is

the Romans in these occupations, for the Roman was always a landlubber'.[52] Their only rivals in commerce and maritime trade were 'the descendants of their own ancestors, the Syrians of the East'.

These different emphases and interpretations notwithstanding, both supporters and opponents of historical materialism agree that what finally emerged from the process of decline was feudalism.[53] Nowhere does this aspect emerge more clearly than in the study by Hardy of the large estates in Byzantine Egypt.[54] Over a period spanning the fifth and sixth centuries, and based on papyri outlining the economic activity undertaken by the landowning Apion family, Hardy records the presence of institutional and relational forms that he accepts – albeit somewhat reluctantly – were no different from those characterizing feudalism.[55] Chief among them was the 'usurpation' by estate landlords of the executive power traditionally vested in the state. This in turn led not just to landlord exercise of control over irrigation, but also to the operation of private prisons and private armies (*brucellarii*), each of which were used to enforce the hereditary unfreedom of the estate tenants (*coloni*).[56]

---

presented by Frank as evidence for his broader view, that imperialism was not driven by economic interests.

52   'In reviewing the status of Roman commerce during the last two centuries of the republic', explains Frank (1914: 289), 'we have found that at first Italians who lived near the Greek seaport towns of Southern Italy were actively engaged in the Mediterranean trade. Roman citizens did not gain importance there until after 130 [B.C.], when they began to exploit their new province of Asia. These citizens, however, always lovers of terra firma, gradually drifted into capitalistic enterprises on land, leaving the freedmen of Oriental and Greek stock in Italy and their sons to gain control of the shipping. In the light of these facts we can readily comprehend the attitude of indifference that the senate regularly assumed toward commerce'.

53   For the emergence of feudalism, see not only Oertel (1939: 254) and Walbank (1946: 35, 54–55), but also – and more briefly – Kantorowicz (1965). About the Egyptian case, Frank (1914: 351) commented: 'The system of serfdom existing in Egypt could not readily be abandoned [by Augustus], and it was not modified to any great extent. Its adoption furnished a precedent for later emperors, who used it at least in the management of other imperial estates. Egypt, then, furnishes the chief, though not the only, link between the feudal system of the ancient Orient and that of medieval Europe'.

54   See Hardy (1931: 22): 'The twin institutions of the colonate and patronage laid the foundations of a new agrarian system. The binding of the peasant to the soil was no novelty in Egypt. It was the substitution of private landowners for the state as the beneficiaries of this binding which made it the basis of a semi-feudal order'.

55   Typical of this reluctance to label as feudal the system he (Hardy, 1931: 50) was describing is the following observation: 'There are admittedly many similarities between the economic and social conditions of Byzantine Egypt and those of mediaeval Europe, and the culture and general atmosphere of the period have much that is mediaeval about them'.

56   See Hardy (1931: 59–60, 65ff., 78). 'Are we justified in drawing any general conclusion from these various semi-feudal phenomena?', he asks (Hardy, 1931: 79), and answers: 'Perhaps

When recaptured, therefore, 'escaped serfs' were imprisoned, as were indebted tenants and their kinsfolk, until what was owed to the landlord was paid off.[57] It was, Hardy concludes, 'the way in which powerful individuals took the law into their own hands'.[58]

III

While the political and ideological conditions that contribute to decline of the Roman Empire are addressed by Rostovtzeff and Frank, for Oertel – as for Walbank – the decline is due mainly to economic causes, specifically the absence of a technological base to support the Empire, a consequence of technical weakness in ancient society arising from the presence of slave labour. Moreover, in the arguments of Oertel and Frank one sees presented – albeit in negative terms – the seeds of what later emerged as positive aspects: namely, the revisionist historiographical interpretations celebrating as empowerment notions of ideological and/or economic 'difference' encountered in Late Antiquity, either of 'other' identities and beliefs, or of economic activity. In the course of this revision, the historiography of the Roman Empire is transformed from the *sturm und drang* of systemic decline into a Pollyanna-type narrative of 'sweetness and light'.[59] As will be seen, both in this and the following chapter, economic decline is replaced with a doubly benign process: empowering religious beliefs combined with flourishing economic development, the latter reinterpreted as evidence for the presence in Late Antiquity of capitalism itself.[60] It is to these kinds of explanation that one now turns.

---

       the safest thing at present would be to say that many of the features of the feudal and manorial systems were present in Egypt in the last days of the Roman Empire'.

57   Hardy (1931: 68–69, 70).

58   See Hardy (1931: 67). 'It is a matter of definition whether we speak of ... manors', he (Hardy, 1931: 133) concludes, adding: 'They were places, in any case, where the system ... was applied in its full force. And the peasant who paid his taxes ... watered his land with an estate irrigating machine, got his bread from an estate bakery and his oil from an estate oil press, and knew that the estate prison was waiting for him if he attempted to leave, this peasant was quite well aware what the system was'.

59   Although describing these views as 'sweetness and light' might be deemed by some as rather harsh (which I deny), it is no more so than the dismissive epithet 'melodramatic' applied by Brown (2012: 9) to the decline thesis.

60   Just before the turn of the millennium, the conquest by those opposed to the decline thesis was announced in the following manner (Bowersock, 1996: 42): 'Now, in 1995, it is probably fair to say that no responsible historian of the ancient or medieval world would want to address or acknowledge the fall of Rome as either fact or paradigm'.

Not Death but Resurrection

Late Antiquity covers the era roughly from AD 200 to 800, designated earlier as the Later Roman Empire, and is a concept formulated from around the 1970s onwards, largely by the historian Peter Brown.[61] Opposed strongly to the notion of general systemic decline previously attached to the *Imperium Romanum*, it is an historiographical approach which challenges – and claims epistemologically to have reversed – all preceding negative interpretations of the social and economic processes associated with the view that the Roman Empire 'fell'. This it does with particular reference to the role of religion, which is transformed from a disempowering to an empowering form of belief.[62] The latter outcome, argue exponents of Late Antiquity, is mainly a consequence of scholarly rediscovery of the period in question as having been an 'authentic' and 'organic' expression of religious faith held by plebeian elements at the rural grassroots. By this criterion, it is inferred, does the revision of the earlier negative interpretation stand – or, indeed, fall.

---

61 As argued in an influential 1971 publication by Brown (1989: 209), 'I wished to bring to the average reader a sense of the richness and excitement of a once-neglected period, now known as "Late Antiquity"', an approach which concentrated 'on the cultural and religious history of the period, and on the social changes'. Its declared object was to direct 'the reader's attention away from areas which had, until then, held the centre of the stage in most accounts of the decline and fall of the Roman Empire ...'. Four decades on, he (Brown, 2012: 8–9) restates this argument even more strongly: 'Taking a wider view of Roman history, many scholars have been tempted to think that the fourth century was an age dwarfed by the achievements of the empire in previous centuries. Romans of the fourth century have often been presented as the inhabitants of a deeply impoverished empire, busied among the ruins of their former greatness and engaged in desperate and violent attempts to hold back, for a moment, an ineluctable process of decline that had begun around the year 200 AD. It used to be widely believed that the decline and fall of the Western empire in the generations after the Gothic sack of Rome in 410 only marked the end of a story of progressive breakdown ... The fourth century was already a sinister prelude to the European middle ages'. His emphatic conclusion is: 'This melodramatic view dominated the historiography of the first part of the twentieth century ... this is not the opinion of this author'. About the pivotal contribution of Brown to discussions as to whether or not the Roman Empire declined, Bowersock (1996: 34) notes: 'The debate and subsequent work have gone on still further to annihilate those secure boundaries with which we all once felt comfortable in contemplating the ancient past.

62 The crux of this revisionist argument is as follows (Brown, 1978: 4–5): 'A period of military defeat and of undeniable insecurity among the governing classes of the Roman Empire may not have had repercussions in Roman society at large sufficiently drastic to produce, by way of immediate reaction, the religious changes we ascribe to this period. It is for this reason that I have long been dissatisfied with the idea of a general "crisis" of the third century as a *passe-partout* explanation for the emergence of the distinctive features of Late Antique religion'.

In the course of this revision, all the main concepts and causes informing materialist analyses – stagnation, economic decline, political crises, the rise of feudalism – are discarded. For Brown, as for other exponents of Late Antiquity, the turn to religion was not an effect of economic and/or political crisis in urban contexts, but rather a 'natural' aspect of daily life in rural areas. The latter, Brown infers, were contexts largely untouched by what happened in the great urban centres: for this reason, he stresses the element of religious continuity, since 'changes did not come as disturbing visitations from outside'. That is to say, the dynamic structuring religious change was gradual and internal, not an effect of sudden and external crisis.[63] In his view, therefore, religious histories of the later Roman Empire tended to over-emphasize the rise of 'superstition' and a corresponding decline of 'rationalism'.[64]

According to Brown, the main transformation that took place over the period AD 200–500 was that humanity now had direct access on earth to 'divine power'. In order to effect this epistemological redirection of the approach to Late Antiquity, he also dismisses earlier interpretations – among them the economic and negative ones advanced by supporters and opponents of historical materialism – in which religion appeared 'as the irruption from the outside' of 'oriental' or 'lower class' beliefs.[65] Building on this rejection of political theory and contemporary social science paradigms, Brown asserts that '[w]ords like "conservative" or "traditionalist"… are inapplicable to the study of this period',

---

63   According to Brown (1978: 9), therefore, 'the changes that come about in Late Antiquity can best be seen as a redistribution and a reorchestration of components that had already existed for centuries in the Mediterranean world … changes did not come as disturbing visitations from outside … [Consequently] we must be careful to avoid melodramatic insistence on sudden and widespread changes inn the climate of religious belief in the Mediterranean world of the second and third centuries'.

64   Brown (1978: 10–11) states that 'I would wish to plead that the modern scholar should, at least, begin his study of [people in Late Antiquity] by setting aside holy dread. Many of the religious histories of the Late Antique period … have spoken of the emergence of Late Antique civilization in terms of the rise of "superstition," of a "failure of nerve," or of a "decline of rationalism," In doing so, they seem to miss the point. …'

65   See Brown (1978: 7–8), whose unwarranted rejection of the element of class in this cavalier fashion has been noticed by other historians of ancient society. His work has been criticized by de Ste Croix (1981: 447) because it 'is marred by blindness to the realities of the class struggle in the Later Roman Empire': in support of this critique, de Ste Croix (1981: 583, n.24) refers, for example, to a case in which 'the shortage of food was due largely to the greed of the rich men [a fact that] does not emerge at all in the treatment of this incident by Peter Brown'. Similarly critical is the view (de Ste Croix, 1981: 584–85, n.42) to the effect that 'Brown, who has never grasped the realities of the class struggle in the ancient world, can see only the good side of patronage, and his bland account of that institution gives only a fraction of the real picture'.

since it is not 'possible to make a distinction between the "unthinking" masses and the sophisticated agonizing of a small leisured minority'.[66]

Not the least of the many ironies licensed by this approach are two in particular. Having ruled out any contribution to an understanding of Late Antiquity by contemporary social and political science paradigms, Brown then endorses the relevance to his kind of approach of both anthropology and (latterly) postmodernism. Furthermore, and as will be seen below, his twofold assertion concerning the irrelevance of political/social theory coupled with the absence of a distinction between the masses and a 'leisured minority' exposes the frailty of his methodological approach to the study of Late Antiquity. This is because 'going to the people' in his case amounts to the study of texts – written within a religious discourse, which hides as much as they reveal – which do not correspond to direct access to the unheard plebeian voice and opinion, about religion and much else, circulating at the rural grassroots.

Hence for Brown the twofold inference is clear. First, that political crisis and economic decline, issues which earlier were central to supporters and opponents of historical materialism, are of negligible significance epistemologically. And second, that consequently over the second and third centuries religion has to be seen differently: not as a reaction to negative exogenous processes/events, but as positive, endogenous and the outcome of slow growth. It was, in short, an 'organic' belief system of long standing at the rural grassroots, where its circulation and reproduction was – and now must be appreciated as – a 'natural' phenomenon. Here Brown sets out what amounts to a methodological agenda, a *de facto* approach based on addressing/understanding the rural grassroots discourse about religious belief which, so he argues, will confound 'much of the conventional political and administrative history of the Later Roman Empire'.[67] This is because religious changes of the third century 'cannot be reduced to so many "reactions" to public calamity', but must be 'sought out in the more intimate areas over a wider time span'.

One of the principal claims buttressing the novelty attributed by Brown not just to Christian religion but also conceptually to Late Antiquity itself, concerns what he presents as a break separating the pagan deity-in-heaven of the *Imperium Romanum* from the later deity-on-earth of Christianity.[68] Central to

---

66   Brown (1978: 9).
67   Brown (1978: 6).
68   '*Epigeios theos*: the term [a god upon earth] sums up the Late Antique revolution', argues Brown (1978: 17): 'Heaven and earth have come to be joined in the figure of a human being, and this joining has been brought about so that other human beings could enter the life of a newly formed group under his guidance. "Heavenly" power is used, on earth, by human beings to rule other human beings'. He concludes (Brown, 1978: 98): 'We are dealing, in

this split is an inferred process of democratization, whereby plebeians, in the shape of the Christian congregation, had as a result a more direct access to the divine, who was now present on earth. On the face of it, this seems to contradict his view that religious belief in Late Antiquity did not entail a 'dramatic "diffusion" of novel ideas'.[69] However, even accepting the distinction Brown makes, problems remain. In religious terms, therefore, no break existed between Emperor-worship and authority on the one hand, and Christian belief in the power/authority of the divine: the Emperor as deity-on-earth becomes God-the-father, whose son – also divine – is born on earth. In each case, therefore, divine power/authority fuses with and is supportive of its temporal equivalent.

IV

Mimicking postmodern support for the culture of the migrant 'other', current historiography of ancient Rome reverses the earlier negative interpretation of Frank and recasts 'otherness' as positive. Accordingly, focus has shifted, both epistemologically and (thus) politically: away from a discourse about locals-as-victims to one about migrants-as-culturally-empowered. The emphasis is no longer on the disadvantages to the (Italian) self, as argued long ago by Frank, but rather on the advantages of incorporation enjoyed by the (non-Italian) 'other'.[70] As in the case of so many other contexts, epochs, and issues, the historiography of ancient Rome has not escaped the desire by postmodern theory to find instances of culturally empowering 'otherness' involving identity politics.[71]

---

the fourth century, with a sensibility that was at once more sombre and yet more stable in its expectations of where the locus of the supernatural was to be found. The Christian bishop, the Christian "holy man,", the physical remains of the Christian martyr stand out al the more clearly because the upward ceiling of human contact with the divine has come to be drawn more firmly'.

69 Brown (1978: 7).
70 Although no mention is made of him by name, it is clear that Beard (2013: 179) has Frank in mind when she makes the following dismissive observation: "No writers today quite echo the strident complaints of early twentieth-century historians who ... lamented the dilution of true Italian stock with the foreign blood of freedman, whose origins often lay in the East."
71 For a somewhat bewildered response to the impact on the historiography of ancient society of postmodernism, and one that is very different from an materialist critique, see Bowersock (1996: 38–39) who writes: 'The move away from the fall of Rome to a creative and vibrant late antiquity must also be seen in the perspective of the fin de siècle in which we are now living ... Now a tide of relativism has made us receptive – arguably, too receptive – to forms of culture ... The seductive powers of rhetoric have been reaffirmed ... to assist the annihilation of historical certainties ... The relativist approach, combined with a new awareness of the force of religion and its highly rhetorical theology, opened up the

Noting that 'scholarly views of Roman imperialism and colonialism have altered considerably in the past few decades', Adler describes the result of this kind of reinterpretation in the following manner: 'Rome the reflective, self-conscious power is out; Rome the self-assured maligner of other cultures is in'.[72] It is not surprising, therefore, to encounter in a number of current analyses influenced by postmodernism a positive reading of the very same processes understood as negative by adherents of the decline thesis.

Postmodernizing Premodernity

This is itself part of a broader trend, away from materialist concepts positing the existence of an objective reality and towards a postmodern aporia, or the notion that historiography of ancient Rome is nothing more than literature.[73] Consistent with the latter approach is the privileging of culture at the expense of political economy, an epistemological break that moves the element of determination from the material base to superstructural phenomena. In what is an unmistakeably Panglossian view, one such analysis – by Beard, an influential present-day historian of ancient society – perceives the extension of citizenship and the consequent increasing ethnic/national 'otherness' of Rome's population as a positive development, evidence simply of success, without asking too closely either about the political implications of this or about its impact on the labour market and working conditions.[74] That such a celebratory approach

---

        possibility of turning one's back on the majesty of the Roman Empire in order to salute Byzantium, Ravenna, and Mecca'.

72   Adler (2011: 1).

73   On this point, see Lendon (2009), who observes that "most contemporary writing in English about Latin historians slights these historians' concern for truth, [an] indifference to so important a part of what historians thought they were doing [that] constitutes a pervasive affliction in the scholarship ...". Aporia is central to the "new" populist postmodernism, since by questioning reality – *all* reality – it bolsters the view that nothing is (or ever can be) real, and consequently history is just competing opinions: epistemologically, no objective reality is possible, or indeed desirable.

74   Significantly, this positive interpretation (Beard, 2016: 330) regarding the 'widespread image of Rome as an open culture [which] made the Roman citizen body the most ethnically diverse that there ever was before the modern world' is itself structured by an idealized/benign view of slavery. The latter takes the form that no clear line separated the free from the unfree, and that slavery was anyway only a 'temporary status'. In short, the familiar revisionist trope to the effect the unfree were essentially no different from the free, a claim based on the observation that both worked together, alongside one another. Such a view overlooks a number of things. To begin with, substantial evidence confirms that in other contexts where free and unfree toiled together, differences did occur, in

fails to engage analytically with political economy invites a riposte to criticism that those who invoke Roman history in order to draw parallels with contemporary developments do so without knowledge of the former.[75] Much rather, it could be said that those who apply to ancient society currently fashionable paradigms drawn from the present invariably do so without knowledge of the latter.[76]

Descriptive terms like 'an open culture' that was 'ethnically diverse', however, tell us little or nothing about *how* ethnic/national 'otherness' was perceived, by whom, and why. Accordingly, there are reasons for questioning the extent to which the presence in Rome of 'multiculturalism' was viewed as positively as the use of this postmodern concept implies. It comes as no surprise that Roman historians and other commentators had mixed opinions about conquered Gauls and Germans, expressing contempt for some of their social practices but admiring their courage in battle. Of significance, therefore, is one particular economic cause that in the case of Rome generated the disdainful invocation of ethnic/national 'otherness'.[77] As projected through the work of Juvenal and Lucian, this xenophobic/racist discourse arose when there was fierce competition for employment, and those who were unsuccessful attributed this to the ethnic/national identity of the ones who succeeded.[78]

---

terms of hours worked and payment received. Moreover, unfreedom coincided largely with the productive life of a slave, and manumission occurred only when this ceased to be profitable.

75   For this criticism, see Gillett (2017).
76   Thus, for example, Beard (2013: 191) invokes the term 'multicultural' in relation to ancient society, without considering whether such a modern concept has the same meaning in the historical period and context to which it is applied.
77   See Sherwin-White (1966: 80): 'At every turn the Italian found himself outfaced by the clever *Graeculus*. The proportion of men of eastern Greek origin in the procuratorial service rises steadily throughout the second century ... [Because the] bitterness of this struggle could not find expression in the set debates of the Senate and the historians [this] conflict has remained silent, except for the outbursts of Juvenal and the echoes in Lucian'.
78   Hence the complaint by Lucian that ' "[t]he doors of Rome are open only to Greeks. Why are *they* preferred to *us*?" ', which as Sherwin-White (1966: 67, 68–69) observes, means that 'the tone of the narrative is decidedly hostile [because Lucian] crystallizes the stresses and strains that developed when the representatives of the two cultures [Greek, Roman] met in rivalry'. Noting that '[w]e feel how unpleasant ... the struggle to make good as professional men of letters at Rome', Sherwin-White (1966: 71–72) continues that 'the Roman dislike of Greeks [is presented in] Juvenal's third satire. It begins, "I cannot endure a Rome that is full of Greeks". It is the Greek professional men that Juvenal dislikes, and he dislikes them because they are successful rivals of the home product for the favours of the great Roman patrons'. Hence the presence of utterances by Juvenal to the effect that ' "there is no room for the sons of Rome when the Greek professor is in charge" [and the] Roman client can only exclaim "Is he to be given a better place than me?". These are the very

The vehemence of the language used in such contexts, and the less acute references to the identity of the 'other' more generally, has been attributed to the absence of economic rivalry: the fact that in the latter instances no job competition was involved.[79]

A somewhat different problem faces those classicists who do indeed possess knowledge of postmodern theory: here the difficulty is a seeming disregard on their part for the limits imposed on the kind of use to which they wish to put it.[80] Buying into postmodernism, therefore, Fowler commends literary theory as a way forward, endorsing the relevance of Foucault, Derrida, and Lyotard for the study of classical texts, as well as the approach to Late Antiquity of Brown and Veyne.[81] He approves especially of the use of deconstruction to

---

complaints that Lucian puts on the lips of his Roman rivals'. The cause of such views is explained thus (Sherwin-White, 1966: 73ff.): 'Those lines assert the main theme: the jealousy felt by the native professional person for his too successful foreign rival ... the latent xenophobia felt for the northern barbarians did not come to a head for sheer lack of occasion. It needs pressure and rivalry to bring it to the boil ... Here in Juvenal and Lucian we find [concern about] professional advancement under Roman patronage at Rome itself. The pressure manifests itself in an outburst of hostile feeling with clear overtones of cultural and national prejudice on both sides ... Juvenal's bitterest complaint is in a context of competition [he] is objecting to the infiltration into Roman life of Greek manners and culture – "linguam et mores" – in any form ... So in Juvenal there is an active ... strain of national and cultural prejudice at work'.

79 On this point see Sherwin-White (1966: 78, emphasis added), who notes that 'Pliny the philhellene could find the same faults [with Greeks] as the hostile [Juvenal]. But as a Roman senator his reaction was naturally very different. *They were not competing with him for a job*'.

80 A case in point is Fowler (2000: vii, ix), a classicist who describes himself in the following terms: 'I remain radically anti-foundationalist, -historicist, and –relativist: or, to put it more simply, I believe that we do what we want with texts ... Meaning is constructed, not discovered'. His approach is that of 'a traditional Rortyite pomo view of the world', although he accepts that: 'Someone who says "This is the way the world was" will always appear to have a stronger position than someone who says "This is the way I construct the past"'.

81 Proclaiming the far-reaching epistemological possibilities of postmodern theory, Fowler (Hornblower and Spawforth, 1998: 421) enthuses that 'there is no further step beyond postmodernism for criticism to take, no more radical position to adopt than the total denial of foundations'. A characteristic of postmodernism, accepts Fowler (Hornblower and Spawforth, 1998: 419), is that '[m]any of the most significant 20th century theories of language and literature stress a slippery indeterminacy is discourse that is at odds with the pretence to scientific objectivity'. Nevertheless, he continues, '[we] believe that 20th century theorizing has a great deal to offer classical studies ...' He concludes (Hornblower and Spawforth, 1998: 423) that 'we would like the version of the story we have offered to be seen as stressing both the foundational and the methodological importance of modern literary theory for the classics, that is, both as an important and salutary invitation to examine the presuppositions and preoccupations of our individual

challenge 'closure' by earlier theories – among them Marxism – to establish fixity of meaning. Invoking aporia in this manner enables Fowler to take the next step: that is, to use the element of ambiguity in order to advocate a shift of focus from the author of the text to the reader. However, the concept of the reader, and the reception by the latter of meaning within the text, involves for Fowler how *we* think about classical texts *now*, not how what they contained or advocated was interpreted by elements of the populace at the time they were composed.[82] Although different, this procedure is no less problematic than the methodological difficulty confronting Brown: the latter is faced with the inaccessibility of the Late Antique plebeian voice (= the reader), and thus also what s/he thinks about the text in question; Fowler, by contrast, appears unconcerned with the plebeian voice, his object being to impose on the text a contemporary subjectivity.

If Fowler turns to an 'anything goes' form of literary theory as a desirable approach to an understanding of classical texts, then Veyne and (latterly) Brown resort to the conceptual apparatus of anthropology. Both the latter draw a picture of Roman society as one of imperial and/or religious gift-giving, an altruistic benefaction (= euergetism) undertaken voluntarily on the part of the rich and powerful.[83] Instead of the earlier and negative view of Frank and Jones, concerning increased state appropriation, in the form of taxation, coupled with civic disengagement by the wealthy upper classes, Veyne and Brown propose an altogether different and positive interpretation of the same political and economic processes.[84] The latter are accordingly recast in their analyses as the antithesis of earlier interpretations: not as a malign practice of surplus extraction by the owners/controllers of the means of production/distribution/exchange, therefore, but much rather as a benign resource flow 'from above' (the emperor, senators, the church) to plebeian elements and/

---

practices, and as a wealth of techniques and approaches which will enable classical scholars to play their full part in the cultural dialogue that is a central justification for the study of antiquity'.

82   'A central tenet of postmodernism is that there is no single right way to do anything', notes Fowler (Hornblower and Spawforth, 1998: 421), adding: 'One aspect of this is that significance is firmly located in the reader, rather than the author or the text, and the reader's own set of beliefs becomes the determining factor in the criticism that he or she produces rather than any objective features of the text or its historical context'.

83   On euergetism, see Veyne (1990) and Brown (2012: 62–68).

84   Attempting to recast in positive terms the extension of taxation to the provinces, Brown (2012: 11) describes this as a 'daring innovation' designed to save the empire, rather than what it was: a sign of desperation occasioned by the very process of economic decline he refuses to recognize.

or the rural poor, bolstering an equally idealized perception on their part of patronage.[85]

Even though Brown aims his criticism at Rostovtzeff, whose views are depicted as the 'other' of Late Antiquity interpretations, it is clear that the critique extends to all those – supporters and opponents alike of materialism – who earlier subscribed to the decline thesis. Specifically, Brown targets the following arguments: that the rural populace was steadily impoverished; that *coloni* were either coerced or serfs; that depopulation and decentralization occurred; and that landed estates were either large in size or precursors of feudal properties. All these claims are dismissed by him in the name of 'new scholarship' which emerged over the past fifty years, and in essence underwrites his benign vision of Late Antiquity. The difficulty with this is that, no sooner has Brown asserted his positive view than he quickly notes the presence of contrary evidence which challenges the very case he seeks to make.

Hence the rejection by Brown of Rostovtzeff's view regarding the existence and wealth of large property-owners, on the grounds that '[a]rchaelogical surveys in many regions have effectively demolished what has been called "The Black Legend of the *Latifundium*", since there was little evidence 'for the existence of huge estates' and anyway 'the greatest villas stood in a landscape dotted with small properties'.[86] However, what Brown fails to ask is the limit to what archaelogical surveys are able to tell us, not least that landowners may well have more than one property. Consequently, small or medium estates – when added together in terms of *ownership* – may reveal precisely what he

---

85 The case made by Veyne (1990: xx) is that '[f]or an essential part of its [= Roman Empire] success was precisely the continuity of that ethic of "noble expenditure" that Mauss describes, which united rich and poor in an alternative to the class struggle'. What such a view overlooks, however, is that such a procedure *was* a form of class struggle, in that it promoted/reproduced an ideology of equivalence between rich and poor fostered by a superficial reciprocity inherent in resource disbursement, supporting thereby a false notion of egalitarianism. It was a way of saying 'we the rich have your interests at heart, because are no different from you', a concern demonstrated by distributing a portion of our wealth. Moreover, posing unity between rich and poor in this fashion served as a form of distraction or deflection from other, more dangerous political and economic issues dividing them. As such, it was a manoeuvre which much later came to be seen as populist.

86 For this view, see Brown (2012: 18). Generally speaking, it is a mistake to equate – as does Brown – oppression of the workforce simply with large properties, the inference being that better treatment and less onerous rents are found on smaller estates. This assumption is not borne out, for example, by the fact that, on this particular issue, no difference existed between large, medium, and small estates in Peruvian lowland rural Amazonia before the agrarian reforms of the 1960s; oppressive conditions, bad treatment, and onerous levels of labour-rent experienced by tenants were as much a feature of small and medium estates as of large ones.

claims is absent: a *de facto* pattern of *latifundia*, albeit not consolidated into a single holding.[87] For this reason, it is necessary to question the assertion about the lack of evidence about huge estates, given that he conflates estate with landholding, whereas the latter can and does cover the ownership of a number of estates.

Linked to this is the attempt by Brown to justify the claim about undersized estates – and thus the absence of *latifundia* – by emphasizing the presence of 'small properties'. This contrast only works for those who remain unaware of the *relationship* between the two, as outlined by Kautsky. The latter showed how small properties historically provide the labour-power on which large ones depend, and as a result are either not dispossessed or, indeed, leased out precisely in order to ensure a guaranteed labour supply. The subsequent observation by Brown, that 'the wealthy drew a large proportion of their wealth from rents of innumerable small farms [so the] *microfundium* and not the *latifundium* was the most prominent feature of the Roman countryside', supports exactly the point made not by him but by Kautsky.[88]

Moreover, having earlier outlined how landowners extracted ever-larger surplus (tax, rents) from their tenants, Brown insists that such proprietors were not 'super-rich', only 'town councillors'.[89] The latter designation is misleading, conveying as it does the image not of landlord power/dominance but rather of insignificant municipal officeholders exercising limited authority over smallscale economic resources. Most oddly, Brown bases his view about the non-existence of 'super-rich' on the size of villas, which were not 'enormous'. Keen to dispel any connection with feudal landownership, he cites architectural style and size of residences belonging to estate proprietors, insisting that such buildings did not match those of the 'medieval seigneurie', nor were they 'the work of proto-feudal lords'.[90] Rather, in his view, the scale and magnificence of the villas operated merely so as to 'radiate ... a sense of luxury enjoyed in a peaceful land'. Equally unpersuasive is his explanation as to why Christian teaching became more acceptable at this conjuncture: namely, that money

---

87 Brunt (1971: 34–35) confirms the common existence of just such a pattern, whereby numerous properties located in different places were in fact held by a single – and consequently, in terms of aggregate rural acreage, sizeable – landowner.
88 Brown (2012: 19).
89 'The stereotype inherited from Rostovtzeff has caused us to imagine that all late Roman landowners [were latifundists]', writes Brown (2012: 20–21): 'They were no such thing. Most were rich town councillors; they were not members of the super-rich'.
90 The villas, Brown (2012: 21) assures us, 'did not stand out as lonely châteaux ... as if they were the centres of a medieval seigneurie ... Rather ... [t]hey radiated a sense of ... luxury in a peaceful land. They were not the work of proto-feudal lords. ...'

now symbolized future riches ('money is future time').[91] This is a contrast with the earlier and negative reason, advanced by Walbank among others, which stressed its role as an avoidance mechanism. Material wealth was suddenly declared to be unimportant and ephemeral, since according to Christianity real riches were only to be found in heaven. In short, a religious discourse justifying existing inequalities.

Continuing his attempt to counter the negative image drawn by Rostovtzeff and others, by replacing it with a positive image of the Late Antique agrarian structure, Brown insists that 'there is little evidence that the rural population became "steadily poorer and more destitute" in the course of the fourth century'.[92] In much the same vein, he expresses doubts over the label 'rural serfs' attached to tenants, because they were not tied to land nor were they subject to landlord coercion.[93] Immediately, however, he concedes that there are difficulties with this interpretation, not least that landowners did not require the state to act on their behalf, as they possessed sufficient power locally to coerce their own workers.[94] Nor was the state needed to enforce debt bondage: indeed, the state made it legally necessary to repay debts, so it already legitimized coercion.[95] Similarly rejected by Brown are economic decentralization, urban depopulation, and aristocratic flight by landlords from the urban to the rural,

---

91 Brown (2012: 15–16).
92 For this see Brown (2012: 19), expressing the kind of view Brunt (1974: 92) may well have had in mind when observing about an earlier period of Roman history: 'It is an illusion that in the late Republic the urban plebs was usually well and cheaply fed by the State. As for the modern scholars who repeat ancient gibes that the doles corrupted the urban population, one must wonder if they would also condemn all modern measures of social welfare; in Rome there were no charitable foundations for the poor, and no unemployment benefits'.
93 'Rostovtzeff spoke of the labour force of the villas as if they were "rural serfs", maintains Brown (2012: 19), since '[h]e had in mind the serfs of the middle ages … But this was not necessarily the case. In the fourth century, tenant farmers were not tied to the land by the Roman government working in collusion with the great landowners … [the Roman colonate] may not have been as widespread or as coercive a system as we had thought'.
94 Accepting both that 'by the time the tax collector and the landowner (who were often one and the same person) had passed by, there was not much left for the farmer', and that '[t]he fourth century [was a time in which] the rural population was driven as hard as, if not harder than, in any other period of ancient history', Brown (2012: 13, 20) seemingly contradicts two earlier assertions. First, that there was no crisis arising from enhanced surplus extracted from 'those below'; and second, his denial of the view that 'the rural population became "steadily poorer and more destitute" in the course of the fourth century'.
95 Ironically, Brown (2012: 538, n.2 chapter 2) cites Banaji in support of these objections, when the latter was much rather one of those who questioned the element of unfreedom.

all of which prefigure the eventual development of feudalism.[96] Once again, he conflates actual residence on the estate, which need not necessarily have been the case, with drawing additional surplus from such properties. Since the latter had always been a source of wealth, in an important sense, landlords never ceased to be a 'ruralized class'.

Conclusion

Seen from the broad perspective of Marxist theory, the difficulties with the Late Antiquity approach are simply put. To begin with, the latter promotes what amounts to a positive image of capitalism, one that – because it is crisis-free and seemingly benign – appears systemically eternal (as will be seen more clearly in the next chapter). Much the same is true of the way religion is depicted. It is a framework, therefore, purged of all the processes which generate transition, among them crisis, struggle, and the non-development of the productive forces. No fundamental systemic transformation means in turn no transition, and thus also no distinguishing characteristics separating one mode of production from another. History – as depicted by this kind of historiography – becomes merely a narrative about an ever-present dynamic that is progress. One cannot be sure that, in the case of some exponents of Late Antiquity, such erasure of Marxist 'negativity' is wholly accidental.

There are a number of distinct ways in which a materialist approach perceives religious discourse: as a pre-modern form of 'from below' false consciousness (Marx and Engels), a call for emancipation (Kautsky on the Christian congregation), a 'from above' method of exercising control (Walbank), and as an economic burden (de Ste Croix). The overlap between these functions suggests they are not mutually exclusive, in that a belief in salvation propagated by the church may project emancipatory objectives amounting to false consciousness, although – given the heterogeneous socio-economic composition of the congregation – the existence of a uniform consciousness applicable in such circumstances is problematic. The same politically debilitating process is also identified by Frank, an anti-Marxist, who linked the end of the Roman

---

96 'Rostovtzeff (and many scholars after him) placed landowners of the later empire firmly in the countryside', notes Brown (2012: 20), adding: 'It was assumed that the later Roman aristocracy took to the land en masse [and] became a ruralised class, whose power over the land anticipated that of feudal lords of later times. One of the great excitements of the scholarship of the last half century has been the realization that, in the fourth and fifth centuries, no such thing happened'.

Republic and the subsequent decline of the *Imperium Romanum* to the arrival of Emperor-worship, installing thereby religiously sanctioned 'from-above' power exercised by a ruler-as-deity.

Systemic decline itself was attributed by earlier materialist approaches to a combination of factors: the availability of cheap/unfree labour-power meant impoverishment, underconsumption, and retardation (= limits to the development of the productive forces). This led in turn to economic crisis, to which religion was a response, together with decentralization and ruralisation. A decline in external sources of labour-power that was cheap/unfree gave rise to tenancy in the form of the colonate, a production relation which prefigured the transition to an eventual feudal stage. Regarding production relations and other phenomena contributing to economic stagnation or growth, however, it is crucial to be aware of two distinct meanings of retardation: to prevent something from starting on the one hand, and on the other stopping it from continuing. Of these two meanings, it is the first that is applied most frequently to ancient society. The second is mistakenly applied to present-day accumulation by exponents of the semi-feudal thesis, despite the fact that – once established – even advanced capitalism is perfectly compatible with labour-power that is cheap/unfree.

This double perception of economic crisis and religion as disempowerment contrasts absolutely with the very different empowering role allocated to economic development and religious belief by historians of Late Antiquity who challenge the very concept of systemic decline. The latter is replaced with continuity, economic stability, and general prosperity, a context and period marked in the approach of Brown and postmodern-influenced historiography by on the one hand the absence of impoverishment, *latifundia*, and the 'super-rich, and on the other the presence of imperial/aristocratic gift-giving and culturally-empowering 'otherness'. In effect, Late Antiquity becomes the site for the celebration of ancient capitalism and Christianity, neither of which in materialist terms recognize or require a form transcendence (worldly salvation, feudalism). Not the least problematic aspects of such a framework is a crucial methodological issue: it is simply not possible to say – as do some exponents of Late Antiquity – either in the case of religion that 'this is what people thought', let alone why they might have thought what they (supposedly) did, or in the case of the economy that trade and currency transactions by themselves negate crisis, decline, and transition, as they do for Banaji (see the following chapter).

CHAPTER 6

From Modern to Ancient Capitalism (*via* Bourgeois Economics)

> There is, of course, no more dangerous illusion than that of novelty, which often reflects nothing more than an ignorance of history
>
> An observation by PIERRE VILAr about the role of money in society.[1]

∴

> Obviously the student of Rome's growth must not rest content with generalisations that have come into vogue in a later day [but] must also give a just evaluation of the opposing factors, which have so often been overlooked.
>
> An observation made a century ago by TENNEY FRANK about the historiography of ancient society, as relevant now as it was then.[2]

∴

Introduction

Unwary classicists may be unaware of the extent to which the analytical framework and arguments about the Late Antique economy can be – and in the case considered below, is – based on extremely problematic assumptions concerning agrarian change in nineteenth and twentieth century India. It was in relation to the latter context/conjuncture, therefore, that Jairus Banaji first identified the existence in what he termed the 'colonial' mode of production of accumulation based on a rural proletariat composed of the 'disguised' wage labour of peasants.[3] This approach led in turn to a reductionist view, whereby

---

1 Vilar (1976: 7).
2 Frank (1914: viii).
3 The term 'proletariat' has two distinct usages. First, it refers to a relationally non-specific concept of toil undertaken by any kind of worker who lives by the physical application of his/her manual labour. This is the meaning used by much historiography of ancient society. Second,

all systemically-specific relational forms were henceforth collapsed into a single a-historical variant, characterized by him as hired labour that was 'free'. Notwithstanding the fact that, when applied to Indian history during the 1970s debate about the mode of production such claims received short shrift from Indian and non-Indian scholars, Banaji now makes the very same claim with regard to ancient society, where he identifies a similar process of accumulation based on 'free' wage labour.[4] Late Antiquity, he maintains, was characterized not by economic decline, but rather by growth, the rise of a 'new' imperial aristocracy that not only invested in irrigation on estates that were not fragmented but also employed 'free' labour and was 'responsive to market opportunities'.

His analysis is aimed at Weber's interpretation of ancient society, and in particular the view about the decline and fall of the Roman Empire, dismissed as a 'moribund dogma'.[5] According to Banaji, therefore, for Weber ancient civilization was urban, coastal, and based on slave labour. Hence the argument of Weber about the economic decline of ancient civilization in the third century A.D. is premised on the contraction in population and the money economy, and thus a reversion to natural economy.[6] Unduly influenced by Bücher, Weber

---

in its specifically Marxist sense as used here, a proletariat refers to a workforce defined by a particular set of characteristics. The most important of these involve property relations: that is, workers who, because they are separated both from their means of labour and from the control of an employer (and as such possessing nothing to sell but a capacity to work), are as a result personally free to commodify/recommodify their labour-power.

4 It is clear from their introduction to a collection about the historical transformation of Egyptian agriculture to which Banaji (1999) also contributes that Bowman and Rogan (1999) are unaware either of the Indian mode of production debate, the deployment then of the very same claims made now by Banaji, or the earlier critique made by others of these arguments. For an analysis of the contradictory nature of his contributions to the Indian mode of production debate, see Brass (2003).

5 Banaji (2010: viii). One might suppose that his objection to Weber is driven by and takes the form of a Marxist critique, but this is far from the case. Ironically, given the attempt by Banaji to replace the Weberian interpretation of ancient society with Sombart's notion of 'business economy' (see below), Weberian historiography actually shares much of its non-Marxist epistemology with Sombartian theory. As the introduction to Sombart (1967: xiv-xv, original emphasis) makes clear, 'Sombart and Weber were at one in their insistence on discovering the special role of religion in forming the spirit of Western capitalism. Both were interested in countering the economic and materialistic determinism of the Marxist interpretation of history; for both the quest for an alternative explanation led to an emphasis on discovering attitudinal factors, the ethos, the *spirit* that infused the newly hightened commercialism of Western Europe'.

6 Banaji's interpretation contrasts not only with that of Weber (1976) but also with that of Vernant (1980: 6–7), who suggests that ancient economy might be classified by the following duality. An opposition between on the one hand agrarian economic activity (*oikonomia*), a combination of peasant cultivation and artisan production undertaken by family labour, and on the other urban-based economic activity (*chrematistike*) involving financial transactions

subscribed to the view of economic decline linked to agricultural stagnation. Hence the multiple and interrelated processes in late antiquity as perceived by Weber: a decline in urbanization, the money economy, agricultural production, and the capacity of the workforce (composed of slaves) to reproduce itself, all of them linked. This in turn led to the rise of an autarchic, subsistence-based and thus economically isolationist peasant economy, as Roman landowners settled slaves on land as tenants, thereby effecting a systemic transition to a feudal mode of production. Each component of Banaji's interpretation is in effect the antithesis of Weber's.[7] What Banaji objects to, therefore, are the interrelated arguments about imperial economic decline giving rise in turn to a transition not just from slavery to the colonate (i.e., from slavery to tenancy) but also to feudalism.[8]

This chapter is composed of four sections, the first of which considers the way in which changing definitions of mode of production are applied to the economy both of Late Antiquity and of capitalism itself, the result being that the Late Antique economy is depicted as a flourishing kind of capitalism. The latter claim rests in turn on the view that rural production relations in Late Antiquity cannot be said to prefigure a feudal stage, a perception examined

---

and maritime trade. He also points out that, although money was important in Greece from the fourth century B.C. onwards, there was no paid labour, since the market that existed was for slaves and not the commodity labour-power (Vernant, 1980: 9, 17 n.18). The latter is of course the antithesis of the position adhered to by Banaji, who equates the presence of money with the existence of paid labour that is 'free'.

7 It is important to be aware of the extent to which Banaji's analysis constitutes the 'other' of that outlined by Weber (1976: 390ff.). For the latter, therefore, production using slave labour possessed a fundamental contradiction: whilst slavery was economically efficient (for better control, slaves were accommodated in non-familial units: barracks on estates), and thus central to market exchanges in ancient society, the slave population was unable to reproduce itself demographically. The institution of slavery, and with it production for exchange, therefore depended on a constantly replenished slave market, which in turn required the continuous supply of war captives. As long as war guaranteed the provision of unfree labour, which was cheap, labour-displacing technological improvements were unnecessary, nor were free workers able to compete (hence their relative absence). When the Roman Empire ceased to expand territorially, the main source of prisoners of war dried up, which resulted in a corresponding shortage of slaves. The scarcer these unfree workers became, the more landlords turned to tenancy, securing labour-rent from those to whom land was leased. Although not free, in the sense of being able to commodify their own labour-power, tenants cultivating smallholdings with family labour were nevertheless able to reproduce themselves (and the estate workforce) demographically. Over time such estates became economically self-sufficient, contributing thereby to a decline in market transactions.

8 Banaji (2010: 197), on whose objection to feudalism see below and also elsewhere (Banaji, 1999: 195). Significantly, perhaps, the 'new' archaeology also objects to the concept 'feudalism' (Francovich and Hodges, 2003: 27ff.).

critically in the second section. Problems with such definitions/exclusions are looked at in the third and fourth sections, where difficulties are seen to stem either from the conflation of Marxist and marginalist economic theory, or from methodological shortcomings.

I

It is perhaps significant that in support of his own benign view of Late Antiquity, Brown cites the work of Banaji: and just as the former seeks to cast religion in a positive light, so the latter attempts in turn to do the same for the economy.[9] On the face of it, however, the most recent analysis by Banaji appears to depart from the assumptions made by Brown, in that its focus is specifically on the Late Antique economy. Sensing, perhaps, that a 'sweetness-and-light' interpretation is problematic, and that consequently issues such as retardation, crisis, and decline – termed by him 'catastrophist models' – cannot be eliminated conceptually from the epistemological agenda, Banaji starts by distancing himself – albeit tentatively – from the kind of hostility expressed by Brown towards the decline thesis.[10] However, this is misleading, and he quickly reverts to an economic approach that is consistent with the antagonistic perception of 'catastrophist models' held by other exponents of Late Antiquity.[11] Like Brown, therefore, these earlier interpretations that fall roughly into the category of a materialist framework are the ones that Banaji, too, dismisses.[12] The object, he announces, is to 'revamp the history of the fourth to the seventh centuries [that] separates Rostozvteff [sic] from the kind of history and archaeology ... of the new scholarship ... from the 1980s onwards'.[13]

---

9   For endorsing references to Banaji, see Brown (2011: 15; and 2012: xxix, 536 n.36, 537 n.42, 538 n.2 chapter 2); these in turn are reciprocated by Banaji (2018: 12, 79).
10 'It is not my intention to deny that [catastrophist] models or forms of description contain *some measure of truth*', accepts Banaji (2018: xii, original emphasis), agreeing with another contemporary analysis that ' "there is a real danger for the present day in a version of the past that explicitly sets out to eliminate all crisis and all decline" '.
11 For Banaji (2018: 63, 74), therefore, 'the "fall" of the western empire is a mere abstraction', and '[c]atastrophist images of the fall of antiquity use biological metaphors like decay and decline ...'.
12 What is termed 'catastrophe flips' (Banaji, 2018: xii) is 'the strongest (and probably the least tenable) form of catastrophism, and basically it is some picture of this sort that underpinned much of the earlier, mainly pre-war historiography that lacked any real notion of late antiquity as a period'. The historians referred to include not just Weber, Rostovtzeff, and Walbank, but also Finley and Jones.
13 Banaji [2018: ix].

Capitalism, Capitalism Everywhere

If an effect of the semi-feudalism of Patnaik is to banish capitalism, and thus also a concept of transition, then the approach to ancient history of Banaji arrives at the same end by a different route.[14] Over the years he has endorsed – and then dropped – a dizzying number of modes: semi-feudalism, the 'colonial' mode, the peasant mode, and the tributary mode.[15] Contrary to what he claims is the case, therefore, Banaji has on many occasions changed his mind about theory, always after – not before – others criticized the views he confidently maintained were Marxist. Having lambasted A.G. Frank's interpretation of the mode of production in Latin America for decades past, Banaji now confesses that 'I've become much more sympathetic to the general perspectives that Frank argued in Capitalism and Underdevelopment in Latin America'.[16]

Nor is it the case, as Banaji asserts, that he has never subscribed to the characterization of India as 'feudal'.[17] During the mode of production debate, Banaji originally commended the semi-feudal thesis as the analytical way forward. It was only when another contributor to that debate pointed out the errors of his analysis that he changed his mind and came out against the view he had initially advocated. Banaji did exactly the same over the 'colonial' mode of production, which he initially espoused, only changing his mind – again – when the mistaken theory he was so enthusiastic about was criticized by others subsequently. To these modes he now adds a couple more: the Late Antique economy is labelled by him as a case, variously, of 'proto-industrialization', 'proto-modernity', 'quasi-capitalism', or 'commercial capitalism'. None of them is found in Marx, nor is Banaji's own interpretation of modes of production, based as it is largely on monetary expansion. This leads to a familiar

---

14 On semi-feudalism and Patnaik, see a previous chapter in this volume. The political affinity between Patnaik and Banaji should not surprise, given that initially the latter was a supporter of the semi-feudal thesis, of which the former remains an adherent.
15 For details, see Brass (2012).
16 The rider he then adds – 'The weakness of Frank's approach was that he didn't have the tools to argue the point in a more sophisticated theoretical way' – is not merely patronizing but, given Banaji's own problems with theory, wholly inappropriate. See www.counterfire.org>Features>Book Reviews, 15 April 2011.
17 Denying that he has ever characterized India as 'feudal', Banaji asserts – see comments by him posted on 15 April 2011 at www.counterfire.org>Features>Book Reviews – that his arguments have altered only in one particular respect ('Where I have changed my position quite substantially is in rejecting the same characterisation ("feudal") for Latin America'). This is an incorrect claim, one that could only be accepted by those who are either unaware of or ignore what he has actually written in the past about the mode of production.

relay-in-statement: money signals the historical ubiquity not only of economic growth and wage-labour (albeit everywhere 'disguised') but also of capitalism itself. It is by means of this pattern that he seeks to explain the nature of the Late Antique economic process.

As with so many of the concepts he deploys, what Banaji understands by the term 'capitalism' is theoretically problematic, and his efforts to rectify this are consequently replete with contradiction. Although he begins by insisting that in all cases ancient economy must be differentiated from modern capitalism, any distinctiveness – never strong – soon recedes into the background. Disavowing the notion of ancient society as capitalist, he nevertheless opts instead for the presence there of 'individual capitalists', on the grounds that their existence was 'well attested throughout antiquity'.[18] For this reason, he settles for the opaque construction that around the start of the Principate an 'unproductive capitalism' amounted to 'a characterization of the economic activities of particular capitalists or groups of capitalists and not of the economy as a whole'. At this point, however, he adopts a more sweeping and all-embracing definition, asserting that 'there was surely no period of Republican, imperial or late antique history when *capitalists* were not active in major sectors of the economy or when indeed some of these, or parts of them, were not organized on capitalist lines'.[19] Additional observations made by Banaji suggest his view is that the Roman economy of Late Antiquity was indeed capitalist.[20]

Support for this contention takes the form of two interrelated claims. First, the deployment by Banaji of an heroic image of the merchant, whose economic importance in the production process exceeds that identified by Marx with regard to the nineteenth century.[21] Together with aristocrats and 'smaller entrepreneurs', therefore, merchants composed the 'business classes',

---

18   Banaji (2018: 48–49).
19   Banaji (2018: 49, original emphasis).
20   Hence expressions (Banaji, 2018: 51) such as the 'relative modernity of the Roman economy', together with the following kind of endorsement (Banaji, 2018: 2): 'Maurice Picon has suggested that … manufacturing [at the Samian potteries in southern Gaul] was organized on a capitalist basis. Even if we agree with this (and I am inclined to) …'. Elsewhere Banaji (Éwanjée-Épée & Monferrand, 2015: 5) states clearly that what is to be found in Late Antiquity is indeed capitalism: 'Marx (inevitably) identified capitalism with the modern capitalism that was rapidly developing in his day. But pre-modern capitalism has been widespread in many parts of the world from China under the Southern Sung to large sectors of the Muslim world … Here is a prototype of the kind of capitalism that flourished … even in antiquity'.
21   The intervention of 'merchant enterprise' in production, argues Banaji (2018: 2), means that the merchant 'emerges … as a more substantial figure than the commercial capitalists that Marx saw being subordinated to industrial capital in the late nineteenth century'.

'businessmen', and 'moderately affluent middle classes' whose activity fuelled the dynamic economy of Late Antiquity. What is seen by Banaji as 'the rational core of the Roman economy' is an 'obsession with money-making', which prompts both his question: 'Did the Roman passion for business simply evaporate, then?', and its answer that 'catastrophist views of the period certainly imply this'.[22] The latter claim is, of course, incorrect: analyses by so-called catastrophists' put forward a different kind of argument. Namely, that the process of 'business' – incidentally, *not* the same as capitalism – was adversely influenced not from voluntary causes (as Banaji infers) but rather for material ones. That is, crisis/decline stemmed not from the intentional/subjective/irrational (= unexplained) withdrawal of 'businessmen' from the market but rather was due to an economic limit posed by a combination of retardation (an obstacle to further development of the productive forces) and underconsumption (an obstacle to further expenditure on the part of slaves and low-paid workers). Moreover, any focus on trade has also to consider additional costs, unmentioned by Banaji, which were considerable: because of the risks (shipwrecks, storms, pirates, bandits), therefore, finance for caravan and sea trade throughout the empire (and beyond) carried a high rate of interest.[23]

And second, so as to back his contention about the presence in Late Antiquity of an economic system akin to capitalism, it is necessary for Banaji to have to identify the forms of the exchanges which his merchants, 'business classes', 'businessmen', and 'moderately affluent middle classes' themselves undertake. This he does in two ways: on the one hand by stressing the multiple and positive aspects fuelling what he claims is unabated economic dynamism, and on the other by downplaying (or denying) any negative economic processes and effects. Vitality is itself embodied in the frequently made interconnection between economic activity, money circulation, and gold currency (*solidus*), a correlation reflected in observations such as 'rigorously maintained gold coinage', '[t]he most striking economic fact about late antiquity is … more money in circulation *per head of the population* than at any previous time in Roman history, the bulk of this in the form of gold', and 'markets were booming'.[24]

---

22   Banaji (2018: xiii, xiv).
23   Simkin (1968: 46–47) records that, whilst the *annual* interest rate on ordinary loans was 15 per cent, on money borrowed for the purpose of trade, by contrast, the rate was *monthly*: five per cent for trade loans, ten per cent for caravan trade, and twenty per cent for sea trade.
24   For these statements, see Banaji (2018: 13, 18, 22, original emphasis). A symptomatic remark (Banaji, 2018: 12) is that 'monetary economy was the backbone of the late empire and the sheer scale on which gold circulated actively is surely the most telling sign … of

Much like Brown, therefore, Banaji denies the existence in Late Antiquity both of impoverishment and of overtaxation, forms of oppression and/or appropriation central to so-called 'catastrophist models' informing earlier historiography.[25] He goes much further, however, and emphasizes the opposite as being the case: according to him, therefore, rural workers in Late Antiquity were being paid in gold. Hence claims to the effect that '[c]ertainly by the sixth century most ordinary groups of rural labourers were being remunerated in *solidi*', that there was 'widespread use of cash payments on rural estates in Egypt (already by the third quarter of the fourth century)', and that '[t]he rural workers ... were paid ... cash wages (paid in gold)'.[26]

Money Makes the World Go Round?

Banaji's views about the systemic role of money are simply put. A desire to interpret modes of production largely in terms of 'the expansion of monetary economy' leads epistemologically to a familiar relay-in-statement: money signals the historical ubiquity not only of economic growth and wage-labour (albeit everywhere 'disguised') but also of capitalism itself.[27] Inexorably, the latter becomes systemically eternal, and thus a-historical; for Banaji, therefore, 'a combination of modes of production' is to be replaced with an 'articulation of forms of capitalism'.[28] Along the way, feudalism more-or-less vanishes, as does the distinction between free and unfree labour, and capitalism is effectively declared ever-present.[29] It is to be found in Egypt during late antiquity, in thirteenth century Sung China, and in seventeenth century Mughal India.[30] Structural or systemic inconsistencies are labelled 'complexity', 'peculiarities' or specific 'configurations', so much so that at times history is reduced to an ensemble of disconnected components left floating in theoretical space.

---

      the general nature of economic activity'. For similar claims, see Banaji (2018: 27, 52, 54, 55, 66).

25   'The economic revival of the late antique period was closely bound up with its monetary history', maintains Banaji (2018: 54), for which reason '[t]he idea that the period saw a general impoverishment is just not true'. Equally categorical is his view (Banaji, 2018: 7, 86), the target of which is the work of Jones, that overtaxation contributed to the decline of the Roman Empire.

26   Banaji (2018: 55, 65, 82).

27   Banaji (2010: 7).

28   Banaji (2010: 360).

29   Banaji (2010: 26, 41–42, 131–154).

30   Banaji (2010: 29, 37–8, 155ff., 358).

Any attempt to elaborate a theory of modes of production runs the risk of what has been characterized, memorably, as an approach whereby 'each Andean valley has its own mode of production, and individuals may change them two or three times a week like underwear'.[31] Unfortunately, the multiple and ever-changing systemic designations adopted by Banaji are an illustration of precisely that kind of approach. Having initially endorsed the semi-feudal thesis and the 'colonial' mode of production, neither of which is a Marxist concept, Banaji discarded both in turn.[32] However, the legacy of each carried over into all subsequent claims made by him. Thus what he now terms 'disguised' wage-labour, or smallholders who continued to operate their own labour process, but no longer as independent units of production, was a characteristic specific to the colonial workforce.[33] Rural households in nineteenth-century India are perceived by Banaji as a unitary form, or peasant-as-cultivator, a concept also shared by the semi-feudal thesis. Another legacy, common to semi-feudalism and the 'colonial' mode of production, is the view of the colonial state as the main exploiter of the Indian peasant.

Despite the fact that 'peasant mode of production' is a populist, not a Marxist concept, elsewhere Banaji mistakenly assumes that '[i]t is not at all incompatible with Marxist theory to posit a specifically peasant mode of production or "peasant economy"'.[34] Equally unconvincing is his claim that no difference exists between neo-populist and Leninist views about the peasantry. Unsurprisingly, therefore, Banaji – like Bernstein (see Chapter 4, this volume) – dismisses the peasant differentiation categories used by Lenin to indicate the fact of class formation in rural Russia and applied by other Marxists to present-day India.[35] To this ever-changing list Banaji adds another mode of production: the tributary, which he asserts 'now looks to me like the best contender for a

---

31   Foster-Carter (1978: 74).
32   Banaji (2010: 68, n.26 Chapter 1). See also Banaji (1972) and his contribution to Rudra (1978: 418, n.24).
33   The reproduction of such units was governed by capital, and the price the producer in the 'colonial' mode received for the enforced sale of his/her crop was deemed 'a concealed wage', as 'disguised' wage-labour worked mainly on its own land and not that of – or for – others.
34   Banaji (1976: 1601). Defending the neo-populist Chayanov against Marxist critiques, he adds to the confusion by first denying that the Chayanovian concept 'equilibrium' derives from neo-classical economics, and then accepting that Chayanov did indeed use 'marginalist notions'. In much the same vein, having endorsed the 'peasant mode of production', Banaji (2010: 94–5, 217) then criticizes Wickham (2005) for using the same concept.
35   About India, therefore, Banaji (1990) has observed that '[s]tratification terminology (rich/middle/poor) is the least helpful way of trying to make sense of this shifting and ambiguous reality'.

Marxist characterization of Asiatic regimes'.[36] It is defined as one in which the state controls everything: the ruling class, all means of production and all surplus labour. In formulating the tributary mode, Banaji not only invokes Bahro but also appears to base much of his criticism of Marx himself on the ideas contained in Wittfogel.[37] What is interesting is that Bahro and Wittfogel were keen to label the soviet system as a form of 'oriental despotism' – embodying the Cold War shibboleth of a "totalitarian state" – so as to condemn both Marxism and socialism *tout court*.

As significant are the reasons for adopting the concept of a tributary mode, and the way it is characterized. Banaji regards tributary economies as dynamic because of money circulation, describing the Mughal regime as a 'formidable achievement' on account of its 'peace, order, and new market opportunities'.[38] Like the case of Late Antiquity, therefore, Mughal India was in Banaji's view a place of sweetness and light, the kind of tension-free socio-economic 'harmony' one finds described in analyses by neo-classical historiography, not in a Marxist text. As such, it not only discounts negative aspects of the Mughal system (famines, crop-failures, oppressive administration, peasant uprisings) but fits rather too neatly into prevailing nationalist discourse about the "rise of the east, decline of the west", whereby the present-day economic dynamism of India and China is projected backwards into history (= eternal capitalism).[39]

II

In order to sustain his interpretation regarding the ubiquitous nature of capitalism, Banaji was previously obliged to erase the concept of a feudal stage from Indian historiography. This proves to be no less true in the case of Late Antiquity.[40] To this end, he erects two contrasting images: between on the one hand his depiction of economic dynamism (its 'sophistication' and

---

36   Banaji (2010: 15–40).
37   Bahro (1978), Wittfogel (1963: 369ff.).
38   Banaji (2010: 37–38).
39   That Mughal India was anything but sweetness and light is clear from many sources, among them Habib (1963: 330–33, 337–51).
40   In answer to a question (Éwanjée-Épée & Monferrand, 2015: 9) as to 'how does one think about transition when one has given up any kind of historicism?', Banaji replied: 'What is denied is any rigid succession of modes of production ... There were whole centuries in the western parts of the former Roman empire when the rural labour force comprised workers who cannot be characterized either as slaves or as serfs ... The main casualty of much of this rethinking has been any simplistic idea of "feudalism" as an all-embracing historical category with a universality almost as great as capitalism's'.

'resilience'), and on the other what is termed 'minimalism', or a countryside bereft of all economic activity.[41] The object is to displace relational forms and economic processes associated historically with feudalism – decentralization, landlordism, serfdom, tenancy, sharecropping, peasant smallholding, subsistence production, payment in kind, ruralisation, the importance of landed property – with ones linked conceptually to capitalism, among them landlord-as-'businessman', the prevalence of wage labour, and payments made in cash. The 'minimalist' position is linked by Banaji to a belief that slave labour was irrational, and that consequently Rome lacked an economically rational form of labour organization. Against this, he maintains that '[t]he Roman economy was as much a proto-industrial economy as an agrarian one'.[42]

Fear of Feudalism

Crucial aspects of the case about Late Antique economic dynamism rest on the way production relations are to be interpreted. Thus, the workforce on the estate is categorized by Banaji neither as serfs, who are unfree, nor as tenants who pay labour-rent to the proprietor leasing them a smallholding, but simply as landless permanent workers in receipt of a cash wage. In keeping with this attempt to find only workers, not peasants, he casts doubt on the way the latter designation is used: the term 'peasant' applied to those who worked the land in Late Antiquity do not, he insists, coincide with the same concept as used today.[43] Instead of rent-paying tenants with usufruct access to portions of estate land, as indicated by Hardy in the account of the Apion family properties, therefore, Banaji refers to such elements merely as 'surplus'

---

41 The purpose of his interpretation, Banaji (2018: xii, 7, original emphasis) points out, is 'to argue strongly for the sheer scale and *resilience* of the late antique economy', and 'defend the *sophistication* of ancient economic behaviour against minimalism' which informs the decline thesis the 'catastrophic model' since 'minimalism simplifies social structures, denies economic complexity to pre-capitalist societies, regards trade and money as of little or no significance in the history of such societies. ...'
42 Banaji (2018: 1).
43 Objecting to the characterization of village populations 'in terms like ..."a middle class of peasants"', Banaji (2018: 79–80) questions the relevance of the latter term altogether: 'These are meaningless characterizations, since they beg the question of who or what "peasants" were in the late antique world. None of the numerous terms used ... to describe people who owned or worked the land maps onto our own (sometimes confused) notions of the peasantry with quite the neatness or symmetry we would like. *Geōrgos* comes closest, but ... it refers often to a purely landless stratum that worked on large estates on a permanent basis. They certainly were not peasants and had little control of the land they worked'.

workers seeking employment.⁴⁴ The impression conveyed is that, as they were not rent-paying tenants but hired workers, the economic system of which they were a part could not have been a precursor to feudalism, being much rather an ancient form of capitalism. In order to challenge the presence of tenure associated with feudalism, he invokes architecture – much like Brown – so as to argue that the *villa* corresponded to a 'discrete block of land' and thus a 'physically coherent entity'. The latter indicated that the estate could not have been subdivided into tenancies, and consequently its workforce must have consisted of landless permanent workers.

Characterized by Banaji as 'a widespread dogma', since production relations were not based on rent-paying tenants to whom estate land had been leased, feudal tenure is 'simply a cliché transferred to late Roman history from the popular idea of the large landowner (everywhere!) as a landlord'.⁴⁵ A number of observations are in order concerning the tone and substance of this kind of rejection. To begin with, it contrasts with the more considered discussions of this issue by de Ste Croix and Finley.⁴⁶ The latter, in particular, gives due weight to the lack of sources plus the different meanings used. In keeping with this, the relationally mixed character of the estate workforce was acknowledged even by those writing the early analyses dismissed by Banaji as 'minimalist', indicating that although the presence of hired labour was accepted, unlike him it was not used to cast doubt on a feudal trajectory.⁴⁷ None of the historians labelled as 'minimalist' go as far as Banaji, who claims with absolute certainty that the estate workforce was not drawn from tenancies.

When considering the definition of estate labour as either tenants or workers, Banaji seems to overlook countervailing information supportive of earlier materialist analyses claims about decentralization, ruralisation, tenancy, and how these kinds of tenure prefigure a feudal stage. Having classified *Geōrgos* as 'a purely landless stratum', it turns out that, after all, such labourers had usufruct access to estate land and were in fact sharecroppers.⁴⁸ Banaji appears

---

44   Banaji (2018: 22). Sharecroppers are identified by Banaji (2018: 76) not as rent-paying tenants cultivating plots of land but rather as part of the rural workforce.
45   See Banaji (2018: 70ff.).
46   Thus, for example, Finley (1976) records that harvesting gangs were composed of smallholders.
47   According to Johnson (1936: 79), therefore, private estates, managed by stewards, 'were either cultivated directly by the owners with the help of slaves or hired labour, farmed on a system of shares [= sharecropping], or leased to tenants … on a fairly large scale'.
48   Banaji (2018: 82). According to Rowlandson (1985), in Egypt crown tenants (*basilikoi geōrgoi*) were rent-paying cultivators of royal land, many of whom 'were essentially small-scale farmers'. As in many other contexts, tenants were differentiated economically, and

to sense the looming contradiction, and attempts to justify his earlier and very different characterization of these same production relations.[49] Endeavouring to salvage the case about estate labour composed not of tenants but of workers, and thus to extract his argument from the teleological problems it now confronts, he invokes a parallel between the Roman estate in Late Antiquity and the Latin American *hacienda*. The former, he explains, 'exploited a landless workforce comparable [to] the *gañanes* in Mexico'.[50] What this underlines, however, is the danger of making a comparison with what for him is an unfamiliar agrarian context. Thus, the depiction by Banaji of *gañanes* as a 'landless workforce' is incorrect, since they were tenants to whom the proprietor of a large estate leased land and – because of debts owed – paid off such loans with their own labour-power and that of their household members.[51] In short, *gañanes* were neither free nor landless.

Equally misleading are terms such as 'sophisticated' and 'resilient' used by Banaji both to denote economic dynamism in the Late Antiquity and to differentiate this from what is presented by him as 'minimalist' (= feudal) depictions of the earlier decline thesis. What such a contrast overlooks is that even a backward rural economy can be 'sophisticated' and indeed 'resilient' in terms of its organization and reproduction, applying solutions to the economic problems faced by so-called 'minimalist' grassroots units. Such labels do not make a system capitalist and could just as easily be descriptions of processes found in a non- or pre-capitalist system, as many ethnographic studies attest. This does not prevent Banaji from dismissing the characteristics – urban crisis, poverty, underconsumption, market contraction – that Weber connects

---

included at the top end better-off elements, some of whom sub-let portions of their holdings to sub-tenants.

49 Stating incorrectly that *geōrgoi* were 'these workers whom I started by defining as a landless peasantry' – what he actually said was that '[t]hey certainly were not peasants' – Banaji (2018: 143–44) goes on to confuse the issue further by saying that 'it is important to realise that in their case the term referred not to a smallholding peasantry but to rural households of whom the majority were clearly dependent on the estate for employment'.

50 Banaji (2018: 153–54).

51 As Góngora (1975: 152–53) makes clear, '[t]he free Indians (*naborios, laborious, gañanes, and peones*), who could hire out their labour to any Spaniard ... soon tended to settle on some *estancia* or *hacienda*, where the owner granted them the use of a plot of land ... the method consisted of advancing wages due for an entire period with a debt which he had to pay off by labour, without being able to leave the *hacienda*'. Much the same is evident from the description of *gañanes* in Duncan, Rutledge, and Harding (1977: 37), where they are referred to as tenants. As to the element of control which *gañanes* are said to lack, the same source records that the landlord 'complained that some acted as if they owned the estate, rarely working [for him] more than one or two days a week'.

with 'ruralization, decentralization, and ultimately decline, insisting only that 'almost nothing in our actual evidence supports such an idea'.[52] Despite seeming to accept the fact of decentralization, therefore, Banaji maintains this was consistent with 'an extraordinary flow of capital into the rural sector, in the process failing to address the reasons for decentralization.

All Modes Lead to Rome

Upholding his opposition directly to Weber, and indirectly to feudalism, Banaji then claims implausibly that the main repository of wealth in Late Antiquity was not land but money.[53] Notwithstanding that such a claim is the linch-pin of his capitalism-not-feudalism case, it is for a number of reasons possibly the most contentious empirical claim he makes. Nearly all historiography of the Roman Empire shows that land was not just the main but the most durable economic asset the rich could acquire.[54] Unlike money, which was subject to inflation, constant fluctuations in value, clipping, and currency debasement (reducing the precious metal content of coins), land kept its value over time. Furthermore, since precise data about the purchasing power of money over the long term is either of questionable accuracy or unavailable, it is as a result extremely difficult to quantify its value in relation to the cost and price of land.

Neither is it the case that adherents of the decline thesis attribute this to the economic irrationality of slavery. Earlier materialist analyses, such as that by

---

52 'Even the notion of a greater emphasis on the rural aspects of life actually expresses the true fact of an extraordinary flow of capital into the rural sector, not the collapse of the urban economy', observes Banaji (2018: 54), adding that '[o]f course, Max Weber argued for a structural crisis of the urban sector, the contraction of markets and a "ruralisation" of the life of the empire. But almost nothing in our actual evidence supports such an idea'.

53 His opposition to the views of Rostovtzeff and Weber, argues Banaji (2018: 61, original emphasis), derives from their perception of 'the late empire as a period of expanding natural economy. Yet the distinctiveness of the late empire lies precisely in the fact that *money*, not land, emerged as the general form of wealth'. This kind of claim is contradicted by Brunt (1988: 270), who points out: 'But is it true that it was not so much land that veterans wanted as the cash value of land? The suggestion does not seem very plausible'.

54 According to Finley (1976: 117), therefore, '[t]he upper strata of Italian society were rich, some very rich ... [a] substantial portion of their incomes – to put it no more strongly than that – came from the land'. In a similar vein, Jones (1940: 266) writes: 'Land was also in antiquity almost the only and permanent form of investment, and all wealth however earned therefore tended to be put into land for the sake of security ...' So, too, argues Brunt (1988: 241): 'In the economic life of ancient Italy agriculture was of dominant importance. Land was the safest investment, and the chief basis of wealth'.

Walbank, did not regard slave labour as irrational; they saw the problem differently – that the cheapness and availability of slaves precluded investment in improved productive techniques. When the source of such unfree workers declined, due to the Augustan era of peace, landlords and employers had to look elsewhere for their labour-power. Hence the colonate, and eventually feudalism. All this has nothing to do with a supposedly irrational organization of labour: much rather it is a systemic issue, one that prefigured a later transition to feudalism. Interestingly, Banaji repeats his initial claim, whereby demographic increase = additional labour for estate work = economic growth = capitalism, without realizing that such a link between the availability and cheapness of labour-power for estate cultivation was precisely the argument made by Walbank (and others) in support of the retarding effect on the development of the productive forces in Late Antiquity.[55]

As problematic is the label of 'proto-industrial' attached by Banaji to the Late Antique economy. Significantly, this concept was inserted by Medick (who formulated it) between feudalism and capitalism over a sixteenth to nineteenth century period, *not* – as does Banaji – in ancient society.[56] Furthermore, 'proto-industrialization' was defined by Medick as a rural phenomenon, whereby peasant-kulaks and merchant-putters-out outsourced tasks to rural households. The latter does not correspond to the description used by Banaji of 'proto-industrial' as a form of 'mass production'; it would seem, therefore, that as deployed by him the term simply functions as a conceptual proxy for the kind of capitalism he wishes to locate in Late Antiquity.[57] Equally problematic is his term 'peasant', which he restricts to a Chayanovian model of self-sufficient, subsistence-oriented independent smallholder (= 'a peasantry proper', 'pure peasants'), thereby wrongly excluding from this categories such as sharecropper and tenant.[58] Regarding as peasants only a Chayanovian ideal-type family farmer is in a sense necessary, since it enables Banaji to exclude them from the estate system, and thus to sustain the fiction of an

---

55 See Banaji (2018: 21), where he writes 'this Middle Byzantine demographic increase in turn fuelled the expansion of large estates because labour was more easily available now'. The same case about population increases was made by him earlier (Banaji, 2001).
56 Medick (1981).
57 Banaji (2018: 13).
58 See Banaji (2018: 157, 158, 164–65), which suggests that he persists in misrecognizing the fact that tenants and sharecroppers were peasants, having usufruct rights on an estate, for which they paid rent (in labour or in kind). They were no less peasants for not owning the land they cultivated. Following the logic proposed by Banaji, one could say a landlord who held an estate granted him by the monarch was as a result not a landlord.

estate workforce composed solely of landless hired labour, on which depends in turn his capitalism-not-feudalism designation of the Late Antique economy.

The privileging by Banaji of exchange relations (trade, market, merchants, money, gold), as distinct from property relations, is open to a number of objections. To begin with, this focus is not new, a similar analysis of the pattern and structure of trade linking western and eastern parts of the Roman Empire having appeared in the late 1960s, nor is it Marxist.[59] Problems with any claim to have discovered evidence for capitalism in ancient society have been underlined by many Marxists, and were highlighted by Trotsky a century ago, in the course of questioning a similar attempt by Pokrovsky to have found 'a trade-capitalist Russia in the sixteenth century'.[60] To say, as does Banaji, that market competition is proof for the existence of capitalism, in effect makes it necessary to argue that the Punic Wars – the struggle between Rome and Carthage over the course of the second century BC for commercial supremacy in the Mediterranean – corresponded to a form of capitalist rivalry. It amounts to nothing more than labelling all trade as capitalist, which is precisely the view that Banaji seems to hold.[61] On this criterion, capitalism has existed everywhere and at all times, a perception espoused not by Marxist theory but rather by neoclassical economists generally, and cliometrician

---

59 Simkin (1968).
60 Writing in 1921, Trotsky (1972a: 341–42) noted: 'Here suffice it to say that in constructing a trade-capitalist Russia in the sixteenth century Comrade Pokrovsky falls into the error of the German professor Eduard Meyer who discovered capitalism in ancient Greece and Rome. Meyer was undoubtedly right in noticing that previous views of the economic structure of Greece and Rome (those of Rodbertus and others) as a series of self-contained natural-economic cells (*oikos*) was a schematic and over-simplified one. He showed that these basic cells were connected with one another and with other countries by a fairly well developed system of commodity exchange. At the same time, in certain spheres and branches there was also mass production. Utilizing modern economic relations and concepts, Meyer retrospectively constructed a Graeco-Roman capitalism. His error consisted in the fact that he failed to appreciate the quantitative, and therefore also qualitative, differences between various types of economies – *oikos*, simple commodity, and capitalist'.
61 The privileging by Banaji (2017: 3, original emphasis) of a dominant form of merchant capital as historically ubiquitous, a feature as much of Late Antiquity as of present-day neoliberalism, is evident from the following: 'It is crucial to see at the outset that Marx treats commercial capital ... strictly as a function of *industrial* capital. The merchant is simply an "agent" of industrial capital ... If Marxists think they [*sic*: not "we"] can use this "theoretical definition"... as the basis for writing the history of capitalism, they will make no progress beyond largely sterile debates about "transition", "world systems", etc'. This underlines the extent of his break, not just with the concept 'transition' but also with Marxist theory itself.

historiography in particular. For them, as now it seems also for Banaji, capitalism is depicted as systemically eternal, an economic form that cannot be transcended.

The claims made by Banaji concerning the widespread use in Late Antiquity of gold currency also face a number of difficulties. To begin with, the assertion that it is an issue not addressed by earlier historiography is quite simply incorrect.[62] Perhaps the most critical assessment of his argument pointed out that, relative to other commodities, gold was far too valuable to circulate as currency on a day-to-day basis, and consequently functioned much rather as a general store of wealth.[63] The disparity between the price of gold and other commodities exchanged was too large for it to operate as anything other than a much narrower repository of value.[64] It is a critique borne out by the economic survey edited by Frank which, contrary to the insistence by Banaji that the Late Antique countryside was awash with hired workers paid in gold, throws doubt

---

62   Thus, for example, the volume on Egypt in the economic survey of ancient Rome edited by Tenney Frank contains a large section on precisely this subject (Johnson, 1936: Chapter III).

63   The criticism, by an economist (Grantham, 2004), of the earlier volume by Banaji where the same case is advanced, merits citing in full: 'Banaji seems to accept the view that in the third century the economy was becoming less monetized, and that this trend reversed itself after the establishment of the solidus. The logic of this argument is very obscure. The value of the solidus relative to the price of ordinary commodities and labour (a semi-skilled worker earned three solidi per year) was so high that it can hardly have been used as a store of wealth or in banking and wholesale commerce. Evidence of its being used in ordinary transactions most likely refers to its use as a unit of account. The value of other coins relative to the solidus varied systematically over time. One should be able to make some sense of the pattern, as the copper coinage was the principal medium of exchange. Unfortunately Banaji is not a trained economist. His monetary analysis is hopelessly contaminated by the attempt to explain the variations in the relative value of copper, silver and gold coinage ... The monetary history of the later Roman Empire deserves better'. It is difficult not to agree with the concluding observation about sources, that the analysis 'does not state hypotheses in a way that might permit the reader to judge whether they are supported or disconfirmed by the facts. This is partly the fault of the facts, which are scattered and hard to aggregate into an empirical argument'. Earlier, Jones (1956: 24, 26) indicated not only that privately-owned gold was used to pay taxes or sold to the treasury in exchange for 'debased denarii', but also that the fourth century government purchased in *solidi*, resulting in an inflation of the denarius, which in Egypt exchanged for the *solidus* at a rate of 30,000,000 to one.

64   Thus, for example, Jones (1956: 31–32) notes that '[t]he Roman Emperors from time to time paid subsidies to various barbarian kings beyond the Rhine and the Danube in denarii ... or later in solidi. These subsidies were fairly regular, and at times very large ... Many of these solidi were no doubt melted down into jewellery or plate ... Solidi found in Norway do not necessarily attest Roman trade with that country'.

on the veracity of such an assumption.⁶⁵ Similarly problematic is his assertion concerning increases in money quantity per head of population, which relies for its veracity on two calculations: the amount of money in circulation, and population levels, neither of which – as Brunt and others have pointed out – can be done with any kind of precision.⁶⁶ On the question of overtaxation, the occurrence of which Banaji denies, it is crucial to note the case that was actually made by Jones: what the latter pointed out was that the taxation system was regressive, in that a peasant smallholder paid the same 'as the great landlord on his wide estates'.⁶⁷ Famines and peasant starvation also contradict assertions concerning the lack of rural impoverishment, a condition that Banaji also denies.⁶⁸

III

In keeping with the view of Late Antiquity as a bountiful economic period, therefore, Banaji reveals his underlying theoretical allegiances. First, the same enthusiasm for the efficacy of the market as did Oertel previously in the case of the early Principate.⁶⁹ And second, underlined thereby is the dissonance

---

65 'Numismatists are in general agreement that gold was not issued from the Alexandrian mint by the Emperors', observes Johnson (1936: 425), 'and records of payments in gold coin are extremely rare'.
66 On difficulties calculating population levels throughout Roman history, see Brunt (1987).
67 See Jones (1966: 22) who 'In the old days when the rate of taxes was fixed the government had to cut its coat according to its cloth. Now if it wanted to spend more it could raise the [tax rate]. In fact we are told by Themistius that in the forty years between 324 and 364 it was doubled ... the whole burden of taxation ... fell on agriculture'. By the sixth century, the tax rate on peasants was 'crushing' (Jones, 1966: 294–95), being 'equivalent to about a third of the crop on arable land'.
68 On famines and peasant starvation, see Jones (1966: 295). Elsewhere he (Jones, 1964: 10) states that: 'A passage in Galen also reveals serious distress ... [s]peaking of the widespread and prolonged famines which had recently occurred, he writes: "The city dwellers, as it was their practice to collect and store enough corn for all the next year immediately after the harvest, carried off all the wheat and barley and beans and lentils, and left what remained to the country people, that is pulses of various kinds, and they took a good deal of these too to the city. The country people finished the pulses during the winter, and so had to fall back on unhealthy foods during the spring; they ate twigs and shoots of trees and bushes, and bulbs and roots of indigestible plants; they filled themselves with wild herbs and cooked fresh grass." As a result, he goes on, practically all of them developed ulcers, which in the majority of cases proved fatal'.
69 Earlier critiques by me (Brass, 2003; Brass, 2005; Brass, 2012) of both the theory and methods used by Banaji pointed out that his approach was not just inconsistent with Marxism but also compatible with an anti-Marxist neoclassical economic framework. His interpretation of ancient society is in terms of its theoretical assumptions comparable to that of the cliometric analysis by Fogel and Engerman (1974) of the southern antebellum plantation system.

between the economic picture Banaji draws and that portrayed by earlier materialist analyses.[70]

Had Marx Lived ...

It is difficult not to see Banaji as the true inheritor of the Oertel argument concerning the presence in the Roman Empire of a benign market system. Thus, for example, Oertel used the same kind of sources (papyri, coinage) as Banaji, yet the latter presents them as 'new'.[71] However, there are a number of differences between them. To begin with, Oertel located what he regarded as a fully functioning urban capitalism in the first century Principate; by contrast, Banaji places a similarly idealised economic system in rural areas from the third century onwards. Whereas Oertel – a neoclassical economic historian – maintains that the subsequent decline was due to state 'interference' in the functioning of the market, Banaji contends that the market did indeed continue to function, and that consequently Late Antiquity – as a *de facto* extension of the Roman Empire (which did not, after all, decline or fall) – represents the ongoing triumph of capitalism. The case made by Oertel in the late 1930s, that 'capitalistic' commerce was moving East, is precisely the same as that advanced now by Banaji.[72]

This theoretical affinity with non- or anti-Marxist theory celebrating the market has deep roots. There is no Marxist or Marxism that escapes Banaji's censure, the epithet 'bad theory' cropping up time and again throughout his publications (a favourite term of disapprobation being the accusation of 'formalism'). Among those castigated in this manner are not just Isaac Ilyich Rubin, Lenin, and Kautsky but also Marx himself. It is in a sense unsurprising, therefore, that such condemnation is then seen by Banaji as a license to reinterpret what they (and others) really meant. Although the distinction between relations of production and relations of exploitation is central to his

---

70 See Walbank (1946: 56–57) for a different view: 'Byzantium remained a rigid caste-state, its rural districts largely desolate and its agriculture feeble, with neither the economic foundations nor the mental atmosphere to foster scientific thought and progress ... Its achievements ... were far from negligible, but they lay rather in the field preservation and the maintenance of equilibrium, than in any new and vigorous undertaking'.
71 On the sameness of these sources, see Oertel (1939: 246).
72 For the earlier case, see Oertel (1939: 238–39, 243, 246), who notes 'the transference to the provinces of that activity, capitalistic in its methods, which was specifically bourgeois'. The latter description coincides with the 'moderately affluent middle classes' of Banaji (2018: 5).

own interpretation, therefore, Banaji nevertheless accepts that he 'do[es] not, of course, claim that the distance was always marked in the work of Marx himself'.[73] Playing fast and loose with Marxist theory extends also to the concept 'primitive accumulation', which according to Banaji 'is no longer the best way to frame the early history of capitalism'.[74] However, it pops back into life subsequently, when he states 'I shall argue that at least some of this was "primitive accumulation"', only to vanish once again later in the same analysis: '"primitive accumulation" of capital ... is not necessarily the best perspective to adopt' when writing the history of capitalism.[75] Like modes of production themselves, 'primitive accumulation' seems to be an issue about which Banaji continues to change his mind.

He goes further, and not only accuses Marx of not 'producing a specifically materialist history' but also maintains that 'there is no specifically Marxist historiography of capitalism'.[76] As in the case of modes of production not found in Marx's analysis, but nevertheless inserted into his own framework by Banaji, the latter assures us that '[h]ad Marx lived to complete the new version of [the third volume of *Capital*], we would no doubt have an even more powerful demonstration of what [exploitation] meant'.[77] The difficulty with this kind of endlessly counter-factual approach is obvious. Hence the point made by Marx in the *Resultate* concerning formal subsumption of labour refers specifically to what happens to apparently pre-capitalist forms (smallholding, slavery, debt bondage, sharecropping) under capitalism, once this has become established.[78] However, this is projected backwards into history by Banaji, who then argues that wherever/whenever such relations are encountered, they are 'disguised' hired workers, and – consequently – there too is found capitalism.

---

73 Cf. Banaji (2010: 2, 4–5, 9) and Banaji (1972: 2498). Marx (1969: 391–2; 1968: 328; 1972: 301–2, 310, 352, 495) uses the term 'exploitation' to describe a *quantitative* relation between capital and labour (the *rate* of exploitation), not – as argued by Banaji – a *qualitative* relational difference (slave-not-sharecropper, worker-not-peasant). The latter meaning was elaborated much rather by the anthropologist Pierre-Philippe Rey, who conducted fieldwork in Africa during the 1960s (Rey, 1975; Dupré and Rey, 1980). Marx's emphasis is on the amount of surplus extracted *within* the context of a given production relation, as distinct from the different institutional forms involved. Hence exploitation can increase or decrease without the production relation itself changing – that is to say, regardless of whether the latter consists of free or unfree labour-power.
74 Banaji (2010: 43–44).
75 Banaji (2010: 261, 272–3).
76 Banaji (2010: 46, 272).
77 Banaji (2010: 42).
78 Marx (1976: 948ff.).

By contrast, he commends and/or endorses the work of many non-Marxist and anti-Marxist authors, including neo-classical economic historians such as Steinfield, Fogel, Engerman, Bauer and Kula.[79] Castigating Marx and other Marxists for 'formalism', therefore, Banaji in effect dismisses what they thought and wrote, putting in their place his own views (based on the assumption, that 'whole swathes of the history of capitalism are ignored by Marxists').[80] The latter turn out to have little or nothing to do with Marxism.

Marginalism Is Not Marxism

Nowhere is the extent of Banaji's break with Marxism, and his affinity with non-Marxist theory, more on show than in his insistence that no difference has existed – or can exist – between free and unfree labour.[81] All working arrangements are for Banaji nothing more than variants of 'disguised' wage-labour, conceptualized by him as 'contract' to which he adds the label 'free'. For a marginalist economic historian such as Steinfeld, whose legalistic definition of contract Banaji endorses, freedom of contract means quite simply the ability of workers *to enter* working arrangements: that they are subsequently unable *to withdraw* from them without the consent of their employer does not affect his meaning.[82] Banaji thereby unwittingly imbibes from neo-classical economic theory the view that a work arrangement is defined simply by the act of recruitment ('entry into').

This contrasts with Marxist theory, for which a work arrangement is defined by a process: the reproduction of the relational form ('entry into' + 'exit from'), as embodied in the ability of a worker personally to commodify and recommodify his/her own labour-power. It is simply not the case that Banaji's interpretation is based on the view that "Marx's Capital can only be understood profoundly if one takes the Hegelian background of the work seriously". Had it been, Banaji would have discovered the crucial role Hegel played in Marxist teleology: namely, the

---

79 This shortcoming is itself compounded by the fact that Banaji falls into the most common of epistemological traps, the failure to question the methods/theory of secondary sources cited. We are left wondering what assumptions structure these analyses, what kinds of concepts they use, and why.
80 Banaji (2010: 272).
81 See Banaji (2010: 131ff.) It does not follow from saying that free wage-labour is not the *sine qua non* of the capitalist mode of production (Banaji, 2010: 11) – these days an uncontroversial proposition, having been advanced over the years by, among others, Maurice Dobb, Ernest Mandel, Sidney Mintz, Daniel Guérin, Alex Lichtenstein and me – that consequently there is no difference between free and unfree labour-power.
82 Steinfeld (2001).

conceptualization by Adam Smith of labour as value, by Hegel of labour as property, and by Marx of labour-power as commodity that can be bought/sold. A distinction between workers who are free and those who are unfree informs the historical process of becoming, being, remaining, and acting as a proletariat, itself the result of class struggle between capital and labour.

In the course of such conflict, agency metamorphoses from that conducted by the (Hegelian) subject-in-general to that by (Marxist) subjects-of-a-particular-class. This in turn gives rise to the bonding by employers of landless workers – regardless of whether they are permanent, seasonal, casual, locals, or migrants. The latter corresponds to deproletarianization, a process whereby labour power is either decommodified or recommodified by someone other than its owner. Even when dispossessed of land, therefore, erstwhile smallholders – not just in India but also elsewhere in the global capitalist system – nevertheless still retain access to another form of personal property: their labour-power. It is precisely this kind of ownership, exercised by workers over their labour-power, that an employer has to deprive them of so as to exert in turn full control over a modern production process.[83]

That Banaji remains unsure as to what, precisely, constitutes unfree labour-power is evident from the way he defines it in relation to the Late Antique economy. Replying to a critic who takes him to task for not recognizing that *coloni* were unfree, he responds weakly by saying that were they unfree, no law would be required to impose this, which misses the point entirely.[84] State-enforced unfreedom is anyway unnecessary, since landlords have the power locally to do so on their own behalf. Similarly mistaken is the equation by him

---

83   Marx (1973: 463) states quite clearly that free labour is in terms of consciousness of labour-power as the property of the self an improvement over the way this relation is perceived by unfree workers. It is therefore a myth that capitalists everywhere and at all times want labour-power to be free. They do initially, it is true, so that they can have access to workers, one of the reasons why the bourgeoisie are opposed to a landlord class which imposes unfree relations on its own tenants, thereby denying capitalists access to this potential workforce. However, once the latter have become separated from the means of production, are transformed into a proletariat, and begin to organize as such against employers with the object of improving pay/conditions, the situation changes. This is especially the case when owners of the means of production come under pressure from two sources as capitalism spreads: on the one hand from workers struggling against cut-backs to pay/conditions, and on the other from rival enterprises that have managed to cut labour costs.

84   For this criticism, and the reply, see Banaji (2018: 162, n.28 chapter 1), where he states that '[c]*oloni* were a category of permanent farm labour [who] were free persons in the legal sense that they were not slaves, but restricted in their movements and subject increasingly to … the control of their employers'. Nearly two decades ago the same element of confusion informed the acceptance by him (Banaji, 2001: 207ff.) that smallholding tenants (*coloni*) were indeed unfree, both 'belonging to their masters by law' and being

of unfreedom only with chattel slavery, a view which he incorrectly thinks is the way Marxism interprets it. Limiting unfreedom only to chattel slavery is to ignore the extent to which a wide variety of non-slave production relations – for example, tenants, sharecroppers, bonded labourers, attached workers, indentured servants – are also unfree.

IV

As noted in the previous chapter, methodological difficulties confront those exponents of Late Antiquity who ascribe the novelty of their different interpretations to previously overlooked information contained in grassroots data of one kind or another. The most obvious of these problems concern the sparse nature and extent of the data required for the case they seek to make, not least regarding both the presence of 'new' categories (landowners, workers) and religious beliefs held.[85] This is a problem that applies with particular force to the claims about Late Antiquity made not just by Banaji but also by Brown.

Building Castles in the Air

Time and again, therefore, one encounters what in such 'new' analyses is a familiar procedure: an initial and tokenistic acceptance of the paucity of the data is quickly followed by the construction of an elaborate theoretical architecture built on precisely these same 'sources'. In such instances, repeated warnings voiced by the author him/herself about fragmentary, absent, or even 'invisible' data are subsequently disregarded, and with them any mismatch between evidence and argument. Long ago, A.H.M. Jones cautioned against the

---

'persons subject to the legal control of others'. These tenants, he then asserts, were nevertheless 'free' labour, because 'such subjection was grounded ... not in slavery but in wage labour'. In brief, because they were paid, such tenants were wage labour, which by definition must be 'free'. Thus *coloni*, over whom he accepts landlords exercised what amounted to property rights, are in his view still 'free' wage labourers.

85 Instead of legal sources, Banaji bases his case about the ubiquity of 'free' wage labour in antiquity on papyri. Notwithstanding the fact that each new claim – about, for example, the existence/presence of casual/seasonal/daily wage labour that is 'free' – is preceded by a disclaimer concerning the scanty and/or partial nature of the sources on which it is based, the subsequent process of theoretical construction on such 'foundations' does not appear to take much account of these empirical limitations. The problem is not just methodological, therefore, since difficulties stemming from inadequate data are accompanied – and, indeed, compounded – by theoretical shortcomings.

attempt to make inflated claims on the basis of what were – and are still – thin, incomplete, or even non-existent archaeological/numismatic data, advice that exponents of Late Antiquity in effect ignore.[86] Much the same point had been made even earlier by Sherwin-White, who observed that '[a]ny argument from silence in the history of the empire is dangerous'.[87] In particular, Jones warned against the tendency by numismatists to over-interpret the meaning of coins found at archaeological digs, and the role/extent of currency in the Roman Empire, remarking that 'the value of the numismatic evidence has tended to be overstrained'.[88] Pointing out that '[a]fter the great inflation of the mid-third century A.D. the currency remained in a chaotic condition for about two centuries', Jones observes that some coins continued to circulate for centuries, and further that copies were struck, which 'shows how dangerous it is to argue from dated coins the dates of economic events'.[89]

In the case of Brown, it is clear not just from his earlier publications but also from his unintentionally revealing autobiographical memoir, that he has been – and increasingly is – faced with an insurmountable problem with regard to the sources for the kind of history that he wishes to see written. This is especially so given the ambitious research agenda he sets now for historians of Late Antiquity: to anchor the study of religious belief at a grassroots level, in 'the social, economic and cultural circumstances of the later empire'.[90] His

---

86 Noting both that the economic data available to ancient historians 'are sparse, inaccurate and vague', and that consequently economic generalizations about Egypt on the basis of papyrological sources are impossible, Jones (1948: 2) commented: 'The task of reconstructing the public finances of Egypt from the papyri is comparable with attempting an estimate of the revenue of the United Kingdom from a few pages torn at random from the ledgers of the inland Revenue Offices of, say, Maidenhead, Gloucester and Chepstow'. Much the same point was made subsequently by Finley (1971) and Stone (1971).
87 Sherwin-White (1939: 190).
88 See Jones (1956: 32). This is accompanied by numerous other and similar caveats (Jones, 1956: 19, 26): for example, '[i]t might be expected that [coins] would be useful evidence for economic history', but '[w]e have scarcely any information on some very elementary questions', and '[h]ow far ... the Roman empire had any currency policy is very difficult to divine. The coins themselves are almost the only evidence, but great caution is needed in building any theories upon them'.
89 Jones (1956: 29, 30).
90 Hence the initial emphasis (Brown, 1972: 17) on the importance of 'more intimate, if prosaic, facts about how Late Roman men grappled with suffering and misfortune in their lives, by what means they maintained their image of themselves, and what they expected in their relations with others', concluding that '[t]he historian of religion, precisely because his is a historian of religion, must keep his eyes firmly on the ground'. More recently he had stated (Brown, 2003: 5, 6): 'I did not conceive of my biography of Augustine as a contribution only to the religious history of late antiquity ... Religion without Society interested me not in the least ... Up to this day, the study of religious experience

dilemma is a methodological one: he is unable to escape the limits which his sources impose on him. Despite the claim by Brown about the centrality to his own work of an anthropological approach, a major gulf separates fieldwork involving the ethnographic practice of participant/observation carried out at the rural grassroots from his own researches. The latter are, and cannot be anything other than, a mediated source of information: texts written not by those at the rural grassroots but about them, by commentators whose ideology (religious) or class position will rather obviously have an impact on what these texts contain.[91]

Necessarily missing from any/every historiography of Late Antiquity, therefore, is a capacity to access, capture, and record the unmediated voice-from-below, a methodological procedure that is indeed open to present-day anthropologists conducting fieldwork at the level of the village, the smallholding, the peasant family, or the individual agricultural labourer. It is precisely this gulf – between on the one hand a desire to 'know' what 'the little people' think, and why, and on the other the absence of direct contact with such unmediated voices – that poses difficulties for the approach to Late Antiquity that Brown regards as necessary.[92] In light of this impasse, it is understandable that he turns to the only available resolution, not a methodological but rather a theoretical one. The deployment of a postmodern approach in order to re-examine the existing texts: 'We still must sift these texts, again and again [for]

---

divorced from a precise social context has always struck me as a singularly weightless exercise. A history of the rise of Christianity that is not rooted in a precise and up-to-date history of the social, economic and cultural circumstances of the later empire and the early middle ages is, quite simply, not history'. Significantly, he then adds: 'Easier said than done'.

91 'The books we read together at those desks ... were our true interlocutors', notes Brown (2003: 7, 12), 'I wanted to make sure that the ancient authors spoke to us quietly, and with their own voices'. This contrasts with the comments made by others on these same kinds of sources. Noting that 'Christian hagiography is arguably the most distinctive literary genre of late antiquity', therefore, Mitchell (2007: 14, 15) continues by saying '[m]uch of this Christian literature is transparently and unabashedly partisan in the way that it portrays the world of late antiquity'.

92 'I have developed a taste for smaller figures, glimpsed in great numbers, against a late antique landscape of greater religious and cultural complexity than we had once supposed', confesses Brown (2003: 16), adding: 'I have found myself, for the moment at least, happy to find myself among the little people, often glimpsed at the very edge of the field of vision of triumphalist Christian texts ... To develop the skills necessary to treat with intelligence and respect persons, little as well as great, caught in this way, on the edge of an unknown future, remains the *ars atrium* of any historian of late antiquity'.

alternative voices lurking on the very margins of evidence'.[93] Many of these same methodological difficulties also face the attempt by Banaji to interpret the Late Antique economy as a form of capitalism.

In his haste to proclaim the validity of a point, therefore, Banaji moves rapidly from one text to another, all mentioned far too briefly. Nowhere does he stop to interrogate the theory – let alone the methods – informing the analyses he endorses, passing over this issue to claim this or that text merely 'shows' or 'demonstrates' the case (or argument) he is attempting to make. Thus, for example, Banaji endorses a paper written in 2008 which states that 'the entire regulatory system is geared to free labourers and free manufacturers and traders', without asking how its author defined these concepts.[94] The problems inherent in this sort of approach have been raised elsewhere, when he commended as models to be followed both the cliometric (= neoclassical economic) revision of the antebellum plantation economy and the work of the anti-Marxist historian Richard Pipes, overlooking the many critiques of those analyses, not just political but also empirical and methodological.[95] An earlier – and methodologically problematic – appeal by Brown to visualize what are non-existent data ('we have to make the considerable imaginative leap of entering into a world where religion was taken absolutely for granted') is reproduced verbatim by Banaji with regard to the economy.[96] Moreover, where the presence of capitalism in ancient society is concerned, despite the fact that Banaji favours the approach of Mommsen (who endorses its existence) over

---

93 Asking '[w]here does all this leave me?', Brown (2003: 15) replies: 'The application of literary theory to the textual evidence of later antiquity has left us with a sober respect for the power of texts in and by themselves to iron out the tensions and anomalies of real life. If each age gets the historical methodology that it deserves, then the Christian writers ... have got what they richly deserved: a stringent dose of post-modern "hermeneutical suspicion" [which] challenges us to look elsewhere ... to the great, untidy "excavation site" of the texts themselves. We still must sift these texts, again and again, for hitherto unconsidered scraps of evidence, for hints of unresolved anomalies and of alternative voices lurking on the very margins of the evidence'.

94 Banaji (2018: x). An additional difficulty, and one he does not mention, is the representativeness of the data about ancient society which does indeed survive. This is a methodological caveat noted by Rowlandson (1985: 329): 'But although precise information is available for one village, we must hesitate to generalise from this single case. Indeed, the whole subject of land tenure in Ptolemaic Egypt is so bedevilled by geographical and chronological concentration of papyrological sources that it is difficult to assess how far the conditions of tenure were themselves subject to regional variation or chronological development'.

95 For details, see Brass (2005: 132ff.; 2012: 714 n.12).

96 Brown (1978: 8–9). For a similar invocation of 'invisible' economic data, see Banaji (2001: 220).

that of Marx (who denies this), the description by Mommsen of provincial economic organization does not quite accord with the notion of widespread economic dynamism.[97]

It is only when the evidence Banaji claims exists is scrutinized that real difficulties emerge. Time after time, therefore, reference is made to proof furnished by archaeological data 'that began to be laid out in the 1990s and certainly by the 2000s', without asking what such evidence (not presented) can tell us; that is, the same methodological problem that confronts Brown.[98] Confident assertions to the effect that 'the archaeological revolution of ... the last three decades throws up a huge challenge for historians of late antiquity', and '[t]he explosion of survey archaeology since the late 1970s has shown ...' remain unaccompanied by explanations as to what precisely the 'archaeological revolution' actually demonstrates.[99] Maybe because of this one encounters an occasionally tentative observation ('My own feeling is ...'), together with equally sporadic admissions concerning the lack of evidence/data/information corroborating the argument, claim, or case that Banaji is making.[100] Ironically, he questions the case made by earlier analyses dismissed as 'minimalist' on the grounds of 'how do we know?', forgetting perhaps that this very question has been raised about the claims he himself makes.[101]

---

97 Mommsen (1867: 220) observes that although 'Celtic industry cannot have been wholly undeveloped', therefore, '[i]n most branches, however, their handicraft does not appear to have risen above the ordinary level'.

98 See Banaji (2018: 8–9), who announces early on that he does not intend to discuss his sources (Banaji, 2018: xvii). For similar references to this sort of evidence, along the lines of 'the archaeology has now made a decisive difference to the way economic histories should be written', 'from the abundant numismatic and papyrological evidence ... it is certain that there was an increase in the "per capita value of the money stock", see Banaji (2018: 11, 18).

99 Banaji (2018: 62–63). Again on a personal note, whilst in Aquileia during September 2013, I visited its Archaelogical Museum where two maps in the numismatic section indicated that the range of trade under Roman rule (North Africa, Germany, the Balkans) reduced considerably under the Patriarchate, when coins which had been encountered far afield were now found only in the vicinity of Aquileia itself.

100 These sort of admissions are encountered intermittently (Banaji, 2018: xv, 58, 68–69, 78 original emphasis). Thus he accepts the absence/paucity of data/sources for his concept 'private economy' (contracts, accounts, correspondence), plus other similar references along the lines of 'we have no way of quantifying the role of direct grants of land', '[o]ne reason there is so little explicit evidence of this side of their economic activities ...', and '[t]he dispersion of merchant colonies throughout the Mediterranean *may* imply a transformation of commerce ... [t]he famous financier ... was bound to have had late antique counterparts, but we know almost nothing about them'.

101 See Banaji (2018: 8–9), of whom the same question has been asked previously on a number of occasions (Brass, 2003, 2005).

Claims about the presence of extensive trade networks, leading initially to notions of economic dynamism and, ultimately, to an interpretation that the particular area concerned represented a form of ancient capitalism, have been brought into question more recently by a detailed analysis of the Cyclades at a much earlier period.[102] In a timely warning against the tendency on the part of some to identify the scantiest of economic activity as evidence for capitalism, a remarkably scrupulous cliometric study of the economy of Delos over the second and third centuries BC, posed methodological questions about access to and meaning of the available economic data – along the lines of 'the uninformativeness of these documents [the proxeny decrees] has not stopped commentators from drawing economic inferences' – together with its implication for theory about the wider economic system in which the island was situated.[103]

Notwithstanding '[t]he idea that the Hellenistic Aegean saw an extensive price-setting market has appealed to many scholars', therefore, not only was it the case that 'prices were set locally and were relatively impervious to the impact of price changes elsewhere', but it was also the fact that '[t]he small scale of the trade is also striking'.[104] Rather than being 'tied into a great trading network' extending from Greece to the Levant – in other words, an ancient

---

102 'Early studies of the Delian economy were influenced by a "modernizing" model of the Hellenistic world that saw capitalism everywhere and emphasized long-distance trade and strong market interconnections', observes Reger (1994: 55–56), who continues that they 'served as a solid substratum on which to build a history of economic change over time for the entire Greek East'.

103 See Reger (1994: 64). Earlier, he (Reger, 1994: 9) made the following apposite comments: '[M]any of the data from Delos, as abundant as they may be, are useless for economic analysis. There are hundreds of instances of payments to unskilled labourers for cleaning, carrying roof tiles, hauling building stone, or transporting wood, but ... [g]eneralizations about the "level of wages" or attempts to reconstruct a budget or cost of living from such data are very hazardous. Likewise, the lack of figures for quantity bought for some goods ... and the absence of any descriptive information (weight, length, cost of manufacture) for other items ... render the abundant recorded prices useless'. In the same vein, he concludes (Reger, 1994: 273): 'Many places offer no data, of course, and the desire to squeeze as much information as possible out of the sources that do exist certainly can lead to over-interpretation, distortion, and generalizations based on inadequate evidence'. Such caveats bear out the earlier methodological caution advised by historians like A.H.M. Jones, Sherwin-White, Brunt and de Ste Croix.

104 See Reger (1994: 75, 79). 'Generally speaking', he notes (Reger, 1994: 80), 'discussions of markets in the Hellenistic economy have not shown much sophistication. A large-scale, long-range, unified price-setting market for a good like grain requires the reliable exchange of local price information, available to all participants; reliable, reasonably quick transportation to respond to local changes caused by local conditions; redistribution and storage centres; and indifference on the part of consumers as to the origin of the goods they buy and on the part of producers as to the ultimate destination of their

form of capitalism – 'Delian economic history ... can be explained perfectly adequately' by reference to local phenomena.[105] Accordingly, from this unexpected quarter – both contextually and theoretically – comes a methodological lesson that it would be wise for historians of ancient society to heed.

Conclusion

Of the many current attempts to redefine both the Late Antique economy and Marxism itself, that by Banaji is by far the most problematic, departing from Marx to the degree that it ceases to be recognizable as having a framework informed by his concepts. From his interpretation of Late Antiquity, one would have difficulty in guessing that Banaji originally subscribed to the semifeudal thesis and the concept of a 'colonial' mode of production, both of which he abandoned only after he was criticized by other participants in the 1970s debate. As easy to miss is the fact that his interpretation of Marxism not only diverges substantially from that of Marx and Lenin, but also is sympathetic to (and informed by) a conceptual apparatus opposed to Marxist theory. Many elements in his analysis (the state, the free/unfree labour distinction, peasant household) are drawn not from Marxism but from non-and anti-Marxist frameworks (neoclassical economic historiography, populism, Cold War notions of the state). Marxism, Banaji would have us believe, is really nothing more than a species of marginalist economic theory, and Lenin is nothing more than an unwitting follower of Chayanovian neo-populism. The obvious question posed is how much Marxist theory can one abandon and still be regarded in all seriousness as a Marxist?

Among the more important Marxist concepts Banaji discards is the distinction between free/unfree production relations, an ironic absence given its centrality to an understanding both of Late Antiquity and of economic development in India. Since capitalism is perceived by him as an eternal systemic form, the 'disguised' wage-labour framework recognizes neither unfree labour nor primitive accumulation. By abolishing the free/unfree distinction and

---

products. The Hellenistic Aegean met only some of these conditions, only in part, and only some of the time'.

105 'In contrast to more traditional approaches, which have regarded Hellenistic Delos as tied to a great trading network reaching from Greece, or even southern Italy, to the Black Sea, the Levant, and beyond', argues Reger (1994: 49), 'Delian economic history, especially prices and rents, can be explained perfectly adequately by appeal to entirely local phenomena'.

maintaining instead that all rural workers – in Late Antiquity no less than in present-day capitalist India – are simply hired labourers who are contractually free, this view breaks with Marxism and is indistinguishable from neo-classical economic historiography. In short, it reproduces the claim made by cliometricians that capital and labour are ever-present, historically non-specific and thus 'natural' economic categories that cannot be transcended.

Given that the approach of Banaji to Late Antiquity has more in common with neoclassical economics than with Marxism, the supposition would be that a degree of overlap exists between his arguments and those of Oertel. And, indeed, this turns out to be the case. As drawn by Banaji, therefore, the picture of Late Antiquity is one of large numbers of happy workers freely wandering around the countryside with their tunic pockets bulging full of gold. It is a comforting image for present-day bourgeois economists interested in proclaiming the advantages that capitalism – systemically eternal, of course – confers on its workforce, members of which might be entertaining negative thoughts as to the lack of economic benefit that accumulation holds for people like themselves. His hostility to Marxism is evident from the attempt to erase the difference between industrial capital and merchant capital: whereas Marx subordinated the latter to the former, Banaji not only reverses this but appears intent on reducing industrial capital to a species of merchant capital. Among other things, this enables him to claim that capital is ever-present, as much a feature of Late Antiquity as of the twenty-first century global economy.

CHAPTER 7

From Class Struggle to Identity Politics (*via* 'Otherness')

> In the titanic battles that must be fought before the emancipation of the American working class is attained it is inconceivable that the Negroes can or will remain a neutral force. They will cast their lot with the ruling whites or with the proletariat seeking to unseat them. If their tremendous power is thrown on the side of the bourgeoisie, it will mean a sure triumph for reaction and a heavy blow at all the aspirations of Negroes themselves. If their weight is added in the scales on the side of the proletariat, their common victory against capitalism will be immensely facilitated, the transition to a new social order will be immeasurably less painful and protracted. In the process of his own liberation the Negro will help emancipate the whole of humanity in freeing itself.
>
> Left Opposition policy on the race/class issue formulated by MAX SHACHTMAN during the early 1930s.[1]

∴

Introduction

On the face of it, there is little to connect the approaches to Late Antiquity considered in the previous two chapters with discussion in this one of the interrelations between identity, belonging, and the reproduction in present-day metropolitan capitalism of the industrial reserve army. In terms of what is missing from Marxism, and why the presence of Marxist theory is missed, however, there is no epistemological break. Accordingly, the focus of this chapter is on the way the process of empowerment/disempowerment has shifted

---

1 See Shachtman (2003: 4). It should be noted that when citing the words not just of Shachtman but also of Robeson and James, the direct language each of them used has been followed, despite the fact that their ways of describing ethnic 'otherness' are nowadays no longer appropriate.

politically: from importance attributed initially to class formation/consciousness/struggle in metropolitan contexts, to the current privileging in the same milieu of essentialist categories of ethnic/national 'otherness'. This change has been accompanied by a corresponding re-conceptualization of systemic empowerment: the latter has moved away from socialism and towards capitalism. The fact and dynamics of this shift is examined with reference to the contrast between the earlier political ideas/agency of two major black intellectuals/activists (Robeson, James), and the later forms involving writers/commentators linked to the post-colonial diaspora.[2]

The dissimilarity in terms of personal background/achievement and forms of agency together with political objectives, between on the one hand Paul Robeson and C.L.R. James, and on the other current writers/commentators on broad issues to do with culture, belonging, identity, politics, and immigration, is marked.[3] Robeson and James were descended from plantation slaves, either in the United States or the Caribbean, and each of them was personally accomplished in a wide range of activities and fields (scholarship, film/theatre, song, academia, sport). Furthermore, both were at ease not just with Western culture – about which each displayed an understanding of its aesthetics, history, politics, and meaning – but also combined such knowledge with a similar appreciation of popular culture. Robeson and James not only advocated direct action in furtherance of socialist political objectives, but – consequently – experienced sustained harassment by security organs of the capitalist state.[4]

---

2 Whilst it is true that the post-colonial diasporic voices considered here are not the only ones, or indeed not even the most representative views regarding 'otherness', they are nevertheless publicly the ones heard more often than not. It is they who occupy media platforms – appearing frequently on television or radio discussion programmes, writing articles in the press or publishing books – and consequently in terms of contributing to, forming, and reproducing a symptomatic discourse about 'otherness', whose voice can be seen as a relatively privileged one.

3 For the life and background of Robeson, see Duberman (1989); that of James can be found particularly in his quasi-autobiographical account (James, 1963) of West Indian cricket, which locates this sport – which he played and about the history of which he wrote extensively – in its wider political, social and economic context.

4 It is important to remind ourselves of the scale, duration, and impact of harassment by the state experienced by Robeson on account of his principled adherence to the political views he held. The negative effects on his ability to earn a living as a result of the HUAC hearings are described by Foner (1978: 4): 'As Robeson refused to succumb, theatre doors and concert halls were closed to him, his books were removed from libraries, and his records no longer played over the air. The State Department's refusal to grant him a passport in 1950 deprived him of the opportunity to perform abroad. Unable to act or sing in the commercial centres of culture, or to appear on radio or television, or to make recordings, or to travel, Robeson saw his income plummet from over US$150,000 annually to US$3,000'. The extent and intensity

For black intellectuals/activists such as them a threefold emancipation was necessary and had to be realized. First, contextually in terms of their own country, either within the United States or ex-colonies in the Caribbean. Second, politically, in the form of a transition to socialism. And third, grassroots struggle and organization based on a collective 'from below' identity (class + ethnicity). Because socialism remained on the political agenda, therefore, emancipation required the inclusion of all members of the working class, regardless of ethnic or national identity.[5]

By contrast, none of these options is any longer on their agenda of their present-day equivalents, composed for the most part of middle-class writers/commentators from the post-colonial diaspora who construct what might be termed a symptomatic discourse. To a large extent, they have similar backgrounds: a number of them come from wealthy and/or business families, have been privately educated, and are employed in the professions (journalism, teaching, media, culture).[6] For them, agency is individual not collective; emancipation and achievement are similarly individual, but contextually these aims are to be realized not in the home nation, as they were for Robeson and James, but rather in another western capitalist one. Again in sharp contrast to either Robeson or James, instead of socialism as a desirable/feasible objective, politically the goal is now to ascend the existing hierarchy of capitalism itself.[7] Not only is there no endorsement of socialism, let alone revolutionary Marxism, but all that present-day exponents of post-colonial discourse seem to want is simply a bigger slice of the capitalist cake; the desire is not to change the way

---

of this harassment is all too clear from the exchanges between Robeson and the Committee of the Judiciary of the US Senate in 1948, and the HUAC during 1956 (Foner, 1978: 413–36, 490–94). James, too, was arrested in the early 1950s, and detained on Ellis Island.

5 This was a view held also by many on the left (e.g., Shachtman, 2003; Guerin, 1956) – regardless of ethnicity/nationality – at the same period, extending from the 1930s through to the 1950s.

6 Seemingly in anticipation of some of the criticisms levelled at present-day post-colonial discourse, James (MARHO, 1983b: 270) has observed: '*Négritude* was not of African origin at all. It was West Indian and could only have come from the West Indies. It was not only a revolt against assimilation, but an assertion of an African civilization. Many Africans today are hostile to *negritude* because they argue that bourgeois and petty-bourgeois intellectuals have taken it up rather than taking part in concrete struggles against the imperialists'.

7 A revealing story by Mehta (2019: 66), which recounts the response of his grandfather to racist humiliation, underlines the extent to which it takes the form not of a desire for socialist equality but rather of pride in the capitalist success of those belonging to the same ethnicity or nationality ('Later, when he was living in London, he took pride in sending me lists of the richest Indians in the UK, some of them richer even than the Queen').

the cake is made, only to ensure that a larger portion of it comes their way.[8] For this reason, class is rarely, if ever, mentioned; mobilizing beliefs and organization are now largely about non-class forms of empowerment, particularly those involving ethnic or national identity.

It is of course true that the issues addressed by Robeson and James were those of a different era, when – it might be argued – the problems were correspondingly distinct. However, the comparison undertaken here is based not on particular issues, which may indeed be historically specific, but on a broader approach that is political, based on principles that transcend any particular conjuncture. Namely, a politics informed by socialist theory which applies as much to the present day as it did to the epoch of Robeson and James. This kind of approach contrasts with current post-colonial discourse about 'otherness', where the solution presented consists for the most part of vapid utterances: that is, moral appeals simply to be 'nice' to one another, without asking too closely why it is that we aren't, and what connects the latter situation to the dynamics of capitalism as a systemic form.[9]

Of the three sections composing this chapter, the first outlines the way the race/class issue informed the political ideas and agency of Robeson and James, together with the emphasis both placed on the importance of class solidarity and socialist objectives that transcended ethnic/national boundaries. The contrast between the latter approach and the more recent one of the post-colonial

---

8 In the words of one post-colonial exponent (Alibhai-Brown, 2018: 53), '[a]ll we want is a share'. Not raised by such views are crucial economic questions regarding the amount and form of this 'share', how is it to be calculated, by whom and why. More importantly, wanting nothing more than a larger slice of the capitalist cake differentiates what is essentially a bourgeois political objective from that of socialists, as Shachtman (2003: 67–68) long ago made clear: 'The Communists do not endeavour ... to divide the fight for full social and economic equality for the Negro from the general socialist struggle of the proletariat as a whole against the capitalist class. On the contrary, they combine the two, thus distinguishing themselves from the petty bourgeois liberals who demand (in words) the abolition of inequality but want to preserve the capitalist class and its system intact, that is, people who want "equal rights for Negroes" without the class struggle. The Negro masses will attain social, political and economic equality only by way of the class struggle'.

9 Thus, for example, Mehta (2019: 25) resorts to a weak form of Social Darwinism, maintaining: 'It is our most elemental drive: to survive; and, having propagated, to do anything and everything to make sure our progeny lives a little better than we have. It is this, more than anything, that is the animating force of global migration'. What this underlines is the poverty of an approach that is bereft of any attempt to situate the issue in terms of political economy. Similarly, outlining what political correctness is trying to achieve, Alibhai-Brown (2018: 25) assembles a jumble of platitudes ('To be a better person. To be a better nation. To be a better world.'), again failing to situate the issue of why 'political correctness' arose, why it elicits the criticism it does, and what to do about this, in terms of political economy.

diaspora is examined in the second section, while the causes and effects of current discourse about the race/class issue with regard to capitalist nations themselves is considered in the third section.

I

Film, Sameness, Otherness

About the political importance of Robeson there can be no question: through extensive cultural activities – in song, theatre, and film – he had an international presence, an influence epitomized by the kind of cinematic persona that he projected during the 1930s. A comparison of two of films in which Robeson starred – *Sanders of the River* (1935), directed by Zoltan Korda; and *The Proud Valley* (1940), directed by Penrose Tennyson – underlines the contrasting politics of the characters he depicted on screen.[10] In *Sanders of the River* Robeson played a Nigerian tribal leader, a role he agreed to undertake so as to be able to portray Africans in a favourable manner on screen. At the editing stage, however, his character was altered, changing from an empowered indigenous authority figure to a disempowered pawn of British imperialism, a revision that led to Robeson disowning the film.[11]

The Proud Valley, by contrast, shows the character he plays – a miner in a Welsh pit village who happens to be ethnically 'other' – in a very different political light: as empowered and a valued member of the community.[12] Whereas

---

10   Among the other films in which he appeared during the 1930s were: *The Emperor Jones* (1933), directed by Dudley Murphy; *Showboat* (1936), directed by James Whale; *Song of Freedom* (1936), directed by J. Elder Wills; and *King Solomon's Mines* (1937), directed by Robert Stevenson.
11   As explained by Robeson himself (Foner, 1978: 107, original emphasis), '[t]he twist of the picture which was favourable to English imperialism was accomplished *during the cutting* of the picture *after* it was filmed. I had no idea that it would have such a turn after I had acted in it ... .I was roped into the picture because I wanted to portray the culture of the African people in which I have the greatest interest ... Nothing would hurt me more than to have the African natives think that I had betrayed them [because] I have seen some types of natives who have gone to Cambridge or Oxford and have been won over to English imperialism'. On his disappointment with *Sanders of the River*, see also Duberman (1989: 178ff.).
12   Significantly, of the films Robeson made, *The Proud Valley* – produced for Ealing Studios – was his own favourite. The character he played is the aptly-named David Goliath, who leaves a ship to seek employment in a small coal mining town in South Wales. Recruited to its male voice choir, he becomes a miner, and refuses to abandon the villagers when – after an explosion closes the pit – its inhabitants experience unemployment and impoverishment. In the course of an attempt to open the mine once more, he and fellow miners

in the former his (altered) role is that of a 'native' subordinated to a dominant imperial class, in the latter he is merely one additional individual who belongs to same class of workers. Throughout this film, therefore, the emphasis is on a solidarity that transcends ethnicity: the subtext to *The Proud Valley* is that white miners from South Wales share with a black American the same kind of history – a common experience of exploitation/oppression by owners of the means of production – and thus also the same kind of (class) enemy and (class) struggle.

In a fundamental sense, the difference between these two films, and the roles within them taken by Robeson, inform the way he viewed the relationship between class and race. Unlike later exponents of post-colonial discourse, Robeson differentiates 'otherness' in terms of class, observing that mixing socially with African students in London 'who were mostly of princely origin', he also encountered 'another class of Africans' consisting of workers.[13] As perceived by him, the character of a nation was determined not by its upper classes but by 'the common people', an identity that – because it transcended borders – constituted not nationalism but rather internationalism. Accordingly, because Robeson differentiated a nation in terms of its opposed class elements and interests, both within and outside the nation itself, he distinguished politically between those inhabitants within a nation who 'lived by plundering colonial peoples' and others inside the same nation who 'earned their bread by honest toil'.[14] It would not normally be necessary to draw attention to what

---

become trapped underground. He dies as a result of successfully rescuing those trapped with him, an act of self-sacrifice on his part. Of particular interest is the way 'otherness' features in the film: racial identity is largely absent as an issue, with a single and notable exception. The latter occurs when one miner queries employing in the pit a 'big stranger' who is black, which another miner dismisses (to much laughter) with the comment that 'he is black, but we are all black down the pit'. That is to say, what might have emerged as a potentially divisive element of racial identity is for the miners of no consequence. What is of importance for them, however, is class solidarity, effectively depicted in an early scene. When the all-white male voice choir is rehearsing in an upstairs room, and David Goliath joins in the singing from the street outside and below, they invite him to join them ('come up, friend'), which of course he does.

13 'Besides these students, who were mostly of princely origin', notes Robeson (1958: 41), 'I also came to know another class of Africans – the seamen in the ports of London, Liverpool and Cardiff'. As noted by Duberman (1989: 172–73, original emphasis), 'even in the early thirties, in the flush of his enthusiasm for Africa, [Robeson was] not parochially insistent on the narrow loyalties and values of of one particular cultural or racial group ... For most of his life he managed to hold in balance a simultaneous commitment to the values ... of cultural distinctiveness *and* international unity'.

14 'It was in Britain – among the English, Scottish, Welsh and Irish people of that land', comments Robeson (1958: 56), 'that I learned that the essential character of a nation is

might seem an obvious, not to say banal, distinction, were it not the case that nowadays, in contrast to Robeson, current post-colonial exponents make no such distinction, tending to equate nations with a specific ethnic identity and a concomitant role as either oppressor/exploiter or oppressed/exploited.

In contrast to views currently promoting empowerment linked only or largely to non-class identity, the 'from below' struggle that Robeson supported – as he himself made clear – was not due simply to the fact that people were ethnically 'other' but because they were oppressed. This was what endeared him not just to black workers in the United States but also to white miners in South Wales.[15] As is true also of later post-colonial exponents, living and working in London was for Robeson a politically formative experience.[16] However, on the basis of the knowledge acquired as a result, and the political use to which it was put, he followed a path that differed greatly from that of post-colonial discourse.[17] Whilst in Britain, therefore, he learned from a friend in Manchester how ancestors of the latter had undergone hardship/toil in the textile mills in the course of weaving cotton produced by black slaves on the Southern plantations in the United States. This particular example, argued Robeson, illustrated the veracity of 'those forces in world life which make for

---

determined not by the upper classes, but by the common people, and that the common people of all nations are truly brothers in the great family of mankind'. He continues: 'If in Britain there were those who lived by plundering the colonial peoples, there were also the many millions who earned their bread by honest toil'. His conclusion is significant: 'And even as I grew to feel more Negro in spirit, or African as I put it then, I also came to feel a sense of oneness with the white working people whom I came to know and love'.

15 As recounted by Robeson in 1958 (Foner, 1978: 453), 'I went down into the mines with the workers, and they explained to me, that "Paul, you may be successful here in England, but your people suffer like ours. We are poor people, and you belong to us. You don't belong to the bigwigs here in this country." And so today I feel as much at home in the Welsh valley as I would in my own Negro section in any city in the United States ... We are a working people, a labouring people – the Negro people. There is a unity between our struggle and those of white workers in the South'.

16 On this, see Robeson (1958: 40): 'It was in London, in the years that I lived among the peoples of the British Isles and travelled back and forth to many other lands, that my outlook on world affairs was formed ... After several trips back and forth, I decided to stay in Europe and to make my home in London ... It must be said, however, that for me London was infinitely better than Chicago has been for Negroes from Mississippi'.

17 'Later, when I changed my base in English life and found myself more at home among the common people, I liked that country even better and, beyond an occasional trip to the States, I thought I was settled for life', notes Robeson (1958: 41), adding: 'But London was the centre of the British Empire, and it was there that I "discovered" Africa'. As Foner (1978: 15) points out, 'this helped Robeson extricate himself from the narrow nationalist viewpoint that the struggle of the people was fundamentally a racial one'.

common interests and make real the concept of international brotherhood'.[18] Even when upholding the rights of oppressed black populations worldwide, therefore, he does not seek to divide them and their interests from the 'common people' of a different ethnicity – a truly internationalist approach.

To Keep Them Divided

The view of James about this same race/class issue is, however, more ambivalent, a difficulty that is evident in the well-known discussion between him (as 'Comrade Johnson') and Trotsky in Mexico during 1939.[19] A decade earlier, the position espoused by Stalin had been that as blacks in America were a nation, they should seek not just equality but also 'self-determination' in the Southern US. This policy initiative was adopted by the American Communist Party, insisting that henceforth 'communists are for a Black Republic'. In the course of the 1939 discussion with Trotsky, James pointed out that, whereas the black populations of Africa and the West Indies desired national independence (= self-determination) because they inhabited colonies, those in the US were different: 'The Negro desperately wants to be an American citizen'.[20] Much in the spirit of Robeson, James then gave as an example how a strike by Chicago meatpackers had been undermined by employers so as to break the unity between white and black workers.[21] Ousting class solidarity with non-class identity in

---

18 This story and its political lesson is recounted thus (Robeson, 1958: 61–62): 'The workers in Manchester had supported the side of Abolition in the American Civil War; though the Union blockade of the South cut off the supply of cotton and resulted in greater hardship for them, while at the same time the mill-owners and their government had supported the side of Slavery. So here was a further insight and understanding of those forces in world life which make for common interests and make real the concept of international brotherhood'.

19 This discussion is included in Trotsky (1972b).

20 See James (Trotsky, 1972b: 24–25), who elaborates: 'In Poland and Catalonia there is a tradition of language, literature and history to add to the economic and political oppression and to help weld the population in its progressive demand for self-determination. In America it is not so'. Earlier, Shachtman (2003: 71, 73, 84) had stressed the same fact, that '[t]he American Negroes do not constitute a nation separate and apart from the rest of the population of the country ... A common territory the Negroes have, but it is the United States as a whole and not any section of it ... [America] which in common with the white workers and poor farmers is the Negroe's homeland'.

21 The divide-and-rule tactic pursued by employers to generate conflict between the different ethnic groups who had withdrawn their labour is illustrated by James (Trotsky, 1972b: 25) thus: '[Workers] had struck and had passed through the Negro quarter in Chicago with the black population cheering the whites in the same way as they cheered the

this manner led to the re-emergence of black nationalist movements, until worker unity surfaced again during the New Deal of the 1930s.[22]

From this historical dialectic between class and non-class struggle in America, James drew a crucial political lesson: supporting a call for black self-determination, he argued, would divert organization away from class-based trade unions and towards race and nationhood, thereby replicating the divide-and-rule tactic pursued by capitalists.[23] It would, in short, simultaneously weaken class solidarity and fuel racial prejudice, thereby playing into the hands of the owners of the means of production. This politically irrefutable case against promoting self-determination as a policy notwithstanding, ironically

---

blacks. For the capitalists this was a dangerous thing and they set themselves to creating race friction ... The capitalist press played up the differences and thus set the stage and initiated the riots that took place for dividing the population and driving the Negro back upon himself'. Much the same point was made earlier by Shachtman (2003: 45), who argued that 'the theory of [black] racial inferiority is of invaluable assistance to the ruling class when it permeates white workers [since it] serves to erect walls of prejudice between black and white wage slaves, to keep them divided, to pit the one against the other so that they may not pit their joint strength against their common adversary'. Crucially, underlined by Shachtman as fuelling prejudice was the role of labour market competition after the Civil War, when employers used black workers so as to undercut white equivalents, a ploy that led to a racist reaction by those in the latter category: 'This prejudice', he observed (Shachtman, 2003: 46), 'was transmitted to succeeding generations, not only in the South, but also in the North, where workers feared the cheap labour competition of the Southern negro who, escaping from the extremely low subsistence level of existence in the South, hired himself out for what was a higher wage to him but a strike-breaking wage to the better-paid northern mechanics', adding that '[t]he failure of the white workers to assist the Negroes in their attempts to organize into the trade union movement only accentuated the friction and difficulties'.

22 In the words of James (Trotsky, 1972b: 25–26): 'The New Deal made [positive] gestures to the Negroes. Blacks and whites fought together in various struggles. These [black] nationalist movements have tended to disappear as the Negro saw the opportunity to fight with the organized workers and to gain something'.

23 See James (Trotsky, 1972b: 26): 'The danger of our advocating and injecting a policy of self-determination is that it is the surest way to divide and confuse the workers in the South. The white workers have centuries of prejudice to overcome, but at the present time many of them are working with the Negroes in the Southern sharecroppers' union and with the rise of the struggle there is every possibility that they will be able to overcome their agelong prejudice. But for us to propose that the Negro have this black state for himself is asking too much from the white workers, especially when the Negro himself is not making the same demand. The slogans of "abolition of debts," "confiscation of large properties," etc., are quite sufficient to lead them both to fight together and on the basis of economic struggle to make a united fight for the abolition of social discrimination'. For his participation subsequently in the 1942 sharecroppers' strike in Missouri, under the slogan 'Black and White Unite and Fight!', see James (1977a: 89–94).

James then proceeded to accept its efficacy: he proposed supporting 'the right of self-determination' if it was advocated by the black population, therefore, but added that no attempt should be made to raise this slogan independently, lest it placed 'an unnecessary barrier between ourselves and socialism'. Having provided an excellent account of the Southern sharecroppers' union, the membership of which cut across ethnicities, and argued cogently against a policy of self-determination on account that it would jeopardize this struggle by dividing black sharecroppers from their white counterparts, James subsequently proposes the adoption (but not the promotion) of this very policy.[24]

Another participant ('Carlos') in the same discussion pressed for self-determination on the grounds that, in a particular context, people 'have a right to decide for themselves'.[25] Denying that self-determination was 'necessarily reactionary', the situation of blacks in the South required autonomy, since they were 'part of the colonial empire'. He drew a parallel with 'the breaking up of large estates into small plots', which although perceived as reactionary, was 'not necessarily so', since the issue was 'up to the peasants whether they wanted to operate the estates collectively or individually'.[26] After further discussion, James concluded – somewhat contradictorily – that self-determination ought to be a slogan, notwithstanding its reactionary nature and antagonistic stance towards socialism.[27] His ambivalence with regard to self-determination can be traced in part to two interrelated causes: first, an over-optimistic endorsement of the kind of nationalism emerging in Third World countries following decolonization; and second, an equally misplaced confidence in the progressive character of peasant cooperatives in such contexts.

---

24 See Woofter (1936) for the economic conditions of white and black sharecroppers in the Southern US during the 1930s. When in the course of an interview (Richardson, Chrysostom, and Grimshaw, 1986) towards the end of his life, James was asked whether he and Trotsky had supported the idea of a separate black state within America, he appeared to remember things differently. His answer now was 'No! No! No! We discussed in some detail plans to help to create and build an independent black organization in the United States. That we did, but we were thinking of a political grouping that would advocate the cause of blacks. But this was taken up by people to mean that we wanted to build a black section of the United States – a black Mississippi!'
25 See 'Carlos' (Trotsky, 1972b: 26–27), the pseudonym of Charles Curtiss.
26 'Carlos' (Trotsky, 1972b: 32).
27 When Trotsky himself queried the application to self-determination of the term 'reactionary', James (Trotsky, 1972b: 31–32) responded: 'If he [the black worker] wanted self-determination, then however reactionary it might be in every other respect, it would be the business of the revolutionary party to raise that slogan'. He went on to say that 'I consider the idea of separating as a step backward so far as a socialist society is concerned. If the white workers extend a hand to the Negro, he will not want self-determination'.

Significantly, much of the 1939 James/Trotsky discussion about self-determination – but not its conclusions – was based on an earlier analysis of the race/class issue by Max Shachtman, who opposed far more resolutely the position of Stalin that in the United States 'the struggle of the Negro masses for liberation ... must take the form of a movement for national liberation'.[28] This, Shachtman pointed out, relocated the issue politically, transferring it from one about working class formation/consciousness/struggle and placing it instead within the teleological domain of the national question. Repositioning the issue in this manner, he maintained, was 'radically wrong and guaranteed to produce the most harmful results in the fight to liberate not only the Negro but the whole American working class', for two reasons in particular. First, that the white bourgeoisie could not be relied on for political support in any black working-class struggle against racism; second, and more importantly, the black petty-bourgeoisie could not be relied on either. The latter problem stemmed from an economic cause: the link between the black petty bourgeoisie and the segregated consumer market.[29]

Unlike many critics of racism – then as now – Shachtman differentiated the black population in terms of class, as a result of which he concluded that the black petty bourgeoisie could not be regarded as progressive. This was due to the economic benefits derived from the monopoly position it exercised over the black consumer. On account of this, the petty bourgeoisie opposed not the ending of segregation per se but only with regard to trade union membership, since the admission of black workers to membership would deliver higher wages, thereby providing both an increased level of purchasing power and (consequently) higher profits for the black petty bourgeoisie.[30] Citing the

---

28   Shachtman (2003: 68–69).
29   At that conjuncture, Shachtman (2003: 55–56) pointed out, no black bourgeoisie existed in the United States: 'A big bourgeoisie the race [cannot produce] because of the conditions of its existence. In the South, the fierce oppression and discrimination permits the Negro to rise only to the level of the petty businessman and small property owner. In the North, the monopoly of financial and industrial capitalism, the domination of the big banks and the big trusts, excludes the possibility of more than an entirely insignificant group of Negroes rising to the rank of the large capitalist class. These circumstances decisively determine the nature and role of the comparatively thin, but active, layer of Negro petty bourgeois, who, it must be remembered, are additionally limited in their possibilities for advancement by the rigorous rules of Jim Crow'. As a result (Shachtman, 2003: 56, 57), the 'segregated market is the very basis of existence for the Negro petty bourgeoisie [which] favours letting down the colour bar in the trade unions so that the Negro workers shall not be so wretchedly paid, and consequently constitute so unprofitable a market for the Negro intellectuals and small businessmen'.
30   According to Shachtman (2003: 62), therefore, 'the Negro petty bourgeoisie gratuitously identifies its own narrow class interests with the destiny and interests of the Negroes as a

authority of Lenin, Shachtman reiterated the central point in this debate, that the right to self-determination must of necessity be subordinated 'to the revolutionary struggle for the elimination of the capitalist order and for the realization of socialism', a task which could be realized only as a result of working class unity across the ethnic divide in America as a whole.[31]

Solidarity, Struggle, Socialism

Struggles arising from class solidarity, or the practice linked to socialist internationalism, also emerged in the course of the response by Robeson and others to the rise of fascism in Europe during the 1920s and 1930s, and the attack on the Spanish Republic.[32] Like other socialists, therefore, he was fully aware of the complicity between on the one hand aristocratic landowners and elements of the capitalist class in bourgeois democracies like Britain, and on the other the fact that destruction of working class movements/organizations, together with rolling back any political and/or economic gains these had managed to achieve, was central to the foreign and domestic objectives pursued by fascist parties in Italy and Germany.[33] For Robeson it was a matter of some pride

---

whole. This convenient identification is aimed to screen the class differentiation within the Negroes themselves, to obliterate the class struggle, to present the narrow economic and social aspirations of the petty bourgeoisie as identical with the broad historical interests of the Negroes as workers and poor farmers and as an oppressed race'. This, he went on to argue (Shachtman, 2003: 64), is because the black petty bourgeoisie 'is a stratum which lives on the reactionary system of segregation [and thus] is an obstacle on the road of the advancement and emancipation of the race. It is not a bridge between the black masses and the white; it is a wall between them'.

31 On this point, see Shachtman (2003: 70, 93–94, 97–98, 99–100), who stressed also that such an objective required in turn maintaining the territorial integrity – that is, no internal self-determination – of America itself (Shachtman, 2003: 85): 'From the historical standpoint, there cannot be the slightest dispute about the progressive character of the establishment of one unified nation'.

32 'I went to Spain in 1938, and that was a major turning point in my life', he stated (Robeson, 1958: 61), because '[t]here I saw that it was the working men and women of Spain who were heroically giving their "last full measure of devotion" to the cause of democracy in that bloody conflict, and it was the upper class – the landed gentry, the bankers and the industrialists – who had unleashed the fascist beast against their own people'.

33 'In England, in the great country houses where I had often been welcomed as a guest, having tea and exchanging smiles with Lord and Lady This-and-that, a quiet serenity prevailed', commented Robeson (1958: 59–60), adding that 'upper-class England was rather pleased by what [fascist] dictators were doing … they were out to save all the great houses of Europe from the menace of "Bolshevism", and in Germany and Italy there was no longer any nonsense from Labour, and business went ahead much better with no trade unions'.

that the International Brigades defending the Spanish Republic included both white and black Americans.³⁴

Although each differed as to its meaning, both Robeson and James were committed politically to the necessity and feasibility of a socialist transition. Crucially, for Robeson a major point of difference between the United States and the Soviet Union was the issue of racial oppression, a distinctiveness expressed by him that 'in Russia I felt for the first time like a full human being – no colour prejudice like in Mississippi, no colour prejudice like in Washington'.³⁵ Socialism, argued Robeson, was the way forward politically and economically for 'newly emancipated nations of Asia and Africa'.³⁶ It is clear that the kind of socialism advocated by him in 1948 was essentially a programme built around the concept of a welfare state that was not so different from that of the 1945 Labour Government in the UK.³⁷

Among the social policies Robeson thought should be introduced to the United States, therefore, was public housing for veterans and the poor, corresponding to an all-embracing social security agenda, one that rested in turn on legislation not only prohibiting specific oppressions (such as lynching) but also promoting equal rights and equal opportunities. This programme would

---

On the support for Hitler among the British upper classes, see the detailed case-study by Kershaw (2004), and more generally 'The Men Behind Munich', *Labour Monthly*, Volume 21 (1939), pp. 26–34. The latter outlined how '[t]he biggest industrialists, the most wealthy financiers and landowners are the "leaders" of the Anglo-German fellowship. They are the same people who for generations have been the backbone of the British Conservative Party'.

34 'My heart was filled with admiration and love for these white Americans [of the Abraham Lincoln Battalion of the International Brigades] who came to defend Madrid', writes Robeson (1958: 61), 'and there was a sense of great pride in my own people when I saw that there were Negroes, too, in the ranks of the Lincoln men in Spain'.

35 See Robeson (1958: 56). As regards his own political beliefs and principles, Robeson (1958: 12) states: 'I care nothing – less than nothing about what the lords of the land, the Big White Folks, think of me and my ideas ... But I do care – and deeply – about the America of the common people whom I have met across the land ... the working men and women whose picket-lines I've joined, auto workers, seamen, cooks and stewards, furriers, miners, steel workers ...' To this he (Robeson, 1958: 38) adds that 'neither the promise of gain nor the threat of loss has ever moved me from my firm convictions'.

36 See Robeson (1958: 45, 47).

37 For these views as delineated by Robeson at that juncture, see Foner (1978: 491–92). 'On many occasions', states Robeson (1958: 47), 'I have publicly expressed my belief in the principles of scientific socialism, my deep conviction that for all mankind a socialist society represents an advance to a higher stage of life – that it is a form of society which is economically, socially, culturally, and ethically superior to a system based upon production for private profit ...'.

require banning cartels and monopolies, and the nationalization of what has been described as the commanding heights of the economy (coal industry, railroads, shipping, atomic energy, and airline companies). Advocating what was in effect state control of utilities and other key industries ('put them in the hands of the people'), such a project in his view was necessary because 'where it is clear that these are public necessities and of national life or death then it seems to me they should be nationalized'.[38]

However, nationalization – which Robeson equated with socialism – was associated by James only with state capitalism. Accordingly, James broke with the two main interpretations of systemic transition: on the one hand that of Stalin, for whom the transformation of private into state property meant that capitalism had become socialism, and on the other the view of Trotsky, that in Russia nationalization of industry signalled the presence of a workers' state.[39] Instead, what James regarded as socialism was 'the emancipation of the proletariat from enslavement to capital'. Ironically, in the case of newly independent African nations, he maintained that it was peasants who constituted a 'new class': in such Third World contexts the focus of economic development would be on the transformative potential of peasant cooperatives, which he accepted would involve 'freedom and rights for capitalism'.[40] Nevertheless, James argued in the 1960s that governments of independent African nations were 'creating a new type of society, based not on Western theories but on the concrete circumstances of African life and its historic past', an example of the latter being in his opinion the 'humanist' approach of Kaunda (= ' a new road for Africa').[41] Despite regarding the peasantry as a class, and arguing that it was not workers but petty commodity producers who were 'creating a new type of society', together with an ambivalence concerning self-determination which privileged nationalism, James – like Robeson – believed in the desirability/feasibility of socialism.

---

38   Making clear that his quarrel was not with the inhabitants of the United States, and that he was opposed to the unequal distribution of income, Robeson (Foner, 1978: 221) pointed out in 1949 that '[w]e are loyal to the America of Lincoln and the abolitionists, but not to those who degrade my people. One percent of the American population gets 59 percent of the national income'.
39   See James (1969: 13, 32), who objected to the position taken by Trotsky that, because the transfer of private property to state ownership could be achieved only as a result of working class agency, the state-property form necessarily corresponded to an achievement of the proletarian revolution.
40   See James (1977b: 202).
41   James (1977b: 215, 219–221).

It is clear that, unlike either Robeson or James, a number of current postcolonial exponents focusing on the disempowerment of 'otherness' do not want to replace capitalism with something better; what they seem to want is only an improved deal under the existing neoliberal system.[42] Advocating an immigration open-door policy because its subjects are 'wealth creators', as does Mehta, is the sort of utterance which these days can be heard from most CEOs of multinational corporations.[43] Indeed, in support of this view he invokes the call by an American billionaire for 'increasing immigration, because it's good for the economy', since it confers market advantages on US businesses engaged competitively with rival enterprises elsewhere in the world.[44] In doing so, Mehta inadvertently reveals one of the main reasons why capital wants migrants: insofar as the latter are cheap/unfree forms of labour-power, such workers enable owners of the means of production to compete more effectively with other capitalists in the global market.

This is what Marxist political economy has long argued, but Mehta appears unaware of this explanation, and quickly passes over the implications of open-door immigration on the labour market on the receiving nation.[45] Accepting that free trade and free movement will empower corporations but disempower local workers, he reproduces in effect a familiar apology for neoliberalism, a project which in his view is necessary because it will in turn 'revitalize' the 'global dominance' of America.[46] Much the same

---

42 Mehta (2019: 145) even denies the existence of capitalism, insisting that '[t]he United States ... cannot properly be called a capitalist society'.

43 'Diversity isn't just a nice thing to have', observes Mehta (2019: 162), 'it is actively essential to attract the kind of people who create wealth'.

44 For this view, see Mehta (2019: 168–69) who maintains that '[t]he self-made billionaire [Bloomberg] laid out the business case for immigration: many other countries are growing their economies faster than the United States is, reversing the century-long advantage America has enjoyed ... He called for increasing immigration, because it's good for the economy ... There's a global consensus among 99 per cent of legitimate [*sic*] economists that immigration is good for the economy'.

45 It comes as no surprise that a billionaire justifies his call for increased immigration by claiming it is good for the economy. It may indeed be 'good', but what benefits from this expansion in the industrial reserve army of labour is profits and dividends, not wages and work conditions. By conflating economy with country in this manner, and declaring that everyone gains, billionaires disguise the fact that it is *they*, not workers, who are the main beneficiaries. Backing up this call with reference to support from '99 per cent of legitimate economists' similarly exposes the latter as neoclassical economic theorists, or those who see virtue in any/every policy contributing to the accumulation process.

46 'There will be winners from free trade and free movement of people – like technology corporations', acknowledges Mehta (2019: 171, 183), but then adds that 'there will be losers – like the unskilled'. This is necessary in his opinion since 'immigrants can revitalize ... the entire economy', an objective linked by him to the fact that 'America has succeeded,

kind of approach and assumptions inform the advocacy of mass migration by Mohsin Hamid, whose humanitarian/culturalist perception of immigration similarly ends up being indistinguishable from *laissez-faire* economic theory.[47]

II

Magical (Un-)Realism

In what is a reiteration of the contemporary variant of 'drain' theory advanced by Patnaik in furtherance of her justification for economic reparations payable to India by erstwhile colonial nations, the case made by Mehta for the adoption of open-door immigration into European countries as a distinct form of reparations for colonial exploitation rests similarly and centrally on what begins as a 'rich'/'poor' country dichotomy.[48] He illustrates this by answering the question 'why are you in my country' with the reply of his grandfather: 'Because we are the creditors ... you took all our wealth, our diamonds. Now we have come to collect'.[49] This kind of 'revenge discourse', based as it is on a simplistic 'rich'/'poor' duality applied to nations soon breaks down, since rather obviously 'rich' countries have people who are poor, while 'poor' ones contain rich – and in some instances, very rich – inhabitants. Indeed, this becomes evident as his argument develops, where the terms 'rich' and 'poor' nations are gradually supplanted by references to the predatory activities in Africa of multinational

---

and achieved its present position of global dominance, because it has always been good at importing the talent it needs'. A clearer endorsement of capitalism is hard to imagine.

47   See Hamid (2014).
48   Objecting to the fact that 'a great many people in the rich countries complain about migration from the poor ones', Mehta (2019: 3) counters that 'the rich countries colonized us and stole our treasure and prevented us from building our industries', a view which ill accords with two points. First, that the wealth referred to as having been 'stolen' belonged not to India but to *rich* Indians (Maharajas, landlords), many of whom were happy to arrange mutually beneficial deals with their colonial masters. And second, as has been outlined by numerous analyses – among them Gadgil (1959), Gordon (1978), Markovits (1985), and Tirthankar (2018) – not only was colonialism compatible with the rise and prosperity of Indian business empires (Tata, Birla), but such capitalist enterprises (Mittal, Hinduja, Ambani) have continued to expand and flourish economically, both within and outside India itself.
49   On this exchange, see Mehta (2019: 3). Of interest is the mention by his grandfather of diamonds as part of the national wealth taken by the colonizer, since according to Mehta (2019: 154, 174) after migrating to the United States his own parents established themselves in New York as diamond merchants.

corporations.⁵⁰ The latter, however, continue to be labelled 'Western', thereby reproducing the 'us'/'them' polarity based on national identity.

In keeping with this, most – if not all – the current social and economic difficulties faced by Third World nations are attributed by post-colonial discourse simply to colonialism. These extend from chattel slavery, conflict, hunger, and poverty, to religious/separatist discord, climate change and environmental degradation.⁵¹ Not only does 'much of the hunger and civil strife that persists in South Asia today [have] its origins in Partition', therefore, but 'Congo's political situation since [Belgian colonialism] has been chaotic, and remains so today'.⁵² Winston Churchill is castigated – rightly – for his imperialist outlook and dislike of Indians, but no reference is made to the fact that he wasn't too keen on the British working class either.⁵³ Similarly unmentioned is opposition within colonizing nations to issues like colonial oppression, slavery, and Third World poverty, and of complicity inside colonies themselves with, for example, the sale of slaves to European traders. After conceding that not everything wrong in ex-colonies is the fault of colonization, and that – along with internal causes – multinational corporations are to blame, Mehta nevertheless reassigns culpability to colonialism.⁵⁴ Like Patnaik, therefore, he maintains that colonialism endures beyond independence, reproducing the nationalist trope that colonial rulers were simply replaced with Western businessmen.⁵⁵

---

50   Mehta (2019: 49, 65, 107) finally differentiates the 'rich', accepting the existence of 'rich versus poor' *within* the United States, the presence of 'a giant Anglo-Dutch conglomerate' in the Nigerian Delta, and that conflicts within Africa 'are fuelled ... by the multinational corporations'. Noting that Guinea's population 'lives in extreme poverty' while the country has extensive mineral resources (bauxite, gold, diamonds) which are exploited by Western corporations that have ' "negotiated" contracts with the country's leadership [and] siphoned off an extortionate share of the profits', Mehta (2019: 42–43) indicates that '[t]he money earned by Guinean locals is mainly accrued by the President and his many wives; and that money, too, follows the company profits out of the country [to tax havens]'. Exactly – it is not the 'rich' countries but international capitalist enterprises that exploit and benefit in this manner: equally, in 'poor countries' there are those who also gain from this process (just as there are in 'rich' countries).
51   Although she is critical of the way the Indian caste system came to the UK via the diaspora, Sarah Sahim (in Shukla, 2016: 169–180) nevertheless assigns sole blame to Britain for its continuation. Nothing is said about its root and reproduction within present-day India itself.
52   Mehta (2019: 62, 71).
53   Mehta (2019: 63ff.).
54   'Of course', accepts Mehta (2019: 72), 'the colonizers aren't responsible for every bad thing that is now happening in the former colonies; some of it is our own damn fault. Many of the issues that make people emigrate are home-grown'.
55   'In any case', insists Mehta (2019: 72–74), 'colonialism isn't over ... Corporate colonialism is the new colonialism. When the colonial regimes withdrew their soldiers and viceroys,

No mention, therefore, of the fact that currently much of the global accumulation project is driven by Asian capital that has, amongst other things, taken over many so-called 'Western' businesses.

However, unlike Patnaik, for whom reparations are a purely economic transaction requiring transfers from ex-colonial nations to erstwhile colonies, for Mehta by contrast reparations involve transfers of labour-power, and take the form of open-door migration from ex-colonies to colonizing nations.[56] The latter is stated explicitly: 'migration today is a form of reparations'.[57] Objections to immigration on this scale are dismissed by him as 'white fear' and 'narrow nationalism', adding that '[a] wall will do nothing to stop them [immigrants]' who 'will keep coming ... whether you want them or not – because they are the creditors – whether you realize it or not'.[58] Much the same view is expressed by Hamid, another exponent of post-colonial discourse, who categorizes migration as a 'human right', arguing that inhabitants of western nations should not oppose but welcome mass immigration and that anyway such movement is unstoppable and the pattern of the future ('The scale of migration we will see in the coming centuries is likely to dwarf what has come before').[59]

---

they replaced them with their businessmen ... what we have is a border-free for multinationals', which 'looted us for centuries [and] took whatever was worth taking ... they continued taking after we became "independent" ... colonial countries enriched themselves at the expense of subject nations, and there's a case to be made for reparations'.

56   'I am angry', confesses Mehta (2019: 8), 'about the staggering global hypocrisy of the rich nations, having robbed the poor ones of their future, now arguing against a reverse movement of peoples – not to invade and conquer and steal, but to work ... I'm tired of apologizing for moving. These walls, these borders, between the peoples of the Earth: they are of recent vintage, and they are flimsy'.

57   Mehta (2019: 193).

58   See Mehta (2019: 9, 11). Although insisting that 'I am not calling for open borders [merely] calling for open hearts', it is clear that he (Mehta, 2019: 29) is doing exactly that. Subsequently, therefore, Mehta (2019: 192) clarifies both the scale and the form reparations will take: 'Globally ... a giant bill is due' since what 'poor countries' want is 'for the borders of the rich to be opened to goods and people'. Opening the borders of 'rich' nations to goods from 'poor' countries overlooks the fact that this will put money in the pockets not of the impoverished in 'poor' contexts but of multinational corporations that control the export trade.

59   See Mohsin Hamid, 'Why Migration is a Fundamental Human Right', *The Guardian* (London), 21 November 2014, and his contribution to a discussion on BBC Radio 4, *The World Tonight*, 12 November 2015. Much the same point has been made by Chibundu Onuzu, who argues that her cousin 'wished to live in Europe simply because he wanted a better life ... we want what you want ... [w]e all want a better job', concluding in the same vein as Hamid that '[t]here are no fences high enough to stop humans from aspiring'. See 'Migrants only want what you want. Why is that so frightening?', *The Guardian* (London), 26 June 2015. Bereft of any conception of the economic impact on workers in receiving

Why it is necessary for post-colonial discourse to maintain the fiction that colonialism is still largely to blame for every form of current oppression/exploitation occurring within Third World nations is not difficult to discern. Without this link, therefore, support for reparations in the form of open-door immigration is not only unsustainable but creates thereby a space for an alternative understanding of both its cause and effect. About the impact, in terms of labour market competition, on the receiving nation of open-door immigration, post-colonial discourse is somewhat contradictory. On the one hand, therefore, Mehta indicates an awareness of the case that 'migrants rob young Britons of jobs', only to dismiss this as 'demonstrably false', and one of the 'threats that aren't'.[60] On the other, however, he accepts that, by keeping wages low and working conditions poor, capitalist enterprises do indeed benefit economically from the employment of immigrant labour-power that is cheap.[61]

Diasporic Discourse

Differences between earlier and current positions on the issue of 'otherness' and immigration are instructive. With the exception of Mehta, none of the post-colonial exponents addresses immigration in any detail – let alone considers its economic dimension on both sending and receiving country – the inference being that, because those who perceive difficulties with open-door immigration are innately racist, there is no point even in discussing the question.

---

nations, what such migrant-centric appeals to common human aspirations or identity do is merely to mimic *laissez-faire* discourse about the 'naturalness' of individualistic competition in the labour market.

60 See Mehta (2019: 106–107, 168). In answer to his own question 'do immigrants steal jobs from the natives?', Mehta (2019: 170) answers that they do not, invoking as evidence a World Bank economist who repeats the oft-heard business argument that immigrants only fill jobs that locals refuse to do. Unmentioned – once again – is the reason for this situation: that as long as immigrants are employed in such jobs, these will remain ones of poor work conditions and low pay, which is precisely why locals choose not to do them. At another point in the analysis, however, he (Mehta, 2019: 175) reveals that in the United States '86 per cent of first-generation immigrant males participate in the labour force, which is a higher rate than the native-born', which does indeed suggest that a degree of displacement is occurring in the labour market, whereby in some instances immigrants are employed in preference to the 'native-born'.

61 Hence the recognition by Mehta (2019: 134, 145) that 'we'll invite you [as immigrants to the UK] when we need your labour, then throw you out when we've done using you', and 'corporations were ... publicly arguing against restrictions on immigration, because it would drive up wages when the supply of cheap foreign labour went down'.

Like post-colonial discourse, Robeson was opposed to anti-immigration policy based on race but unlike post-colonialism, the way he fought it was to promote *worker* solidarity across the ethnic divide. Post-colonial discourse, by contrast, tends not only to apply the accusation of racism uniformly to everyone belonging to a different national/ethnic identity, but also to leave it at that.[62] Insofar as current forms of empowerment involve championing non-class identity politics, post-colonial discourse about 'otherness' has been transferred from the street to the university, thus replicating the ideological path followed earlier by many on the left. It is a transformation that culminates in the emergence and consolidation of the 'new' populist postmodernism.

Although he hints at the presence of what Marxists define as the industrial reserve army of labour, and immigration as a source of this, Mehta does not link it to class struggle waged 'from above' by employers, to the intensity of labour market competition, to restructuring/outsourcing/relocation, to the rise and consolidation of rival populisms, or the need for the accumulation process of such labour-power in order to sustain or increase profitability. That post-colonial discourse misunderstands the fundamental systemic connection between immigration, accumulation, and labour market competition, therefore, is evident from the somewhat naïve approval by Mehta of the migrant 'work ethic' as positive.[63] It is hardly surprising that the capitalist regards migrant labourers in a favourable light, since they work harder for less pay than locals. Rather than seeing immigration as a 'from above' endeavour to cut costs so as to maintain or enhance accumulation, and anti-immigrant ideology as a 'from below' reaction to such labour market competition, however, there is a tendency for post-colonial discourse to dismiss the latter response simply as racist.

Among the old canards deployed in support of this view is that in the UK opposition to immigration exists in rural areas where no migrants settle, the inference being that such antagonism is straightforwardly racist.[64] What such an argument overlooks, however, is that although not affected economically by the presence of migrant workers in the immediate vicinity, such opposition

---

62   Consistent with arguments made in this volume (and elsewhere), Haider (2018:12, original emphasis) also describes identity politics as 'the *neutralization* of movements against racial oppression. It is the ideology that emerged to appropriate [the] emancipator legacy in service of the advancement of political and economic elites'.

63   Such optimism is evident from the observation (Mehta, 2019: 108) that '[m]ultiple studies have found that people who have direct contact with immigrants have much more positive views about their work ethic'.

64   See Mehta (2019: 163). This view, which is not confined to post-colonial discourse, can also be found in Burgin (2017: 54).

is nevertheless still based on concerns about labour market competition. The latter process occurs not locally but in large urban centres far away – most notably London – to where those who oppose immigration would themselves (or their children) once have gone in search of work. This is especially true of regions where, due to industrial decline, there are no jobs for the young, who consequently have to travel to the metropolis in order to find employment. Because of increases in the industrial reserve army, and the resulting enhanced labour market competition in the distant urban centres, this option which used to be feasible is currently more difficult, not to say impossible. In short, antagonism in places where there is little or no migrant presence can still be based on economic considerations linked to the deployment by capital elsewhere in the same nation of a workforce composed largely or solely of migrants who are cheaper to employ.

Noting that '[t]hese days, the [immigration] debate is about culture', Mehta argues that '[a]n essential prerequisite to denying entrance to the migrant is to posit a dualism, a clash of civilizations, in which one is far superior to the other, and is therefore entitled to dominate the other'.[65] Not the least of the many ironies is that he then proceeds to chronicle the superiority of Asian immigrants in terms of educational achievement, in the process asserting the kind of dominance which earlier he decried in the case of the 'clash of civilizations' framework.[66] That the latter is simply about the superiority or inferiority of particular cultures, as presented by Mehta, is anyway incorrect: the clash is much rather between (in the case of migrants from Islamic nations) a theocratic culture and (in the case of receiving European nations) a secular one, and how – if at all – such political incompatibility is to be resolved.[67] This has nothing at all to do with a view that one culture is 'far superior to the other', or that consequently the West is 'therefore entitled to dominate'.

Since in his view it offends against cultural pluralism, Hamid similarly objects to the term 'civilization', which misses the fact that the same term encompasses also a non-cultural dimension.[68] Unlike Mehta, however, he limits migration conceptually to a question of culture, which is false. To equate opposition to immigration with a defence of Western 'civilization' misunderstands that the problem linked to the former is not so much cultural as *economic*. An increase

---

65 Mehta (2019: 118).
66 Mehta (2019: 126).
67 As Mehta (2019: 72) himself accepts, Islamic teaching about female subordination is not exactly progressive, and as such poses difficulty in secular contexts where gender equality is a political given.
68 See Hamid (2014: xvi).

in the supply of labour cannot but undermine the standard of living gained as a result of class struggle waged by workers over generations, to obtain and then protect not just wage levels and working conditions but also things like welfare provision, housing, education, and health care. Ignoring all this, he asserts merely that 'civilizations are illusions', which wrongly overlooks the material aspect of this term.

By framing the question of 'civilization' simply in terms of culture, Hamid plays straight into the hands of capital. His view about British society, and the prevalence/innateness of what he takes to be its positive aspects – including the mistaken perception of the media as 'open to dissenting voices' – highlights one of the more important, but least mentioned, attributes of migration that makes it so attractive to capital.[69] Namely, the idealization of the socio-economic character of the receiving nation as benign, and consequently the less likely the emergence of or political support for a systemic challenge from this source, when compared with existing workers who have long experienced austerity/oppression. In short, the 'post-civilization' world desired by Hamid seems to be a place where international capitalism reigns supreme, as a result of a global reserve army exercising a continuous and unrelenting downwards pressure on wages, work conditions, and livelihoods, constantly adjusting them to the lowest common denominator.[70]

On the Shoulders of Giants?

Uncontroversially, political correctness endorsed by post-colonial discourse calls for more 'respect, dignity, and real equality' to be extended to the 'other' – a view with which no one would quarrel – but ignores the way such positive objectives are then applied to the negative economic agenda of capitalism.[71] Accordingly, political correctness makes it difficult to voice opposition to the economic policies that favour – and on occasion, are promoted by – business interests. What Alibhai-Brown and Malik seem not to understand is that extending the kind of absolute cultural protection to 'other' identities in the manner they want slides imperceptibly into a ban also on criticism of

---

69 See Hamid (2014: 28, 40–41).
70 Among the processes which Hamid (2014: 102, 112) regards as desirable are rapid capitalist accumulation, privately-owned media, and 'a soaring stock market'. His endorsement of an unthreatening agenda where capitalism is concerned ('mutual respect, greater engagement and more openness') is one with which few employers would disagree.
71 Alibhai-Brown (2018: 61).

economic policies sought by employers so as to further more intense accumulation. Presenting the issue in terms of ethnicities arraigned for-and-against cultural 'otherness', therefore, disguises and simultaneously renders unassailable a crucial plank in the capitalist agenda.[72] In effect, this defence of cultural empowerment ends up defending the presence or augmentation of what is the industrial reserve army.

Unsurprisingly, therefore, Alibhai-Brown mentions immigration only in passing, and – in sharp contrast to Shachtman – remains silent as to its negative economic impact in the form of enhancing labour market competition, dismissing those who draw attention to the latter as 'a surge of self-pity'.[73] As predictable is the denial by her of a connection between political correctness and far-right reaction; about this link, she observes merely that 'do we blame Germany's Chancellor Merkel for neo-fascist revivalism because she did her Christian duty [sic] by accepting a million asylum refugees'.[74] The absence of an economic dimension to her defence of political correctness, plus the endorsement of open-door migration in moral terms only (= 'Christian duty'), underlines the extent to which argument that focuses only on 'the cultural' is incapable of addressing the link between 'otherness', identity politics, the rise of populism, and the neoliberal project.[75] Malik, too, regards political correctness simply as a moral issue: 'Until we achieve that moral universe, political correctness is a must'.[76]

Much the same is true of Hamid, who upholds his idealist perception of neoliberalism as enabling everyone to choose to be whatever they want by reference to literature, a realm of make-believe where in his opinion reality

---

[72] 'It seems to me', writes Alibhai-Brown (2018: 74, 85–6), 'that white power relinquishes nothing. So long secure and proud, it is determined to define and control the forces now ranged against that power, including cultural protests and desires ... resistance to perfectly reasonable political correctness [has] become a national obsession. White people, on the left and right, made common cause. They could not tolerate those who opposed or deconstructed their certainties, their shared sense of what it was to be British. Beneath their differences there was a stronger bond than many of us challengers realised'.

[73] See Alibhai-Brown (2018: 146) who notes: 'Globalisation and reckless capitalism, mass migration from unfamiliar lands and the loss of old ways are all causing disorientation and a surge in self-pity'.

[74] See Alibhai-Brown (2018: 146–47). Symptomatically, when criticizing Farage as 'a folk hero in white heartlands because [his] anti-PC persona persuaded millions to vote for Brexit', she (Alibhai-Brown, 2018: 141) fails to mention that he mobilized in a populist fashion the already-present opposition to open-door immigration.

[75] Hence the assertion (Alibhai-Brown, 2018: 97) that '[t]he danger comes not from PC espousers, but from the raging right and nationalism'.

[76] Malik (2019: 93).

asserts itself.[77] Avoiding the issue of what actually exists and is reproduced materially, therefore, he too follows postmodernism in arguing that because an aspiration is declared by literature to exist, in reality it does indeed exist. Rather like Alibhai-Brown, therefore, rather than considering issues raised by immigration within a political economy framework, Hamid instead justifies what is in effect a neoliberal position on the industrial reserve army in terms of a 'common humanity'.[78]

Similar difficulties inform the attempt by Malik to distinguish between identity politics that are defensive and benign, and those that are aggressive and negative.[79] Hence the supposedly benign version, the defensive variant, can be extended from an uncontroversial safeguard of 'others' already in the UK to – more controversially – of 'other' migrants who wish to live and work in the country. The latter, seen from the viewpoint of Marxist theory about the link between capitalist accumulation and the industrial reserve army, is not as defensive/benign as Malik supposes. Equally problematic is her view that 'defensive identity politics' is merely a response by the 'other' to the 'dominance and ubiquity of a white identity': in short, the claim that it was whites who first played the race card, to which 'others' responded in kind. The trouble with this chronology is, once again, that furnished by the industrial reserve army: when capital resorts to 'other' forms of labour-power, in order to cut costs and compete more effectively, the raising of the race issue by white workers is itself defensive, in the sense that it is seen by them as a way of protecting their own jobs and livelihoods.

III

Placid Multiculturalism

Just as the economic case for open-door immigration rests on its being a form of reparations for colonialism, so the cultural one – privileging 'otherness' – depends centrally on the relativistic epistemology of postmodernism.

---

77 See Hamid (2014: xi–xii, 87ff.).

78 See Hamid (2014: 22–23), a theme reproduced by him subsequently in fictional mode (Hamid, 2017). A 'common humanity', it should be noted, is not the same as the class solidarity endorsed by Robeson.

79 That the two variants of identity politics, as proposed by Malik, are problematic is evident from the fact that her antagonistic/negative variant, conveying as it does an element of dominance, could just as easily be applied to post-colonial discourse itself, as some of the views held by a number of its exponents attest.

Combining the latter with the notion of 'political correctness', therefore, post-colonial discourse rejects both the Enlightenment as a valid source of universal values and the explanations by political economy of immigration.[80] Labelling the Enlightenment as specifically 'Western', and thus of limited applicability where the identity of the 'other' is concerned, Alibhai-Brown rejects the validity of claims about universality that derive from Enlightenment discourse about the desirability/feasibility of modernity, in the process absurdly characterizing Marx himself simply as a 'white supremacist'.[81] Elsewhere, however, she contradicts this by equating political correctness with leftism/Marxism.[82] In doing so, Alibhai-Brown is not merely wrong but seemingly confirms the accusation made by the Great Replacement approach that political correctness is a distinctively leftist ideology (see next chapter).

Like Alibhai-Brown, Malik is an ardent post-colonial proselytizer, but unlike the former she regards political correctness as a myth which, because it is 'a challenge [to] male, white and heteronormative power', generates moral panic among those in the latter category.[83] Political correctness is used as 'a cudgel with which to beat back basic advances towards equality', maintaining in the process that it merely replaces old prejudices with new ones empowering 'women, people of colour and those who are "other" '.[84] Like Alibhai-Brown, who sees the concept as positive, and political correctness as an approach to be encouraged, Malik views the debate it generates as 'manufactured outrage', a negative outcome of the reaction against 'otherness'.[85] For her, opposition to political correctness is not just based on a myth but one that has been turned 'into a culture war weapon' used by the political right in the debate about immigration.[86] What she objects to, therefore, is not political correctness per

---

80 For the PC/postmodernism link, see Alibhai-Brown (2018: 106, 136) who revealingly outlines its non-economic dynamic: 'Since the 1980s, PC has pushed through bold, overdue and radical cultural shifts in the arts, popular culture, politics and power, ideas and actual practice'.
81 Alibhai-Brown (2018: 124).
82 Alibhai-Brown (2018: 56–57, 111).
83 According to Malik (2019: 58, 60), political correctness is defined as 'rendering everyone hesitant to express views that could be misconstrued as prejudicial', which in turn gives rise to 'the myth of political correctness [that] is the oldest and most pedigreed of contemporary political myths'.
84 Malik (2019: 61–62).
85 For the dismissal of any/all opposition to political correctness as 'manufactured outrage', see Malik (2019: 88).
86 Over the past half century (Malik, 2019: 66, 75) 'there has been a concerted attempt ... to turn political correctness into a culture war weapon ... In the UK, a culture war was brewing around immigration, identity and class'.

se but rather to the debate about it: the latter is perceived as a chimera, and opposition to its impact as being essentially about a non-issue (= an 'imaginary tide').

Attributing the Brexit vote to imperialist nostalgia and 'just plain old racism', Malik argues that such dissent was directed at the European Union (= 'epitome of political correctness') because it 'represents an imposed freedom of movement'.[87] In an attempt to upend the debate about immigration, Malik then contends that similarly mythical is 'the grievance industry' linked to 'white identity politics': consequently, 'anti-immigration rhetoric' is regarded by her as nothing more than 'contemporary white grievance mythologies'.[88] Opposition to open-door immigration is – like that to political correctness – unfounded, baseless, irrational, and proof of an unthinking racism. This view depends in turn on the way Malik defines identity politics: on the one hand, as defensive, or 'the effort to secure the rights denied to some on the basis of their identity'; and on the other, aggressive, or 'that which seeks domination on the basis of identity'.[89] The inference is that, whereas the defensive variant is benign (= good/positive/justifiable), the aggressive one is not (= bad/negative/unjustifiable).

Equally clear is the way respective ethnicities and chronologies feature in this post-colonial oppositional framework. Arguing that defensive identity politics 'is mistakenly seen as [dividing] the electorate, and has pushed white voters into the embrace of populists', Malik insists that this same label should be attached instead to 'a response [by the 'other'] *against* the dominance of a white identity'.[90] In effect, the chronology of this process is reversed: not whites responding defensively to the advance of 'otherness', but rather a defence by the 'other' to white aggression/dominance.[91] The same kind of argument has been advanced by Afua Hirsch, who labels those who accuse her, too, of 'playing the race card' – that is, defining victimhood solely in terms of ethnic 'otherness' – as themselves being 'deeply racist'.[92] About these definitions and how

---

87   Malik (2019: 69–70).
88   For the 'grievance industry', see Malik (2019: 72). What is termed 'white identity politics' is condemned by her (Malik, 2019: 139) as a phenomenon that has been 'a cornerstone of domestic and overseas American and European politics for the last two centuries', thereby extending inferentially the accusation of racism to wholly undifferentiated populations over many epochs.
89   Malik (2019: 139–40).
90   Malik (2019: 141, emphasis added).
91   In the words of Malik (2019: 144): 'White identity politics came first and is aggressive, while identity politics by non-whites came second and is defensive'.
92   See 'The "race card" is how they try to silence us', *The Guardian* (London), 16 January 2020. For a different, yet relevant, take on this view, see the following observation by

they give rise to opposed characterizations (virtuous/malign) of both politics and identities, a number of observations are in order.

Celebrating Otherness?

Post-colonial sentiments about the achievements of immigrant selfhood are in some instances matched with negative characterizations of people inhabiting metropolitan countries. In a section entitled 'a brief history of fear', therefore, criticism of immigration is depicted as being the result of 'a rich vein of hysterical European, particularly French, literature on the subject'.[93] Opponents of immigration generally are referred to as 'bigots [who] brayed in full chorus', while views that Muslims do not assimilate is attributed to 'a bunch of Islamophobes'.[94] In keeping with this, an opponent of unregulated immigration to the United States, who is white, is described as a 'wild-eyed extremist' belonging to a 'rag-tag bunch of nativist vigilantes'.[95] Across the Atlantic, it seems, things are no better. Those in Britain who fear the impact of immigration are dismissed simply as 'poorly-educated or right-wingers'.[96] Of the post-Brexit United Kingdom, the same source asks 'why should they [ex-colonies like India] make a deal with a cold, windswept bunch of Islands in the North Sea?'.[97] One can only

---

Haider (2018: 18–19, 20): '[I]f you talked about racism without talking about capitalism, you weren't talking about getting power in the hands of the people ... that was clearly the situation we were getting into in the United States, as optimistic liberals celebrated the replacement of mass movements, riots, and armed cells with a placid multiculturalism. Over the course of several decades, the legacy of anti-racist movements was channelled toward the economic and political advancement of individuals like Barack Obama and Bill Cosby ... Within the academy and within social movements, no serious challenge arose against the cooptation of the anti-racist legacy. Intellectuals and activists allowed politics to be reduced to the policing of our language, to the questionable satisfaction of provoking white guilt, while the institutional structures of racial and economic oppression persisted'.

93 Mehta (2019: 110).
94 Mehta (2019: 122–23, 164).
95 Mehta (2019: 129).
96 Mehta (2019: 108). Similarly, the inference by Alibhai-Brown (2018: 87) is that the UK population at large is uniformly ignorant ('I bet most Brits have no idea about the censorship and self-censorship that operates secretly in all walks of life'). She also describes a critic of her own politically correct views (Alibhai-Brown, 2018: 96) as 'a man-boy with a redundant life map who needs to get a grip'.
97 Mehta (2019: 187). As problematic is the description by Hanif Kureishi of what he terms 'the master race' as composed of 'the usual knuckle-dragging, semi-blind suspects with their endlessly repeated terrors and fears [whose] stupidity and the sound of their

with difficulty avoid the conclusion that were Europeans currently to use these same kind of terms and descriptions in print about inhabitants of erstwhile colonies belonging to a different ethnicity, demonizing them in an undifferentiated manner as unthinking, swivel-eyed, and innately dim-witted, it would very quickly – and rightly – attract condemnation.[98]

Nor is it the case that celebration of 'otherness' by post-colonial exponents is static. Where this might lead is evident from the analysis by Mehta, in which this process undergoes a politically worrying shift: the original case advanced by him, that 'I am like you', is replaced increasingly with a subtext proclaiming 'I am better than you'.[99] Realizing perhaps that sentiment of this kind is not merely alienating but also confirms the fears expressed by those who adhere to the Great Replacement framework (see the next chapter), he clarifies that such achievements do not mean 'Indians are some master race'. Nonetheless, the impression created is that he may think they are. When coupled with other arguments made by him, the inference that might be drawn – and indeed is drawn by Great Replacement exponents – is that a discourse 'we are better than you' licenses as its next step a claim that 'we deserve to be in your country'.[100] When combined with negative representations by post-colonial discourse of those in European nations, moreover, an argument such as '[t]he future of

---

pathetic whining would be funny if it weren't so tragic ... ' See 'The whining about diversity is driven by fear and ignorance', *The Guardian* (London), 16 June 2018.

98 Even imperialists such as Sir Harry Johnston, a late nineteenth century colonial administrator who held the stereotypically racist views of his era and class, ascribed positive characteristics to the non-white populations about whom he wrote (Johnston, 1920: vi), noting that Africans possessed 'an equality in brain-power with some of the cleverest and ablest White men living in the present day'.

99 Hence the proliferation of statements (Mehta, 2019: 126, 176, 188, 190–91) such as the following. 'The fastest-growing race in the country [the United States] is now Asian: we are increasing ... There's also the fear that, once non-whites are let in, we'll do better than them ... immigrants overall are much better educated'; 'in almost all categories, immigrants do better than the native-born'; '[t]he east African Asian refugee community [that came to the UK from Uganda] is one of the wealthiest communities of any colour in the UK; their educational achievements eventually outrun those of native-born whites;; and 'Indian Americans are the most successful group of any kind in the United States: we have the highest per capita incomes, the highest educational attainment'.

100 See Mehta (2019: 187), who dismisses Great Replacement discourse as 'poisonous', '[t]he false stories of populists, their fearmongering, their bigotry' (Mehta, 2019: 29, 113–15) without being aware of the extent to which his own views, and the way these are expressed, play directly into the hands of this 'other' discourse. Equally, he (Mehta, 2019: 128) describes immigration policies as 'ethnic cleansing', seemingly oblivious to the fact that the same term is applied by Great Replacement discourse to account for the impact on white Americans of immigration.

our species, like our past, is African', hints at a potential continuation along the lines of 'more so than you, in fact', a possibility which in turn fuels Great Replacement reaction.[101] Once again, it hardly seems necessary to underline just how large a gap exists between this sort of post-colonial approach, one that stresses 'otherness' to the degree and in the terms it does, and the contrasting emphasis placed earlier by Robeson and James on the importance of class solidarity uniting workers of different ethnicities.

Migrant achievement projected by post-colonial discourse is nevertheless tempered by what is felt by its subject to be the taint of migrant 'otherness', in the form of non-recognition by white colleagues in the same hierarchy, along the lines of 'I am just like you, but am not acknowledged as such (by you)'.[102] What post-colonial exponents making this case object to, therefore, is not so much capitalist exploitation as two specific but interconnected types of status diminution.[103] On the one hand, their lack of social status parity with those in the receiving country who belong to a different ethnicity yet occupy the same (relatively exalted) class position as themselves. And on the other, a failure on the part of those in the receiving country to differentiate immigrants in terms of hierarchical position (the wealthy or 'successful' ones from those who are poor). Hence the frequency of the assertion by Mehta that 'I am American', which signals the importance attached by him to the element of sameness as

---

101 Both the fact and tone of some assertions by Mehta (2019: 182) – for example, that 'I claim the right to the United States, for myself and my children and my uncles and cousins ... We're here, we're not going back ... It's our country now ... It's our America now' – construct as powerful a sense of entitlement as that of its 'other': the equally-powerful sense of nationalist selfhood informing Great Replacement ideology.

102 'On the NYU campus, everyone speaks Hindi but the Sahibs', observes Mehta (2019: 37), who then laments that 'I am one of the Sahibs, but I am also brown'. Similarly, Reni Eddo-Lodge (in Shukla, 2016: 77–83) notes that 'I wrote about whiteness from the perspective of an outsider who – despite my university education, well-spoken relative privilege – has always been locked out of whiteness's exclusivity clause'. So, too, Riz Ahmed (in Shukla, 2016: 159–168), who – 'a scholarship to private school' notwithstanding – describes his problems getting through airport security on his travels to and from film shoots, and regrets that '[i]n one way or another you are all saying, "I'm not like the rest of them"'.

103 In an account of this sort of liminal existence, Kieran Yates (in Shukla, 2016: 108–118) describes how uncomfortable she feels in her home village in Punjab where '[e]ven my long, perfectly pointed acrylic nails give away my cushy life, devoid of manual labour'. Her focus is on the difficulties of 'belonging' either in the UK or in India, and consequently 'how anomalous I am in both worlds'. Similarly, Musa Okwonga (in Shukla, 2016: 224–234), whose parents fled from Uganda, and was educated subsequently at Eton and Oxford, was considered at home 'too posh to hang out with most of the locals', yet also told by another Etonian that '[I] will never be one of them'.

regards his American peer group, and difference from other, less educated/ prosperous immigrants who have still to gain citizenship.[104]

In many ways, post-colonial views correspond to a familiar reaction by erstwhile colonial subjects to what is perceived as disdain on the part of those who used to be colonizers. The position taken by some of these exponents, therefore, replicates a move away from what has been termed the 'cultural cringe', a phenomenon described by its originator as 'an assumption that the domestic cultural product will be worse than the imported article', and applied by him to the positive way – verging on awe – which an erstwhile colonized nation perceives the cultural achievements of its one-time colonizer ('the centrifugal pull of the great cultural metropolises works against us').[105] Of relevance to the case made by post-colonial discourse is not the 'cultural cringe' *per se* but rather its 'other'; the latter is a mirror image of the former, and arises as a reaction to it, thereby replacing a sense of cultural subordination with one of cultural autonomy ('the Cringe Inverted').[106] It entails a twofold process: not

---

104 Reminding us that he is educated, an American, and not like other immigrants, Mehta (2019: 7, 39, 47, 155) recounts variously that 'I have been in America for forty-three years. For thirty of those I have been an American citizen. Every year, my confidence in my position in the country grew. When I went abroad – a summer in London, nine months in Paris, even when I went back to India for a couple of years – I would return to America with relief, because there I could be a American'; 'I go back to my lavish NYU campus [in Abu Dhabi] and sit that evening by the sea at the Hyatt [hotel], paying more for drinks in one day than [my taxi driver] earns in a week. Because I am an American'; 'Flashing my American passport, I get on a fast, comfortable ferry … '; and, finally, 'I've been living in lower Manhattan on and off since 1980, when I studied at NYU'. Asked whether he was an Indian, Mehta (2019: 129) replied: 'Originally, yes, but now I'm American'. For him (Mehta, 2019: 107) the United States is 'the country I call home'.

105 The term 'cultural cringe' was outlined during 1950 by Phillips (1958: 89–95) and used by him to depict the asymmetrical intellectual relationship between Australia as an ex-colony and the UK as an ex-colonizer, a link the inequality of which he described as an 'internalised inferiority complex [which] causes people to dismiss their own culture'.

106 On 'the cringe inverted' as the 'other' of 'the cultural cringe', see Phillips (1958: 89–90). An essay dealing with Australian folk-song where this reverse variant is described observes (Phillips, 1979: 50): 'A generation ago, aesthetically U-minded Australians averted their eyes from the vulgarities of their country's past; today those vulgarities have become history to be sought out and cherished'. It could be argued that, in effect, there are not two but three variants of 'the cringe'. First, the privileging by the erstwhile colonized of the culture of the ex-colonizer ('your culture is so much better than ours') – the 'cringe' proper; second, the privileging in a positive way by the erstwhile colonized of their own culture ('we know and understand our own culture, you don't') – the 'cringe' inverted; and third, the privileging by the erstwhile colonized of their own critiques about the culture belonging to the ex-colonizer ('we know and understand your culture so much better than you do yourselves') – the 'cringe' relocated. The last variant, it could be argued,

only the assertion by those from a previously colonized nation of its own ideological and cultural independence, but also and simultaneously the opposite; deprivileging the same characteristics of the earlier colonial power.[107] Whatever is linked to the experience and/or history of colonization is *ipso facto* condemned, regardless of its wider theoretical provenance and politics, a view not so different from that of the 'new' populist postmodernism.

Accordingly, what is significant are the following. First, that both the 'cultural cringe' and its reversal project an identity not of class but of nation. Second, in doing so, each creates a space for a discourse about related institutional forms as emblematic of long-standing national tradition, and consequently essentializing them as innate. This in turn sanctifies rival cultures as being 'authentic', a process reifying a specifically national identity of both colonizer and colonized. And third, attempts then to invoke a similar kind of 'difference' with regard to economic organization/behaviour do no more than deflect attention from the sameness of class formation/struggle imposed by the process of accumulation. The point about Marxist political economy is that its scope is international: since the rules it applies transcend frontiers, its teachings about capitalism as a system are not restricted to any one context, and cannot thus be regarded as specific – or, indeed, inapplicable – to a particular nation, region, or locality. It is precisely this element of universality that is denied both by much present-day writing/comment supportive of unregulated immigration and by a 'new' populist postmodernism that similarly privileges national/ethnic 'otherness'. Each unsurprisingly rejects not just Marxism, but also its core theoretical elements such as class analysis and socialism.[108]

Conclusion

Outlined here has been the manner in which discourse about consciousness/struggle linked to class and race altered in a number of interconnected ways, together with and reasons for such change. As a result, concepts of political

---

informs many 'new' populist postmodern analyses encountered in higher educational institutions of metropolitan capitalist nations.

107 Hence the kind of reaction by Alibhai-Brown (2018: 53) when, having had her candidacy doubted by 'white, male dons' at the interview stage, proclaims 'I did get into Oxford [University] and I showed them'.

108 As has been seen elsewhere in this volume, to some degree this rejection of Marxism and socialism is also consistent with views expressed by Patnaik, Bernstein, Dhanagare, and Banaji.

and ideological empowerment have themselves been transformed: from class to non-class identities, and to ethnic/national forms of 'otherness' in particular; and from the attainment of socialism as a desirable/feasible objective, to ascending the existing hierarchy of capitalism. All this has been accompanied by a change in the locus of empowerment itself; from erstwhile colonies, now independent countries, to within a metropolitan capitalist nation itself. These shifts are embodied in the contrast between the earlier views of Paul Robeson and C.L.R. James, and the later ones held by writers/commentators belonging to the post-colonial diaspora.

The 1930s debate about self-determination underlines the political importance which Robeson and James – as well as others on the left during the first half of the twentieth century – attached to the construction and reproduction of unity between workers of different ethnicities. Stalin attempted to categorize the black population in the United States as a separate nation, consequently presenting the struggle as one of national liberation that licensed self-determination, a separateness that in many ways was no different from the Bantustans favoured by the South African apartheid regime. Opposing this, leftists supported class unity that transected ethnic (or 'national') 'otherness, pointing out that to subordinate working-class solidarity to the formation of multi-class alliances overlooked the fact that the bourgeoisie and/or petty-bourgeoisie of whatever ethnicity were unreliable partners in the struggle. Accordingly, the pursuit of identity politics was not just a method of negating emancipation, but also diverged from the Leninist dictum about combatting national oppression but not promoting national identity.

For Robeson and James, therefore, the difference of ethnic/national identities were necessarily transected by the sameness of class: solidarity generated by the latter took the form of internationalism, whilst empowerment required both the transcendence of capitalism and a transition to socialism in advanced and less developed economic contexts. By contrast, what writers/commentators of the post-colonial diaspora want is not socialism but rather a better deal under capitalism. Whereas historically exponents of the 'drain' theory argued for economic reparations payable to ex-colonies, reparations in current diasporic discourse take the form not of money but of labour-power: that is, open-door immigration from ex-colonies to the advanced capitalist nations of erstwhile colonizers. Such arguments are justified additionally by an undifferentiated concept of rich/poor nations, a duality which reproduces the nationalist claim that colonialism endures beyond decolonization.

Just as the economic case for open-door immigration depends on the efficacy of the reparations-for-colonization argument, therefore, so the combined political correctness + identity politics of 'otherness' advanced by diasporic discourse rests on its being a response to a prefiguring non-'other' identity politics, that of white selfhood. This, too, is presented by some exponents of diasporic discourse as a colonial legacy which requires amends. In an important sense, the justification of open-door immigration depends centrally on the acceptability of the prefiguring case about colonialism being a method whereby 'rich' countries 'stole' the treasure of 'poor' countries, a variation of the 'drain' thesis that is a staple nationalist trope. If this discourse about immigration-as-a-form-of-reparations fails, then so does the justification for open-door immigration. Based on the questionable view that the experience of colonization prevented economic development in colonized nations, claims for reparations overlook the emergence and consolidation in such contexts of what is now recognizably a dynamic that is Asian capitalism.

Barely mentioned, if at all, by its proponents is an alternative explanation as to who else benefits from open-door immigration, and why. That is, the centrality to the accumulation process of an expanding industrial reserve army in order to divide the working class, suppress wage costs, increase profitability, and maintain competitive advantage over rival producers in what is now a global economic system. The identity politics of the post-colonial diaspora, based as it is on culture-as-empowerment, ignores the way championing 'otherness' in this fashion is supportive of neoliberalism. This it does through hindering economic critiques of the accumulation process in metropolitan capitalist nations by facilitating the defence of open-door immigration made by employers who need to augment the industrial reserve. This poses no difficulty to those in the post-colonial diaspora who perceive capitalism as positive; for Marxists opposed to the accumulation process in such contexts, it does.

CHAPTER 8

Great Replacement, or Reaping the Capitalist Whirlwind (*via* Populism/Nationalism)

The question of identity is a question involving the most profound panic – a terror as primary as the nightmare of the mortal fall. This question can scarcely be said to exist among the wretched, who know, merely, that they are wretched and who bear it day by day – it is a mistake to suppose that the wretched do not know that they are wretched; nor does this question exist among the splendid, who know, merely, that they are splendid, and who flaunt it day by day: it is a mistake to suppose that the splendid have any intention of surrendering their splendour. An identity is questioned only when it is menaced, as when the mighty begin to fall, or when the wretched begin to rise, or when the stranger enters the gates, never, thereafter, to be a stranger: the stranger's presence making *you* the stranger, less to the stranger than to yourself.

> A still relevant observation made almost half a century ago by JAMES BALDWIN concerning the historically undiminished power, role, and contextual specificity of identity politics.[1]

∴

No one in the West will ever be happy again ... never again; happiness today is nothing but an old dream, the past conditions for its existence are simply no longer being fulfilled.

> A cry of despair evoked by MICHEL HOUELLEBECQ that is widely thought to be symptomatic of despondency currently prevalent among inhabitants of advanced capitalist nations.[2]

∴

---

1 See Baldwin (1976: 77, original emphasis).
2 See Houellebecq (2019: 87).

Introduction: The Last Taboo

If there is one process that rivals climate change for the label of an inconvenient truth, it is the current migration pattern from Third World and erstwhile Soviet bloc countries into the metropolitan capitalist nations of Europe. Hence the importance of understanding and accounting for this process, and in particular what – if anything – differentiates Marxist from non-Marxist approaches to the issues involved.[3] As conceptualized both by its exponents and by those addressing its discourse, causes, and impact, the Great Replacement (hereafter GR) refers to a process of ethnic/national displacement by an incoming population of an existing one, a supplanting effected by means of mass immigration from one country (or continent) to another.[4] It is a transformation that is

---

3   The importance of differentiating these two political views stems from the fact that, on the subject of surplus labour, GR and Marxism appear to share a common narrative. As will become clear, however, the assumption that such an overlap extends also to politics is incorrect.

4   This process of ethnic displacement has historical precedents, not least in nineteenth century America, when in 1827 Henry Clay, a prominent American politician, made a speech in which he advocated planting a colony in West Africa to which free blacks from the United States could be sent and settled. That project involved what was in effect a reverse displacement: not just removing an existing population, but also consciously making space for a new set of incomers. Instead of the current pattern, whereby according to GR black migrants from Africa replace the white inhabitants of metropolitan capitalist nations, the nineteenth century variant transposed this, black members of the population being sent to African colonies so as to create room in the United States for white immigrants from Europe. As described by Clay (1843: 281), 'by the annual withdrawal of fifty-two thousand persons of colour, there would be annual space created for an equal number of the white race'. Of particular interest are the reasons for and justifications of this colonization. Clay (1843: 281) made no attempt to disguise what he saw as the potential danger of black workers and poor smallholders who might make common cause with white equivalents: with colonization, 'the proportion of the African to the European race will be so small that the most timid may then for ever dismiss all ideas of danger from within or without'. The reason for this fear was outlined by him in pathological terms: 'Of all the classes of our population, the most vicious is that of the free coloured. It is the inevitable result of their moral, political, and civil degradation. Contaminated themselves, they extend their vices to all around them, to the slaves and to the whites. If the principle of colonization should be confined to them; if a colony can be firmly established, and successfully continued in Africa ... much good will be done [which] will be felt by the Africans who go, by the Africans who remain, by the white population of our country, by Africa, and by America'. With regard to justification, Clay (1843: 282) was equally forthright, presenting this both as virtuous and as consistent with religious teaching: 'There is a moral fitness in the idea of returning to Africa her children, whose ancestors have been torn from her by the ruthless hand of fraud and violence. Transplanted in a foreign land, they will carry back to their native soil the rich fruits of religion, civilization, law, and liberty. May it not be one of the great designs of the Ruler of the universe [= God] ... thus to transform an original crime [= slavery] into a signal blessing. ...'

perceived to be total: not just confined to demography, therefore, but involving also a change in ethnic composition, in religion, in culture, in language, and in politics.

In metropolitan capitalist nations, GR is deemed largely responsible for generating a populist backlash, at the centre of which are disputes about national/ ethnic identity and belonging. It could be argued, ostensibly, that in terms of teleology GR is a mirror image of the kind of post-colonial discourse examined in the previous chapter, its 'other' in all respects save one: politics. However, rather than regarding these two approaches as belonging to separate ideological traditions, GR and post-colonial discourse should be seen instead as forming two sides of the same populist coin. For reasons that will become clear, this is the interpretation followed in this chapter.

Accordingly, examined here is the way GR and its related issues/processes/ outcomes are addressed in four recent analyses: that by Eric Kaufmann, Stephen Smith, Renaud Camus, and Bret Easton Ellis.[5] Although there are significant differences between them in terms of approach, each attempts to explain the emergence and consolidation of all or particular aspects of the immigration/GR/populism combination, without considering in any detail the connection either to capitalist accumulation, to its neoliberal variant and the accompanying *laissez-faire* project, or to the formation, expansion and role of a global industrial reserve army of labour. Missing or downplayed, consequently, is a link between GR and ever more intense labour market competition, plus the kinds of non-class identity and struggle this has generated historically, a dynamic and its attendant conflict that continues into the present.

Approaches to GR in either positive or negative terms, tend to interpret it chiefly in Malthusian terms, and focus on the ethnic/national/cultural identity both of those inhabiting the host context and of the migrant. Marxism, by contrast, perceives the latter subject principally in economic terms, as part of the industrial reserve army. Whereas in the Malthusian variant the migrant features largely as a potential/actual consumer, for Marxism s/he appears mainly in the role of potential/actual worker. Implicitly or explicitly, therefore,

---

5 See Kaufmann (2018), Camus (2018), Smith (2019), and Bret Easton Ellis (2019). It must be stressed that, with the exception of Camus, none of the others is a GR advocate. Hence the term GR exponent refers simply to those who address the issue without necessarily endorsing all its ideological, economic and political claims, a distinction that is absolutely crucial. Whereas the focus of Smith is principally on causes of migration from the sending context, that of Camus, Kaufmann, and Bret Easton Ellis is mainly on the debates/impact of this same process in the receiving context. Not considered here at the same level of detail, however, are other analyses which also address – in part or in whole – the case made by GR (Esman, 2010; Murray, 2018, 2019).

GR theory adopts a Malthusian reading, linking immigration into metropolitan capitalist nations to population growth in the so-called Third World.[6]

The presentation which follows is divided into three sections, the first of which examines the components of GR discourse. Blaming what is claimed to be the political left for promoting 'otherness' as empowerment, the second part considers cultural arguments and disagreements as to the responsibility for GR, and specifically how/why the 'new' populist postmodernism has empowered its discourse. Questioning the view that the left is complicit with GR, the third section looks at economic aspects of the immigration debate, with particular reference to Marxist theory about the industrial reserve army.

I

White Fright, White Fight

Denying that he is 'an alarmist Eurocentric', Smith examines 'Africa's importance as a reservoir of migrants', and maintains that over the next two generations one hundred million Africans 'are likely to cross the Mediterranean Sea', warning that 'neither Europe nor Africa has yet taken the full measure of the challenge that lies ahead [since the] two continents are still unprepared for a migratory encounter of unprecedented magnitude'.[7] In his opinion, therefore, Africa will soon become 'a departure hall'.[8] Whereas historically the main pattern of migration has been an internal one, within Africa itself, now it has become largely an external process, with Europe as its objective. Currently the path followed begins with rural exodus to the cities, and from thence to Europe.[9] The main reasons encountered inside Africa for this transformation, argues Smith, are a combination of rapid demographic growth, the youthfulness of the population, urbanization, development aid, and the entrenched political power at the grassroots of gerontocracy.

Ironically, therefore, one result of development aid has been a 'burgeoning middle class', the components of which will migrate in search of better paid

---

6 Although he disavows being a demographer, Smith (2019: 39, 45, 49–50) nevertheless focuses on population data/projection, and invokes Malthus. In keeping with this, and responding to his own question 'Why is all this happening now?', Kaufmann (2018: 12) answers: 'Population change – demography – lies at the heart of the story'.
7 Smith (2019: 4, 131).
8 Smith (2019, 132).
9 Smith (2019: 118–19).

employment in Europe.[10] According to Smith, therefore, migrants will consist of two categories: those belonging to the bourgeoisie, who can afford to pay the passage, and will go in pursuit of improved lives and jobs; and – to a far less extent – the poor and/or unemployed, who hope to find any kind of work, well-paying or otherwise.[11] Accepting that such population movement is composed for the most part of economic migrants, Smith highlights an obvious difficulty: the jobs sought in Europe will be the ones that are automated, confronting migrants with no other prospect than joining the ranks of the unemployed in another country.[12] He contrasts this bleak economic future with that of Europeans who migrated to the United States in the late nineteenth century, when there was a strong demand for labour-power in the host nation.

Challenging the view that the fundamental structural divide within Africa is the persistence of ethnic/tribal politics, Smith maintains instead that the 'significant obstacle to democracy' is much rather the 'principle of seniority'.[13] Arguing that 'the postcolonial state in Africa represents the pursuit of "gerontocracy" by other means', he insists that it is the latter (and not ethnicization/tribalization of politics) that not just undermines the democratic process, but by doing so blocks the prospects of African youth, who then turn to Europe in order to realize their hopes. Among the pull factors are welfare provision, which enable migrants without a family support network to survive during the search for employment.[14] That such labour market competition possesses negative implications for European workers is clear, since 'in traditionally wealthy countries of the North, the least qualified workers – increasingly exposed to international competition – have sunk into the "precariat"'.[15] In this, Smith

---

10 See Smith (2019: 86). In what he (Smith, 2019: 107) terms the development paradox, 'the countries of the North subsidize the counties of the South with development aid so that the poor can live better lives and – though this is rarely said so directly – stay where they are. By doing so, however, rich countries shoot themselves in the foot [because] development aid subsidizes migration'.

11 'Not everyone in Africa who wishes to migrate to Europe can simply pack up and head out', observes Smith (2019: 103, 104), so it is 'a less indigent stratum of Africans – the continent's middle class – that migrates'. Anticipating just such a process, and writing ironically, Baldwin (1976: 81, original emphasis) has observed: 'The necessity, then, of those "lesser breeds without the law"... is this: one must not become more free, nor become more base than they: must not be used as they are used, nor yet use them as their abandonment allows one to use them: therefore, they must be civilized. But when they *are* civilized, they may simply "spuriously imitate [the civilizer] back again," leaving the civilizer with "no satisfaction on which to rest."'

12 Smith (2019: 15, 123, 149).
13 Smith (2019: 69, 83, 91).
14 Smith (2019: 145).
15 Smith (2019: 100–101).

agrees with Camus, for whom the disadvantages affect not just those in the host nation but also the migrants themselves, since the attractions which the latter hope to find in the destination are rapidly dissipated by the very fact of migration itself.[16]

Unlike Smith, whose focus is principally on the sending context, and the causes there of outmigration, Camus explores the impact on the host nations in Europe. Lamenting what he regards as a process of de-authentication operating across the whole of European culture – affecting everything from language, music, and art, to food, images, and gestures – Camus assigns blame internally: not to migrants from Africa but rather to the political and ideological spread within Europe itself of the idea of equality, which has proscribed any/all criticism of immigration.[17] Cultural erosion is an effect of what he terms 'the dictatorship of the petty-bourgeoisie', or the consolidation of an inclusiveness 'whose limits more or less coincide with the world itself' and consequently 'knows practically no outside world'.[18] Exercising as a result an ideological hegemony (equality = deculturation = de-authentication) which it is impossible politically to challenge, the 'petite bourgeoisie is *par excellence* the class of replacement'.[19] Most significantly, what led Camus towards GR theory in the first place was when in the 1990s he encountered Muslims in a French village setting; that is, the presence of 'otherness' not just in France but in its pristine rural areas, a situation he interpreted as an almost sacrilegious encroachment onto the physical and ideological terrain that symbolized the agrarian myth.[20]

---

16   This paradox is outlined by Camus (2018: 41) in the following way: 'Their real opinion of what French and European colonialism was about, Africans express it with their feet, as they run to France and to Europe to settle down here with the French and the Europeans ... They think they are rushing to paradise, at least by comparison. They are running into a wall of illusions, as what made Europe so desirable for them was ... the simple fact that they were not there. As soon as they are present in sufficient numbers, Europe is lost for Europeans, because they are being replaced, and lost for the Africans, because it becomes just another Africa, plagued with the same kinds of problems, be they religious, political ... For them the whole European continent is like one of those fabled alchemical treatises where the text on each page vanishes as soon as the book is opened at it'.

17   Regarding this locus of blame, see Camus (2018: 88–89). On GR as a process of cultural de-authentication, see Camus (2018: 139, 146, 147). 'If there is no culture', he observes (Camus, 2018: 98), 'culture will be the name of whatever there is'. He continues (Camus, 2018: 114): 'Equality between century-old local traditions and mores and imported ways of life and foreign traditions will let nothing standing, or worth standing, of any nation'.

18   Camus (2018: 111, 121–22).

19   Camus (2018: 128).

20   In the course of a discussion, Camus told his interviewer that '[i]n the late nineties, he began writing domestic travel books, commissioned by the French government. The work

Cultural erosion/de-authentication is also central to the investigation by Kaufmann into the dynamics of GR fears now circulating among the inhabitants of developed societies. Rightly linking immigration to the rise of populism, he nevertheless attributes the latter development simply to the numerical decline in western nations of populations constituting a hitherto dominant white ethnic group (= 'whiteshift'), insisting that populism is determined by 'concern over identity, not economic threat'.[21] As a framework for analysing GR issues, however, problems with this kind of approach surface quickly; political differences in such contexts are explained in psychologistic terms, a difficulty that stems in part from a methodology based on attitudinal surveys. Thus both supporters and opponents of immigration are categorized as belonging to distinct psychological types, since in his opinion 'all social systems work with the grain of some of our evolutionary psychology'.[22] Denying that they are informed by inequality, wealth, and power, Brexit voting patterns are instead ascribed by him to 'psychological quirks'.[23]

Demography, Culture, Civilization

Upholding the view that political organization in Africa is an effect of generational power, Smith overlooks the fact that in many instances ethnic/tribal identity has been mobilized in a populist fashion, either from within (to secure electoral support or to lay claim to a better share of existing resources) or from without (to divide and rule, by focussing on non-class identities). In cases where 'old men rule', therefore, and equate tribal/ethnic identity with that of the nation, this can be linked to imperialism, which installs and keeps in power those such as Mobutu in order to further its own economic and political

---

took him to the department of Hérault, whose capital is Montpellier. Although Camus was familiar with France's heavily black and Arab inner suburbs, or *banlieues*,... his experience in Hérault floored him. Travelling through the medieval villages, he said "you would go to a fountain, six or seven centuries old, and there were all these North African women with veils." A demographic influx was no longer confined to France's inner suburbs and industrial regions; it was ubiquitous, and it was transforming the entire country'. See Thomas Chatterton Williams, 'The French Origins of "You Will Not Replace Us" – The European thinkers behind the white-nationalist rallying cry', *The New Yorker*, November 27, 2017.

21 Kaufmann (2018: 2, 4). Lest it be thought that 'other'-culture-as-disbarment is applied just by Europe to migrants from the Third World, it was also applied by colonies to immigrants from Europe itself (Lochore, 1951).
22 Kaufmann (2018: 20, 295).
23 Kaufmann (2018: 196–7, 200).

interests. Although he decries the concept of migration as a form of 'revenge colonization' on the part of a 'resentful Africa', Smith nevertheless comes close to endorsing this very notion.[24] Hence the inference by him that where European workers experience a descent into the ranks of the 'precariat', they were lucky to have a decent standard of living in the first place, and should neither be surprised nor complain when as a result of globalisation this is taken away from them.[25] This is a politically reactionary argument, one that is heard frequently from some who see development as a zero-sum process. In this discourse those belonging to the European working class currently enduring a decline in living standards are perceived as undeserving victims, now that they are being replaced (both at home and abroad) by the Third World 'other', a politically more deserving case.[26]

The pejorative description by Smith of the post-1945 welfare provision enjoyed by working class in Europe as 'a well-cosseted exception in an otherwise more exposed world', suggests that he does indeed regard this as in some sense illegitimate, despite the fact that what there remains still of such provision ('a social safety net') has had to be fought for in the course of class struggles waged 'from below' throughout history.[27] What is not mentioned in this variant of 'revenge colonization' discourse is to whose advantage it really is: namely, capitalists undertaking labour process restructuring, undermining any consciousness of class (and thus solidarity) by playing workers of different ethnic/national identities against each other. Where this 'divide-and-rule' strategy is combined with economic restructuring, the political outcome throughout Europe has been, unsurprisingly, the rise of populism. This is particularly relevant to the contrast Smith makes between two historically distinct migration flows. Whereas the 1880s migration to the United States corresponded largely to a situation in which migrants were an addition to existing workers, and thus not in the main competitors with them, early twenty-first century migration to Europe by contrast is – and is perceived to be – informed by a different economic dynamic. Instead of simply labour-power added to the existing workforce, it is in many cases 'instead of' the latter. As such, it can be seen by those in employment, or hoping to enter this, as an unwarranted source of labour market competition, designed to drive down wages and working conditions.

---

24 Smith (2019: 139).
25 Smith (2019: 101).
26 This is because European workers are seen as complicit historically in the colonization by imperialism – and thus exploitation – of the Third World 'other', a view held by – among others – Patnaik (see Chapter 3, this volume).
27 Smith (2019: 145).

A similar refusal to address economic determinants generally, and more especially those generated by accumulation, its dynamics and attendant forms of class struggle, means that Kaufmann must confine within capitalism any political remedies he suggests. Hence the anodyne nature of his political solutions to the issues raised by GR, along the lines of different attitudes towards immigration 'need to be respected', 'I set out a vision for a new centre, which entails accepting the legitimate cultural interests of reconstructed, open ethnic majorities. This can pave the way towards a more relaxed, rational political conversation', and 'Conservative whites need to have a future and I believe most will accept an open form of white majority identity'.[28] His conclusion – that the 'appropriate policy response is … a compromise between equity and efficiency' – underlines the extent to which Kaufmann remains trapped within the epistemological and political limits imposed by capitalism, and thus an inability to resolve the contradictions it reproduces.[29] Without, that is, addressing either what accumulation entails systemically, or its need to restructure the labour process by creating and then taking advantage of an industrial reserve army. Contrary to the claim by Kaufmann, that GR is an effect simply of demographic growth, throughout history population change has always occurred – and continues to do so – within specific contexts; what is happening now is not so much demographic growth *per se* as population *movement*. This is what has to be explained, in economic terms: that is, the systemic dynamic governing/preventing such movement, and with it the contradiction between workers who want to protect their wage levels, jobs, and living standards from yet more competition, and the need of capital to force down these same wage levels and conditions in order to compete (and even, perhaps, to survive). In short, the systemic contradiction which generates populism.

Equating culture with civilization, Camus – like so many others – uses the latter term in its restricted sense: that is, civilization without its economic and political dimensions, and their achievements. In keeping with this, he conflates 'race' and 'people', concepts which for him 'are more or less exchangeable'.[30] As

---

28 For these views, see Kaufmann (2018: 4, 27, 28).
29 Kaufmann (2018: 330).
30 Camus (2018: 75). Much of the GR discourse about cultural erosion was anticipated in the early 1920s by Stoddard (1922: 5), as with Camus a proponent of 'white fright', and who like him expressed the same kind of concerns: 'Today, the progress of science may have freed our own civilization from the peril of armed conquest by barbarian hordes; nevertheless, these peoples still threaten us with a subtler menace [since they are] able to migrate easily, owing to modern facilities of transportation, the more backward peoples of the earth tend increasingly to seek the centres of civilization, attracted thither by the high wages and easier living conditions which there prevail. The influx of such lower elements into civilized societies is an unmitigated disaster'.

with Kaufmann, this in turn takes Camus directly onto the theoretical terrain of populism, for which the words 'race' and 'people' are similarly interchangeable. What is interpreted by Camus as a process of *de*culturation is much rather one of *re*culturation, or a combination of extending cultural inclusiveness while at the same time forbidding Marxist political economy. This of course is a project that brings together neoliberalism (= the sacredness of individual economic choice), the 'new' populist postmodernism (= the sacredness of individual identity choice), and deregulated market capitalism. For this reason, the contention that everything is allowed is linked to – and indeed generates – the kindred argument that nobody may criticize any cultural/ideological position one chooses to take.[31] In turn, this licenses the empowerment of identity politics, which combines everything-is-allowed with no-criticism-is-permitted, since non-class identities (and their advocates) cease to be the object of critique. Hence the emergence – or re-emergence – of a politics linked to these identities, and the ensuing fusion of postmodernism and populism.

II

Who/What Is Responsible?

If immigration results in cultural erosion/de-authentication, contributing thereby to GR, then how is it to be explained in terms of who or what is deemed to be ideologically and politically supportive of – and thus in an important sense responsible for – this process? With the exception of that by Smith, all the approaches examined here are clear about where to place the blame for the emergence and consolidation of GR: on the promotion by the left of identity politics, championing any/every anguished ethnic/national 'other' by means of a victim narrative.[32]

Hence the focus of the approach to GR by Kaufmann is on conflict from the 1960s onwards between 'white tribalism' and what he terms 'left-modernism'.[33]

---

31 Among those who also make this case is Vargas Llosa (2015).
32 Others that similarly blame the left for the rise of identity politics include not just Wolfe (2000: 113ff.), who labels those responsible for this process 'Rococo Marxists', and Murray (2019: 51ff.), who conflates Marxism with post-Marxism and indicts them all, but also many journalists. Thus, for example, in a long analysis of the crises facing the global economic system currently, one finds the following: 'Meanwhile, a dominant thrust of the left's politics is based not on policy but on identity, asserted against the conservative and nativist ideologies of the right. With such politics, the chances of a consensus on creating a better world … appears minimal'. See 'Covid exposes society's dysfunctions', *Financial Times* (London), 15 July 2020.
33 Kaufmann (2018: 21).

The latter is defined by him as a combination of 'modernist anti-traditionalism' and 'cultural egalitarianism', a synthesis which he accepts 'meshed nicely with capitalism and globalization'. This 'left-modernist cosmopolitanism, which rejected both communism and fascism in favour of cultural radicalism and social democracy, emerged victorious from the war'.[34] In terms of effect, the twofold political impact of 'left-modernism' was to move debate from 'tolerating to mandating diversity' which in turn banished discussion of immigration, 'keeping it off the political agenda'.[35] Equated by Kaufmann with the 'cultural turn', 'multiculturalism', and the New Left, among the main characteristics he ascribes to 'left-modernism' are 'political correctness' and privileging 'subaltern ethnic narratives'.[36] Describing himself as a 'liberal and moderate egalitarian', he is nevertheless critical of 'the excesses of left-modernism': in particular, its exclusionary account together with support for subaltern ethnicity/'otherness' while at the same time decrying non-subaltern ethnic identity. As will be seen below, Kaufmann rather spoils his critique by insisting that all these characteristics are a specifically leftist vice, rather than what they in fact are: a conservative form of anti-capitalism that has a long history.

Like other approaches to GR, and especially that of Camus, Bret Easton Ellis resents having to apologize for being white, a sense of guilt inculcated in his view as a result of cultural democratization which encourages blandness and conformity.[37] Again like them, he attributes such developments to what he regards as the political left, responsible in his opinion for the rise and consolidation of identity politics which on the one hand castigate those like him, simply on the grounds of belonging to a privileged ethnicity, and on the other favour all those categorized as ethnically/nationally 'other'. Again like other approaches to GR, Bret Easton Ellis perceives the main attack on his identity as coming from the younger generation in the same society, an age-group he regards with contempt (millennials = 'Generation Wuss') for having in his view succumbed unjustifiably to an all-embracing concept of victimhood, and consequently being unable to engage critically with the world they inhabit.[38]

---

34 Kaufmann (2018: 313).
35 Kaufmann (2018: 22).
36 On these points, see Kaufmann (2018: 298, 305–6, 321, 338, 341, 345).
37 According to Bret Easton Ellis (2019: 117–18), therefore, 'the logical endgame of the democratization of culture and the dreaded cult of inclusivity, which insists everybody has to live under the same umbrella of rules'.
38 Hence the view (Easton Ellis, 2019: 139–40, original emphasis) about the way in which the left always and uncritically accepts the way the 'other' defines itself: 'This widespread epidemic of self-victimization – defining yourself in essence by way of a *bad* thing, a trauma that happened in the past that you've let *define* you. ...'

Unsurprisingly, in this discourse generational difference fuses with political difference, and Bret Easton Ellis ends by blaming millennials on the left – 'social justice warriors' – for generating/reproducing/endorsing the social ills to which he objects.[39]

Camus blames the left in similar terms, arguing that its promotion of egalitarianism has culminated in an alliance between the left and 'high finance' (= 'Davocracy', or the very rich, 'the great paymasters of the world, bankers and giants of finance'), enabling the latter to justify as benign/progressive the 'great replacism' policy from which it benefits.[40] This it does by the creation of additional consumers – in the form of migrants – to whom it can then sell commodities. Accordingly, to the right-wing trope of 'high finance' (code for 'Jewish' in this discourse) Camus adds the proponents of anti-racism, seen by him as providing 'Davocracy' with protection against the historical accusation that, because it has always been seen as rootless cosmopolitanism, finance has no loyalty to any nation. Hence the fusion of high finance/money/power on the one hand, and on the other anti-racism/virtue/righteousness is for him a combination of right and left ('traditional business interests of the right' + 'traditional moral ideals of the left').[41]

Like Bret Easton Ellis and Kaufmann, therefore, Camus is strongly critical of the left, which he censures for combining with and providing a justification for the GR policies followed by neoliberalism.[42] An analogous connection – but with one important difference – is made by Houellebecq, who argues that responsibility for the rise and consolidation in France of Islam lies with the

---

39 'The high moral tone seized by the social justice warriors, and increasingly an unhinged Left', he maintains (Easton Ellis, 2019: 181, 184), 'is always out of scale with whatever they're actually indignant about [and] had begun to create an authoritarian language police ... we were entering into an authoritarian cultural moment fostered by the Left'. Much the same criticism of 'social justice warriors' is expressed by Kaufmann (2018: 304, 340), Murray (2019: 231ff.), and Camus. 'Yet if the absence of serious discussion and the innate contradictions alone were enough to stop this new religion of social justice', argues Murray (2019: 245, 247), 'it would hardly have got started. People looking for this movement to wind down because of its inherent contradictions will be waiting for a long time [because] they are ignoring the Marxist substructure of much of this movement ... [social justice] desire is not to heal but to divide, not to placate but to inflame, not to dampen but to burn. In this again the last part of a Marxist substructure can be glimpsed'.

40 Camus (2018: 114ff., 134).

41 'That unique combination, money and virtue (or the image thereof), power and righteousness, traditional business interests of the right and no less traditional moral ideals of the left', notes Camus (2018: 163), 'is in my opinion what makes replacism such a formidable enemy, so formidable indeed that one often wonders if there is any point in trying to fight it. ...'

42 See, for example, Camus (2018: 107).

left: instead of depicting this development as evidence for the power of the left (as do Camus, Kaufmann and Bret Easton Ellis), however, Houellebecq regards it as an effect of the ideological weakness of socialism.[43] The critique of Camus is not confined to the left, but extends to include the State. Again like Houellebecq, therefore, Camus draws a historical parallel between collaboration with the German invasion of France by the Vichy regime in 1940s, and the inability or unwillingness of 'collaborationist circles' – 'a tiny minority (of radicals)' – to oppose/resist GR, for him an analogous process of occupation.[44] This equivalence, he explains, stems from a situation 'where the government of an invaded or occupied country, having admitted defeat, applies its best efforts to befriend the invader, usually with little success quite simply because the invader despises him …'.[45]

Rival Ethnicities, Rival Populisms

Contrary to what Kaufmann claims is the case, his concept 'left-modernism' is neither left nor modern: all the defining characteristics he ascribes to it – 'mandated diversity', 'ethno-traditional nationalism', 'subaltern ethnic narratives', and 'political correctness' – are more accurately those which inform the discourse of the 'new' populist postmodernism.[46] The latter deprivileges concepts such as modernity, materialism, class, and even economic development, all dismissed as illegitimate Enlightenment/Eurocentric forms of 'foundationalism' inapplicable to an understanding – let alone empowerment – of 'other' cultural identity and agency, either in the so-called Third World or within metropolitan capitalism itself. Instead, 'new' populist postmodernist discourse re-essentializes historical (and in some instances pre-capitalist) forms of cultural

---

43 See Houellebecq (2015) and also Brass (2017: Ch. 9).
44 In 'two recent occupations of France – the shorter German one in the 1940s and the longer African one of the past forty years', argues Camus (2018: 58–59, original emphasis), 'the two collaborations serving the respective occupying forces are perfect look-alikes … it soon became clear that as far as the term *collaboration* was concerned, it appeared to be decidedly legitimate and appropriate to refer to the successive French governments which, after the Vichy government during the previous occupation, constantly displayed a typical eagerness to anticipate and meet the occupants' wishes and whims half-way. …'
45 See Camus (2018: 63).
46 As indicated earlier in this volume, the 'new' populist postmodernism refers to a variety of discourses (post-development, the Subaltern Studies project, post-colonialism, everyday-forms-of-resistance, post-structuralism, multitudes, etc.) which have in common hostility towards the theoretical apparatus of Marxism.

and economic identity. It is opposed (or resistant) to state power supportive as much of *laissez-faire* accumulation as of socialist central planning and property.[47]

Again contrary to the claim by Kaufmann, that the 'cultural left' pursues 'radical social transformation (as does Marxism, with its 'going beyond' capitalism to socialism), the 'new' populist postmodernism advocates recuperating traditional non-class (= lost) grassroots institutions and authority structures, in much the same way as populism does. Culture wars that he rightly criticizes are no more than an attempt by populists to find a non-Marxist form of grassroots empowerment that does not pose a fundamental threat to existing property relations and wealth. As such, it is the mirror image of what Kaufmann labels 'white tribalism', invoking not just the same arguments concerning the need to empower 'those below' (but not in class terms), but also promoting claims to empowerment using different kinds of ethnic/national/'other' identity. The ideological role of the cultural turn is that it enables one to claim to be a participant in a struggle that is ostensibly radical (for example, objecting to statues of colonizers, slave-owners, or Confederate soldiers), whereas it is actually a substitute for struggle, since the latter process is confined merely to acts of symbolic opposition. This is misrecognized by Kaufmann, who maintains wrongly that 'left-modernism triumphed despite the retreat of socialism', whereas in fact it triumphed not despite but much rather *because* of this retreat.[48]

---

47 As outlined elsewhere (Brass, 2000, 2014), in rural Latin America and India grassroots ethno-nationalism harks back to a mythical Golden Age informed by agrarian myth ideology, which – among other things – entails the restoration of pre- or non-capitalist hierarchy/authority and its attendant institutions/practices, most of which are fundamentally anti-democratic and non-progressive (e.g., subordination of women, concentration of landownership, the presence of unfree production relations). To some degree, and under the label of 'gerontocracy', this is the same kind of problem as that raised by Smith with regard to Africa. In his latest novel, Houellebecq (2019) invokes and laments the demise of agrarian myth ideology in the French countryside. He traces the decline of an aristocratic family as capitalism penetrates rural France; the son of the family embodies this decay, having moved from selling off plots of land to foreigners to running a failing business (bungalows as holiday lets). Deserted by his wife, who takes their daughters with her, the trajectory of decline is represented by the dilapidated state both of the chateau he still occupies and of his appearance. Reproducing the same kind of views about French farmers and farming held by John Berger (on which see Brass, 2019: Chapter 10), Houellebecq (2019: 237, 276–77) endorses the agrarian myth by contrasting the happiness of 'the rural' with the unhappiness of 'the urban', and expresses despair that nothing can be done to stop the onward march of *laissez-faire* capitalism.

48 Kaufmann (2018: 299).

Although the politically divisive aspect of identity politics traced by Kaufmann is also well captured by Bret Easton Ellis, because the latter – again like Kaufmann – mistakenly attributes its origin to the left, and blames the latter for its spread, he overlooks two crucial issues: the question of who/what benefits from this discourse, and the fact that identity politics (= the cultural turn) is a characteristic not of Marxism but rather of the 'new' populist postmodernism.[49] Equating postmodern identity politics with Marxism is profoundly mistaken, since the two positions are epistemologically incompatible: because it deals principally with ethnic/national identity, the 'new' populist postmodernism tends especially in its post-colonial guise to attack not the rich and powerful owners/controllers of the means of production, distribution, and exchange – as does Marxism – but rather all those belonging to an erstwhile colonial/imperial power.

In the recent past, and continuing into the present, therefore, postmodernism makes no distinction between the ruling class and its plebeian components in what were once colonizing nations. Consequently, struggle as interpreted by this kind of approach is mainly or only about national (or ethnic) empowerment on the part of countries and/or populations that were once colonies. As such, the 'new' populist postmodernism is a theory that is largely unconnected with the formation/consciousness/agency of those whose identity is based on class: namely, struggle undertaken by workers that necessarily transcends national/ethnic boundaries.

For the 'new' populist postmodernism, therefore, class is at worst an Eurocentric concept inapplicable outside its geographical area, and at best an add-on, to be addressed and resolved (if at all) only when all other non-class identities have been empowered. In many cases, however, it is only the latter, not the former, that interest exponents of the 'cultural turn'. Splitting working class identity/consciousness/empowerment along ethnic/national lines is the project of capital, not of the left. Yet this is precisely what the 'new' populist postmodernism entails. In keeping with this epistemology are those who align themselves with the 'cultural turn' simply because it is against neoliberalism.

---

49   'I was increasingly reminded by a certain faction', notes Easton Ellis (2019: 243, original emphasis) about what he regards as the Left, 'that we *should* be defining ourselves by our white identity because that was itself a real *problem*. Actually, this faction *demanded* it, without bothering to recognize that identity politics of any kind might be the worst idea in our culture right now, and certainly one that encourages the spread of alt-right and all-white organizations. Across the board, identity politics endorse the concept that people are essentially tribal, and our differences are irreconcilable ... This is the toxic dead-end of identity politics: it's a trap'.

Among those who regard populism as progressive, and consequently advocate what is conceptualized by them as 'left populism', is Chantal Mouffe.[50]

This is a view that emerged from earlier post-Marxist theory, which championed multi-class alliances based on hegemony, with the object of achieving a politically non-specific form of radical democracy (= a return to a 'kinder'/ 'caring' capitalism). Not the least problematic aspect of building multi-class alliances is that as soon as their object is achieved (the defeat of feudal proprietors), capitalist producers turn on their erstwhile allies (workers, poor peasants). Categorizing populist movements as the way forward politically, simply because such mobilizations oppose *laissez-faire* accumulation, overlooks the fact that their bourgeois components are just as – if not even more strongly – hostile to any form of socialism.

III

The economic background to the rise of immigration and populism, one that GR analyses tend to avoid or downplay, is clear. An effect of labour's stronger position in the immediate post-1945 era was that hours worked fell and industrial conflict increased. Class struggle 'from below' in metropolitan capitalist nations – the results of which were full employment, higher wages, and the welfare state – led in turn to class struggle 'from above', in the form of the new international division of labour. From the 1960s onwards, therefore, the Green Revolution drove peasants off the land and made them available to capital as workers, thereby enabling the outsourcing/downsizing of capitalist production. This was compounded in the late 1980s by the provision of additional sources of cheap and available labour-power nearer Europe, from countries previously part of the USSR and now members of the EU. Whereas development theory deploying the 'precariat' concept worries about the inability of temporary and low-paid labour-power to reproduce itself economically, this does not arise as long as capital can draw on an industrial reserve army that is global. Hence the need to preserve the well-being of its workers is no longer a major concern.

Political Economy and/as Great Replacement

Like their cultural equivalents, economic arguments about the GR/immigration/populism connection, divide into two: between those who, because they

---

50 Mouffe (2018).

support capitalism, perceive an expanding industrial reserve army as either non-existent or – since it contributes to economic growth – as positive; and those critics of accumulation who regard the same process as negative.[51] On the one hand, therefore, are the early pro-market liberal theorists and later neoclassical economists who endorse the market, and are supportive of the historical project of capitalism. On the other are Marxists opposed to the impact of the industrial reserve army on the solidarity, consciousness and struggles of the working class.

From the mid-eighteenth century to the mid-nineteenth, liberal political economists in France, such as Dunoyer and Turgot, formulated a *laissez-faire* project in defence of 'pure' capitalism, leading to neo-classical economic theory and culminating in present-day neoliberalism. At its centre was the economic argument that, like any other kind of trade involving the circulation of commodities, the free movement of labour could – and, indeed, should – operate not just at the national level of a nation (= within a country) but also amongst nations (= between countries), thus paving the way for the globalization of the capitalist system.[52] By advocating the principle of a free labour market, one that was not confined to workers of a particular nationality but extended also to include foreigners coming to or residing within the nation concerned, therefore, liberal political economy established the rationale underwriting the formation and operation – on a world scale, eventually – of what Marxism, its

---

51 Broadly speaking, where negative discourse is concerned, the overlap between cultural and economic theory can be illustrated in the following way:

Theory	*Discourse*	*Process*	*Cause*	*Beneficiary*	*Victim*
Marxist	economic	Industrial reserve army	Over-accumulation	employer	worker
Anti-/ Non-Marxist	culture	Great Replacement	Over-population	'other' identity	self

A Similar overlap informs cultural/economic theory taking a positive approach:

Theory	*Discourse*	*Process*	*Cause*	*Beneficiary*	*Victim*
neoliberal	economic	empowerment	(economic) choice	society	none
postmodern	culture	empowerment	(identity) choice	individual subject	none

52 For additional details about the post-1789 emergence of this liberal economic discourse, see Brass (2019: Chapter 4).

main theoretical opponent, came to regard as the industrial reserve army of labour.

Among those who during the immediate post-1945 era dismissed the efficacy of the industrial reserve army, on the ground that it was no longer a capitalist requirement, were Aron and Rostow. Along with the latter, Aron recognized both the economic role and political implications of the industrial reserve. Invoking the dichotomies structuring Cold War ideology, Aron presented the alternatives in terms of the (good) capitalist market versus the (bad) socialist plan, which in turn licenses the corresponding positive/negative dualism: namely, capitalism = freedom, whereas socialism = coercion.[53] Although conceding that '[i]f capitalism involved a substantial degree of permanent unemployment it would obviously be condemned', he offset this in two ways. First, by warning that '[i]n order to get rid of this reserve army entirely in a developed industrial society a total planning of labour would be necessary' – that is, by epistemologically linking the elimination of the reserve army to socialist planning. And second, by declaring both the industrial reserve and its cause banished.[54]

According to Aron, therefore, 'the industrial reserve army is no longer a decisive factor' in the accumulation process of 1950s Europe, an absence he attributes in turn to the ending of economic crises. Because for him the industrial reserve is an effect only of capitalist development which throws people out of work, Aron failed to consider a different cause, nowadays the predominant one: the active resort by employers to the industrial reserve as part of the class struggle waged against labour, a very different process from the one he identifies. For him it was simply economic crisis, not capitalist competition *per se*, that generates and reproduces the industrial reserve. Since he also

---

53   '*Either* the labour supply is planned, in which case workers who have lost their jobs in one sector of the economy are obliged to go where they will find work – and this implies the limitation or elimination of the free choice of employment', states Aron (1967: 91–2, original emphases), '*or* everyone is allowed to choose his work freely, the distribution of workers depends on demand and on relative wage levels, and there will be a reserve of unemployed workers'.

54   The views of modernisation theorists like Rostow and Aron are misunderstood by Mudde (2019: 102), who describes the causes of populist/far-right support as 'the iteration of modernization theory [because each] entails that globalization has caused winners and losers and the latter vote for far-right parties'. This is absolutely incorrect, since post-war modernization theory argued that capitalism no longer required an industrial reserve army, because rising real wage levels had solved the issue of economic crisis and with it the resort to the combined ideologies of nationalism, populism and fascism. In short, modernization theory advanced views that are the complete opposite of those attributed by Mudde to current variants of populism and the far-right.

perceived economic crisis as a thing of the past ('it has not been shown that the instability inherent in the market economy is of a kind that condemns the system itself'), it followed that the industrial reserve was no longer considered an economic feature central to the reproduction of the capitalist system itself.

Where immigration is concerned, current support for an open-door policy combined with opposition to any criticism of it, extends from international financial institutions (the World Bank, the International Monetary Fund), via national business organizations and *laissez-faire* think-tanks, to NGOs and academia. This support divides into two distinct kinds of defence: arguments that are based either on culture (as outlined above) or economics – and sometimes both (as outlined in the previous chapter). More recently, therefore, academic supporters of the neoliberal project have argued that, as labour-power is the main commodity those in developing nations have to sell, its appearance unprotected by minimum wage or other legislation in deregulated global markets – whether at home or abroad – is justified politically and necessary to the well-functioning of the capitalist system.[55] Thus, for example, Bhagwati champions the use of child labour, which in much of the Third World is unfree, since it enables producers who employ it to undercut and outcompete those who do not.[56] Moreover, he justifies this by claiming that 'diversity of labour practices and standards is widespread and reflects ... diversity of cultural values', maintaining that such relational forms are no more than culturally-specific kinds of national 'otherness'.[57] In all but name, such endorsements of *laissez-faire* approaches to the labour market, combining economic and cultural discourse, amount to a positive view of the cost-effective dynamics informing GR theory.

In a sense, it could be argued that the focus of Marxist theory is and has always been on the process of replacement, great or otherwise: of feudalism by capitalism, and of the latter by socialism. Such an historical process involves

---

55 Some economists who are not neoliberals also support open door immigration, simply on the grounds that it contributes to efficient and cost-effective national growth. Maintaining that 'immigrants bring dynamism' because they are 'entrepreneurial', and that 'immigration is an opportunity', Portes (2016: 176–79) insists that 'free markets should mean free movement'. Again, no mention is made by this kind of approach either of the association between migration and increases in the industrial reserve army, or of the link between the latter combination and the political and ideological rise of populism. Significantly, in the end such advocacy of the free movement of labour is no different from the view taken by libertarians such as von Mises, Hayek, Friedman, and Rothbard.

56 This is but one aspect of the ongoing case made by him and other neoclassical economists (Bhagwati, 1993, 2007; Bhagwati and Panagariya, 2013a, 2013b) against 'State interference' with free trade.

57 See Bhagwati (1995: 28).

economic, political, and ideological changes that correspond to the totality of a transformation as perceived by GR. For Marxism, therefore, systemic transition – from feudalism to capitalism, and from the latter to socialism – could be seen as entailing a great replacement, particularly since as in the case of GR it is accompanied by social conflict. An important difference, however, exists: Whereas change as interpreted by GR is demographic and structured by the empowerment/disempowerment of different ethnic/national categories and identities, that of Marxism by contrast entails a struggle culminating in the replacement not of one ethnicity or nationality by another but rather of one class by another. Thus, for Marxism, the post-1980s process of capitalist restructuring corresponds to a double replacement: initially, production was outsourced to third world countries, where labour-power was cheap; now, however, labour-power from the same (and other) contexts is being insourced to metropolitan capitalist nations, in the form of immigration into Europe.[58]

It is significant, therefore, that the approaches considered here which examine GR discourse either fail to mention the role of the industrial reserve army, or note this briefly and in passing, without naming it as such. Thus accumulation, both as creator of surplus labour and as necessitating this resource, escapes observation and condemnation. Only far into his analysis does Smith hints at a possible connection between cost-cutting, immigration and surplus labour, but says nothing about who benefits (capital) and what in systemic terms currently generates such a development.[59] Unmentioned, therefore, is the necessity of the industrial reserve so as to enhance competitiveness and profitability in a global context where failure to do this on the part of corporations risks going out of business. Avoiding mention of capitalism and class struggle, like the other approaches considered here, Camus maintains that what causes GR is too complex a process to comprehend, let alone oppose.[60]

---

58 As noted above (Chapter 1, this volume), the position of Marxist theory on nationalism, and its difference from that taken by the varieties of non-Marxism considered here, is best summed up in the view expressed by Lenin that the struggle has be not only against national oppression but also and at the same time against nationalism and national culture in general. The importance of this position cannot be stressed too often, since invariably it is only the first part of this twofold struggle that is observed by many of those who regard themselves as Marxists.

59 Smith (2019: 148). Like him and Camus, Kaufmann (2018: 208) also recognizes that immigration exercises a downward pressure on wages/conditions of those already in work, but like them both omits to connect this to the presence/role of (and from the viewpoint of capital the necessity for) the industrial reserve army.

60 Outlining both the causes and thus the possibility of impeding GR, Camus (2018: 165) observes: 'I would rather think of some enormous, bizarre and complex processes, so

Nevertheless, Camus recognizes the difficulty for his argument about a desire for additional consumers rather than workers as the dynamic informing GR, given that immigrants have little money with which to consume, and filling poorly paid jobs is not going to give them much spending power anyway. Accordingly, he shifts the focus onto public spending (schools, health, etc.), arguing this kind of state expenditure to meet their needs will amount to the increased consumption sought.[61] The problem with this is that the capitalist state is following the opposite path: using the availability of cheap immigrant labour-power not to build up but rather to run down public spending generally, and welfare provision in particular. Coming from contexts where social benefits and/or state expenditure are absent or negligible, neoliberalism counts with the fact that new workers will not miss these resources when absent or largely unavailable. In any case, were such workers to demand better provision and resources, they, too, would quickly be replaced by yet more recent additions to the labour market. So, the connection between public spending and consumption linked to immigration is not made. The old argument, a Marxist one, about the cheapness of labour-power – not its capacity to consume – necessary to restore or enhance competitiveness and profitability at the centre of the accumulation process, still holds.

Migration and/as Surplus Labour

Apart from GR exponents, opponents of the neoliberal project fall into two categories: those who to some degree share the assumptions of neoliberals themselves, and Marxists who reject its epistemology. Among the former are those who subscribe to a moral discourse and criticize accumulation for not caring sufficiently about its workforce. Thus, for example, Davis – much influenced by Jan Breman – insists analogously that 'there is no official scenario for the reincorporation of this vast mass of surplus labour into the mainstream of the world economy'.[62]

---

intricate that no one can understand perfectly how they work and why, and no one can master and stop them once they are started'. Elsewhere – in a 2016 interview – he has stated that 'I have very little interest in determining who is responsible for our fatal situation [= GR], except for general statements about it'.

61   Camus (2018: 153–54).
62   See Davis (2006: 199) who, because he was writing before the upsurge in migration towards metropolitan capitalist nations, maintains incorrectly that (Davis, 2006: 200–201): 'With a literal "great wall" of high-tech border enforcement blocking large-scale migration to the rich countries, only the slum remains as a fully franchised solution to the problem of warehousing this century's surplus humanity'.

To present it in this fashion, however, is in effect to agree with the way supporters of capitalism interpret the process: namely, as a residual population lacking any economic role or prospects. In this discourse of despair, therefore, surplus labour appears as some form of accidental or 'natural' occurrence, regrettable but unavoidable. The solution espoused by those adhering to a moral discourse is to advocate a return to a 'caring'/'kinder' capitalism that eschews the highly exploitative market regime of neoliberalism. Such an approach departs from that of Marxism, which regards the industrial reserve as neither accidental nor 'natural', but rather as outcome of an increasingly acute form of class struggle between capital and labour, a situation in which the enlargement of an available pool of actual/potential workers has been engineered politically, economically and ideologically. In short, a conflict in which surplus labour is itself a non-accidental creation of the accumulation process, in the furtherance of which it discharges a crucial economic role.

Where migration is concerned, Marxism distinguishes between two dissimilar processes: labour bought in *to supplement* the existing workforce, because the latter is insufficient to meet the needs of production. This is termed an 'as well as' arrangement. The second form possesses a very different dynamic: migrants are recruited in order *to displace* the existing workforce, because the latter subjects either won't work for the low pay and poor conditions on offer, or – if in post – are deemed too costly to employ, the object being to replace them with cheaper foreign labour. This is termed an 'instead of' arrangement, one that historically and currently generates huge antagonism within the ranks of the working class affected, an hostility that frequently resorts to discourse about ethnic, national or gender 'otherness'.

The combination of the global spread of capitalist development, the internationalization of the industrial reserve army, and the restructuring of the labour process, has been accompanied by the 'instead of' form. Regarding the first kind of liberty taken, and as Marxist theory has long pointed out, this combination generates a resurgence of unfree labour-power – of locals as well as migrants – and corresponds to deproletarianization.[63] The latter involves workforce decomposition/recomposition, whereby in the course of class struggle employers replace free labourers with (or convert them into) unfree equivalents. Significantly, perhaps, this transformation does not prevent employers from continuing to insist that they recruit migrants only because no locals are available or willing to do the work, a thinly disguised attempt to represent

---

63   For the view that deproletarianization is an *integral* aspect of the accumulation process itself, see Brass (1999, 2011).

merely as supplementing what is actually its 'other' – displacing the existing workforce.[64] Clearly, it is the latter form that drives capitalist restructuring, given the importance of cost considerations where accumulation occurs in a global *laissez-faire* environment. Unsurprisingly, therefore, when asked why they prefer a migrant workforce, capitalists deploy the politically less contentious 'addition to' version rather than the 'instead of' form.

Marxism and the Industrial Reserve

Appearances to the contrary notwithstanding, therefore, Marxism departs substantially from all earlier and/or later arguments supportive of or opposed to immigration. That is, from modernisation theory which banished crisis and the industrial reserve; from economic theory which endorses neoliberal globalization; from approaches to GR theory informed either by (non-economic) cultural determinants or by Malthusian assumptions; and from Malthus himself, for whom population growth was defined as a general phenomenon linked epistemologically and politically to the food supply. Unlike them all, Marxist theory deploys the concept of the industrial reserve army of labour, which is based on the growth not of population per se but rather on its economic implications: the impact of under- or unemployed plebeian elements both on the labour market and thus on class formation and struggle.[65]

Hence the centrality to the accumulation process of the industrial reserve army is (and always has been) key to Marxist theory, not just about the reproduction and development of the capitalist system, but also about the possibility (or otherwise) of struggle leading to a socialist transition.[66] Merely by its

---

64   If jobs are taken by migrants at existing low pay levels and poor conditions, then employer incentive to pay more and improve working conditions so as to attract non-migrants vanishes. In short, the 'logic of job competition' – or potential/actual displacement of existing workers as distinct from supplementing them – very much determines labour migration policy in *laissez-faire* contexts, as pro-business governments have frequently conceded. It is a difficulty that the mere extension of citizenship fails to address. As a solution to what is a wider systemic process, therefore, citizenship limits the response to the political and ideological domain, leaving intact a capitalist economy that generates and reproduces such problems in the first place.

65   Despite almost recognizing the presence and economic role of the industrial reserve, Camus (2018: 116, 139, 153, 173) nevertheless omits to do so, not least because he cannot bring himself to blame the capitalist system *per se* – as distinct from its financial/foreign variants (= 'Davocracy') – for creating and reproducing surplus labour.

66   See not just Marx (1969: 257; 1968: 17, 477, 554, 557, 559–61; 1972: 350) but also Trotsky (1940), Luxemburg (2013), Dobb (1955: 215–225), and Glyn (2006). Along with other

presence, let alone by its expansion, the industrial reserve permitted employers not just to keep wages down – thereby depressing payment below the value produced by labour-power – but also avoid having to improve work conditions. According to Marx himself, therefore, the reserve army comes into its own once the early stage of capitalism – that generally associated with primitive accumulation – has been left behind.[67]

The threat an increasing reserve army posed not just to hard-won wage levels and employment conditions but also to the protection of these gains – by means of solidarity among and capacity of an existing workforce to organize – was such that Marx gave serious consideration to opposing further immigration.[68] In ways that anticipate current argument about withdrawal from EU membership so as to stem competition from the industrial reserve army, a century and a half ago Marx advocated severing the link with Ireland precisely in order to prevent migrants from competing with and undercutting English workers.[69] He insisted that working class emancipation in England depended ultimately on Ireland following its own path of capitalist development, and to this end international solidarity would take the form of support from English workers for Irish equivalents in their struggle for economic and

---

        Marxists, Lenin (1960c: 179, original emphasis) regarded the industrial reserve army as the *sine qua non* of capitalism, 'which could neither exist nor develop without it'. Accordingly, for him the industrial reserve 'being an inevitable result of capitalist accumulation, is at the same time *an indispensable component part of the capitalist machine*'. This, he goes on to argue, is the opposite of the view held by populists ('romanticists'), who saw the presence of surplus labour as an extraneous aspect ('a mistake') of the accumulation process.

67   Marx (1976: 784–85).

68   Among those who recognized this was Engels (Marx and Engels, 1934: 496–7). In the course of a visit to the United States during 1920s, a British trade unionist (Cramp, 1924: 19) recorded his views on the way controlled access to the American labour market was to the benefit of the existing workforce: 'This question of immigration is one which has exercised the minds of American Statesmen and Labour leaders for years past. Until a few years ago about one and a half million aliens arrived in the United States annually. Now only 175,000 are given admittance each year ... [i]t will at once be seen how much the hand of organized labour is strengthened by this stringent organization. Frequently the employing class make a demand for some relaxation of these regulations, but the American federation of Labour is emphatic upon the necessity of maintaining what has become a safeguard for the American workers' standard of life, and public opinion appears solidly in favour of the present position'.

69   For details, see Marx and Engels (1934: 289–90). Observing that '[t]he average English worker hates the Irish working man as a competitor who lowers his wage and his standard of life', Marx (Collins and Abramsky, 1965: 170) argued that the Irish Question was central to the interests of the labour movement in England, adding that 'to forward the social revolution in England ... the decisive blow must be struck in Ireland'.

political independence, as distinct from migrating to where this had already occurred.

When Marxists depart from the strategy of opposing more labour market competition and endorse not a class and internationalist approach but much rather one based on national/ethnic identity, history teaches a sharp lesson. In the case of late nineteenth and early twentieth century Austria, therefore, a burgeoning industrial reserve army had a deleterious impact on the solidarity of a working class differentiated in terms of ethnicity/nationality.[70] When capitalists turned to Czech migrants so as to displace unionized German workers, fuelling thereby the rise of nationalism (much like GR theory nowadays), the response on the part of Austrian Social Democracy and trade unions was to advocate organizational separatism reflecting this national/ethnic 'otherness'. The result was that not only did proletarian institutions and politics split along ethnic/nationalist lines, but labour market competition between Czech migrants and German workers, together with the intense economic rivalry to which it gave rise, laid the ground for the emergence and consolidation during the 1920s and 1930s of the far right in Austria and Germany.[71]

Equally sharp is the same lesson as currently taught to Marxists and other leftists from metropolitan capitalist nations. In the case of the UK, not only was the Brexit vote determined in part by working class anxieties concerning the level of immigration, but this was itself compounded by the disdain of 'New Labour' for the impact on labour market competition of a burgeoning industrial reserve. Predictably, therefore, just as Labour discarded its commitment to representing the interests of a working class already ravaged by inequality, unemployment, austerity, and poor remunerated jobs – ending Clause 4, downgrading the Trade Union connection, and failing to repeal Thatcherite anti-labour legislation – so the political right moved to occupy the same ground, championing the 'forgotten'.

---

70   See Brass (2019: Chapter 3).
71   On this see Whiteside (1962, 1975), who outlines why an expanding capitalist market in 1890s Austria, which pitted workers and migrants of different ethnicities against one another, led to the addition of the word 'national' to the term 'socialism'. Rapid capitalist development generated labour market competition and intense antagonism between Germans and Czechs, relatively well-paid local and cheaper migrant components of the same industrial workforce, a situation benefiting – and taken advantage of by – employers. Internationalism, social democracy, working class solidarity, trade unions, leftist political parties and socialism itself were all undermined as a result. That the same kind of process can be seen happening in Europe today, where the continuing expansion of *laissez-faire* capitalism and an industrial reserve army fuel the rise both of nationalism and of far right political parties, is clear.

In the prevailing context, where *laissez-faire* capitalism seemed unstoppable, where Labour no longer seemed troubled by this, and where a socialist programme was lacking, many in working class areas saw the nationalist/populist alternative (UKIP, the Brexit party, and latterly the Conservative Party) as the least-worst option on offer. Not the least of the many ironies arising in the course of current debate about Brexit is that, advocating a no-deal approach has not prevented those on the political right continuing to promote the necessity of yet more immigration so as to enhance competitiveness of capitalist producers in a post-Brexit UK.[72] This of course is precisely what those belonging to the working class who voted to leave the EU were against.

Conclusion

Ostensibly, there is an overlap between GR discourse and Marxism, in that conceptually each deals with systemic totality, its mode of transformation, and its effects. However, unlike Marxism, GR discourse examined here focuses on demographic aspects, as embodied in large-scale migration to metropolitan capitalist nations, and the rise there of populism. The latter, such analyses of GR maintain, is a political response to non-economic issues such as cultural erosion/de-authentication and population displacement. This externally-driven dynamic is blamed in turn on the complicity of internal advocacy: that of the political left, deemed culpable for GR on account of the ideological support it extends to any/all forms of 'otherness'. Such an approach, it is argued, is problematic for two reasons in particular: what GR regards as the political left is itself much rather a rival form of populism, and consequently the

---

72 Following the leave vote in the 2016 referendum, the desire of employers for continued access to a reserve army composed of immigrant workers has been a constant refrain. See '[Conservative Home Secretary] Rudd promises door will be kept open to EU workers after Brexit', *Financial Times* (London), 27 July 2018; 'CBI wants new rules to keep open pipeline of EU workers after Brexit', *The Guardian* (London), 10 August 2018; 'Farmers say visa scheme will not solve shortage of staff after EU departure', *The Guardian* (London), 7 September 2018; 'Business anger at "elitist" plan to axe visas for lower-paid', *The Guardian* (London), 19 September 2018; 'Fear of skills shortages prompts business to plan moves abroad', *Financial Times* (London), 29–30 September 2018; 'Immigration waiver allows cheap labour to build windfarm', *The Guardian* (London), 22 October 2018; 'Ease entry rules for Indians to win deals after Brexit, say MPs', *The Guardian* (London), 24 June 2019; 'International graduates to be offered two-year work visas', *The Guardian* (London), 11 September 2019; 'Visa climbdown allows overseas students to stay for longer', *The Times* (London), 11 September 2019; 'Foreign students to get longer visas', *The Telegraph* (London), 11 September 2019.

misrecognition of the economic issues structuring both GR and a resurgent populism.

As framed in these two narratives, for and against GR, it appears at times as if the struggle is simply over rival claims to victimhood – who is the more oppressed and disadvantaged, and thus more worthy of support. Insofar as it privileges cultural identity as empowering, therefore, postmodern theory is complicit with the kind of nationalist ideology informing populism. The latter feeds off *laissez-faire* accumulation where economic crisis – generating both an expanding industrial reserve army of migrant labour and also more intense competition between capitalists themselves and between workers seeking employment results inexorably in political crisis. To the postmodern argument emphasizing the cultural identity of the migrant-as-'other'-nationality, therefore, populism counterposes an argument similarly emphasizing cultural identity, only this time the nationality of the non-migrant worker.

In the discourses opposed to and supportive of GR, hostility towards anti-racism licenses as a reaction an endorsement of another ethnic/national identity. As recognized by some GR analyses, anti-racism is itself transformed thereby into a narrative sustaining nationality/ethnicity, albeit of an 'other' kind, to the extent that it becomes in turn a defence of such identities. Pushed to its logical conclusion, it becomes in effect a form of what might be termed pro-'otherness'. Ideologically, white identity is itself counteracted by an analogous form of difference; politically, therefore, one kind of populism confronts another variant of the same kind of discourse. The difficulty is, and remains, that the analyses examined here misattribute this transformation: it is regarded as emanating from – and thus an ideology belonging to – the left, whereas it more correctly it has to be placed at the other end of the political spectrum. This difficulty possesses as a corollary the unwillingness of many on the left to engage with GR via the lens of political economy, rather than share with populism an approach the focus of which is only on culture.

Accordingly, much analysis purportedly from a leftist position simply attaches a label of racism to any/all GR argument, and – having refused to engage with it, and overlooking what Marxism has said about it – moves on to other things. Ironically, this is itself a mirror image of what exponents of the GR themselves do, which is to attach a label of mistaken/naïve leftist thinking to their political opponents, similarly overlooking what Marxism says about both the presence and the impact of the industrial reserve army. In short, about this particular issue neither approach is correct: leftist dismissal of GR argument ignores an economic dimension that GR itself overlooks or demotes, while the blame that GR attributes to the left should more accurately be attached to the 'new' populist postmodernism.

Rather than an indictment of Marxism, therefore, the kind of view held by the GR analyses considered here is more accurately a critique of the 'new' populist postmodernism. It is the latter, *not* the former, which – like GR itself – privileges ethnic/national (= non-class) 'otherness', to the extent that its theory by inference legitimizes the *laissez-faire* position of 'high finance' regarding the desirability of the free movement of labour. By contrast, the argument here is simple: whether owners of the means of production bring additional potential/actual workers into the labour process of metropolitan capitalist nations, or instead employs them in outsourced enterprises where they already are, in their own countries, the economic function and outcome of the industrial reserve army is in all cases the same. In whatever the context, surplus labour is available to replace those in employment who may ask for – let alone organize in pursuit of – higher wages and better working conditions.

Conclusion
Beyond Marxism, What?

Tracing the extent to which Marxism is missing but necessary across a variety of seemingly unconnected debates within (and beyond) the social sciences, extending from Third World development, via the historiography of ancient society, to how and why the capitalist system takes the form it currently does, reveals the unavoidable presence of contradictory processes. Of these perhaps the most egregious is the way adherence to a Marxist approach merges with views that are incompatible with – or indeed antagonistic to – Marxist political economy. It is clear from the outset, therefore, that a departure from Marxist theory combined with an endorsement of non- or anti-Marxist epistemology does not of itself preclude a continued identification as a Marxist, and on occasion the claim (by self and others) to be an influential one. This in turn licenses a number of further steps: first, to insist that the element of contradiction is itself unimportant; second, to maintain that non- or anti-Marxist epistemology is in the end compatible with Marxism; and third, to privilege these non- or anti-Marxisms, in effect discarding a theoretical approach that is recognizably Marxist. Politically, it could be argued that such change results in a double misrecognition: the wrong kind of friends (populism, a 'benign' capitalism) coupled with the wrong kind of enemies (Marxism, socialism).

This transformation is discernible not just in the larger desertion from Marxist theory *per se* but also in smaller and apparently insignificant conceptual departures: the advocacy by Stalin, and later Hobsbawm, of multi-class alliances in furtherance of capitalism instead of struggle against the latter by workers; the thinly disguised nationalism of Patnaik underneath the carapace of opposition to imperialism; the support of Bernstein and Dhanagare for agrarian populist and/or nationalist discourse, coupled with a rejection by them of peasant differentiation and of class formation/consciousness/struggle; the casting aside by Brown (and others) of the Roman Empire decline thesis, supported by Marxists, in which economic stagnation leads to systemic transition, in favour of a Late Antiquity composed of prosperity and social harmony, as upheld by postmodernism; the discarding by Banaji of the same decline thesis, in its place substituting an a-historically ubiquitous merchant capitalism; the celebration of capitalism by current post-colonial discourse plus its essentializing of identity politics, a contrast with the earlier advocacy by Marxists (Robeson, James, Shachtman) of class solidarity/struggle that opposed capitalism and transcended ethnic/national boundaries; and, finally, the reaction to this by populist Great Replacement theory, countering immigrant 'otherness' by privileging non-migrant selfhood.

Marxist theory is based on the concept of systemic transition: from ancient society to feudalism, from the latter to capitalism, and ultimately to socialism. Addressed thereby is the formation or dissolution of class, together with its impact on the division of labour in different places and different ages, as this refers to labour processes that are nationally and regionally specific. Central to this dynamic is the transformation of peasant into worker, in the course of which the subject is converted from a seller of the product of labour to labour-power itself. For Marxism, therefore, peasant differentiation along class lines poses crucial questions about the direction taken by economic development, not least about the kind of production relation that emerges as a result. Among them is whether the labour-power of erstwhile petty commodity producers is free or unfree, whether the labouring subject is employed on a permanent, casual, temporary, migrant or local basis, and the manner in which such a workforce is inserted into the labour process. Hence the significance attached by Marxists to the connection between depeasantization and the creation of surplus labour, and how – as part of the industrial reserve – it is positioned with regard to those already employed, together with the degree to which any reserve components become competitors of those currently in the labour market.

As capitalism develops and becomes global, these questions become correspondingly more important. This notwithstanding, the approaches examined in this volume – whether supportive of or antagonistic to Marxism – analytically negate the historical dynamic based on class formation/consciousness/struggle involving systemic transition. As does populism, by constituting as progressive any/every form resistance designed to reproduce peasant economy; by regarding through nationalist lens all instances of struggle against capital; and by declaring capitalism as either absent or systemically ever-present. Under constant attack, the relevance of Marxist theory about class is viewed negatively: as inapplicable to an understanding either of ancient society or of the Third World; and as responsible for the rise of identity politics. One way or another, capital escapes a similar attack: either it is only a 'foreign' presence: then again, it has always been present historically; or beyond neoliberalism there is only a more benign version of what currently exists. As systemically there is no alternative to capitalism, both a transcendence of the accumulation process and a transition to socialism are in effect off the political agenda.

Apart from theoretical difficulties that stem from non-engagement with or misunderstanding of Marxist interpretations, critiques aimed at the latter which nevertheless fail to hit their target (= missing Marxism) are additionally a consequence of problematic methods. Hence the claim about the progressive nature of populism in Russia and India fails because sources are either not consulted or misrecognized, whilst the case for the existence in Late Antiquity of 'new' socio-economic categories and religious beliefs either lack data or are unable to access the requisite grassroots voice. Attempts to supplant the negative characteristics informing the decline thesis as applied by Marxists (and others) to the Roman Empire with positive ones about Late Antiquity as an epoch marked by widespread social harmony and economic dynamism rest on the kind of substantial and detailed evidence contained in ethnographies, but which histories of ancient society cannot provide.

Why such political and epistemological changes – amounting to a Marxism that is missing – make necessary a revolutionary socialist Marxism is just as clear. Where development in both the Third World and metropolitan nations is concerned, social sciences have become a hotbed of populists, arguing either for a better deal for the undifferentiated rural producer (rich peasants and commercial farmers as well as smallholders) under capitalism, or for boosting the industrial reserve army in the latter contexts by means of open-door migration. This is in sharp contrast to Marxist theory, for which the main problem involved the way peasant differentiation and the reserve army hindered prospects for a socialist transition. Many of those in the social sciences engaged in the study of capitalist development no longer accept this as a problem – let alone the main one – for the simple reason that the majority have given up on either the possibility, the desirability, or the feasibility of a socialist transition. This is something that those who remain Marxists have not done.

The claim levelled most frequently against Marxism, that it has no satisfactory theoretical framework for the study of resistance against global neoliberalism, is quite simply wrong. Much rather the opposite is true, in that much of the debate – both for and against Marxism – in development studies over the past four decades has been about little else. Equally problematic is the framework – along the lines of 'a struggle for survival' – offered as an alternative to Marxism and other kinds of modernity. Development paths that are proposed currently as alternatives to Marxism – including Third World resistance against globalization – are not new, but much rather familiar and very old arguments. The latter correspond for the most part to a populism informed by nationalist ideology, a combination that has a very long history in Europe, North America and Russia (from the 1890s onwards) and also in Third World countries themselves (throughout the twentieth century). What such populism attempts to do is to unite the different class interests within a given nation – a domestic bourgeoisie and petty bourgeoisie no less than urban workers plus rural labour and peasant smallholders – in a common form of resistance against capital that is international (= 'foreign'). This is does, moreover, by avoiding potentially divisive class distinctions within the nation thus mobilized and focusing instead on the process of cultural erosion as a denial of national selfhood.

Historically the 'other' of Marxism, agrarian populism is a discourse that is simultaneously anti-capitalist and anti-socialist. It is a 'from above' attempt to mobilize the rural grassroots on the basis of the agrarian myth, thereby obtaining support among peasants and farmers opposed to the effects of industrialisation, urbanization and capitalist crisis. In the context of economic depression, the invocation of anti-foreigner sentiment or the town/country divide permits landowners and/or rich peasants to deflect, distort or displace class consciousness by emphasizing loyalties not antagonistic to capital (and thus compatible with the continued process of accumulation). Politico-ideologically, the resulting 'peasant-ness' – which agrarian populism claims is culturally innate and unchanging – comes to symbolize the 'nation' itself, and depeasantization becomes synonymous with deculturation and the erosion (or loss) of national identity.

It was this task which all historical varieties of populism – both the 'old' variants of the late nineteenth and early twentieth centuries, and the 'new' postmodern variants from the late twentieth century onwards – have sought to effect by merging the agrarian myth with 'popular' culture. Embodied in new social movements theory and the 'everyday-forms-of-resistance' framework, as well as in the Subaltern Studies project, the 'new' populism influenced by a postmodern cultural analysis not only questions the necessity/possibility of economic development ('post-development') but rejects Marxism, meta-narratives/universals, and 'Eurocentric' Enlightenment discourse ('post-Marxism'). The resulting intellectual retreat, both from the analysis of political economy and from socialist ideas, and their replacement in development theory and historiographical debate with an idealist postmodern relativism possessing epistemological roots in the innate 'peasant-ness' of the agrarian myth, has been justified in academic/intellectual circles by reference to the supposed unfeasability/undesirability/unworkability of socialism itself.

This process underlined two things: the strong connection between on the one hand the antagonism shown even by progressive opinion in metropolitan capitalism to revolution and socialism, and on the other that the rise and consolidation in such contexts of the 'cultural turn' has deep historical roots. Some abandoned Marxism in favour of the 'new' populism for reasons to do with the intellectual fashion of postmodernism, jumping onto a bandwagon because everyone else was on it, without examining too closely what this transition involved theoretically or politically. Others changed paradigms because they lacked an understanding of Marxism, and thus failed to recognize – or to appreciate the importance of – the epistemological distinctiveness between it and its 'new' populist 'other'. For specifically historical reasons, yet others shifted their allegiance because they had forgotten – or perhaps never learned – about the dangers posed by the political right. Increasingly, the latter has moved onto the ground occupied historically by the left, but which the latter appears to have abandoned. This is perhaps the most worrying aspect of the intellectual realignment that has occurred during the past forty years.

Many of those whose arguments have been examined here, and claim their views are located theoretically within the Marxist tradition, turn out not just to have rejected its basic precepts and concepts, but also to have opted instead for varieties of nationalist and/or populist ideology. Since the latter advocate the protection or restoration of peasant economy in Third World countries, they are disguised as critiques of imperialism or particular kinds of capitalism (foreign, financial), but rarely – if ever – of capitalism *per se*. Accordingly, calls for the restoration of petty commodity production have reconstituted the peasantry as a unitary category, reproducing the interpretation favoured historically and currently by agrarian populism. No mention is made of socialism, either as a desired objective or as a central emplacement of longstanding historical debate about agrarian change and the role in this of rural producers. This contrasts with Marxist theory, which argues that in the course of capitalist development the peasantry is differentiated along class lines, its top stratum (= rich peasants) consolidating means of production and becoming small capitalists, while its increasingly landless bottom stratum (= poor peasants) joins the ranks of the proletariat. For this reason, to regard peasants as a uniform category – as does populism – is mistaken, since these distinct rural strata possess economic and political interests that are not just different but antagonistic.

Among those who regard themselves as Marxists, therefore, are Worsley and Patnaik, both of whom appear to subscribe to an idealized view about the economic viability of pre-colonial peasant agriculture, despite the fact that historically such forms of traditional 'subsistence' insurance tend to collapse when famine threatens. In keeping with the 'middle peasant' thesis, moreover, smallholders are perceived simply as 'autonomous' or 'independent cultivators' meeting their own subsistence requirements, a view that what existed prior to colonization was a viable peasantry, capable of reproducing itself economically regardless of the wider system. This in turn is consistent with the claim that, prior to the era of imperialism, a situation of agrarian balance and environmental sustainability existed, a state of affairs which had long predated colonialism.

For rather obvious reasons, bourgeois nationalist discourse tended to depict exploitation as something that started with the British, and that only British landlords did to African and/or Indian peasants. Unsurprisingly, a consequence was both to downplay the exploitative role of indigenous producers (landlords, capitalists), and thus also to idealize the pre-colonial past. At the centre of this discourse was an idealized image of the self-sufficient smallholder, a crisis-free and culturally pristine socio-economic entity the more recent manifestations of which have taken the form of the 'middle peasant' thesis. Without the intervention of British colonialism, it is implied, everything in rural India and Africa would have been fine, and village-level coping mechanisms ensured that when food shortages occurred, the worst effects of famine were successfully contained, not least by the intervention of a benign indigenous landlord class disbursing largesse to all and sundry. Worsley and Patnaik seem to accept all these claims at their face value, in the process endorsing the myth of a pre-colonial/pre-British/pre-capitalist 'golden age' when kind rulers ensured that peasants and workers all obtained subsistence provision.

Much the same is true of Hobsbawm. Because of an initial focus on the transition from feudalism to capitalism, in Britain and Latin America, he interpreted nationalism as a necessarily 'progressive' force politically, a process whereby actual/potential capitalists aligned the power of the state with – as they saw it – the interests of the nation as a whole, as embodied in accumulation and economic development. However, he failed to spot – as did so many on the left during the period following the 1960s development decade – that progress, once achieved, can be reversed. In the course of class struggle waged 'from above', therefore, not only have economic/political/ideological advances realized by workers been rolled back, but such a process is the very essence of conflict waged 'from above'. Hence the reversal of emancipatory trends (higher wages, better working conditions, welfare provision, the social wage, etc.) is the *sine qua non* of historical struggles undertaken by capital.

What Hobsbawm failed to notice was the meaning of nationalism and its kindred concepts informing the 'cultural turn', which he endorsed as a result. Once the 'new' populist postmodernism was the object of criticism from Marxists, he jumped on the bandwagon, long after others had drawn attention to the conservative and reactionary underpinnings of postmodernism. Although theoretical inclusiveness is notionally attractive, in practice it can – and does – open the door to views that are incompatible with Marxism and a socialist transition. The reason for such caution is that theoretical openness was how postmodernism gained a foothold leading to hegemonic dominance: many Marxists – among them Hobsbawm – who thought it would be a good idea to admit its claims, conceptual apparatus, and arguments, in the specific form of social history, ended up being taken over by postmodern theory. The way the latter was able to colonize debate, not just about the peasantry but also about the desirability/undesirability of economic development itself, confirms the accuracy of suspicions harboured by many early twentieth-century Marxists toward academia, an institution they regarded as too complicit with capitalism to mount a thorough critique of bourgeois political economy.

That Marxism is missing, and is itself in turn missed, is nowhere so evident as in the way the global spread of the market generates in turn two interconnected phenomena: the growth worldwide both of the industrial reserve army, and – as a politico-ideological reaction to this – of populism. Attempts to distance what is depicted as a 'progressive' form of populism from the taints either of the 'cultural turn', of conservatism, or of the far right, overlook the extent to which the structure and political discourse of the former inescapably mimics that of the latter. For this reason, those who contend that unlike Marxism, populism now offers a political way forward in Third World countries and metropolitan capitalist ones alike do so in defiance of its history of reaction and its current trend in that same direction. Ironically, this kind of position is one that the anti-globalization movement shares not only with postmodern and post-colonial theory, but also with much of the political right in Europe and elsewhere. Much recent development theory that has been informed by this kind of populism is unaware of its reactionary roots, and the fact that the political right also has an anti-capitalist discourse. Consequently, many of those undertaking the study of Third World development initially signed up uncritically to a populist/nationalist/postmodern critique of neoliberalism.

Historically and over the recent past, Marxism has made substantial interventions in debates about peasants, migrants and unfree labour, linking them to processes such as class differentiation of petty commodity production, the expansion and class composition of the industrial reserve army, and the acceptability to capital of workers who are unfree, together with their role in the class struggle obstructing or making possible a socialist transition. The frequency with which labour market competition triggers an ideological and political reaction taking the form of prejudice against the ethnic/national identity of rivals for the same jobs, a process discernible in epochs and debates extending from those about Roman imperial decline and/or Late Antiquity, via late nineteenth and early twentieth century Austro-Marxism, to modern post-colonial discourse and Great Replacement theory, suggests it is too serious an occurrence to ignore or dismiss simply as bigotry. This is underlined by two interconnected issues: that currently grassroots mobilization based on identity politics is becoming the norm in terms of opposition to the global spread of the industrial reserve as capitalism develops; and that Marxist theory about this process is now being sidelined or ignored by many present-day contributions to these same debates.

CONCLUSION: BEYOND MARXISM, WHAT?

Thus, for example, the theoretical model applied by Banaji to economic development ancient and modern is consistent not with Marxism, but much rather a number of non- or anti-Marxist approaches. His insistence on a capitalist presence in ancient society is consistent with the neoclassical economic historiography of Oertel who, like Banaji, sees the Roman Empire as an example of benign, tension-free accumulation. The crucial political distinction between on the one hand Brown and Oertel, and on the other Banaji is that whereas the latter maintains he is still a Marxist (but isn't), the former make no such claim. Furthermore, the privileging by Banaji of merchant capital over its industrial counterpart, with regard not just to pre-/non-capitalist modes but also to advanced capitalism itself, mimics the claims advanced currently by those who apply the fashionable concept 'financialization' to the global economic system. Each insists that merchant capital is the dominant form at every conjuncture, in effect denying the presence any longer in the world economy of what Marxism recognizes as 'proper' capitalism. The inference is that, as a result of the 'wrong' kind of capitalism, any transition to socialism has to be postponed until the 'proper' sort is deemed present.

Not the least of the many ironies is that, while many currently deny the existence of capitalism, preferring instead to label it 'financialization', those such as Banaji have now 'discovered' the self-same systemic form – capitalism – in Late Antiquity. The fact of trade and hired labour-power both in ancient society and in feudalism has long been known about, but this does not constitute evidence for the presence at such epochs of capitalism, merchant or otherwise. Significantly, the revisionist interpretation of Banaji – whereby Late Antiquity = economic dynamism = market opportunities = peace, order – is in step with a much wider pattern of nationalist appropriation. In an important sense, the case made by him about Roman Imperialism complements that made by Patnaik about its later British counterpart. Whereas for Patnaik it was British imperialism that persisted in India beyond the end of the colonial era, for Banaji it was capitalism that endured beyond the fall of the Roman Empire. What each seems to be saying is that western forms of imperialism and/or colonialism notwithstanding, economies in the east could have or, indeed, did, prosper and flourish historically in a benign/tension-free manner on their own account. Despite the claim by each of them to be a Marxist, the approach of both to their respective time periods and historical contexts is underwritten by a positive view of national 'otherness' and – more broadly – nationalist discourse.

This nationalist trend took off during the 1980s, when the Subaltern Studies series attempted to replace an historical materialist approach as this applied to grassroots mobilizations in Asia with a 'new' populist postmodern one.

A hitherto dominant Marxist conceptual framework – based on class formation/struggle, modernity, working class internationalism and a socialist transition – was replaced with nationalism and a concept of an undifferentiated peasant as an 'authentic' but unheard South Asian voice. In a similar vein, the attempt by Banaji to relocate an 'authentic' capitalism outside its historic birthplace replicates this shift (along the lines of 'we always had a propensity to economic dynamism, in the past no less than the present'). It is difficult not to see these Third-Worldist/nationalist appropriations as fitting into the prevailing triumphalism of the 'decline of the West, the rise of the East' variety, an ideological accompaniment to the outsourcing of capitalist production from metropolitan contexts (Europe, the USA) to Asia (China, India). In short, a celebration of non-Western ideological or economic power, an approach that has nothing to do with Marxist theory, let alone a socialist outcome.

Broadly speaking, much recent writing about Asia – especially that in the social sciences – tends to fall into two categories, both celebratory. The first looks upward, so to speak, focusing on macro-level issues, and perceives as wholly admirable the economic success of the nation as measured in data on output, production, trade, etc.; the second by contrast looks downward, and extols as an achievement any/every instance of rural grassroots mobilization and/or resistance. In sharp contrast to Marxist political economy, these two celebratory approaches have not a lot to say about the formation/consciousness/struggle specifically of class, either as this occurs within the Indian countryside or in terms of its impact on the wider capitalist system (= national + international). Aspects of both categories are found in some of the approaches – projecting national victimhood and/or exceptionalism – examined critically in this volume. Whereas the nationalism of Patnaik is *internal* (nationalism on behalf of but within its own national context), that of the post-colonial diaspora is an *external* phenomenon. The latter amounts to a proxy discourse, whereby the nationalism that is deployed no longer occurs within its own defined space but now is expressed on behalf of a nation left behind.

As problematic, therefore, is that aspect of the development debate which concerns the impact of a growing industrial reserve on workers in metropolitan capitalist nations. Inhabitants of less-developed countries, who have to some degree benefitted from economic development (education, skill acquisition, etc.), may nevertheless perceive their livelihood prospects by remaining in such contexts as unenticing. Their eyes turn, naturally, abroad, to metropolitan capitalist nations where living standards for people like them are much higher, and income/salary levels correspondingly large. They migrate to these places, and in the process exert a downward pressure on wages/conditions for workers already in these labour markets, in effect handing an advantage to capitalists engaged in a twofold struggle, both with their own workforce and with rival producers.

Not the least difficulty raised by this standoff is that each component of the workforce may – for different reasons – side with capital: the upper stratum in order to maintain its existing 'privilege', and the lower so as to obtain employment. Why this is problematic is not so much an upper stratum protecting wages/conditions won by class struggle over epochs, as the siding by these workers with employers in the hope of defending such gains. The outcome is class collaboration (= 'opportunism') licensing populism and nationalism. It was the latter development, fuelling the 'social-chauvinism' of the 1914–18 war, that concerned Lenin in a more general sense: namely, the extent to which imperialism was able to generate working class rivalry through the resort by capital to the reserve army of labour. Now, however, many of those who are (wrongly) perceived as Marxists conceptualize the industrial reserve simply as a form of cultural empowerment on the part of the migrant, a view which plays into the hands of the far right. Of the many difficulties in their confrontation with Great Replacement theory, therefore, not the least significant is that hostility from such 'Marxists' permits its target to erect Marxist theory as a straw man opponent. This despite the fact that the theory classified by Great Replacement as Marxism, in order to be dismissed as such, not being Marxist.

It is, of course, the case that throughout history a workforce composed of migrants has over time become class conscious, and thus open to mobilization/organization by trade unions and leftist political parties. However, as the example of the United States underlines, once this occurs, employers and the capitalist state quickly resort to new sources of 'green' labour in order once again to repeat the same process. All that happens, therefore, is that the cycle based on displacing radicalized workers with malleable equivalents continues unabated, a pattern that controlling/regulating immigration would make difficult, if not impossible. For this reason, a Marxist response would be to advocate more not less control over the labour market, by means of extending the regulation of labour-power and economic planning on a global scale, not – as a number of the present-day writers/commentators of the post-colonial diaspora exponents themselves suggest – simply to adopt a *laissez-faire* policy in the name of 'a common humanity'. Since the latter approach tends to be migrant-centric, it consequently makes little or no mention of the deleterious impact such a process would have in receiving countries, in terms of either wages/conditions/livelihoods of existing workers, or of the advantages such a process confers on employers and far right politics in these contexts.

This is not to say that, in theory, writers/commentators of the post-colonial diaspora *could* make 'defensiveness' an issue of class, as Marxists do, rather than (or perhaps as well as) race. However, such an approach is faced with a self-evident obstacle. Because its exponents generally come from business and/or more privileged backgrounds, post-colonial discourse unsurprisingly tends to advocate not socialism but a capitalism which not only accepts them but rewards their success. In a fundamental sense, therefore, they cannot appeal to a common *class* identity (since this is clearly absent), only to one of ethnic or national 'otherness'. It is hardly necessary to repeat how different this approach is from the Marxism of Robeson and James. Hence the case made by post-colonial discourse for open-door immigration into metropolitan capitalist nations, as reparations for 'treasure' acquired by the latter during the colonial era, is in effect the 'other' of the Great Replacement framework, the very view to which post-colonial discourse is opposed. Each of these antagonists – post-colonial discourse, Great Replacement ideology – is in a fundamental sense a version of nationalist/populist ideology, based on essentialist categories of ethnicity and victimhood.

As Marxism in general, and Lenin in particular, long argued, 'from below' political mobilization entails internationalism rooted in secularism and class unity *across* national boundaries, not the promotion of identity politics – based on religion, ethnicity, or nationality – as the sole or main form to be taken by empowerment *within* countries. Whereas both the Great Replacement and the 'new' populist postmodernism view immigration mainly as a question of culture – the former against, the latter for – Marxism by contrast looks at the same process in terms of political economy, and its contribution to the formation/reproduction of the industrial reserve. While Great Replacement indicts open-door immigration but leaves out capitalism, so the 'new' populist postmodernism indicts (some forms of) capitalism but leaves out the industrial reserve army. In effect rival populisms, each one of which is the mirror image of the other. Trapped by its support for a Thirdworldist and an empowering cultural identity, much development theory in general, and especially that influenced by the 'new' populist postmodernism, has been unable (or perhaps unwilling) to see immigration through the lens of political economy; that is, as a process leading to acute levels of labour market competition which in turn generate a politico-ideological response that takes the form of populism.

Hence the importance of how core elements of Marxist theory – among them the process of class formation/consciousness/struggle, the cultural/economic identity of peasants and workers (as perceived by themselves and others), the impact on the latter categories of potential/actual systemic transition, plus whether (and why) capitalism and socialism are seen as desirable or undesirable – have been and are inserted into debates about populism, nationalism, and postmodernism. This, it is argued here, reveals the degree to which

CONCLUSION: BEYOND MARXISM, WHAT?

Marxism is indeed missing, yet necessary. In short, not just that views advanced by those who regard themselves (and are regarded by others) as socialists are incompatible with – and thus undermine – Marxism, but also why this has happened, and what form it has taken. This is the reason why significance is attached to the way in which not just the politics but also the epistemology informing the approach examined in each chapter breaks with crucial aspects and/or concepts that are fundamental to Marxist analysis, and departs thereby from Marxist theory, broadly defined,

Bibliography

Adler, Eric, 2011, *Valorizing the Barbarians: Enemy Speeches in Roman Historiography*, Austin, TX: University of Texas Press.
Alibhai-Brown, Yasmin, 2018, *In Defence of Political Correctness*, London: Biteback Publishing Ltd.
Amis, Kingsley, 1970, *What became of Jane Austen? And other Questions*, London: Jonathan Cape.
Amis, Kingsley, and Robert Conquest, n.d., 'A Short Educational Dictionary', in C.B.Cox and A.E.Dyson (eds.), *Black Paper Three*, London: The Critical Quarterly Society.
Andolina, Robert, Nina Laurie, and Sarah Radcliffe, 2009, *Indigenous Development in the Andes*, Durham, NC: Duke University Press.
Andrews, R.F. [ps. Andrew Rothstein] 1934. *The Truth about Trotsky*. London: Communist Party of Great Britain.
Applebaum, Anne, 2020, *Twilight of Democracy: The Seductive Lure of Authoritarianism*, London and New York: Allen Lane/Doubleday.
Aron, Raymond, 1967, *18 Lectures on Industrial Society*, London: Weidenfeld & Nicolson.
Attridge, Derek, Geoff Bennington, and Robert Young (eds.), 1987, *Post-structuralism and the question of history*, Cambridge: Cambridge University Press.
Babington, Bruce, 2002, *Launder and Gilliat*, Manchester: Manchester University Press.
Bahro, Rudolf, 1978, *The Alternative in Eastern Europe*, London: NLB.
Baldwin, James, 1976, *The Devil Finds Work*, London: Michael Joseph Ltd.
Banaji, Jairus, 1972, 'For a Theory of Colonial Modes of Production', *Economic and Political Weekly*, Vol. 7, No. 52.
Banaji, Jairus, 1976, 'Chayanov, Kautsky, Lenin: Considerations towards a Synthesis', *Economic and Political Weekly*, Vol. 11, No. 40.
Banaji, Jairus, 1990, 'Illusions About the Peasantry: Karl Kautsky and the Agrarian Question', *The Journal of Peasant Studies*, Vol. 17, No. 2.
Banaji, Jairus, 1999, 'Agrarian History and the Labour Organization of Byzantine Large Estates', in Bowman and Rogan (eds.).
Banaji, Jairus, 2001, *Agrarian Change in Late Antiquity: Gold, Labour, and Aristocratic Dominance*, Oxford: Oxford University Press.
Banaji, Jairus, 2010, *Theory as History: Essays on Modes of Production and Exploitation*, Leiden: Brill.
Banaji, Jairus, 2017, 'Merchant Capital', http://www.historicalmaterialism.org/reading-guides/merchant-capital/jairus-banaji/.
Banaji, Jairus, 2018, *Exploring the Economy of Late Antiquity: Selected Essays*, Cambridge: Cambridge University Press.
Beard, Mary, 2013, *Confronting the Classics*, London: Profile Books.

Beard, Mary, 2016, *SPQR: A History of Ancient Rome*, London: Profile Books.

Bernstein, Henry, 2018, 'The "Peasant Problem" in the Russian Revolution(s), 1905–1929', *The Journal of Peasant Studies*, Vol. 45, Nos. 5–6.

Bethell, Leslie (ed.), 2016, *Viva la Revolución: Eric Hobsbawm on Latin America*. London: Little, Brown.

Bhagavani, Manu, and Anne Feldhaus (eds.), 2008, *Claiming Power from Below: Dalits and the Subaltern Question*, New Delhi: Oxford University Press.

Bhagwati, Jagadish, 1993, *India in Transition: Freeing the Economy*, Oxford: Clarendon Press.

Bhagwati, Jagadish, 1995, *Free Trade, 'Fairness' and the New Protectionism*, London: Institute for Economic Affairs.

Bhagwati, Jagadish, 2007, *In Defense of Globalisation*, Oxford: Oxford University Press.

Bhagwati, Jagadish, and Arvind Panagariya, 2013a, *India's Tryst with Destiny*, London: HarperCollins.

Bhagwati, Jagadish, and Arvind, Panagariya, 2013b, *Why Growth Matters*, New York: Public Affairs.

Bierce, Ambrose, 1967 [1906], *The Enlarged Devil's Dictionary* (edited by Ernest Jerome Hopkins, Preface by John Myers Myers), London: Victor Gollancz Ltd.

Blok, Anton, 1988 [1974], *The Mafia of a Sicilian Village 1860–1960: A Study of Violent Peasant Entrepreneurs*, Cambridge: Polity Press.

Borras, S.M., 2019, 'Agrarian Social Movements: The Absurdly Difficult but not Impossible Agenda of Defeating Right-wing Populism and Exploring a Socialist Future'. *Journal of Agrarian Change*, https://doi.org/10.1111/joac.12311.

Bowersock, Glen W., 1996, 'The Vanishing Paradigm of the Fall of Rome', *Bulletin of the American Academy of Arts and Sciences*, Vol. XLIX, No.8.

Bowman, Alan K., and Eugene Rogan (eds), 1999, *Agriculture in Egypt: From Pharaonic to Modern Times*, Oxford: Oxford University Press.

Brass, Tom, 1994, 'Some Observations on Unfree Labour, Capitalist Restructuring, and Deproletarianization', *International Review of Social History*, Vol. 40, Part 1.

Brass, Tom, 1995, 'Reply to Utsa Patnaik: If the Cap Fits …', *International Review of Social History*, Vol. 39, Part 2.

Brass, Tom, 1999, *Towards a Comparative Political Economy of Unfree Labour: Case Studies and Debates*, London: Frank Cass Publishers.

Brass, Tom, 2000, *Peasants, Populism and Postmodernism*, London: Frank Cass Publishers.

Brass, Tom, 2002, 'Rural Labour in Agrarian Transitions: The Semi-Feudal Thesis Revisited', *Journal of Contemporary Asia*, Vol. 32, No. 4.

Brass, Tom, 2003, 'Why Unfree Labour is Not "So-Called": The Fictions of Jairus Banaji', *The Journal of Peasant Studies*, Vol. 31, No. 1.

Brass, Tom, 2005, 'Late Antiquity as Early Capitalism?', *The Journal of Peasant Studies*, Vol. 32, No. 1.

Brass, Tom, 2011, *Labour Regime Change in the Twenty-First Century: Unfreedom, Capitalism and Primitive Accumulation*, Leiden: Brill.

Brass, Tom, 2012, 'Jairus Banaji's Mode of Production: Eviscerating Marxism, Essentialising Capitalism', *Journal of Contemporary Asia*, Vol. 42, No. 4.

Brass, Tom, 2014, *Class, Culture, and the Agrarian Myth*, Leiden: Brill.

Brass, Tom, 2015, 'Peasants, Academics, Populists: Forward to the Past?', *Critique of Anthropology*, Vol. 35, No.2.

Brass, Tom, 2017, *Labour Markets, Identities, Controversies: Reviews and Essays 1982–2016*, Leiden: Brill.

Brass, Tom, 2019, *Revolution and Its Alternatives: Other Marxisms, Other Empowerments, Other Priorities*, Leiden: Brill.

Brassey, Thomas, 1872, *Work and Wages*. London: Bell and Daldry.

Brassey, Thomas, 1879, *Foreign Work and English Wages*. London: Longmans, Green, and Co.

Brenton, Tony (ed.), 2016, *Historically Inevitable? Turning Points of the Russian Revolution*, London: Profile Books.

Brown, Geoff, 1977, *Launder and Gilliat*, London: British Film Institute.

Brown, Peter, 1972, *Religion and Society in the Age of Saint Augustine*, London: Faber and Faber.

Brown, Peter, 1978, *The Making of Late Antiquity*, Cambridge, MA: Harvard University Press.

Brown, Peter, 1989 [1971], *The World of Late Antiquity AD 150–750*, London: Thames and Hudson Ltd.

Brown, Peter, 2003, 'A Life of Learning', *Charles Homer Haskins Annual Lecture*, Philadelphia, PA: ACLS Occasional Paper, No. 55.

Brown, Peter, 2011, 'The Field of Late Antiquity', in David Hernández de la Fuente (ed.), *New Perspectives on Late Antiquity*, Newcastle upon Tyne: Cambridge Scholars Publishing.

Brown, Peter, 2012, *Through the Eye of a Needle: Wealth, the Fall of Rome, and the Making of Christianity in the West, 350–550 AD*, Princeton, NJ: Princeton University Press.

Brunt, P.A., 1971, *Social Conflicts in the Roman Republic*, London: Chatto & Windus Ltd.

Brunt, P.A., 1974 [1966], 'The Roman Mob', in M.I. Finley (ed.), *Studies in Ancient Society* (Past and Present Series), London and Boston: Routledge and Kegan Paul.

Brunt, P.A., 1987 [1971], *Italian Manpower, 225 B.C. – A.D. 14*, Oxford: The Clarendon Press.

Brunt, P.A., 1988, *The Fall of the Roman Republic and related essays*, Oxford: The Clarendon Press.

Burgin, Andrew, 2017, 'Oppose Little Brexit Britain – Defend Free Movement', in Kate Hudson (ed.), *Free Movement and Beyond: Agenda Setting for Brexit Britain*, London: Public Reading Rooms.

Burke, Peter (ed.), 1998, *New Perspectives on Historical Writing*, Pennsylvania, PA: The Pennsylvania State University Press.

Byres, T.J., 1996, *Capitalism from Above and Capitalism from Below*, London: Macmillan.
Campbell, J.R., 1937. *Spain's "Left" Critics*. London: Communist Party of Great Britain.
Camus, Renaud, 2018, *You Will Not Replace Us!* Plieux: Chez l'auteur.
Cannadine, David, 1992, *G.M. Trevelyan: A Life in History*. London: HarperCollins.
Carrillo, Santago, 1977, *'Eurocommunism' and the State*, London: Lawrence and Wishart.
Christie, Ian, 1985, *Arrows of Desire: The Films of Michael Powell and Emeric Pressburger* (Foreword by Martin Scorsese), London: Waterstone & Company Limited.
Clay, Henry, 1843, *Life and Speeches*, Volume I, New York: Greeley & McElrath, Tribune Buildings.
Cochrane, Regina, 2007, 'Rural Poverty and Impoverished Theory: Cultural Populism, Ecofeminism, and Global Justice', *The Journal of Peasant Studies*, Vol. 34, No. 2.
Collins, Henry, and Chimen Abramsky, 1965, *Karl Marx and the British Labour Movement*, London:Macmillan & Co. Ltd.
Cox, Caroline, Keith Jacka, and John Marks, 1977, 'Marxism, Knowledge and the Academies', in C.B.Cox and Rhodes Boyson (eds.), *Black Paper 1977*, London: Maurice Temple Smith Ltd.
CPGB (Communist Party of Great Britain), 1925. *The Errors of Trotskyism: A Symposium*. London: Communist Party of Great Britain.
Cramp, C.T., 1924, *My Trip to the Western Hemisphere*, London: Co-operative Printing Society Limited.
Croix, de Ste., G.E.M., 1981, *The Class Struggle in the Ancient Greek World, from the Archaic Age to the Arab Conquests*, London: Duckworth.
Davis, Mike, 2006, *Planet of Slums*, London: Verso.
Debray, Regis, 1970, *Strategy for Revolution: Essays on Latin America* (edited by Robin Blackburn), London: Jonathan Cape.
Debray, Régis, 1979, 'A Modest Contribution to the Rites and Ceremonies of the Tenth Anniversary', *New Left Review*, No.115 (May-June).
Dhanagare, D.N., 1983, *Peasant Movements in India 1920–1950*, Delhi: Oxford University Press.
Dhanagare, D.N., 1995. 'The Class Character and Politics of the Farmers' Movement in Maharashtra during the 1980s', in Tom Brass (ed.) *New Farmers' Movements in India*, London: Frank Cass.
Dhanagare, D.N., 2014, *The Writings of D.N. Dhanagare: The Missing Tradition – Debates and Discourses in Indian Sociology*, New Delhi: Orient Blackswan.
Dhanagare, D.N., 2017, *Populism and Power: Farmers' movement in Western India, 1980–2014*, London: Routledge.
Dobb, Maurice, 1955, *On Economic Theory and Socialism*, London: Routledge & Kegan Paul.
Drage, Geoffrey. 1904. *Russian Affairs*. London: John Murray.
Duberman, Martin Bauml, 1989, *Paul Robeson*, London: The Bodley Head.

Duncan, Kenneth, Ian Rutledge, and Colin Harding (eds.), 1977, *Land and Labour in Latin America*, Cambridge: Cambridge University Press.

Dupré, Georges, and Pierre-Philippe Rey, 1980, 'Reflections on the Pertinence of the Theory of the History of Exchange', in Harold Wolpe (ed.) *The Articulation of Modes of Production*, London: Routledge & Kegan Paul.

Easton Ellis, Bret, 2019, *White*, London: Picador.

Emmanuel, Arghiri, 1972, *Unequal Exchange: A Study of the Imperialism of Trade* (translated from the French by Brian Pearce), London: New Left Books.

Engels, Frederick, 1976, 'Principles of Communism [1847]', in *Karl Marx Frederick Engels Collected Works*, Volume 6, London: Lawrence & Wishart.

Escobar, Arturo, 1995, *Encountering Development: The Making and Unmaking of the Third World*, Princeton, NJ: Princeton University Press.

Esman, Abigail, 2010, *Radical State: How Jihad is Winning over Democracy in the West*, Santa Barbara, CA: Praeger.

Evans, Richard J., 2002, *Telling Lies About Hitler: The Holocaust, History and the David Irving Trial*, London: Verso.

Evans, Richard J., 2014, *Altered Pasts: Counterfactuals in History*, London: Little, Brown.

Evans, Richard J., 2019, *Eric Hobsbawm: A Life in History*, London: Little, Brown.

Éwanjée-Épée, Félix Boggio, and Frédéric Monferrand, 2015, 'Jairus Banaji: Towards a New Marxist Historiography', http://www.historicalmaterialism.org/interviews/jairus-banaji-towards-a-new-marxist-historiography/.

ffrench, Patrick, and Roland-François Lack (eds.), 1998, *The Tel Quel Reader*, London: Routledge.

Finley, M.I., 1968, 'Christian Beginnings: Three Views of Historiography', in M.I. Finley, *Aspects of Antiquity: Discoveries and Controversies*, London: Chatto & Windus.

Finley, M.I., 1971, 'Archaeology and History', *Daedalus*, Vol. 100, No. 1.

Finley, M.I., 1976, 'Private Farm Tenancy in Italy before Diocletian', in M.I. Finley (ed.), *Studies in Roman Property*, Cambridge: Cambridge University Press.

Fogel, Robert William, and Stanley W. Engerman, 1974, *Time on the Cross: Volume I – The Economics of American Negro Slavery*, London: Wildwood House.

Foner, Philip S. (ed.), 1978, *Paul Robeson Speaks: Writings, Speeches, Interviews, 1918–1974*, London and New York: Quartet Books.

Foster-Carter, Aidan, 1978, 'The Modes of Production Controversy', *New Left Review*, Number 107.

Foucault, Michel, 1996, *Foucault Live: Collected Interviews, 1961–1984* (edited by Sylvère Lotringer, translated by Lysa Hochroch and John Johnston), New York, NY: Semiotext(e).

Fowler, Don Paul, 2000, *Roman Constructions: Readings in Postmodern Latin*, Oxford: Oxford University Press.

Francovich, Ricardo, and Richard Hodges, 2003, *Villa to Village: The transformation of the Roman Countryside in Italy, c.400–1000*, London: Gerald Duckworth & Co. Ltd.

Frank, Tenney, 1914, *Roman Imperialism*, New York: The Macmillan Company.

Frank, Tenney, 1920, *An Economic History of Rome*, Baltimore, MA: The Johns Hopkins Press.

Fudge, Judy, 2019, '(Re)Conceptualising Unfree Labour: Local Labour Control Regimes and Constraints on Workers' Freedoms', *Global Labour Journal*, Vol. 10, No. 2.

Gadgil, D.R., 1959, *Origins of the Modern Indian Business Class*, New York: Institute of Pacific Relations.

Garzetti, Albino, 1974, *From Tiberius to the Antonines: A History of the Roman Empire AD 14–192* (Translated by J.R. Foster), London: Methuen & Co. Ltd.

Genovese, Eugene D., 1984, 'The Politics of Class Struggle in the History of Society: An Appraisal of the Work of Eric Hobsbawm', in Pat Thane, Geoffrey Crossick, and Roderick Floud (eds.).

Gillett, Andrew, 2017, 'The Fall of Rome and the Retreat of European Multiculturalism: A Historical Trope as a Discourse of Authority in Public Debate', *Cogent: Arts & Humanities*, Vol. 4, No. 1.

Glyn, Andrew, 2006, *Capitalism Unleashed*, Oxford: Oxford University Press.

Góngora, Mario, 1975, *Studies in the Colonial History of Latin America*, Cambridge: Cambridge University Press.

Goodman, David, and Michael Redclift, 1981, *From Peasant to Proletarian*, Oxford: Basil Blackwell.

Gordon, A.D.D., 1978, *Businessmen and Politics: Rising Nationalism and a Modernising Economy in Bombay, 1918–1933*, New Delhi: Manohar Publicaions.

Grantham, George, 2004, 'A Review of Agrarian Change in Late Antiquity: Gold, Labour and Aristocratic Dominance', *EH.NET* (May).

Guerin, Daniel, 1956 [1951], *Negroes on the March: A Frenchman's Report on the American Negro Struggle*, New York and London: Grange Publications.

Guha, Ranajit (ed.), 1982–89, *Subaltern Studies I-VI*, New Delhi: Oxford University Press.

Gupta, J.N., 1911, *Life and Work of Romesh Chunder Dutt* (with an Introduction by His Highness the Maharaja of Baroda), London: J.M.Dent & Sons, Ltd.

Habib, Irfan, 1963, *The Agrarian System of Mughal India*, Bombay: Asia Publishing House.

Haider, Asad, 2018, *Mistaken Identity: Race and Class in the Age of Trump*, London and New York: Verso.

Hall, Stuart, 1960, 'The Supply of Demand', in E.P. Thompson (ed.), *Out of Apathy*, London: New Left Books.

Hamid, Mohsin, 2014, *Discontent and Its Civilizations: Dispatches from Lahore, New York, London*, London: Hamish Hamilton.

Hamid, Mohsin, 2017, *Exit West*, London: Hamish Hamilton.

Hardy, Edward Rochie, 1931, *The Large Estates of Byzantine Egypt*, New York: Columbia University, Faculty of Political Science.
Haslam, Jonathan, 1999, *The Vices of Integrity: E.H. Carr, 1892–1982*, London: Verso.
Hobsbawm, Eric J., 1962, *The Age of Revolution: Europe 1789–1848*, London: Weidenfeld & Nicolson.
Hobsbawm, Eric J., 1968, *Industry and Empire: An Economic History of Britain since 1750*, London: Weidenfeld & Nicolson.
Hobsbawm, Eric J., 1973, *Revolutionaries: Contemporary Essays*, London: Weidenfeld & Nicolson.
Hobsbawm, Eric J., 1987, *The Age of Empire 1875–1914*, London: Weidenfeld & Nicolson.
Hobsbawm, Eric J., 1989, *Politics for a Rational Left: Political Writing, 1977–1988*, London: Verso.
Hobsbawm, Eric J., 1998, *Behind the Times: The Decline and Fall of the Twentieth Century Avant-Gardes*, London: Thames and Hudson.
Hobsbawm, Eric J., 2000, *On the Edge of the New Century: In conversation with Antonio Polito*, New York: The New Press.
Hobsbawm, Eric J., 2002, *Interesting Times: A Twentieth-Century Life*, London: Allen Lane.
Hobsbawm, Eric J., 2011, *How to Change the World: Tales of Marx and Marxism*, London: Abacus.
Hodgson, Geoff. 1975. *Trotsky and Fatalistic Marxism*. Nottingham: Spokesman Books.
Hornblower, Simon, and Antony Spawforth (eds.), 1998, *The Oxford Companion to Classical Civilization*, Oxford: Oxford University Press.
Houellebecq, Michel, 2015, *Submission*, London: William Heinemann.
Houellebecq, Michel, 2019, *Serotonin*, London: William Heinemann.
Hughes, H. S. (ed.), 1954, *Teachers of History: Essays in Honor of Lawrence Bradford Packard*, New York: Cornell University Press.
Ignatieff, Michael, 1998, *Isaiah Berlin: A Life*, London: Chatto & Windus.
Ilife, John, 1983, *The Emergence of African Capitalism*, London: The Macmillan Press, Ltd.
James, C.L.R., 1963, *Beyond a Boundary*, London: Hutchinson & Co. Ltd.
James, C.L.R., 1969 [1950], *State Capitalism and World Revolution*, Detroit, MI: Facing Reality Publishing Committee.
James, C.L.R., 1977a, *The Future in the Present: Selected Writings*, London: Allison & Busby Limited.
James, C.L.R., 1977b, *Nkrumah and the Ghana Revolution*, London: Allison & Busby Limited.
Johnson, Allan Chester, 1936, *An Economic Survey of Ancient Rome – Volume II: Roman Egypt to the Reign of Diocletian*, Baltimore, MD: The Johns Hopkins Press.
Johnston, Sir Harry H., 1920, *The Negro in the New World*, London: Methuen & Co. Ltd.

Jones, A.H.M., 1940, *The Greek City: From Alexander to Justinian*, Oxford: The Clarendon Press.
Jones, A.H.M., 1948, *Ancient Economic History*, London: H.K. Lewis.
Jones, A.H.M., 1956, 'Numismatics and History', in R.A.G. Carson and C.H.V. Sutherland (eds.), *Essays in Roman Coinage – Presented to Harold Mattingly*, Oxford: Oxford University Press.
Jones, A.H.M., 1964, *The Later Roman Empire 284–602* (Volume I), Norman, OK: University of Oklahoma Press.
Jones, A.H.M., 1966, *The Decline of the Ancient World*, London: Longmans, Green & Co Ltd.
Kantorowicz, Ernest H., 1965, 'Feudalism in the Byzantine Empire', in Rushton Coulborn (ed.), *Feudalism in History*, Hamden, CT: Archon Books.
Kaufmann, Eric, 2018, *Whiteshift: Populism, Immigration and the Future of White Majorities*, London: Allen Lane, Penguin Random House.
Kautsky, Karl, 1925, *Foundations of Christianity: A Study in Christian Origins*, London: George Allen & Unwin Ltd.
Kautsky, Karl. 1984. 'The Competitive Capacity of Small-scale Enterprise in Agriculture [1894/95]', in Athar Hussain and Keith Tribe (eds.), *Paths of Development in Capitalist Agriculture,* London: Macmillan.
Kershaw, Ian, 2004, *Making Friends with Hitler: Lord Londonderry, the Nazis and the Road to War*, New York: The Penguin Press.
Keuneman, Peter, 1982 [1939], 'Eric Hobsbawm: A Cambridge Profile 1939', in Raphael Samuel and Gareth Stedman Jones (eds.).
Kulikowski, Michael, 2019. *Imperial Tragedy: From Constantine's Empire to the Destruction of Roman Italy, AD 363–568.* London: Profile Books.
Laibman, David, 2015, *Passion and Patience: Society, History, and Revolutionary Vision*, New York: International Publishers.
Leader, Zachary (ed.), 2000, *The Letters of Kingsley Amis*, London: HarperCollins Publishers.
Lendon, J.E., 2009, 'Historians without History: Against Roman Historiography', In Andrew Feldherr (ed.), *Cambridge Companion to Roman Historians*, Cambridge: Cambridge University Press.
Lenin, V.I., 1960a, 'Explanation of the Law on Fines Imposed on Factory Workers [1895]', *Collected Works*, Vol. 2, Moscow: Foreign Languages Publishing House.
Lenin, V.I., 1960b, 'Draft and Explanation of a Programme for the Social-Democratic Party [1895–96]', *Collected Works*, Vol. 2, Moscow: Foreign Languages Publishing House.
Lenin, V.I., 1960c, 'The Characterization of Economic Romanticism [1897]', *Collected Works*, Vol. 2, Moscow: Foreign Languages Publishing House.
Lenin, V.I., 1963, 'The Three Sources and Three Component Parts of Marxism [1913]', *Collected Works*, Vol. 19, Moscow: Foreign Languages Publishing House.

Lenin, V.I., 1964a, 'The Development of Capitalism in Russia [1899]', *Collected Works*, Volume 3. Moscow: Foreign Languages Publishing House.
Lenin, V.I., 1964b. 'Critical Remarks on the National Question [1913]'. *Collected Works*, Volume 20. Moscow: Foreign Languages Publishing House.
Lenin, V.I., 1964c, 'Imperialism, the Highest Stage of Capitalism [1917]', *Collected Works*, Vol. 22, Moscow: Progress Publishers.
Lenin, V.I., 1964d, 'Tasks of the Left Zimmerwaldists in the Swiss Social-Democratic Party [1916]', *Collected Works*, Vol. 23, Moscow: Progress Publishers.
Lévy, Bernard-Henri, 2008, *Left in Dark Times: A stand against the new barbarism*, New York: Random House.
Littlejohn, Gary, 1973a, 'The Peasantry and the Russian Revolution', *Economy and Society*, Vol. 2, No. 1.
Littlejohn, Gary, 1973b, 'The Russian Peasantry: A Reply to Teodor Shanin', *Economy and Society*, Vol. 2, No. 3.
Littlejohn, Gary, 1977, 'Peasant Economy and Society', in Barry Hindess (ed.), *Sociological Theories of the Economy*, London: The Macmillan Press, Ltd.
Lochore, R.A., 1951, *From Europe to New Zealand*, Wellington, NZ: A.H. & A.W. Reed.
Luxemburg, Rosa, 1976 [1916], *The National Question: Selected Writings* (Edited with an Introduction by Horace B. Davis), New York: Monthly Review Press.
Luxemburg, Rosa, 2013, *The Complete Works: Volume I, Economic Writings 1* (Edited by Peter Hudis, translated by David Fernbach, Joseph Fracchia and George Shriver), London and New York: Verso.
Mackenzie Wallace, Donald, 1877, *Russia*, London: Cassell & Company, Limited.
Mahajan, Gupreet, 2011, *Accommodating Diversity*, New Delhi: Oxford University Press.
Malik, Nesrine, 2019, *We Need New Stories: Challenging the Toxic Myths Behind Our Age of Discontent*, London: Weidenfeld & Nicolson.
MARHO (The Radical Historians Organization), 1983a, 'Interview with Eric Hobsbawm', in *Visions of History*, Manchester: Manchester University Press.
MARHO (The Radical Historians Organization), 1983b, 'Interview with C.L.R. James', in *Visions of History*, Manchester: Manchester University Press.
Markovits, Claude, 1985, *Indian Business and Nationalist Politics 1931–39*, Cambridge: Cambridge University Press.
Marx, Karl, 1969, *Theories of Surplus Value – Part I*, London: Lawrence & Wishart.
Marx, Karl, 1968, *Theories of Surplus Value – Part II*, London: Lawrence & Wishart.
Marx, Karl, 1972, *Theories of Surplus Value – Part III*, London: Lawrence & Wishart.
Marx, Karl, 1973, *Grundrisse*, Harmondsworth: Penguin Books.
Marx, Karl, 1976, *Capital – Volume I*, Harmondsworth: Penguin Books.
Marx, Karl, and Frederick Engels, 1934, *Correspondence 1846–1895*, London: Martin Lawrence Ltd.

Marx, Karl, and Frederick Engels, 1957, *On Religion*, Moscow: Foreign Languages Publishing House.

Marx, Karl, and Frederick Engels, 1976, 'The Communist Manifesto [1848]', in *Karl Marx and Frederick Engels Collected Works*, Volume 6, London: Lawrence & Wishart.

Marx, Karl, and Frederick Engels, 2001a, 'Engels to Pasquale Martignetti in Benevento, January 1887', in *Karl Marx Frederick Engels Collected Works*, Volume 48 (Engels: 1887–1890), London: Lawrence and Wishart.

Marx, Karl, and Frederick Engels, 2001b, 'Engels to Conrad Schmidt in Berlin, April 1890', in *Karl Marx Frederick Engels Collected Works*, Volume 48 (Engels: 1887–1890), London: Lawrence and Wishart.

Marx, Karl, and Frederick Engels, 2001c, 'Engels to Vera Zasulich in Mornex (France), April 1890', in *Karl Marx Frederick Engels Collected Works*, Volume 48 (Engels: 1887–1890), London: Lawrence and Wishart.

Mattick, Paul, 1967, 'The Limits of Integration', in Kurt H. Wolff and Barrington Moore, Jr. (eds.), *The Critical Spirit: Essays in Honor of Herbert Marcuse*, Boston, MA: Beacon Press.

Mavor, James, 1914, *An Economic History of Russia: Volume Two – Industry and Revolution*, London: J.M. Dent & Sons, Limited.

Mavrakis, Kostas, 1976. *On Trotskyism* (translated by John McGreal). London: Routledge & Kegan Paul Ltd.

Medick, Hans, 1981, 'The Transition from Feudalism to Capitalism: Renewal of the Debate', in Raphael Samuel and Gareth Stedman Jones (eds.), *Culture, Ideology and Politics: Essays for Eric Hobsbawm*, London: Routledge & Kegan Paul Ltd.

Mehta, Suketu, 2019, *This Land is Our Land: An Immigrant's Manifesto*, London: Jonathan Cape.

Mignolo, Walter, 2012, *Local Histories/Global Designs: Coloniality, Subaltern Knowledges, and Border Thinking*, Princeton, NJ: Princeton University Press.

Mitchell, Stephen, 2007, *A History of the Later Roman Empire AD 284–641*, Oxford: Blackwell Publishing.

Mommsen, Theodore, 1867, *The History of Rome – Vol. IV, Part 1* (Translated by the Rev. William P. Dickson, D.D.), London: Richard Bentley, New Burlington Street.

Mouffe, Chantal, 2018, *For a Left Populism*, London & New York: Verso.

Mudde, Cas, 2002, 'In the Name of the Peasantry, the Proletariat, and the People: Populisms in Eastern Europe', in Y. Mény and Y. Surel (eds.), *Democracy and the Populist Challenge*, London: Palgrave, Macmillan.

Mudde, Cas, 2019, *The Far Right Today*, Cambridge: Polity.

Murray, Douglas, 2018, *The Strange Death of Europe: Immigration, Identity, Islam*, London: Bloomsbury.

Murray, Douglas, 2019, *The Madness of Crowds: Gender, Race and Identity*, London: Bloomsbury.

Nanda, Meera, 2004, *Prophets Facing Backward: Postmodern Critiques of Science and Hindu Nationalism*, New Brunswick, NJ: Rutgers University Press.

Naoroji, Dadabhai, 1901, *Poverty and Un-British Rule in India*, London: Swan Sonnenschein & Co., Ltd.

Oertel, F.W., 1934, 'The Economic Unification of the Mediterranean Region: Industry, Trade and Commerce', in S.A. Cook, F.E. Adcock, and M.P. Charlesworth (eds.), *The Cambridge Ancient History: Volume X – The Augustan Empire, 44 BC – AD 70*, London: Cambridge University Press.

Oertel, F.W., 1939, 'The Economic Life of the Empire', in S.A. Cook, F.E. Adcock, M.P. Charlesworth, and N.H. Baynes (eds.), *The Cambridge Ancient History: Volume XII – The Imperial Crisis and Recovery, AD 193–324*, London: Cambridge University Press.

Olgin, M.J. 1935. *Trotskyism: Counter-Revolution in Disguise*. New York: Workers Library Publishers.

Patnaik, Utsa, 1978, "On the Mode of Production in Indian Agriculture – A Reply", in Ashok Rudra *et al.*, *Studies in the Development of Capitalism in India*, Lahore: Vanguard Books.

Patnaik, Utsa, 1995, 'On Capitalism and Agrestic Unfreedom', *International Review of Social History*, Vol. 40, Part 1.

Patnaik, Utsa, 1997, 'Capitalism and Unfreedom', *International Review of Social History*, Vol. 42, Part 3.

Patnaik, Utsa, 1999, *The Long Transition: Essays on Political Economy*, New Delhi: Tulika.

Patnaik, Utsa, 2007, *The Republic of Hunger and Other Essays*, Monmouth: The Merlin Press.

Patnaik, Utsa, 2017, 'Revisiting the "Drain", or Transfers from India to Britain in the Context of the Global Diffusion of Capitalism', in Shubhra Chakrabarti and Utsa Patnaik (eds.), *Agrarian and Other Histories*, New Delhi: Tulika Books.

Patnaik, Utsa, and Prabhat Patnaik, 2017, *A Theory of Imperialism*, New York: Columbia University Press.

Peacock, Thomas Love, 1895, *Maid Marian* and *Crotchet Castle*, London and New York: Macmillan & Co.

Pegg, Simon, 2011, *Nerd Do Well*, London: Arrow Books.

Petras, James F., 1978, *Critical Perspectives on Imperialism and Social Class in the Third World*, New York: Monthly Review Press.

Petras, James F., 1981, *Class, State, and Power in the Third World; with Case Studies on Class Conflict in Latin America*, London: Zed Press.

Phillips, A.A., 1958, *The Australian Tradition: Studies in Colonial Culture*, Melbourne: F.W. Cheshire.

Phillips, A.A., 1979, *Responses: Selected Writings*. Balmain, NSW: Australia International Press.

Pollitt, Harry, and R. Palme Dutt, 1937. *The Truth about Trotskyism: Moscow Trial January 1937*. London: Communist Party of Great Britain.
Pollitt, Majorie, 1937. *Defeat of Trotskyism*. London: Communist Party of Great Britain.
Portes, Jonathan, 2016, *Capitalism: 50 Ideas You Really Need to Know*, London: Quercus Books.
Prakash, Gyan (ed.), 1995, *After Colonialism: Imperial Histories and Postcolonial Displacements*, Princeton, NJ: Princeton University Press.
Prakash, Gyan, 1999, *Another Reason: Science and the Imagination of Modern India*, Princeton, NJ: Princeton University Press.
Radkey, Oliver H., 1963, *The Sickle under the Hammer*, London and New York: Columbia University Press.
Reger, Gary, 1994, *Regionalism and Change in the Economy of Independent Delos, 314–167 B.C.*, Berkeley, CA: University of California Press.
Rey, Pierre-Philippe, 1975, 'The Lineage Mode of Production', *Critique of Anthropology*, No. 3.
Rhys, Ernest, 1917, *The Old Country: A Book of Love and Praise of England*, London: J.M. Dent & Sons, Ltd.
Richardson, Al, Clarence Chrysostom, and Anna Grimshaw, 1986, 'C.L.R. James and British Trotskyism', http://www.revolutionary-history.co.uk/jamesmen.htm.
Rioux, Sébastien, Genevieve LeBaron, and Peter J. Versovšek, 2020, 'Capitalism and Unfree Labour: a review of Marxist perspectives on modern slavery', *Review of International Political Economy*, Vol. 27, No. 3.
Robeson, Paul, 1958, *Here I Stand*, London: Dennis Dobson.
Rosenberg, Arthur, 1934, *A History of Bolshevism*, London: Oxford University Press.
Rostovtzeff, M., 1927, *A History of the Ancient World: Volume II – Rome*, Oxford: The Clarendon Press.
Rowlandson, Jane, 1985, 'Freedom and Subordination in Ancient Agriculture: the Case of the *Basilikoi Geōrgoi* of Ptolomaic Egypt', in P.A. Cartledge and F.D. Harvey (eds.), *Crux: Essays in Greek History Presented to G.E.M. de Ste. Croix on His 75th Birthday*, London: Gerald Duckworth & Co. Ltd.
Roy, Tania, and Craig Borowiak, 2003, 'Against Ecofeminism: Agrarian Populism and the Splintered Subject in Rural India', *Alternatives*, Vol. 28, No.1.
Rudra, Ashok *et al.*, 1978, *Studies in the Development of Capitalism in India*, Lahore: Vanguard Books Ltd.
Samuel, Raphael, and Gareth Stedman Jones (eds.), 1982, *Culture, Ideology and Politics: Essays for Eric Hobsbawm*, London: Routledge & Kegan Paul Ltd.
Schmitt, Carl, 2004, *Legality and Legitimacy*, Durham, NC: Duke University Press.
Schmitt, Carl, 2005, *Political Theology: Four Chapters on the Concept of Sovereignty*, Chicago, IL: The University of Chicago Press.

Scott, James C., 1976, *The Moral Economy of the Peasant: Rebellion and Subsistence in Southeast Asia*, New Haven, CT: Yale University Press.
Scott, James C., 2012, *Decoding Subaltern Politics: Ideology, Disguise, and Resistance in Agrarian Politics*, London: Routledge.
Scott, James C., 2017, *Against the Grain: A Deep History of the Earliest States*, New Haven, CT: Yale University Press.
Sender, John, and Sheila Smith, 1986, *The Development of Capitalism in Africa*, London: Methuen & Co. Ltd.
Seregny, Scott J., 1989, *Russian Teachers and Peasant Revolution: The Politics of Education in 1905*, Bloomington, IN: Indiana University Press.
Serge, Victor, and Natalia Sedova Trotsky, 2015, *The Life and Death of Leon Trotsky*, Chicago, IL: Haymarket Books.
Shachtman, Max, 2003, *Race and Revolution* (edited and introduced by Christopher Phelps), London: Verso.
Sherwin-White, A.N., 1939, *The Roman Citizenship*, Oxford: The Clarendon Press.
Sherwin-White, A.N., 1966, *Racial Prejudice in Imperial Rome*, London: Cambridge University Press.
Shukla, Nikesh (ed.), 2016, *The Good Immigrant*, London: Unbound.
Simkin, C.G.F., 1968, *The Traditional Trade of Asia*, London: Oxford University Press.
Singh, Charan, 1964, *India's Poverty and Its Solution*, London: Asia Publishing House.
Sisman, Adam, 1994, *A.J.P. Taylor: A Biography*, London: Sinclair-Stevenson.
Sisman, Adam, 2010, *Hugh Trevor-Roper: The Biography*, London: Weidenfeld & Nicolson.
Sitwell, Edith, 1962, 'Pride', in Angus Wilson, Edith Sitwell, Cyril Connolly, Patrick Leigh Fermor, Evelyn Waugh, and W.H. Auden, *The Seven Deadly Sins*, London: Sunday Times Publications Ltd.
Smith, Horace, 1890 [1836], *The Tin Trumpet*, London: George Routledge and Sons, Limited, Broadway, Ludgate Hill.
Smith, Stephen, 2019, *The Scramble for Europe: Young Africa on its way to the Old Continent*. Cambridge: Polity.
Snow, C.P., 1951, *The Masters*, London: Macmillan & Co. Ltd.
Sombart, Werner, 1967, *Luxury and Capitalism*, Ann Arbor, MI: The University of Michigan Press.
Soria, George, n.d. (c.1937), *Trotskyism in the Service of Franco*, London: Lawrence and Wishart.
Stalin, Joseph, 1928. *Leninism*. London: George Allen & Unwin Ltd.
Stalin, Joseph, 1940. *Marxism and the National and Colonial Question*. Moscow: Foreign Languages Publishing House.
Stalin, Joseph, 1952. *Problems of Leninism*. Moscow: Foreign Languages Publishing House.

Steinfeld, Robert, 2001, *Coercion, Contract and Free Labor in the Nineteenth Century*, Cambridge: Cambridge University Press.

Stepniak, Sergius, 1905, *The Russian Peasantry: Their Agrarian Condition, Social Life and Religion*, London: George Routledge & Sons, Limited.

Stoddard, Lothrop, 1922, *The Revolt Against Civilization: The Menace of the Under-Man*, London: Chapman & Hall, Ltd.

Stone, Lawrence, 1971, 'Prosopography', *Daedalus*, Vol. 100, No. 1.

Sukhanov, N.N., 1955, *The Russian Revolution 1917*, London: Oxford University Press.

Thane, Pat, Geoffrey Crossick, and Roderick Floud (eds.), 1984, *The Power of the Past: Essays for Eric Hobsbawm*, Cambridge: Cambridge University Press.

Thorner, Alice, 1982, 'Semi-Feudalism or Capitalism? Contemporary Debate on Classes and Modes of Production in India', *Economic and Political Weekly*, Vol. XVII, Nos. 49–51.

Tirthankar, Roy, 2018, *A Business History of India: Enterprise and the Emergence of Capitalism from 1700*, Cambridge: Cambridge University Press.

Tomlinson, John, 1991, *Cultural Imperialism*, London: Continuum.

Trevor-Roper, Hugh, 1965, *The Rise of Christian Europe*. London: Thames and Hudson.

Trotsky, Leon, 1932, *Problems of the Chinese Revolution* (Translated with an Introduction by Max Shachtman), New York: Pioneer Publishers.

Trotsky, Leon, 1934, *The History of the Russian Revolution*, London: Victor Gollancz, Ltd.

Trotsky, Leon, 1936, *The Third International After Lenin,* New York: Pioneer Publishers.

Trotsky, Leon, 1940. *The Living Thoughts of Karl Marx, based on Capital: A Critique of Political Economy*, London: Cassell and Company, Ltd.

Trotsky, Leon, 1967 [1936], *The Revolution Betrayed: What is the Soviet Union and Where is it Going?* London: New Park Publications Ltd.

Trotsky, Leon, 1969, 'The Three Conceptions of the Russian Revolution', *Writings 1938–39,* New York: Merit Publishers.

Trotsky, Leon, 1972a, *1905*. London: Allen Lane, The Penguin Press.

Trotsky, Leon, 1972b [1967], *On Black Nationalism and Self-Determination*, New York: Pathfinder Press, Inc.

Trotsky, Leon, 1973, *The Spanish Revolution* (1931–39), New York: Pathfinder Press.

Trotsky, Leon, 1975, *The Struggle Against Fascism in Germany* (Introduced by Ernest Mandel), Harmondsworth: Penguin Books.

Trotsky, Leon, 1979a, *Leon Trotsky on France*, New York: Monad Press.

Trotsky, Leon, 1979b, *Military Writings and Speeches: How the Revolution Armed* (Volume I – The Year 1918), London: New Park Publications.

Trotsky, Leon, 1980, *The Challenge of the Left Opposition (1926–27)*, (edited by Naomi Allen and George Saunders, with an introduction by Naomi Allen). New York: Pathfinder Press.

Trotsky, Leon, 1999. 'On the Intelligentsia [1912]', *Revolutionary History*, Vol. 7, No. 2 (Special Issue on: *Culture and Revolution in the Thought of Leon Trotsky*).
Truffaut, François, 1968, *Hitchcock*, London: Secker & Warburg.
Tugan-Baranovsky, M. I., 1970 [1898], *The Russian Factory in the 19th Century*, Homewood, Illinois: The American Economic Association.
Vargas Llosa, Mario, 2015, *Notes on the Death of Culture*, London: Faber and Faber.
Varshney, Ashutosh, 1995, *Democracy, Development and the Countryside: Urban-Rural Struggles in India*, Cambridge: Cambridge University Press.
Vernant, Jean-Pierre, 1980, *Myth and Society in Ancient Greece*, Brighton: The Harvester Press Limited.
Veyne, Paul, 1990, *Bread and Circuses: Historical Sociology and Political Pluralism* (Translated by Brian Pearce, Introduction by Oswyn Murray), London: Allen Lane, The Penguin Press.
Vilar, Pierre, 1976, *A History of Gold and Money 1450–1920*, London: New Left Books.
Vogt, Joseph, 1993 [1967], *The Decline of Rome: The metamorphosis of ancient civilization*, London: Weidenfeld.
Walbank, F.W., 1946, *The Decline of the Roman Empire in the West*, London: Cobbett Press (Past and Present Series: Studies in the History of Civilization).
Walling, W. E., 1908, *Russia's Message*, New York: Doubleday, Page & Company.
Wankankar, Milind, 2011, *Subalternity and Religion*, New York: Routledge.
Wark, Mckenzie, 2019, *Capital is Dead*, London: Verso.
Weber, Max, 1976, *The Agrarian Sociology of Ancient Civilizations*, London: New Left Books.
Whiteside, Andrew Gadding, 1962, *Austrian National Socialism before 1918*, The Hague: Martinus Nijhoff.
Whiteside, Andrew Gadding, 1975, *The Socialism of Fools: Georg Ritter von Schönerer and Austrian Pan-Germanism*, Berkeley, CA: University of California Press.
Wickham, Chris, 2005, *Framing the Early Middle Ages: Europe and the Mediterranean 400–800*, Oxford: Oxford University Press.
Wiener, Martin J., 1981, *English Culture and the Decline of the Industrial Spirit, 1850–1880*, Cambridge: Cambridge University Press.
Wilson, A.J., 1909, *An Empire in Pawn: Being Lectures and Essays on Indian, Colonial, and Domestic Finance, 'Preference', Free Trade, etc.* London: T. Fisher Unwin.
Wittfogel, Karl, 1963, *Oriental Despotism: A Comparative Study of Total Power*, New Haven: Yale University Press.
Wolfe, Tom, 1970, *Radical Chic & Mau-Mauing the Flak Catchers*, New York: Farrar, Straus, and Giroux.
Wolfe, Tom, 1976, *Mauve Gloves & Madmen, Clutter & Vine*, New York: Farrar, Straus, and Giroux.

Wolfe, Tom, 2000, *Hooking Up*, London: Jonathan Cape.
Woofter, T.J., 1936, *Landlord and Tenant on the Cotton Plantation*, Washington, DC: Works Progress Administration Division of Social Research, Monograph V.
Worsley, Peter (ed.), 1971, *Two Blades of Grass: Rural cooperatives in agricultural modernization*, Manchester: Manchester University Press.
Worsley, Peter, 1957, The Trumpet Shall Sound: A Study of 'Cargo Cults' in Melanesia, London: MacGibbon & Kee.
Worsley, Peter, 1960, 'Between Two Worlds: Imperial Retreat', in E.P. Thompson (ed.), *Out of Apathy*, London: New Left Books.
Worsley, Peter, 1964, *The Third World: A Vital New Force in International Affairs*. London: Weidenfeld & Nicolson.
Worsley, Peter, 1969, 'The Concept of Populism', in Ghiţa Ionescu and Ernest Gellner (eds.), *Populism*, New York: The Macmillan Company.
Worsley, Peter, 1984, *The Three Worlds: Culture and World Development*, London: Weidenfeld & Nicolson.
Worsley, Peter, 1989, *Marx and Marxism*, London: Routledge.
Worsley, Peter, 1997, Knowledges: What Different Peoples make of the World, London: Profile Books.
Worsley, Peter, 2008, *An Academic Skating on Thin Ice*. New York: Berghahn Books.
Yeats, William Butler, 1933, *The Winding Stair and Other Poems*, London: Macmillan and Co., Limited.
Youngblood, M., 2016, *Cultivating Community: Interest, Identity, and Ambiguity in an Indian Social Mobilization*, Pasadena, CA: South Asian Studies Association.
Zene, Cosimo, 2013, *The Political Philosophies of Antonio Gramsci and B.R. Ambedkar: Itineraries of Dalits and Subalterns*, London: Routledge.
Zunz, Olivier (ed.), 1985, *Reliving the Past: The Worlds of Social History*, London and Chapel Hill, NC: The University of North Carolina Press.

Author Index

Abramsky, C. 253
Adler, E. 158
Alibhai-Brown, Y. 200, 218 *passim*, 227
Amis, K. 44, 228
Andolina, R. 59
Andrews, R.F. 42
Applebaum, A. 14
Aron, R. 247
Attridge, D. 62

Babington, B. 21
Bahro, R. 176
Baldwin, J. 31, 230, 234
Banaji, J. 7, 25–26, 139, 144, 164, 166, 167 *passim*, 177 *passim*, 185 *passim*, 195–96, 227, 259, 265ff.
Beard, M. 138, 139, 157ff.
Bennington, G. 62
Berger, J. 87, 243
Bernstein, H. 25, 41, 90, 115 *passim*, 125 *passim*, 175, 227, 258
Bethell, L. 69, 80
Bhaduri, A. 19
Bhagavani, M. 59
Bhagwati, J. 248
Bierce, A. 55
Blok, A. 73
Borowiak, C. 118
Borras, J. 110, 120
Bowersock, G.W. 153, 154, 158
Bowman, A.K. 168
Brass, T. 2, 5, 7, 8, 13, 16, 18, 23, 36, 37, 71, 75, 77, 81, 87, 92, 99, 100, 104, 106, 112, 142, 168, 171, 184, 192, 193, 242, 243, 246, 251, 254
Brassey, T. 70
Breman, J. 2, 7, 8, 250
Brenton, T. 119
Brown, G. 21
Brown, P. 139, 153 *passim*, 165–66, 170–71, 174, 178, 190, 258, 265
Brunt, P.A. 164, 180, 184, 194
Burke, P. 60
Byres, T.J. 7

Campbell, J.R. 42
Camus, R. 150, 232, 235–36, 238 *passim*, 249ff
Cannadine, D. 64
Carrillo, S. 30
Chayanov, A.V. 175, 86–87, 115, 116, 122, 129, 175, 181, 195
Christie, I. 19
Chrysostom, C. 206
Clay, H. 231
Cochrane, R. 118
Collins, H. 253
Conquest, R. 2
Cox, C. 1
CPGB 42
Cramp, C.T. 253

Davis, M. 250
de Ste Croix, G.E.M. 139, 145ff., 155, 165, 178, 194
Debray, R. 4, 5, 18, 57
Dhanagare, D.N. 25, 90, 115 *passim*, 129ff., 227, 258
Dobb, M. 187, 252
Drage, G. 126
Duberman, M.B. 198, 201, 202
Duncan, K. 179
Dupré, G. 186

Easton Ellis, B. 232, 240ff., 244
Emmanuel, A. 92
Engels, F. 2, 35, 69, 139ff., 145, 165, 253
Engerman, S.W. 184, 187
Escobar, A. 77, 114–15
Esman, A. 232
Evans, R.J. 2, 56, 64 *passim*, 75ff.
Éwanjée-Épée, F.B. 172, 176

Feldhaus, A. 59
ffrench, P. 62
Finley, M. 137, 170, 178, 180, 190
Fogel, R.W. 184, 187
Foner, P.S. 198ff., 203, 209, 211
Foster-Carter, A. 175

Foucault, M.   47, 58–59, 73, 76, 160
Fowler, D.P.   139, 160–61
Francovich, R.   169
Frank, T.   137ff., 147, 149ff., 157, 161, 165, 167, 183
Friedman, M.   248
Fudge, J.   8

Gadgil, D.R.   212
Garzetti, A.   150
Genovese, E.   68
Gillett, A.   159
Glyn, A.   252
Góngora, M.   179
Goodman, D.   57
Gordon, A.D.D.   212
Grantham, G.   183
Grimshaw, A.   206
Guérin, D.   187, 199
Guha, R.   130–31
Gupta, J.N.   94, 96ff.

Habib, I.   176
Haider, A.   216, 223
Hall, S.   4, 67
Hamid, M.   212, 214, 217ff.
Harding, C.   179
Hardy, E.R.   145, 152ff., 177
Haslam, J.   64
Hayek, F.A.   248
Hilferding, R.   48
Hirsch, A.   222
Hobsbawm, E.J.   2, 24, 56, 60, 62 *passim*, 72 *passim*, 82–83, 87, 258, 263
Hodges, R.   169
Hodgson, G.   56
Hornblower, S.   160–61
Houellebecq, M.   230, 241ff.
Hughes, H.S.   70

Ignatieff, M.   64
Iliffe, J.   104

Jacka, K.   1
James, C.L.R.   26, 197ff., 204ff., 209ff., 225, 228, 258, 268
Johnson, A.C.   178, 183–84
Johnston, Sir H.   224

Jones, A.H.M.   139, 150, 161, 170, 174, 180, 183–84, 194

Kantorowicz, E.H.   152
Kaufmann, E.   232–33, 236, 238 *passim*
Kautsky, K.   48, 90, 113–14, 139 *passim*, 163, 165, 185
Kershaw, I.   209
Keuneman, P.   73
Kulikowski, M.   138
Kureishi, H.   223–24

Lack, R-F.   62
Laclau, E.   115, 117
Laibman, D.   29–30
Laurie, N.   59
Leader, Z.   2
LeBaron, G.   8–9
Lendon, J.E.   158
Lenin, V.I.   1, 24, 30, 31, 35, 45, 48 *passim*, 55, 76, 83, 87, 89, 90–91, 116, 119, 123–24, 133–34, 175, 185, 195, 208, 249, 253, 267, 268
Lévy, B-H.   117
Lichtenstein, A.   8, 187
Littlejohn, G.   115
Lochore, R.A.   236
Luxemburg, R.   76, 81, 139, 143ff., 252

Mackenzie Wallace, D.   125
Mahajan, G.   59
Malik, N.   218ff.
Mandel, E.   187
Marcuse, H.   4
MARHO   76, 199–200
Markovits, C.   212
Marks, J.   1
Marx, K.   1, 2, 4, 35, 45, 67, 69, 75, 76, 86, 90, 99, 100, 105, 106, 117, 139ff., 145, 165, 171–72, 176, 182, 185 *passim*, 195–96, 221, 252–53
Mattick, P.   4
Mavor, J.   126
Mavrakis, K.   56
Medick, H.   181
Mehta, S.   199–200, 211 *passim*, 223ff.
Mignolo, W.   59
Mintz, S.   187

AUTHOR INDEX

Mitchell, S. 191
Mommsen, T. 137, 192–93
Monferrand, F. 172, 176
Mouffe, C. 115, 117, 133, 245
Mudde, C. 10–15, 247
Murray, D. 232, 239, 241

Nanda, M. 118
Naoroji, D. 91 *passim*, 104, 107

Oertel, F.W. 139, 147ff., 152–53, 184–85, 196, 265
Olgin, M.J. 43

Palme Dutt, R. 42
Panagariya, A. 248
Patnaik, P. 91ff., 100–101
Patnaik, U. 7, 25, 48, 82ff., 91 *passim*, 101–102, 104ff., 171, 212, 213, 214, 227, 237, 258, 262, 263, 265, 266
Peacock, T.L. 109
Pegg, S. 22
Petras, J.F. 57
Phillips, A.A. 226
Piccone, P. 117, 118
Pollitt, H. 42
Pollitt, M. 42
Portes, J. 248
Prakash, G. 61, 62
Prasad, P. 7

Radcliffe, S. 59
Radkey, O.H. 120
Ranger, T. 69
Redclift, M. 57
Reger, G. 194–95
Rey, P-P. 186
Rhys, E. 19
Richardson, A. 206
Rioux, S. 8–9
Robeson, P. 26, 66, 197 *passim*, 208ff., 211, 216, 220, 225, 228, 258, 268
Rogan, E. 168
Rosenberg, A. 127
Rostovtzeff, M. 139, 147–48, 153, 162, 163, 164, 165, 170, 180
Rostow, W. 247
Rothbard, M. 248
Rowlandson, J. 178, 192

Roy, T. 118
Rudra, A. 57, 175
Rutledge, I. 179

Samuel, R. 60, 63
Schmitt, C. 117
Scott, J.C. 59, 138
Sedova Trotsky, N. 127
Sen, A. 7
Sender, J. 104
Seregny, S.J. 116
Serge, V. 127
Shachtman, M. 197, 199–200, 204, 205, 207, 208, 219, 258
Shanin, T. 90, 115, 119–20
Sherwin-White, A.N. 159–60, 190, 194
Shukla, N. 213, 225
Simkin, C.G.F. 173, 182
Singh, C. 122–23
Sisman, A. 64
Sitwell, E. 55
Smith, H. 81
Smith, Sheila 104
Smith, Stephen 232 *passim*, 243, 249
Snow, C.P. 70
Sombart, W. 143, 168
Soria, G. 42
Spawforth, A. 160–61
Stalin, J. 24, 29, 30, 31, 34, 39, 40 *passim*, 52
Stedman Jones, G. 60, 63
Steinfeld, R. 187
Stepniak, S. 125ff.
Stoddard, L. 238
Stone, L. 190
Sukhanov, N.N. 127

Thorner, A. 57
Tirthankar, R. 212
Tomlinson, J. 61
Trevor-Roper, H. 64, 90
Trotsky, L. 24, 30 *passim*, 42ff., 46–47, 52–53, 55ff., 68, 76, 89, 119, 128, 182, 204ff., 207, 210, 252
Truffaut, F. 18
Tugan-Baranovsky, M.I. 119

Vargas Llosa, M. 239
Varshney, A. 117

Vernant, J-P. 168–69
Versovšek, P. 8–9
Veyne, P. 139, 160ff.
Vilar, P. 167
Vogt, J. 144
von Mises, L. 248

Walbank, F.W. 139, 144 *passim*, 164–65, 170, 181, 185
Walling, W.E. 125, 127
Wankankar, M. 59
Wark, M. 3
Weber, M. 143, 168ff., 179–80
Wiener, M.J. 151

Whiteside, A.G. 254
Wickham, C. 175
Wilson, A.J. 95
Wittfogel, K. 176
Wolfe, T. 4, 16–17, 239
Woofter, T.J. 206
Worsley, P. 2, 24, 82 *passim*, 101 *passim*, 262–63

Yeats, W.B. 29
Young, R. 62
Youngblood, M. 131

Zene, C. 59
Zunz, O. 60

Subject Index

academia
  as 'ivory tower' 3, 77
  Bristol University 22
  British School at Rome 138
  Cambridge University 66, 70, 73, 201
  debates within 3, 5, 6, 13
  Intelligentsia 30, 36, 44, 117, 128
  katheder-socialism 16
  New York University (NYU) 225–26
  Oxford University 201, 225, 227
  Students 1, 77, 167, 202, 255
Africa 24, 26, 83 *passim*, 102, 103, 106, 107, 115, 140, 143, 186, 193, 199, 201ff., 210, 212, 213, 224–25, 228, 231, 233ff., 242, 243, 263
  Congo 213
  gerontocracy 233, 234, 244
  Guinea 213
  Nigeria 201, 213
  Uganda 224, 225
  (see also Great Replacement)
agrarian myth 10, 18ff., 23, 34, 128, 235, 243, 261
  Darwinian 18, 21, 23
  nature 12, 18, 19, 23, 32, 34, 73, 121, 128
  pastoral 18, 23
  (see also nationalism, populism)
agrarian question 113, 119
  American path 46
  Prussian path 46
agrarian reform 41, 57, 111, 149, 162
Alegría, Ciro 104
anthropologists
  Mauss, Marcel 162
  Palerm, Ángel 104
  Redfield, Robert 104
  Warman, Arturo 104
Aron, Raymond 247
Asia 85ff., 103, 111, 115, 132, 146, 150, 153, 176, 209, 213–14, 217, 224, 229, 265, 266
  (see also India)
Australia 226
Austria 254

Bagehot, Walter 70
Baldwin, James 19, 230, 234
Benn, Tony 65
Bernstein, Eduard 31
Bernstein, Leonard 16–17
Black Panthers 16–17
Blair, Tony 66–67
bourgeoisie 2, 4, 6, 7, 16, 17, 24, 29ff., 35, 44, 46–47, 50, 53, 56–57, 63, 68, 74, 81, 85, 86, 95, 97–98, 102, 105, 108, 121, 126, 127, 130, 147, 148, 149, 150, 188, 197, 207–8, 228, 234, 235, 260
  (see also capitalism, class, development)
Brass, Anna Luisa xii, 28, 136, 138
Britain 4, 8, 23, 42, 63, 71, 83, 91, 94, 95, 104, 202, 203, 208, 213, 223, 263
  'New Labour' 66ff., 254
  austerity 106, 218, 254
  Brexit 13, 219, 222–23, 236, 254–55
  CPGB (Communist Party of Great Britain) 42
  Liberal Party 91
  London 199, 202–3, 217, 226
  Manchester 95, 203–4
  UKIP (United Kingdom Independence Party) 15, 255
  Victorian 67, 70, 151
bureaucracy 32, 34, 149

capital, agribusiness 34, 35, 84, 90, 114, 132
capital, foreign 7, 25, 32, 34, 35, 37, 52, 75, 76, 79, 84, 90, 103, 107, 108, 132, 253, 260, 262 (see also imperialism)
capital, industrial 19, 26, 32, 34, 48, 68, 73, 84, 91, 124, 129, 144, 151, 172, 182, 196, 207, 208, 209, 247, 261, 265
  (see also class, development, Marxism, labour-power, mode of production)
capital, merchant 26, 37, 104, 125, 151–2, 172–3, 181, 182, 194, 196, 258, 265
capital, usury 32, 34, 35, 47, 48, 52, 73, 124, 126, 132, 193, 207, 209, 241, 248, 252, 257, 262, 265
capitalism
  'Davocracy' 241, 252
  'nicer'/'kinder' xi, 10, 12, 29, 46, 57, 80, 112, 114, 153, 245, 251, 258–59, 265

capitalism (cont.)
  crises 3, 4, 5, 9, 11, 33, 47–48, 165, 247–48, 252, 256, 261
  International Monetary Fund 248
  laissez-faire 9, 15, 47, 67, 148, 212, 215, 232, 243, 244ff., 252, 254ff., 267
  monopoly 49, 207
  primitive accumulation 186, 195, 253
  World Bank 215, 248
  (see bourgeoisie, class, democracy, development, feudalism, industry, Keynesianism, kulaks, labour, Marxism, mode of production, political economy, rich peasants, socialism, transition)
Caribbean 26, 198–99
Carrillo, Santiago 30
Castro Pozo, Hildebrando 104
Chattopadhyay, Paresh 99
Chayanov, A.V. 86–87, 115, 116, 122, 129, 175, 181, 195
  (see also peasant, populism, Russia)
China 29, 47, 53, 172, 176, 266
Churchill, Winston 213
class
  alliances xi, 6, 7, 24, 29, 30, 38, 39, 41 passim, 53, 57, 68, 74, 78, 122, 228, 241, 245, 258
  aristocracy 17, 18, 20, 23, 35, 36, 147, 164, 165, 166, 168, 172, 208, 243
  landowners 34, 35, 37, 38, 40, 44ff., 57, 71, 78, 85–6, 91, 102–3, 116, 124ff., 131, 134, 143ff., 152–3, 162 passim, 177ff., 184, 188–89, 208, 209, 212, 243, 261, 263
  (see capitalism, development, land tenure, Lenin, Marxism, mode of production, political economy, reserve army, revolution, state, Trotsky, workers)
class consciousness xi, 6, 7, 31, 33, 35, 53, 60, 62, 85, 102, 131, 134, 165, 188, 198, 207, 227, 237, 244, 246, 258, 259, 261, 266ff.
class formation xi, 16, 32, 33, 34, 119, 175, 198, 207, 227, 252, 258, 259, 266, 268
class struggle xi, 1, 2, 4, 6, 7, 8, 9, 16, 17, 18, 30, 31, 32, 34, 37, 38, 44 passim, 59, 63, 68, 81, 94, 102, 106, 110, 117, 118, 119, 121, 122, 125, 131, 133, 134, 146, 147, 155, 162, 188, 197 passim, 208, 216, 218, 227, 237, 238, 244 passim, 258–59, 263ff.

Clay, Henry 231
Cobbett, William 70
Cobden, Richard 70
colonialism 23, 59, 61, 63, 77–78, 83, 85, 88, 92 passim, 103, 105, 107–8, 112, 158, 212ff., 220, 228–29, 235, 262–63, 265 (see also imperialism, post-colonialism)
  'revenge' 212, 237
  pauperization and 85, 99–100, 107
communism 14, 21, 30, 35, 39, 42, 46–47, 57, 62, 65–66, 68ff., 83, 88, 102, 142, 200, 204, 240
  (see also capitalism, feudalism, Lenin, Marxism, revolution, socialism, transition, Trotsky)
conservatism 1, 3, 4, 5, 10, 14ff., 24, 30, 31, 34, 37, 58, 60, 61, 71, 75, 88, 109, 118, 131, 134, 141, 155, 209, 238ff., 255, 263, 264
  (see also bourgeoisie, capitalism, culture, identity, neoliberalism, populism)
cults 101, 145
  (see also religion)
culture
  'authentic' 24, 26, 32, 34, 59, 73, 75ff., 84ff., 101, 102, 104, 129, 154, 227, 235–36, 239, 255, 266
  as 'cultural cringe' 226–27
  civilization and 22, 61, 91, 138, 144, 147ff., 155, 168, 200, 217–18, 231, 236, 238
  (see capitalism, film, Great Replacement, nationalism, peasant, postmodernism, identity, immigration, race, religion, subaltern studies)

David, Eduard 31
democracy 10 passim, 29–30, 42 passim, 52–53, 57, 74, 76, 78, 85, 110, 150, 157, 208, 234, 240, 243, 245
  citizenship 9, 15, 140, 146, 148ff., 158, 204, 226, 252 87, 169, 181, 232ff., 236, 238, 249, 255 (see also Africa, Great Replacement)
  (see also bourgeoisie, capitalism, class, nationalism, socialism)
deproletarianization 7ff., 254
  decomposition/recomposition 7, 251, 264
  downsizing 7, 245

SUBJECT INDEX   293

outsourcing/relocation   7, 106, 149, 181, 216, 245, 249, 257, 266
restructuring   7, 11, 48, 100, 106, 216, 237–38, 249, 251–52
(see also capitalism, class struggle, development, industrial reserve army, labour-power, lumpenproletariat, Marxism, socialism, transition, workers)
Deutscher, Isaac   65
development
  as modernity   32, 46, 61, 62, 76, 79, 81, 86, 104, 107, 110ff., 114–15, 122, 129, 130, 147, 172, 221, 241. 252, 260, 266
  end-of-ideology   4
  'food security'   36, 92
  'food sovereignty'   36, 92
  paradox   68, 86, 144, 234–5
  retardation   142, 144, 149, 151, 166, 170, 173, 181
  stagnation   25, 127, 144–45, 155, 166, 169, 258
  underconsumption   25, 144, 149, 166, 175, 179–80
  (see agrarian question, capitalism, class, land tenure, Marxism, mode of production, peasant, political economy, production relations, productive forces, reserve army of labour, transition, workers)
Dobb, Maurice   4, 187, 252
Dodd, William   70
Dunoyer, Charles   246
Dutt, Romesh Chunder   91, 94, 96ff., 100

emigration   49, 213
  (see also capitalism, colonialism, Great Replacement, immigration)
empire   23, 25, 74, 75, 125, 137, 138 passim, 161 passim, 173 passim, 185, 190–91, 203, 206, 258, 260, 265
  (see also ancient Rome, Britain, capitalism, imperialism, late antiquity, Russia)
Engels, Frederick   2, 35, 69, 139ff., 145, 165, 253
ethnicity   (see cultural turn, far-right, Great Replacement, identity, nationalism, politics, postmodernism, race)

Europe   11, 12, 13, 14, 23, 26, 36, 37, 53, 60, 71, 73, 76, 85ff., 90, 92ff., 104, 106, 117, 119, 124, 132, 140, 152, 154, 168, 203, 208, 212ff., 218, 222ff., 231 passim, 245, 247, 249, 254, 260, 264, 266
  Enlightenment and   32, 58, 59, 112, 115, 221, 242, 261
Eurocentric   3, 54, 58, 59, 77, 78, 88, 110, 112, 114, 233, 242, 243, 261
Eurocommunism   30
  (see also capitalism, development, Great Replacement, immigration)

famine   38, 94, 176, 184, 262, 263
Fanon, Franz   86
farmer movements   35, 90, 91, 109, 116ff., 121, 124, 128, 129, 130, 133–34
  Bharat v. India   116, 118, 134
  Joshi, Sharad   116–17, 119, 130–31, 134
  remunerative prices and   91, 109, 116, 122ff.
  Shetkari Sanghatana   131
  sugar lobby   123, 129
  Via Campesina   124, 127, 128
  (see also agrarian myth, agrarian question, agrarian reform, India, peasant movements)
far-right   5, 9, 10, 11, 12, 13–14, 15, 24, 26, 30 passim, 45, 53, 68, 70, 75, 103, 107–8, 110, 114, 118, 120–21, 131ff., 154, 197, 205ff., 216, 219, 225, 237, 254, 258–59, 263, 264, 267
  anti-capitalism of   15, 16, 33–34, 49, 52, 58, 108, 132, 240, 261, 264
  fascism   23, 30, 32, 33–34, 46–47, 53–54, 58, 68, 88, 111, 121, 208, 219, 240, 247
  Hitler, Adolf   73, 209
  Schmitt, Carl   117
  (see also capitalism, class struggle, conservatism, Great Replacement, immigration, identity politics, neoliberalism, populism, race)
Fawcett, Henry   70
feudalism   3, 6, 29, 32, 35, 53, 57, 76, 78, 91, 102, 103, 143ff., 152–53, 155, 162–63, 165–66, 169, 171, 174, 176 passim, 195, 245, 248–49, 259, 263, 265
  (see also capitalism, development, Marxism, semi-feudalism, socialism, transition)

Figes, Orlando   115, 119
film
   A Canterbury Tale (1944)   18–20, 23
   A Matter of Life and Death (1946)   18
   Black Narcissus (1947)   18
   Chinatown (1974)   21
   Hot Fuzz (2007)   18, 20–23
   King Solomon's Mines (1937)   201
   Monty Python's Life of Brian (1979)   104
   Night Train to Munich (1940)   21
   Ring of Spies (1963)   21
   Sanders of the River (1935)   201
   Showboat (1936)   201
   Song of Freedom (1936)   201
   Star Wars (1977)   22
   State Secret (1950)   22
   Tawny Pipit (1944)   18–19, 23
   The Emperor Jones (1933)   201
   The Lady Vanishes (1938)   18, 21
   The Life and Death of Colonel Blimp (1943)   18
   The Proud Valley (1940)   201–2
   The Red Shoes (1948)   18
   The Thief of Bagdad (1940)   18
   The World's End (2013)   18, 21–23
   Wicker Man (1973)   20
film directors
   Coppola, Francis   19
   de Palma, Brian   19
   Gilliat, Sidney   21
   Hardy, Robin   20
   Hitchcock, Alfred   18, 21
   Jones, Terry   104
   Korda, Zoltan   21
   Launder, Frank   21
   Miles, Bernard   18
   Murphy, Dudley   201
   Powell, Michael   18–19
   Pressburger, Emeric   18–19
   Scorsese, Martin   19
   Stevenson, Robert   201
   Tennyson, Penrose   201
   Tronson, Robert   21
   Whale, James   201
   Wills, J. Elder   201
   Wright, Edgar   18
film genre
   detective   20

Ealing studios   201
film noir   20
zombie apocalypse   22
France   48, 62, 68, 235–6, 241ff., 246
   Corsica   73
   Gauls   159, 172
   May   1968, 4
   Paris   4, 11, 18, 226
   Vichy   1940, 242
Frank, Andre Gunder   171

Germany   19, 21, 32, 36, 50–51, 58, 66, 69, 117, 149, 160, 183, 193, 208, 209, 219, 242, 254
gold   95, 173–74, 182ff., 196, 213
Gramsci, Antonio   76, 118, 133–34
   hegemony   22, 48, 118, 122–23, 130, 133–34, 235, 245, 263
Great Replacement   26, 62, 151, 221, 224–25, 231 *passim*, 238ff., 245 *passim*, 255–57, 259, 265, 267–68
   'grievance industry'   222
   'white fright'   150, 233, 238
   'white tribalism'   239, 243
   'whiteshift'   236
   de-authentication   235–6, 239, 255
   de-culturation   235, 239, 261
   (see also capitalism, culture, demography, far-right, identity, immigration, populism, racism, reserve army of labour)
Greece   146, 151–2, 159–60, 169, 182, 194, 195
   Delos   194–5
   (see also ancient Rome)
Green, F.E.   70
Groves, Reg   70

Hannington, Wal   70
Hasbach, W.   70
Heath, Richard   70
Hegel, G.W.F.   187–88
historians
   Annan, Noel   65
   Ashton, T.S.   71
   Beard, Mary   138, 139, 157ff.
   Berlin, Isaiah   64–65
   Brown, Peter   139, 153ff., 160 *passim*, 170, 174, 178, 189, 190ff., 258, 265

SUBJECT INDEX

Bücher, Karl   143, 168
Carr, E.H.   64–65
de Ste Croix, G.E.M.   139, 144, 146–7, 155, 165, 178, 194
Elton, Geoffrey   64
Engerman, Stanley M.   184, 187
Finley, M.I.   137, 170, 178, 180, 190
Fogel, Robert W.   184, 187
Frank, Tenney   137, 138, 139, 147, 149ff., 157, 165, 167, 183
Gay, Peter   64
Jones, A.H.M.   139, 150, 161, 170, 174, 180, 183–4, 189–90, 194
Meyer, Eduard   137, 182
Mommsen, Theodor   26, 137, 192–3
Oertel, F.W.   139, 147ff., 153, 184–5, 196, 265
Pipes, Richard   192
Pokrovsky, M.N.   182
Rostovtzeff, M.   189, 147–8, 153, 162ff., 170, 180
Rudé, George   69
Sherwin-White, A.N.   159–60, 190, 194
Tawney, R.H.   71
Taylor, A.J.P.   64
Thompson, E.P.   69
Trevelyan, G.M.   64
Trevor-Roper, Hugh   64, 90
Walbank, F.W.   139, 144 *passim*, 164–5, 170, 180–81, 185
(see also academia, historiography, Eric Hobsbawm, C.L.R.James)
historiography
  'minimalist'   177ff., 193
  cliometrician   182, 184, 192, 194, 196
  Communist Party Historians Group   69
  Subaltern Studies   12, 13, 36, 59, 112, 118, 129, 130, 242, 261, 265
  Whig   29, 68
Hobsbawm, Eric   2, 24, 56, 60, 62, 63 *passim*, 68 *passim*, 76 *passim*, 82, 87, 258, 263–4
  'paradoxical compromise' and   68
  British Academy and   68
  British Establishment and   2, 24, 65ff., 72, 79–80
  Companion of Honour   66–67
  (see also Marxism, New Labour, social history, the cultural turn)
Houellebecq, Michel   230, 241ff.
Howitt, William   70

identity, non-class   xi, 3, 14, 16, 31, 35, 47, 54, 56, 58, 60, 63, 79, 86, 88, 89, 101, 111, 114, 121–22, 131ff., 200, 203ff., 216, 228, 232, 236, 239, 243–44, 257
  Arab   236
  Caste   116, 129, 130, 185, 213
  gender   60, 63, 79, 121, 217, 251
  Hindu   121, 130
  Indigenista   104
  Muslim   121, 172, 223, 235
  Négritude   85, 87, 199
  (see also class struggle, Great Replacement, identity politics, immigration, nationalism, postmodernism, subaltern studies)
identity politics   xii, 13, 14, 15, 17, 24, 26, 58, 60, 70, 88, 98, 110, 113, 157, 197, 216–17, 219ff., 228–29, 230, 239 *passim*, 258–59, 264, 268
  (see also immigration, Great Replacement, far-right, populism, post-colonialism, post-modernism, racism)
immigration   10 *passim*, 26, 48ff., 99, 138, 150, 198, 211 *passim*, 219 *passim*, 228–29, 231 *passim*, 245 *passim*, 255, 259, 267–68
  as asylum/refuge   11, 12, 219ff., 224
  as human right   214
  competition and   12, 13, 15, 23, 47, 53, 205, 215ff., 219, 232, 234, 237, 254, 264, 268
  labour-displacing   252, 267
  morality and   11, 219, 241, 250–51
  open-door   13, 211 *passim*, 228–29, 248, 260, 268
  (see also capitalism, class struggle, Great Replacement, reparations, reserve army of labour, restructuring)
imperialism   xi, 24, 29, 31, 33, 42, 44 *passim*, 53, 61–2, 71, 75, 77, 81, 83ff., 91ff., 96, 102, 105, 107–8, 152, 158, 201, 236, 237, 258, 262, 265, 267
  drain thesis   25, 50, 83, 91 *passim*, 104–5, 107–8, 212, 228, 229
  Roman   25, 152, 158, 264, 265
  unequal exchange   92
  (see also empire, Lenin, Marxism, reparations)

India 7, 24, 25, 35, 57, 59, 61, 75, 78, 83, 85, 90 passim, 105ff., 109, 111, 115ff., 121–22, 124, 129–30, 133–34, 167–68, 171, 174ff., 179, 188, 195–6, 212–13, 223, 225, 226, 243, 260, 263, 265, 266
  Ambani 212
  Andhra Pradesh 124
  Bharatiya Janata Party (BJP) 118, 130, 134
  Birla 212
  Congress Party 91, 95
  Gandhi, M.K. 61
  Hinduja 212
  Maharashtra 116, 121, 123, 130, 131
  Mittal 212
  Mughal 174, 176
  Punjab 225
  Rashtriya Swayamsevak Sangh (RSS) 130
  Shiv Sena 130, 134
  Swatantra Bharat Paksha (BSP) 130
  Tata 212
  Uttar Pradesh 122
  (see also Asia, farmer movements, Naoroji)
Ireland 253
Italy 69, 140, 143, 144, 148, 149, 151, 152, 180, 195, 208
  Campania 151
  Naples 73
  Ravenna 158
  Sicily 73, 140, 144
  (see also ancient Rome, late antiquity)

James, C.L.R. 26, 197 passim, 204 passim, 225, 228, 258, 268
  'Comrade Johnson' 204
  (see also Marxism, Paul Robeson, Trotsky)

Kautsky, Karl 48, 90. 113, 114, 139 passim, 163, 165, 185
  (see also ancient Rome, Marxism)
Kay-Shuttleworth, James 70
Keynesianism 3
kulak 24, 38ff., 52, 57, 90, 117, 119 passim, 133, 181
  'mir-eaters' 126
  (see also capitalism, Lenin, Marxism, rich peasant, Russia, Trotsky)

labour
  aristocracy 71
  bonded 7, 126, 127, 140, 142, 164, 186, 189
  child 248
  corvée 124, 143
  female 38, 208, 209, 243
  freedmen 149, 150, 152
  gañanes 179
  indentured 189
  rent 162, 169, 177
  serf 125, 145, 152–53, 162, 164, 176–77
  slave 50, 125, 140 passim, 151ff., 158–59, 169, 173, 176 passim, 188–90, 198, 203ff., 210, 213, 231, 243
  sweatshop 8, 29
  (see also capital, class, communism, development, labour-power, Marxism, socialism, workers)
labour-power 6, 7, 24, 25, 33, 48, 52, 100, 105, 113, 114, 122, 126–7, 142ff., 163, 166, 168–69, 179, 181, 186ff., 214ff., 220, 228, 234, 237, 247, 248ff., 253, 259, 265, 267
  as commodity 127, 169, 188, 246, 248
  unfree 6, 7, 8, 9, 10, 15, 62, 71, 99ff., 127, 142ff., 146, 151, 152, 158–59, 164, 166, 169, 174, 177, 181, 186ff., 195, 211, 243, 248, 251, 259, 264
Laclau, Ernesto 115, 117
land tenure
  collectives 32, 34, 39–40, 110, 122, 124, 132, 199, 206
  colonate 152, 164, 166, 169, 181
  communal 126, 140
  cooperatives 38ff., 46, 57, 86–87, 101, 206, 210
  latifundia, estates 71, 90, 140, 143ff., 152–53, 162ff., 166, 168–69, 174, 177 passim, 206
  plantation 84, 90, 184, 192, 198, 203
  sharecropping 134, 145, 177, 178, 181, 186, 189, 205–6
  tenant/sub-tenant 43, 78, 102, 123, 124, 134, 145, 152–53, 162ff., 169, 177ff., 188–89
late antiquity 23, 25–26, 62, 137 passim, 153ff., 160, 162, 165–66, 168 passim, 179 passim, 190–91, 193, 195–96, 197, 258, 260, 264–65

SUBJECT INDEX 297

'catastrophist' models and   147, 170, 173, 174, 177
as 'commercial capitalism'   171, 172, 182
as 'new scholarship'   162, 170
as 'proto-industrialization'   171, 177, 181
as 'proto-modernity'   171
as 'quasi-capitalism'   171
Byzantium   145, 152, 158, 181, 185
(see also ancient Rome, development, capitalism, empire, transition)
Latin America
  Amazonia   162
  Bolivia   104
  Brazil   71
  Chile   70
  Mexico   37, 104, 179, 204
  Peru   71, 78, 87, 104, 115, 162
Lenin, V.I.   1, 24, 30–31, 33, 35, 45, 48 *passim*, 55, 76, 83, 87, 89, 90, 116, 119, 123, 124, 133–34, 175, 185, 195, 208, 228, 249, 253, 267, 268
(see also capitalism, Marxism, revolution, socialism, Trotsky)
lumpenproletariat   11, 47, 58, 73, 76, 142
(see also capitalism, deproletarianisation, development, Marxism, reserve army of labour)
Luxemburg, Rosa   76, 81, 139, 143, 145, 252

Malthus, T.R.   51, 232–33, 252
Mariátegui, José Carlos   104
Marx, Karl   1, 2, 4, 35, 45, 67, 69, 75, 76, 86, 90, 99, 100, 105, 106, 117, 139ff., 145, 165, 171–72, 176, 182, 185 *passim*, 195–96, 221, 252–53
(see also capitalism, class, communism, development, Engels, Kautsky, Lenin, revolution, socialism, transition, Trotsky)
marxism   (see class, communism, development, Engels, Marx, Lenin, socialism, Trotsky)
media   1, 16, 17, 61, 77, 105, 198, 199, 218
  BBC   66, 214
methodology   11, 51, 60, 68 *passim*, 82, 107, 111, 119, 126, 138, 156, 159, 161, 166, 170, 184, 187, 189 *passim*, 236, 260
Middle East   29, 106

Egypt   145–46, 152–53, 174, 178, 183, 190, 192
Syria   146, 150, 151, 152
mode of production   57, 82, 99, 165, 167 *passim*, 187, 195
(see also capitalism, development, feudalism, Lenin, Marx, socialism, transition)
Mouffe, Chantal   115, 117, 133, 245

Naoroji, Dadabhai   91 *passim*, 104, 107
(see also drain thesis)
national liberation   207, 228
national question   81, 207
national self-determination   204ff., 208, 210, 228
nationalism   xi, xii, 5, 13, 24, 29ff., 37, 43 *passim*, 52, 59, 61, 71, 74ff., 78, 81, 83, 85, 88–89, 93, 99, 101–2, 104, 107, 113, 116, 118, 132, 134, 202, 206, 208, 210, 214, 219, 230, 242, 243, 247, 249, 254, 258, 263, 266, 267, 268
  'social-chauvinism'   49, 267
  'social-patriotism'   50
(see also capitalism, identity, populism, Stalin)
neoliberalism   5, 7, 9, 15, 33, 71–2, 76, 104, 111, 112, 114, 132–33, 182, 211, 219–20, 229, 232, 239, 241, 244 *passim*, 259, 260, 264
  Friedman, Milton   248
  Hayek, F.A.   248
  market, free   95, 248
  neoclassical economics   182–83, 184, 185, 192, 195–6, 211, 246, 248, 265
  Rothbard, Murray   248
  von Mises, Ludwig   248
(see also bourgeoisie, capitalism, class, conservatism)
New Left   4, 84, 240
NGOS   248

Page Arnot, R.   70
peasant
  'disguised' wage labour   175, 187, 195
  differentiation   24, 30, 32ff., 36, 37, 39, 41, 52–53, 56, 58, 60, 73, 76, 78, 79, 83ff., 90, 93, 105, 107, 114, 119–20, 123–24, 129, 133, 175, 178–79, 258 *passim*

peasant (cont.)
  economy   15, 16, 33, 75, 81, 86, 87, 92, 106, 113, 122, 132, 169, 176, 259, 262
  essentialism   3, 14, 24, 31ff., 53, 58, 75–6, 79, 100, 107, 110, 113, 129
  family farm   24, 32, 34, 52, 103, 114, 181
  household   25, 87, 120, 125–26, 175, 179, 181, 195
  middle   24, 31, 32, 38ff., 87, 108, 119–20, 124, 125, 128, 131, 133, 262, 263
  patriarchy   35, 119–20, 125
  poor   33, 38–39, 41, 52, 63, 73, 75, 97, 102, 113, 114, 121, 122, 126, 134, 245, 262
  rich   7, 35, 37, 38, 41, 57, 63, 73, 86ff., 90, 102, 103, 114, 117, 120 passim, 131, 133–34, 260ff.
  (see agrarian myth, agrarian question, agrarian reform, capitalism, Chayanov, class, culture, development, farmer movements, identity, kulak, labour, land tenure, Lenin, Marx, mode of production, nationalism, populism, postmodernism, transition)
peasant movements   24, 42, 111, 116, 117, 118, 129
  Green International   124, 128
  Peasant Leagues (Brazil)   71
Poland   204
political economy   xii, 9, 11, 12, 14, 17, 36, 54, 57, 63, 70, 82, 98, 109, 111, 129, 143, 227, 239, 245, 246, 256, 258, 261, 264, 266, 268
  (see also capitalism, class, Keynesianism, Marxism, socialism)
populism
  'authoritarian'   15, 241
  'bad/nice' variants   15, 110, 111, 114, 132
  'land sovereignty'   36, 128
  'left/right' variants   245
  'peasant autonomy'   128
  anti-semitism   13
  ecofeminism   112, 118, 129
  everyday-forms-of-resistance   13, 58, 59, 60, 63, 112, 118, 242, 259, 261, 266
  pro-peasant/farmer-first   25, 35, 83, 89, 104, 119
  Radical Chic   15ff.
  rurality   14, 16–17

(see agrarian myth, capitalism, Charan Singh, Chayanov, class struggle, development, far right, postmodernism, post-colonialism, post-Marxism, Subaltern Studies, Teodor Shanin)
populism, agrarian   12, 24–25, 29, 31 passim, 52, 61, 73, 78, 88, 92, 103, 109 passim, 115, 117, 119 passim, 127 passim, 258, 261–62
  (see also agrarian myth, Chayanov, culture, farmer movements, identity, India, kulak, land tenure, nationalism, peasant movements, postmodernism, Russia, Teodor Shanin)
post-capitalism   112, 129
post-colonialism   26, 35, 46, 83, 99, 112, 129, 198ff., 213 passim, 223 passim, 232, 242, 244, 258, 264, 266ff. (see also identity politics, populism, postmodernism)
post-development   36, 112, 114, 242, 261
post-Marxism   112, 129, 239, 245
post-modernism
  aporia   62, 158, 161
  as 'cultural turn'   xii, 2, 26, 30, 37, 45, 50, 53, 55, 56, 58, 62, 70, 72 passim, 82, 109ff., 132, 134, 139, 240, 243–44, 261, 263, 264
  as 'left-modernism'   239–40, 242, 243
  as 'social justice warriors'   241
  Baudrillard, Jean   58
  Derrida, Jacques   58, 160
  Foucault, Michel   47, 58–59, 73, 76, 160
  inclusivity   235, 239, 240, 263
  Kristeva, Juliet   62
  Lyotard, Jean-François   58, 160
  multiculturalism   159, 220, 223, 240
  political correctness   200, 218ff., 229, 240, 242
  Spivak, Gayatri   62
production relations   6, 7, 8, 10, 29, 62, 71, 94, 100, 125, 166, 169, 177, 178, 179, 189, 195, 243
  (see also capitalism, class, feudalism, labour, land tenure, Marx, peasant, workers)
productive forces
  canals   94
  irrigation   94, 105, 124, 152, 168

SUBJECT INDEX 299

railways   43, 94, 210
technology   22, 76, 143, 146, 153, 169, 211
proletariat   (see capitalism, class, deproletarianisation, labour, labour-power, Marxism, political economy, production relations, revolution, socialism, workers)

race   43, 54, 197, 200 *passim*, 216, 220, 222, 224, 227, 231, 238–39, 268
  discrimination   205, 207
  emancipation   197, 199, 208, 216
  racism   63, 207, 216, 222, 223, 241, 256
  riots   205, 223
  segregation   207–8
  (see also anti-semitism, class, Great Replacement, identity politics, populism, nationalism)
reformism   xi, 4, 9, 30, 46, 57, 60
Reinaga, Fausto   104
religion   5, 14, 18, 25, 32, 34, 36, 45, 60, 72, 79, 88, 124, 129, 130–31, 137 *passim*, 153 *passim*, 165–66, 168, 170, 189ff., 213, 231, 232, 235, 241, 260, 268
  Bali Raj   131
  Christian   138, 140 *passim*, 156–57, 163ff., 191–92, 219
  congregation and   140–41, 157, 165
  Emperor-worship   146, 150, 157, 166
  gift-giving   161, 166
  Islam   141, 217, 223, 241
  Messiah   142, 145
  Mithraism   145
  Nicene Council   141
  (see also culture, identity, nationalism, race, populism, Rome)
reparations   23, 25, 92, 104, 105, 212, 214–15, 220, 228–29, 268
  (see also colonialism, immigration, imperialism, post-colonialism)
reserve army of labour   3, 7, 9, 11, 13, 25, 31, 33, 47, 49ff., 63, 76, 83, 99ff., 105ff., 113, 197, 211, 216ff., 229, 232–33, 238, 245 *passim*, 255ff., 260, 264, 267, 268
  metropolis/periphery   25, 53, 100–101, 105ff.
  (see also capitalism, class struggle, deproletarianisation, lumpenproletariat)

revolution   xi, 3, 4, 5, 10, 16, 30 *passim*, 42–43, 52–53, 56, 71, 78, 80, 86–87, 104, 107–8, 112, 117, 119, 120, 127, 140, 147, 148, 156, 199, 206, 208, 210, 253, 260, 261
  1789 French   32
  1917 Russian   37, 40, 90, 119–20, 148
  1962 Cuban   104
  Green   119, 245
  Permanent   30, 37, 42
  (see also capitalism, class, development, Lenin, Marxism, transition, Trotsky)
Robeson, Paul   26, 66, 197 *passim*, 209ff., 216, 220, 225, 228, 258, 268
  HUAC and   198–99
  internationalism of   202, 208, 228
  travel ban   66, 198
romanticism   17, 32, 51, 73, 75, 89, 129, 253
Rome, ancient   25, 104, 137 *passim*, 150 *passim*, 164, 167, 177, 180ff.
  'state-socialism' in   148–49
  Aquileia   193
  Augustus   146, 148, 149, 152, 181
  barbarians and   138, 147, 160, 183
  Caesar, Julius   146
  Caracalla   148
  Claudius   151
  Constantine   145, 146
  Juvenal   159–60
  Lucian   159–60
  Pliny   160
  Republic   149, 150, 151, 152, 164, 166, 172
  Trajan   138
  Vespasian   148
Rostow, W.W.   247
Rubin, Isaac Ilyich   185
Russia   25, 32, 35, 36, 38, 40, 42, 45, 51–2, 57, 87, 89–90, 103, 111, 115ff., 119–20, 124 *passim*, 133, 147, 175, 182, 209, 210, 260
  Bolsheviks   38, 45, 115, 116, 148
  Cossacks   38, 126
  Czar   125
  mir   120, 126, 133
  Molotov-Ribbentrop pact   70
  Moscow trials   70
  Narodnism   35, 37, 51–52
  New Economic Policy   39, 127
  Soviet Union   42, 57, 70, 148, 176, 209, 231

Scargill, Arthur   65
semi-feudalism   6, 7, 29–30, 56–57, 63, 74, 75, 78, 99, 100, 152, 166, 171, 175
(see also feudalism, Stalin)
Shanin, Teodor   115, 119, 120
Sidgwick, Henry   70
Singh, Charan   122–23
Sismondi, Jean Charles Léonard de   51–52
Smith, Adam   188
social history   24, 55 *passim*, 67–68, 72–73, 77, 79–80, 263
  bandits   71, 73, 87, 173
social sciences   1, 2, 89, 104, 112, 155, 258, 260, 266
  anthropology   82, 104, 107, 156, 161, 186, 191
  sociology   1, 2, 11, 82, 90, 107, 118, 122
socialism   xi, 3, 5, 7, 8, 9, 16, 23, 24, 29, 30ff., 38, 39, 40ff., 46–47, 52, 56ff., 62, 66, 67, 68, 75, 78, 80, 83, 88, 89, 103, 111–12, 128, 132, 140, 148, 149, 176, 198, 199, 206, 208ff., 227–28, 242, 243, 245, 247, 248–49, 254, 258ff., 265, 268
(see also capitalism, class, communism, conservatism, feudalism, Lenin, Marx, revolution, Trotsky)
Sombart, Werner   143, 168
Spain   42, 47, 54, 208, 209
  Catalonia   204
  Franco   42
  International Brigades   209
  Republic   208, 209
Stalin, Joseph   24, 29ff., 34, 39, 40 *passim*, 52–53, 55ff., 68, 74, 76, 78, 83, 204, 207, 210, 228, 258
  Comintern   30
  Popular Front   29ff., 34, 46, 47–48, 53, 68, 74
State   7, 8, 9, 15, 21, 30, 32, 34, 38, 39, 40, 44, 45, 47, 57, 58, 59, 64, 68, 77, 79, 82, 85, 86, 91, 103, 110, 114, 124, 127, 128, 132, 133, 140, 142, 146 *passim*, 161, 164, 175, 176, 185, 188, 195, 198, 205, 206, 209, 210, 211, 234, 242, 243, 245, 248, 250, 263, 267
  Independent   210, 228
  New   85, 86, 102
  public spending   106, 250

welfare   4, 164, 209, 218, 234, 237, 245, 250, 263
Switzerland   21, 50

taxation   91, 104, 147, 161, 174–5, 184
trade unions   205, 207, 208, 253–4, 267
transition
  agrarian   23, 32, 132
  capitalist   13, 23, 57, 75, 249
  feudal   23, 166, 181, 249
  socialist   xi, 3, 5, 6, 9, 15, 16, 30, 34, 42, 46, 47, 75, 76, 78, 111, 199, 209, 228, 252, 259 *passim*
  systemic   3, 23, 25, 26, 30, 32, 52, 61, 68, 75, 113, 132, 139, 142, 165, 169, 181, 210, 249, 255, 258ff., 268
Trotsky, Leon   24, 30 *passim*, 40 *passim*, 52–53, 55ff., 68, 76, 89, 119, 182, 204ff., 210, 252
  Left Opposition   38, 40, 41, 45, 52, 127, 197
(see also capitalism, class, communism, Lenin, Marx, revolution, Russia, socialism, transition, workers)
Turgot, Anne-Robert-Jacques   246

United States   4, 15, 23, 26, 42–43, 93, 198–99, 203 *passim*, 215, 223ff., 228, 231, 234, 237, 253, 267
  American Communist Party   204
  Chicago   104, 203–4
  Mississippi   203, 206, 209
  New Deal   205
  Northern   205, 207, 260
  Southern   43, 140, 184, 203ff., 207, 213

villages   19ff., 32, 34, 38ff., 59, 61, 81 *passim*, 101, 116, 120, 125–26, 133, 177, 191–92, 225, 235, 236, 263

Wales   201–3
war
  1914–18   19, 267
  1939–45   16, 124
  American civil   94, 204, 205
  captives   143
  Cold   82, 176, 195, 247
  Punic   151, 182
  Spanish civil   208ff.

SUBJECT INDEX

Weber, Max 143, 168ff., 179–80
West Indies 199, 204
workers 4, 6, 7, 8, 9, 10, 11, 12, 15, 33, 38, 40, 41, 42 *passim*, 58ff., 68, 71, 74ff., 78, 81, 86, 93–4, 97, 100 *passim*, 113, 121, 126–7, 140, 142, 147, 164, 168–69, 173–4, 176ff., 183, 187ff., 196, 202 *passim*, 216, 218, 220, 225, 228, 231, 234, 237–8, 244, 245ff., 250 *passim*, 258, 260, 263 *passim*
  agricultural 53, 63, 79, 94, 97, 112, 114, 129, 191
  deskilled 106, 142
  miners 65, 201ff., 209
  skilled/unskilled 71, 101–2, 106, 183, 194, 211, 255, 266
  (see also capitalism, class, deproletarianisation, immigration, labour, labour-power, Marxism, reserve army)
Worsley, Peter 2, 24, 82 *passim*, 101 *passim*, 262, 263

Yugoslavia 71

www.ingramcontent.com/pod-product-compliance
Lightning Source LLC
Chambersburg PA
CBHW070910030426
42336CB00014BA/2358